Retro Active Television

An In-Depth Perspective on Classic TV's Social Circuitry

Herbie J Pilato

Foreword by Eric Scott (*The Waltons*)

Headline Books
Terra Alta, WV

Retro Active Television
An In-Depth Perspective on Classic TV's Social Circuitry

by Herbie J Pilato

To order additional copies of this book or for book publishing information, or to contact the author:

Headline Books
P.O. Box 52
Terra Alta, WV 26764
www.HeadlineBooks.com
Email: mybook@headlinebooks.com

Author photo on page 240 by Dan Holm

ISBN 13: 9781958914083

Library of Congress Control Number: 2022949378

PRINTED IN THE UNITED STATES OF AMERICA

Dedicated to the communicative magic of positive classic television programming; may its core messages of humanity, understanding, compassion, and loving-kindness help to transmit and unify all people from every culture, heritage, creed, political party, gender, sexual orientation, or religious or spiritual belief.

Content

"The one great problem that has perplexed television experimenters for years–how to synchronize the transmitter and the receiver...."

Popular Mechanics Magazine
April 1928, Volume 1, Number 4

Foreword

I love television.

I grew up with it in my living room, watching a black and white "TV set" with rabbit ears, sitting in front of it, enthralled for endless hours a day.

I was born in 1958, so I don't remember the 1960 Presidential debates. But I do recall the assassinations of President John F. Kennedy in Dallas, his brother Bobby in Los Angeles, and Martin Luther King in Memphis. In 1969, I watched in awe when Neil Armstrong spoke his first words upon landing on the Moon: "One small step…"

I loved watching game shows followed by comedies such as *I Dream of Jeannie*, *The Flying Nun*, *The Munsters*, and *The Dick Van Dyke Show*. It's no wonder that when I was seven years old, my mom asked me if I wanted to do some acting, and I said, "Yes!"

Fast forward to February 1971, when I was cast in an episode of *Bewitched*, which was one of my other favorite shows.

I arrived at Stage 4 on the Columbia Studios lot and entered a familiar sight: The living room and kitchen of Samantha and Darrin Stephens. I met the cast, including Elizabeth Montgomery and Dick Sargent (who by then was playing Darrin, following Dick York's exit two years before). Everyone was so welcoming and kind. It was wonderful to observe how the "magic" was done. "Breaking the fourth wall" didn't ruin it for me, but made me appreciate the technical side of filmmaking; in this case, of course, "television-making."

Eight months later, I found myself playing Ben Walton in a TV-movie titled, *The Homecoming: A Christmas Story*. Written by Earl Hamner, Jr. and adapted from his best-selling novel of the same name, *The Homecoming* received rave reviews and ignited a follow-up weekly family TV series called *The Waltons*, on which I was honored to appear for nine beautiful years.

My life as an actor was and remains exciting and rewarding. I have met and continue to meet many terrific individuals in the entertainment industry, as well as fans of my work and the shows I have performed in.

One of those special people is Herbie J Pilato. He began his career in the industry as an NBC-TV Page in Burbank, close to the Columbia Ranch where I filmed *Bewitched*. While some would have been happy just to be on the studio lot, Herbie observed and studied the surroundings and those involved in the production of television shows. His passion for the industry inspired him to share his thoughts and feelings in an exciting and informative way, authoring several books on popular shows, including *Bewitched*. You can tell Herbie loved watching television as much as I did.

Today, *Retro Active Television: An In-Depth Perspective of Classic TV's Social Circuitry* brings it all full circle. This book is a must-read for anyone who wants to know about the history and impact that television has on American society. Whether you enjoy sitcoms, dramas, talk shows, music-variety hours, or game shows, Herbie brings them all back to life and explains with great detail the evolution of each genre.

I smile with every reference he makes to all the amazing shows that have aired over the decades. His memory is uncanny and his perspective is spot-on.

This book needed to be written and deserves to be read and discussed. For me, it's a road down memory lane. For younger readers, it's a historical document that offers a new perspective with a "retro-spective" twist on a remarkable invention and its influence.

When I first met Herbie, he shared with me his love and affection for *Bewitched* and Elizabeth Montgomery. He remembered me from the episode I appeared in and asked what it was like to work with Elizabeth and to be on the show. In turn, I shared with him the joyful memories of my time on the set and reminded him that the character that I played on the show was named "Herbie."

That was another full-circle moment, like now, in writing the Foreword to this book.

Eric Scott
Encino, California
September 15, 2022

Eric Scott today *[Credit: Courtesy of Eric Scott]*

Preface

In past generations, television loomed large in American households and around the world. There were no video games, internet connections, smartphones, or any number of such communication devices available today. At its genesis, TV was a means of entertainment and a window into domestic and foreign lands and imaginations. Educational programming was presented on networks like PBS, but society benefited in other ways from that shining box of light in the living room. The cultural conversation about and around television's positive social influence has expanded in countless productive and illuminating ways regarding racial issues, domestic problems, women's rights, those with disabilities, and more.

The Seal of Good Practice set the standard for quality family television [Credit: The Classic TV Preservation Society]

While those of a certain age have lived and identified with a TV show like *The Wonder Years*, the modern consumer has also embraced that 1960s-based series, which, when it first aired in the mid-1980s, was nostalgic from the onset. As a result of ABC's success with recent reboot specials of *All in the Family* and *The Jeffersons*, the network has ordered an African-American redo of *The Wonder Years*. And while HGTV continues to reap ratings-gold from new shows that celebrate old shows like *A Very Brady Renovation*, reruns of *The Golden Girls and I Love Lucy* frequently find new young fans.

In 2020, the new Peacock streamer rebooted *Saved By the Bell* to ratings victory, while its parent network NBC readies a sequel to *Night Court* (starring original cast member John Larroquette). Zoom cast reunions of other NBC classic shows like *Frasier* and *Family Ties* are fast becoming the most popular form of programming on digital platforms like YouTube and beyond. Remakes of *Dynasty*, *Charmed*, *MacGyver*, and *Magnum P.I.* have captured all-new contemporary viewers of *The CW* and CBS networks (respectively).

Retro networks like ME TV, Cozi TV, and Antenna TV continue to be more popular than ever as the big TV picture expands, right beside our consciousness of its social ties.

Are we more tolerant of those who happen to be different because *Star Trek* "makes us so"? Has your father's television set developed into today's hip moms and dads because they reaped the benefits of solid TV parentage? Is today's watcher better prepared to acquire lessons on how not to be a mother by screening Nancy Walker as Mrs. Morgenstern on *The Mary Tyler Moore Show* or *Rhoda*?

Channels switch, signals cross, and the focus is clear:

While some research has shown that extensive binge-watching of classic TV shows may cloak deeper issues, other experts say the mainstream affection for such programming simply helps us feel more connected, particularly in these increasingly chaotic times.

Will Meyerhofer, a New York-based psychotherapist and author, has long believed watching our favorite classic TV shows can help us cope with anxiety and mild depression. "For many clients," he said, "...[the] old shows are like the food they grew up with. *The Brady Bunch* or *The Facts of Life* or *The Jeffersons* are like that beloved baloney sandwich on Wonder Bread with just enough mayo the way Mom used to make." Meyerhofer, who finds solace *in Star Trek: The Next Generation*, explained further, "In therapy terms, it's an instant—and for the most part healthy—regression in the service of the ego."

Krystine Batcho, a licensed psychologist and professor at Le Moyne College in Syracuse, New York, has researched nostalgia. She said watching our favorite retro television programs soothes our "nostalgic need" with legitimate emotional benefits. "When people are stressed or anxious or feeling out of control, nostalgia helps calm them down. It's comforting. It's analogous to a hug from your mom or dad or being cuddled."

Columbo is Batcho's TV retro series of choice, but she has also enjoyed "big and clumsy" computers, VCRs, and other such technology and tidbits of the 1970s. For her, it all harkens back to "what we might, even erroneously, perceive as a simpler time in our life with fewer responsibilities and obligations and... worries."

For those who have experienced trauma or loss, the classic TV connection may be a crucial prescription. Reassurance about our identities can be "critical," Batcho said. Re-viewing shows like *Friends* or *Beverly Hills, 90210* has the potential to "bring back memories and feelings of the friends you had back then and at the fun times you had together."

Kimberly M. Wetherell, a fortysomething audiobook narrator from Brooklyn, New York, has always enjoyed "comfort TV" from the past. "When I go to bed, my mind is still racing," she said. "My brain will be going over the anxiety of the day...start overanalyzing things...just won't turn off." But watching a show like *The Golden Girls* is "...like hanging out with old friends."

With its pulsating images and rhythms, stories and conversations, scripted and real, classic TV has guided some to their very life's purpose. For others, with its every sight and sound definition, nostalgic television has become a solid state of social circuitry worn with a harmonic armor of honor. With both whimsy and reality, amidst its many outlets of influence, and in the most productive ways, classic television has plugged into and become a conduit of potential, both established and untapped, teaching its viewers along the way how to be retroactive while living for today.

Retro Active Television: An In-Depth Perspective On Classic TV's Social Circuitry helps to bring it all home, full-circle, with an in-depth perspective of a medium that began as a square tube.

Introduction
A Brief History of Television

Some reports claim television began in 1925.

That's when John Logie Baird and Charles Francis Jenkins worked independently on both sides of the Atlantic and produced weak and blurry images on a screen no larger than one inch in length. Other reports said it was 1928, when WGY, Schenectady, began broadcasting three days a week. After that, things progressed quickly:

The Dumont Network began it all *[Credit: The Classic TV Preservation Society]*

1930—NBC opened an experimental television transmitter in New York.

1931—WICR, operated by Gimbel Bros., went on the air in New York.

1932—CBS reported on the Presidential election broadcast over an estimated 7,500 television sets.

1937—Seventeen experimental stations commenced operation.

1938—NBC telecast *Susan and God*, starring Gertrude Lawrence.

1939—Allen B. DuMont placed the first all-electronics sets on the market, the opening of the New York World's Fair is televised, and a Princeton-Columbia baseball game is TV's first sportscast.

1940—*Pagliacci* was telecast from the Met, the Republican Convention aired live, and CBS marked the first colorcast.

1941—Commercial telecasting began July 1, while WNBT took to the airwaves with a Dodgers-Pirates game from Ebbets Field. The first commercial was the face of a clock made by Bulova (which is charged $9.00 in advertising), as an announcer uttered the time. Other programs that first day included a Lowell Thomas newscast, a USO show, *Uncle Jim's Question Bee*, and a radio/TV simulcast of *Truth or Consequences*.

1945—VE Day celebrations were telecast, as was the first commercial intercity event—the Army-Navy Game, from Philadelphia to New York.

1946—The DuMont network aired *Faraway Hill*, the first soap opera (referred to as such because various brands of soap are advertised during their broadcasts).

1947—Approximately 1400 homes now had sets, while TV created its first schedule of regular programs: *Juvenile Jury*; *Kraft Television Theatre*; *Leave It to the Girls*; *Kukla, Fran, and Ollie*; *Meet the*

Press; *Howdy Doody*; and *A Woman to Remember* (TV's second daytime serial). Viewers also saw the opening of the 80th Congress, President Truman's State of the Union Address, and, later that year, a visit to Truman at the White House; and the World Series (Yankees vs. Dodgers) was watched for the first time by set owners in New York, Philadelphia, Washington, D.C., and Schenectady.

In 1949, the family sitcom was introduced with *Mama* and *The Goldbergs*, along with *Beulah*, the first series to feature an African-American lead (performed by three different actresses: Ethel Waters, Hattie McDaniel, and Louise Beavers.)

In the 1950s, the domestic semi-bliss of *I Love Lucy* and *The Burns and Allen Show* were joined by more such home-based sitcoms like *The Honeymooners*, *My Little Margie*, *I Married Joan*, and *Our Miss Brooks*.

The variety show format went wide in the late-'40s and early '50s with programs like *Toast of the Town* (later *The Ed Sullivan Show*), *Texaco Star Theatre* with Milton Berle, *The Jackie Gleason Show* (originally on the DuMont network), *The Steve Allen Show*, *The Colgate Comedy Hour* (with rotating hosts Martin and Lewis, Abbott and Costello, Eddie Cantor, Donald O'Connor), and *The Garry Moore Show*, which introduced a young Carol Burnett.

Miley Cyrus may have rocked the *MTV Music Video Awards* in 2013, but in 1956 and 1957, Elvis shook his hips on *Berle* and *Sullivan*, the latter on which he was photographed from only the waist up. Journalist Edward R. Murrow and his famous *See It Now* program, exposed Senator Joseph McCarthy, and the game show *Twenty-One* triggered more infamy with a quiz-show scandal twist.

By 1956, the DuMont Network was out of business, and game shows, in general, became a popular pastime of the American viewer, with titles like *You Bet Your Life* (with Groucho Marx), *Beat the Clock*, and *The $64,000 Question*.

Kraft Theatre and *Robert Montgomery Presents* gave life-extension to the 60-minute anthology format, which was cut in half with *Alfred Hitchcock Presents* (and his signature opening: "Good eeevveniiiinnnng"). *Hitchcock* wisely and wryly delivered somewhat of a comedy/drama combo, as did *Father Knows Best*, and *Maverick*, one of the many Westerns that dominated this era.

Gunsmoke, the pilot episode of which was introduced by John Wayne, moseyed its way onto the small screen, and James Arness (as Marshal Matt Dillon) solidified his status as one of TV's most popular Western heroes. *The Roy Rogers Show* added a hodge-podge of classic Western stories in a modern age with a musical element. Soon joining the posse were shows including *Bonanza*, *The Legend of Wyatt Earp*, *Wagon Train*, and others that rode on and off into the TV sunset.

The 1950s "Golden Era" of television brought with it the massive popularity of *Davy Crockett* (as played by Fess Parker, who resurrected a similar persona one decade later with *Daniel Boone*); the musical genius of Arturo Toscanini, the artistic talents of Paddy Chayefsky (and his stellar teleplay *Marty*), Ernie Kovaks, *Omnibus* with Alistair Cooke (later the host of PBS's *America*); *Life is Worth Living* (with the charismatic Bishop Sheen, TV's first self-help, spiritual/religious leader), *The Adventures of Ozzie and Harriet* (Nelson, and son Ricky's teen-idol sensationalism), and Rod Serling and *The Twilight Zone*.

The Donna Reed Show arrived in 1958 when women were supposed to be only at home cooking, cleaning, and raising the children. The many delights of Gale Storm and *My Little Margie* were in full force, as was Liberace and his wavy hair, nimble fingers, and sparkling teeth; *Victory at Sea* (with its spectacular score by Richard Rodgers); Andy Griffith in the film *No Time For Sergeants* (before his monumental '60s series, *The Andy Griffith Show*—and its follow-up, *Mayberry, RFD*).

Joining the '50s fray: *The Loretta Young Show*, Red Skelton ("Good night and may God bless"), Jimmy Durante ("Good night, Mrs. Calabash…wherever you are"), *Lassie* and *Rin Tin Tin*, Mary Martin in a live TV version of *Peter Pan*, Phil Silvers in *You'll Never Get Rich*, and pre-fame performances by James Dean, Paul Newman, Robert Redford, and Grace Kelly (among many other future superstars) in early television drama.

The Wizard of Oz landed on the small screen, along with *Zorro*, as did esteemed big-screen performers like Julie Harris, while Julie Andrews starred in Rodgers and Hammerstein's *Cinderella*, Fred Astaire presented his first special, and *The Untouchables* became a massive hit (and one of the most violent shows of TV's early era).

Daytime delivered children from the doldrums with continued showings of *Bozo the Clown*; *Kukla, Fran and Ollie*; *The Mickey Mouse Club*; and *Captain Kangaroo*.

The 1960s began with the Nixon-Kennedy debates, *My Three Sons*, a double dose of doctors in the guise of *Ben Casey* and *Dr. Kildare*; Gary Cooper hosted *The Real West*, *Sing Along with Mitch* (Miller), and a special with Julie Andrews and Carol Burnett at Carnegie Hall. Viewers were invited to visit *Peyton Place*, TV's first hit prime-time soap (which makes stars of Mia Farrow and Ryan O'Neal), each airing during an overabundance of war, social upheaval, race riots, and political assassinations.

The age of Camelot began with President John F. Kennedy's inauguration and ended with his assassination (allegedly) by Lee Harvey Oswald. From there on, TV viewers sought solace with all forms of escapism entertainment.

Sci-fi/fantasy shows take their cue from the 1950s-induced *Superman* series. *My Favorite Martian* invaded living rooms across the country. A sardonic talking horse giddy-upped on *Mister Ed*. The ghoul-geared sitcoms *The Addams Family* and *The Munsters* debuted in 1964, alongside the affable *Gilligan's Island*—and *Bewitched* (which became the most sophisticated supernatural sitcom of its time). *The Dick Van Dyke Show* elegantly reminded us of the sophisticated Kennedys in the White House, while *The Beverly Hillbillies* made us laugh at the unsophisticated Clampetts.

By the mid-'60s, *I Dream of Jeannie* materialized in the fantasy/sci-fi realm, as did *Batman*, *The Ghost and Mrs. Muir*, *The Flying Nun*, and TV's top science fiction classic: *Star Trek*. The equally-ground-breaking *Julia* jumped courageously into the fold as the first sitcom to feature a non-stereotypical African-American female lead played by Diahann Carroll (as a single-working-mom-nurse-professional no less!), shortly after Marlo Thomas infused TV sets with the energetic endeavors of an aspiring and single actress with two first names (Ann Marie). *The Monkees*, a manic musical sitcom inspired by The Beatles' feature films *A Hard Day's Night* and *Help!*, was scheduled alongside the slower-paced country charms that were ignited by *The Beverly Hillbillies*, which were by now joined by *Petticoat Junction*, and *Green Acres*.

Heavy drama from *The Fugitive* was accented by uplifting shows like *Flipper* and silly sitcoms like *F Troop*. *Tarzan* swung into action with Ron Ely; *Family Affair* with Brian Keith and Sebastian Cabot played it straight (if with mild, heart-warming laughs). *The Smothers Brothers Comedy Hour* attempted to laugh at history and swirled topical political talk with controversy and innovative comedians such as Pat Paulsen (and his run for Presidency), George Carlin, and Richard Pryor.

There's the big mid-'60s change from black and white television to color, which lent its aesthetic to weekly shows like *He & She*, *Gidget*, *The Flying Nun*, *Gentle Ben*…and with musical specials in which Petula Clark touched Harry Belafonte's arm (which aggravated bigots across the country).

By 1968, a black-leather clad Elvis had made a significant NBC "comeback" special; Neil Armstrong walked on the moon; Jacques Cousteau the seven seas (with a series of specials that frequently interrupted ABC's Thursday night lineup), and Marlin Perkins safaried throughout his *Wild Kingdom* (with Mutual of Omaha).

Circumventing the colorful characters and images projected on these shows were the animated adventures of *The Flintstones* and, by 1969, the near-surreal-looking pastel hues, blues, bell bottoms, high heels, and uplifting sentiments of *The Brady Bunch*. Action-adventure shows were injected into the ebb and flow with every *Mission: Impossible* and episode of *It Takes A Thief* and *I Spy*, as did Jack Webb's *Dragnet* (now in color and carried over from his 1950s black-and-white edition) and *Adam-12* (a more serious take on the two-man comedic police team introduced a decade before with *Car 54, Where Are You?*). Comedy, sci-fi, and adventure combined on shows like *The Man from U.N.C.L.E.*, *Batman*, and *Get*

Smart, and more thought-provoking, although no less-entertaining, programs like *The Twilight Zone* and *Route 66*, with their literate morsels of morals and spiritual-centered premises found their own comfort zone and highly-revered niche.

Adding bite to the era is daytime's *Dark Shadows*, arguably the most unique serial, primetime or otherwise, in history, defined by its gothic premise and the brilliance of Jonathan Frid's heart-wrenching performance as Barnabas Collins, the vampire with a sensitive and tortured soul. Saturday daytime animation catered to *The Herculoids*, the musical-laden and comic-book born *The Archies*, while the genius of mysterious and action-powered *Johnny Quest* aired in prime time on ABC for one season from 1964-'65.

Live-action and adventure thrust forward full-throttle with *Hawaii Five-0* and *The Mod Squad*; The Beatles began a British musical invasion, and other UK imports transmitted waves of appeal with intensely-driven shows like *The Prisoner* and *The Forsythe Saga* and, in 1971, *Upstairs Downstairs* (to which *Downton Abbey* pays a measure of homage decades later).

By the mid-'70s, *Then Came Bronson* wheeled in as TV's answer to *Easy Rider*; *The Partridge Family* on Friday nights reignited the music beat that Dick Clark played in the 1950s with *American Bandstand* during the week while Saturday morning became populated by animated editions of *The Osmonds* and *The Jackson Five*.

Sonny & Cher proved they can do more than sing, and the innovative and innate likeability of comedian Flip Wilson wigged-out as Geraldine and other genius characterizations on his comedy variety show. Taking both cartooned and live shelter from the barrage of regular weekly adult-geared programming was the extremely popular Saturday morning lineup for kids including Sid and Marty Krofft's live-action productions of *H.R. Pufnstuf* and *Lidsville*, along with *The Banana Splits, Here Come the Double Deckers* (another BBC import), and the animated *Scooby-Doo, Where Are You?* (a mystery series that features a [sort of] talking dog that becomes a staple in pop-culture for decades to come).

Back in primetime new TV-movies become the staple with *Brian's Song, That Certain Summer*, and *The Autobiography of Miss Jane Pittman*, which made stars of James Caan and Billy Dee Williams, Martin Sheen and Cicely Tyson (respectively). A new kind of reality comedy began reflecting and defining the socially and politically aware, as CBS and innovative writer/producer Norman Lear introduced *All in the Family*, which begat *The Jeffersons* and *Maude*, which in turn begat *Good Times*, while Lear's *Sanford and Son* stands alone on NBC.

The elevated comedy format continued with additional textures on *The Mary Tyler Moore Show* and *The Bob Newhart Show* both of which, among others, were produced by MTM Enterprises, headed by Moore and then-husband (and former and future NBC employee) Grant Tinker. Audiences tune into Sandy Duncan on *Funny Face* (then *The Sandy Duncan Show*), *The Governor and JJ*, and the popular if controversial *Bridget Loves Bernie* (she was Catholic; he was Jewish), which was unfortunately canceled after only one season (despite its Top Ten ratings).

Social relevance reached its peak in the 1970s with the onset of the miniseries manifested by a number of multilayered productions based on best-selling novels. Syndicated in 1974 was the heralded miniseries, *QB VII* (starring Ben Gazzara and Anthony Hopkins), then on ABC in January 1976 with Irwin Shaw's *Rich Man, Poor Man* (which made stars of Nick Nolte and Peter Straus), and *Rich Man, Poor Man, Book II* (Fall, 1976); Alex Haley's *Roots* (1977), and *Roots: The Next Generation* (1979), each of which was broadcast over various consecutive weeknights within seven-day periods. Through it all and after, former *Dr. Kildare* heartthrob Richard Chamberlain became the miniseries king with *Centennial, Shogun, The Thorn Birds*, and *The Bourne Identity*.

Into this mix kicked *Kung Fu*—TV's first Eastern-Western, a monthly-turned-weekly show that began as a 90-minute TV-movie created by Ed Spielman and Howard Friedlander. The series featured David Carradine as Kwai Chang Caine, a half-American/half-Chinese martial arts monk who roamed the Old West on the run from the Far East. Authority and detective shows policed the airwaves with patrols by *Mannix, Cannon, Barnaby Jones, Columbo, McMillan & Wife, McCloud, Kojak,* and *The Streets of San Francisco,* and soon within the half-hour comedy format of *Barney Miller* (the *Brooklyn Nine-Nine* of its day).

TV's golden age of anthology programs were somewhat revived, if ever slightly incognito, with one-hour weekly editions of *Police Story,* and ABC's 90-minute-long *Tuesday* and *Wednesday Movies of the Week* (e.g. *Daughter of the Mind, Love Hate Love, The Last Child, The Victim,* to name only a few).

The '70s continued its sway between family and so-called jiggle shows. *The Waltons* and *Little House on the Prairie* competed with the titillation of *Three's Company* and *Charlie's Angels,* which introduced and made superstars of Suzanne Somers and Farrah Fawcett (respectively). The poster/pin-up motion picture-induced-phenomenon of the Bette Grable/Rita Hayworth era of the 1940s returned and turned heads by way of the small screen (as both Somers and Fawcett created million-selling, full-wall photos for fans).

The strong, and fiercely female independent image and spirit introduced in the '50s (with *I Love Lucy* and *The Donna Reed Show*), and embraced in the '60s (with *That Girl* and *Bewitched*) expanded in the prime time of the '70s with superhero shows like *Wonder Woman* and *The Bionic Woman,* and on Saturday mornings with *Isis* and *Electra Woman and Dyna Girl.* Comedies like *Alice* and *One Day at a Time* continued to take the female lead, as did *The Mary Tyler Moore Show,* which became a staple on Saturday night, where it was eventually joined *The Carol Burnett Show.* The Burnett series secured its spot as the first female-led variety show, expanding upon a format that up until then was made popular only by men.

Marcus Welby, M.D. and *Medical Center* resuscitated the medical drama, while *The New Perry Mason* (with Monte Markham) took over the courtroom reins from Raymond Burr, and *Owen Marshall, Counselor at Law* (which, like *Welby,* was produced by David Victor), lobbied for lawyers on TV. *Welby* and *Marshall's* ABC network leveled itself off with sitcoms like *The Odd Couple* and *Room 222* which, along with *The Courtship of Eddie's Father,* became one of the first dramedies (a comedy with drama, filmed like a movie, without a laugh track or studio audience). Also joining the ABC fun: *Welcome Back, Kotter* (which made a star out of John Travolta), and producer Garry Marshall's Tuesday night double-bill of *Happy Days* (which made a name of Henry Winkler) and *Laverne & Shirley* (which did the same for Penny Marshall and Cindy Williams).

Two other formats solidified their status in the first and second sectors of the '70s: the game show and the talk show. *Let's Make A Deal, The Price is Right, The Dating Game, The Newlywed Game,* and a wildly-popular updated edition of *Match Game* parleyed their way before and/or after daytime's *The Merv Griffin Show, Dinah!* and *The Mike Douglas Show.*

The Tonight Show Starring Johnny Carson explained how late-night talk shows should be done, and *The Donny & Marie Show* filled the primetime gap left by Carol Burnett. By the end of the '70s, audiences found it increasingly challenging to be satisfied with just one program on any one station for any one period of time. Pressing world issues, the increasing desire for personal success, and the expanding selection of broadcast and cable TV shows were to blame, as were new commercial-free cable TV networks. HBO, Cinemax, and Showtime began to offer viewers multiple choices, while the broadcast networks produced shows with multiple storylines (e.g. the Aaron Spelling/Douglas S. Cramer hybrid *The Love Boat*).

Into the '80s, *Magnum P.I.* became a solid weekly entry with the charismatic Tom Selleck, as did Bill Bixby's multi-colored performance and Lou Ferrigno's green muscles on *The Incredible Hulk.* Group discussions and theme shows continued to chime away on chat shows like those hosted by Merv Griffin, who by now had expanded his media empire to include *Wheel of Fortune* and *Jeopardy!,* which joined the high-rated game show stakes of *Password* and *The Hollywood Squares.*

As the '80s continued, the nighttime soap made a comeback with the '70s-ignited *Dallas* (and "Who shot JR?"), *Knots Landing, Falcon Crest,* and *Dynasty.* By the mid-'80s, the domestic sitcom had also returned to the spotlight in the form of *The Cosby Show,* which catapulted itself (and NBC) with top ratings. Female independence continued its horizontal hold with CBS shows like *Kate & Allie,* which marked a TV resurrection for '70s stars Jane Curtain, late of *Saturday Night Live,* and Susan St. James, Rock Hudson's delightful co-star in *McMillan & Wife.* Long comedy runs were also in store for MTM's *WKRP in Cincinnati,* which introduced the world (and Burt Reynolds) to the many feminine wiles of Loni Anderson.

McMillan (and *Thin Man*)-like romantic comedy/crime/mystery shows peaked in the '80s with *Remington Steele* and *Moonlighting,* both of which played well due to the vibrant, sparkling chemistry between their co-ed leads. The senior population was nicely represented with *Newhart, The Golden Girls,* and *Murder, She Wrote.*

Television in the '90s flip-flopped into the '60s with period pieces like *The Wonder Years* and *China Beach,* both set in the so-termed Age of Aquarius. Many shows inadvertently reflected or copied one another (*Hearts Afire* and *Love & War*), while others recycled old-school ideas with new-school formats (*The Bradys*). The family show concept resurfaced with half-hour sitcoms like *Home Improvement* and one-hour dramas like Michael Braverman's ground-breaking's *Life Goes On,* which became the first weekly series to feature a male actor with a disability (Corky Thacher, played by Chris Burke, who has Down syndrome).

Earlier shows like *Gunsmoke* and *Ironside* showed characters with disabilities, but its respective stars, Dennis Weaver and Raymond Burr were not disabled in real life, whereas Geri Jewell was the first actress who happens to have a disability to play a character who happens to have a disability on *The Facts of Life. Life Goes On* inspired producer Aaron Spelling to create *Beverly Hills, 90210,* which featured young, wealthy, self-absorbed characters who addressed serious topics on a regular basis.

As the '90s continued, programming once more began to replicate itself with spin-offs: *Buffy, the Vampire Slayer* begat *Angel,* and *Hercules* begat *Xena: Warrior Princess* (like *The Six Million Dollar Man* begat *The Bionic Woman* in the '70s). The superhero returned to weekly TV, firmly grounded in success with the likes (and some dislikes) of *Lois and Clark: The New Adventures of Superman.*

Joining the '90s lineup was the ever-affable Dick Van Dyke who, absent far too long from weekly TV (following brief returns in 1976 with the Emmy-winning *Van Dyke & Company* and in 1988 with *The Van Dyke Show*), made a more triumphant return with *Diagnosis: Murder* (a male-medical edition of *Murder, She Wrote,* both of which aired on CBS for years).

The unique New York-based non-sitcom ("no hugging, no kissing") *Seinfeld* reignited the ensemble comedy format that inspired shows like *Friends* (the younger *Seinfeld*), *These Friends of Mine* starring Ellen DeGeneres—and later retitled *Ellen* (the female *Seinfeld*), and *Everybody Loves Raymond* (the married *Seinfeld*).

One character from an '80s sitcom proved to be more popular (and sophisticated, from the scripts to the sets) than the show that spawned him: *Frasier,* a spin-off of *Cheers,* is arguably defined in the annals of classic TV history as the last great sitcom (before characters became caricatures and situations became skits).

The unlikable aspects of the *Seinfeld* characters mistakenly made their way into the once-likable performances of the *Seinfeld* actors and by the 2000s a measure of mean-spiritedness pervaded all television shows and characters. The same kind of unwelcome nastiness percolated with the growing popularity of a format first introduced as the reality show in the '80s with one-hour series such as NBC's *Real People* and ABC's *That's Incredible.* This once-uplifting format now translated into competitively nasty, self-serving shows like Fox's *American Idol* and CBS's *Survivor.*

A few examples include *Extreme Makeover: Home Edition*, which helped tip the scales towards sensitivity and heartwarming real-life tales of how new homes transformed the worthy lives of needy families.

The family sitcom was nicely revamped in 2001 with the multi-talents and natural charms of country music superstar Reba McEntire who takes the graceful center stage on The WB with *Reba*. More contemporary half-hour comedies find success in the 2000s (and shortly thereafter) include *Curb Your Enthusiasm, The Office, Sex and the City, 30 Rock, The Middle,* and *Modern Family.*

Science fiction/fantasy shows were on the upswing with *Supernatural, Smallville* (yet another take on *Superman*), and *The Vampire Diaries,* all on The CW. Other networks such as the Sci-Fi Channel (later rebranded as Syfy) brought their fan-boy/girl specific genre into the 21st Century (and beyond) with shows like *Farscape* and *Stargate SG-1* (which originated on Showtime); and Gene Roddenberry's *Andromeda* (executive produced in syndication by his widow and original *Star Trek* star Majel Barrett).

The good ghosts of TV's past joyfully haunted nostalgic-oriented networks like TV Land, which aired all-new programs with secured leads like *Hot in Cleveland*, which stars Betty White (*Date with the Angels, The Mary Tyler Moore Show, The Golden Girls*), Valerie Bertinelli (*One Day at a Time*), and Jane Leeves (*Frasier*). Even '80s stars like *Blossom* vets Mayim Bialik and Joey Lawrence returned to weekly series of their own (*The Big Bang Theory* and *Melissa and Joey*, respectively).

Hopping on the retro ride are new "old-geared" networks like Antenna TV, Cozi TV, and the Hub, all of which began to fill their variant schedules with classic programming like *Bachelor Father, It Takes a Thief, I Spy, Hazel, The Partridge Family, McHale's Navy, Benson, Happy Days, Laverne & Shirley, Barney Miller*, and more.

Cozi TV brought back *Charlie's Angels* and *The Bionic Woman*, while networks like NBC carted out reboots such as *Knight Rider* and *Ironside* for the small screen, and classic TV favorites such as *Star Trek* continue to reboot themselves with shows like *Star Trek Discovery* and *Picard*.

PART 1
FREQUENCIES

"Hailing frequencies…open"
—Lt. Uhura, *Star Trek*
(in several episodes)

Nichelle Nichols blazed the way for female African-Americans on television *[Credit: Courtesy of Nichelle Nichols/Author's Collection]*

Chapter 1

The Nielsen Company, based in New York City, is the leading global information organization that has measured television ratings for years. According to its website, today's consumers are watching more TV than ever, which makes understanding what and how they're watching an essential part of any marketing campaign. With their expansive and representative television panels, Nielsen measures viewing habits "down to the second," uncovering detailed programming and commercial interaction. Because viewers now have multiple platforms from which to choose what and how they watch, Nielsen integrates audience measurement across TVs, PCs, and mobile phones to assist its client-base [the TV viewers] in creating and selecting succinct "cross-platform" strategies.

Into this mixology of technology arrived Mindset Media, also based in New York City. As explained on its website, this company produces the world's first and only "psychographic ad" technology. That means Mindset harnesses interactivity to take media targeting beyond demographics and into 21 specific personality traits that drive consumer choice. The company also operates its own ad network online and offers research products (some in partnership with Nielsen) that help blue-chip marketers better understand their consumers and campaigns.

In 2010, *Advertising Age* magazine studied how Mindset does its job, concluding "we are what we watch," whether we choose to view *Mad Men*, a rerun of *Mad About You*, or a Blu-ray release of the 1963 movie *It's A Mad, Mad, Mad, Mad World*.

Age writer Beth Snyder Bulik put it this way: More reserved individuals are more likely to watch a blue-collar-based series like *Deadliest Catch,* while magnanimous people lean towards less-intense programs such as *The Rachael Ray Show* or *The Bachelor*. Then-Mindset Media CEO Jim Meyer said our personality determines what we consume, watch, buy, and all other decisions, even including political leanings. "We didn't invent psychographics or personality traits…they are really the things that separate buyer groups where demographics fail." As when, for example, specific cars are purchased by certain people with individual tastes.

Mindset accumulated its data from approximately 25,000 viewers of more than 70 shows, measuring common personality traits among the audience. It then detailed the common personality traits that each series was most likely to attract and offered a sample of advertisers that were more or less likely to appeal to those personalities. The results of that study were as follows:

Mad Men (A&E, 2007-2015): Creative individuals, mostly emotional and intellectual idealists, are 41% more likely (than less creative people) to watch this series (which just so happens to be based in the advertising industry—of the 1960s). Advertisers with core market appeal in this category include the computer-driven Apple Corporation, and the luxury-auto-driven Audi A6 car brand, while the Microsoft and GMC Sierra sectors were less interested in getting *Mad*. Also, *Mad Men* fans are 124% more likely to be Liberals, as opposed to Conservatives or members of any other political group; they use American Express cards and haven't a taste for Campbell's Soup.

Family Guy (Fox, 1999-Present): Created by Seth MacFarlane, this non-family-oriented animated series is littered with rebellious, angry, and sarcastic characters who question authority. Fans of this show drive Harley-Davidson motorcycles and eat DiGiorno Pizza, not Dannon Light & Fit Yogurt.

Glee (Fox, 1999-2015): "Gleeks" (as the show's fans are called by a moniker created from the words "glee" and "geek") tend to be open-minded "experientialists" who believe creative and intellectual pursuits contribute to a contented life. Brands that connect with this group include Evian water and Volkswagen Jetta, while Quaker cereals don't work, and, as with *Mad Men*, creative types are 17% more likely to watch *Glee* than less creative sorts.

Dancing with the Stars (ABC, 2005-Present): Traditionalists are 21% more likely to watch this show as opposed to *Glee*; they prefer stability and hardcore facts and respect authority. They dig Kraft Foods, Fiber One, the Buick Regal, and the Chrysler Town & Country van.

The Office (NBC, 2005-2013): "Alpha dog" take-charge types love this show. They prefer Starbucks and BMWs over McDonald's and Lincoln Town Cars. Like Gleeks, they welcome new experiences, which they believe lead to a more fulfilling life. They also always wish they had a V8 juice and the VW Beetle, but Doritos and the Dodge Caravan—not so much.

The Biggest Loser (NBC, 2004-2016; USA Network, Present): This show attracts practical, emotionally stable people who live in the present, work with what they have, and are less prone to manic behavior. They enjoy Bud Light Beer and the Cadillac CTS, as opposed to Newman's Own and the Nissan Leaf. They're the more conservative viewers who also enjoy *Dancing with the Stars*.

The Real Housewives of Orange County (Fox, 2006-Present): Jim Meyer called this reality series "very advertiser-friendly," while Mindset classified *Real* viewers as take-charge types who prefer straight-talkers who keep an even keel in relationships. Applicable brands: Botox and Apple, Nike and Crest Whitestrips. There are no Maxwell House Coffee drinkers or Hyundai Accent drivers in this quadrant.

Bulik said, "Many humble people adore *The Office* and plenty agenda-following realists love *Mad Men*," while Mindset measured statistical group tendencies, and involved the increased likelihood that a group of people who watch a particular show tended to have one or more similar personality traits. That isn't to say that every individual watcher of a show like *Glee* is "open-minded and longs to buy a Volkswagen."

Three years after the *Advertising Age*/Mindset study of modern shows, *Reader's Digest* (RD) published a broader stroke of the big picture, combining both contemporary and classic series with its profile of "Five Great TV Shows That Changed the World," and "made us safer, healthier, quippier and more tuneful."

RD claimed *The Simpsons* (which, like *Family Guy*, is an adult-oriented, if less mean-spirited animated series) "transformed how we talk." In 2005, Linguistics Professor Mark Liberman of the University of Pennsylvania said the show has "taken over from Shakespeare and *The Bible* as our culture's greatest source of idioms, catchphrases, and sundry other textual allusions." *Simpsons* characters like Milhouse Van Houten (voiced by Pamela Hayden) offer "a quote for every occasion." Even the Oxford English Dictionary has a place for trademark phrases like "D'oh!" (which is frequently exclaimed by Homer Simpson, by way of Dan Castellaneta).

RD noted how *Glee* helped ignite the record industry, while Fox, its home network, scored its first "sleeper hit," even though *Glee's* real impact transpired between screenings. As most of the record industry struggled to survive (despite the assistance of musical competition fare like Fox's very own *American Idol* and NBC's *The Voice*), *Glee's* popularity soared by way of iTunes. The show's manifold, multi-racial cast became the fastest act to earn 20 Top-40 hits, surpassing Elvis Presley.

RD's profile also covered shows like *America's Most Wanted* (Fox, 1988-Present), which "cleaned up our streets" by helping to capture more than 1,100 fugitives since its debut, and *Sex and the City* (HBO, 1998-2004), which "encouraged teens to communicate." In 2011, Ohio State University undergraduates who watched any segment of *SATC* were more than twice as likely to converse with their partners about sexual health issues. In 2008, the Rand Institute of Santa Monica, California discovered that girls between 12 and 17 who watched *SATC* and other shows with "high sexual content" were more than twice as likely to become pregnant (as sound an endorsement as any for enforcing the "Mature Audience" rating).

The RD study also addressed the impact of *ER*, which aired on NBC from 1994 to 2009, and made a star out of George Clooney. This show "made us healthier." Clooney starred in a previous NBC medical series with the similar title of *E/R*, a half-hour comedy that lasted one season (1984-1985), in which he played a young smart aleck named Ace, while his second *ER* residency became the long-running, career-changing one-hour drama in which he was a more refined, though equally complicated, Dr. Doug Ross.

It was the second *ER* series that RD marked as a great influencer on society. The show altered the eating habits of its audience—at least in North America. An arc of episodes from 2004, in particular, focused on this prescription for a teen with high blood pressure: exercise and eat more fruits and vegetables. While the plot was somewhat standard, it carried viewer impact. In 2007, researchers from the University of Southern California's medical school found that those who watched these *ER* segments started walking and exercising more, ingesting a healthier diet, or checking their blood pressure.

The *Reader's Digest* study concluded, "How can anyone say watching TV is bad for you?"

Chapter 2

Writer Ed Spielman experienced firsthand television and its influence on society. He began his career as an NBC page in the early 1960s. He later became the only writer/producer in history to have created (or co-created) a Western for TV in each of three subsequent decades: *Kung Fu* (on ABC in the '70s, when the genre was no longer in vogue); *The Young Riders* (also on ABC, in the '80s), and *Dead Man's Gun* (on Showtime in the '90s).

The origins of television, in general, and the anthology Western series in particular, began with *Death Valley Days* in 1952 and *Dick Powell's Zane Grey Theatre*. Both shows followed the demise of classical dramatic radio around 1950 or 1951 when Spielman was just a boy growing up in Brooklyn. His Uncle Irving purchased a small black and white Tele-Tone television that cost enough to be "a down payment for a used car." Irving's apartment was soon jammed with family, friends, and neighbors who were mesmerized by a strange contraption in the living room, covered with some form of Plexiglas screen. Though television technology had been around since the '30s, it didn't arrive as a consumer product until 1946. In that beginning, there was little to watch. "A lot of it was either kid shows or recycled films," Spielman said,

Ed Spielman [pictured], and Howard Friedlander created *Kung Fu [Credit: Author's Collection]*

"…or inexpensive programming like *Rocky King, Inside Detective*, which aired on the DuMont Television Network [from 1950-1954]." Back then, "…it wasn't really about the programming. DuMont was in the business of selling TVs."

Television shaped the viewer's mindset that has since been studied and documented by Nielsen and Mindset Media, and now Neotrope Entertainment. In the early days, TV reaffirmed an American public standard of deportment and morality. It promoted rules of good citizenship for children. Nothing directly or intentionally offensive appeared on television. The medium was heavily regulated. "That's why kids would watch mythological heroes like cowboys or *Superman* [which reaffirmed] 'Truth, Justice and the American Way,'" Spielman said.

During the '50s and the '60s, certain TV comedies became pillars of American culture and helped to create what Spielman called "an orderly society." Sitcoms like *The Andy Griffith Show* and *The Dick*

Van Dyke Show reaffirmed what many held to be very specific American values. When the Vietnam War erupted, the "Sex, Drugs & Rock 'n'Roll" generation began to deconstruct a public standard, not only of morality but of deportment, language, and culture. "So, that today," Spielman observed, "…there isn't a public standard of morality or culture, and you see television reflecting this. There's been a dreadful coarsening of the culture along with what must be observed as a moral decline. It's undeniable."

An artifact of a bygone era is the demise of television's leading role in reaffirming the standard. A significant shift in society occurred whereby generations of Americans were taught "not to be judgmental," Spielman said, minus any more standards. "It simply reflects the moral decline. You can turn on your TV and see Miley Cyrus 'twerking' alongside Robin Thicke during their controversial performance at the 2013 MTV Video Music Awards. Such images were foreign to television viewers until the "Sex, Drugs and Rock 'n' Roll generation deemed them acceptable."

"If there's nobody to say what Miley Cyrus did was disgusting and inappropriate," Spielman continued, "…you're going to get a steady diet of it because Miley Cyrus got a desirable result. She was on every newscast and in every magazine. She got exactly what she wanted. So, what's it going to come to? That somebody will go onstage and bite the head off a chicken?"

Speilman likened it all to "freak shows" from a century before when the mentally ill were utilized as circus performers. Was it a coincidence that *Freak Show* was party to NBC's fourth installment of its popular *American Horror* series, created by *Glee's* Ryan Murphy? Spielman believed so. "Well, now your freak show is on TV…your freak show is in the movies…your freak show is all over the place, because of the removal of a public standard of morality."

He blamed his generation for the Federal Communications Commission's relaxing these codes and believes there was a technological reason they were lifted. "When television was basically just three networks, with their programs later sold into syndication, it was easier to keep standards and practices under control." Remembering a more stringent time, he referred to the Motion Picture Production Code or "Hays Code" utilized for the big screen, though he said he's not "in any way advocating for its return."

Under that code, for example, a male movie star filming a bedroom scene with a female movie star had to keep both of his feet safely on the floor. Any scene not following the code would be deleted from the film's final edit. The Hays Code was a much-maligned set of rules defined for motion picture producers and actors. "Understandably so, because certain things could be said on screen and certain other things could not." From his perspective, everything changed with the classic 1939 feature film *Gone with the Wind*, when Clark Gable, as Rhett Butler, uttered a ground-breaking line to Vivien Leigh's Scarlett O'Hara: "Frankly, my dear, I don't give a damn!"

"The word *damn* was extremely controversial," Spielman said.

A few decades later, a visual mainstream performance on TV introduced other boundaries, or lack thereof, into question: Elvis Presley's appearances on CBS-TV's *The Ed Sullivan Show* (September 9, 1956; October 28, 1956; and January 6, 1957, during the last of which he was allowed to be photographed from only the waist up). Presley's dancing had earned him the nickname Elvis the Pelvis, and the network considered his gyrating as overtly sexual. At the time, some people said rock 'n' roll would debauch whole generations of children. Were they right?

"Willing to sound judgmental," rock 'n' roll fan Spielman wrestled with the answer and replied: "Probably. You take [Elvis's] appearance…and how many years has it been? Sixty? Compare that to Miley Cyrus or Janet Jackson having a wardrobe malfunction and flashing [during the latter's halftime performance at *Super Bowl XXXVIII* in 2004]. There's a phrase: *It's not appropriate*. When was the last time you heard somebody say, 'Excuse me, that's not appropriate'?"

In modern times, television is littered with excessively violent and graphic images in prime time while racy morning and afternoon talk shows, said Spielman, parade "the lower depths and cultural sewage of society to be viewed as entertainment and diversion. There is nothing anymore where somebody would say, 'Oh, that's not appropriate.' Are we saying it's appropriate to have the kind of human behavior that Jerry Springer or for that matter Howard Stern constantly [showcase]?"

"What sounds like a negative opinion is really a cultural critique," Spielman continued. When he was growing up, "any kid could stay home from school if you had the flu. You could turn on the TV, and there would be nothing on that would harm your morals, your citizenship, or your view of life. There was a lovely naiveté involved. I would watch kid shows, cartoons, a game show, or whatever. There were wonderful shows, and you'd watch people who could win a refrigerator, a car, or Tourister luggage if they didn't get the big bonanza."

"Today," he said, "…a kid who stays home from school and flips on the TV—and not on cable—is in danger of losing their childhood immediately. Because if they flip on *The Maury Povich Show*, they'll see some girl who has no idea who the father of her child is. And at the end of the show, instead of winning Tourister luggage, they open an envelope with DNA evidence that says, 'You, Joe Blow—you're the father of the child.'"

In the early days of TV, Spielman added, "We didn't have a choice because there was a societal standard. You couldn't choose something that was disgusting and degrading and societally harmful because it wouldn't be broadcast." He acknowledged the pervading tension in Hollywood between the current standards and the pursuit of artist freedom and said, "The rules have always been under attack. Now, is that a bad thing? No, because some of the rules were a little over the top. But now we've gone the other way so that there's virtually nothing that is inappropriate. That's why a sex tape is now considered marketing."

Has TV's newfound freedom led to the lack of values audiences see today? For Spielman, stand-up comedian Lenny Bruce defined those who justify and define outrageous behavior as creative or artistic freedom. A once-personal-favorite of Spielman's, Bruce, like Miley Cyrus, was hailed as innovative and attacked for being contentious. "When I was a younger guy, we thought it was very cool what Lenny Bruce did," Spielman said. "He was considered a comic genius by a lot of people and really a kind of anarchist in a way. At a very low ebb, he got into [a style of performing that] gave him some degree of notoriety."

Bruce's style was similar to that of Howard Stern's today. "He decided to destroy any norms of civilized deportment." On one occasion, Bruce brought on stage a box of cremated ashes that had once been someone who was in his show. Bruce opened the box and picked through the ashes on camera. Spielman viewed this morbid spectacle and wondered how the comedian would have reacted if "heaven forbid, one of his children had died," and some performer began picking through *those* ashes for the edification of the audience? "Would Bruce have viewed that spectacle as simply breaking a taboo about what was decent?"

When Spielman was a child, "America had a standard. But the people who liked Lenny, and, unfortunately, I was one of them, thought he was interesting. Since then, things have only gotten worse."

"After Lenny Bruce, there was a steady coarsening of the use of language," Spielman said. "There were other comedians like Richard Pryor, who I knew briefly and who, in my eyes, was an utter genius. But you look at the language that Richard Pryor used… Before him, there were no four-letter words…no vulgar expression ever came out of anyone's mouth—not onstage. Some performers were known as *blue comics*, but they were relegated to the lower strata of nightclubs and certainly not the airwaves [of television]. Redd Foxx was the dirtiest [-mouthed] comic in the nightclub circuit, but he never used a four-letter word or *any* rough stuff on TV as an actor. *Sanford & Son* [the 1970s NBC sitcom on which Foxx took the lead] was a big hit. But he cleaned up his act because he had to…because what he did for a living in nightclubs you couldn't do on TV. Today, you see the networks using highly sexualized material and a change in language to the degree that they can. The bar keeps getting lower."

The '60s, the era in which Bruce found fame, was a revolutionary period, "the Vietnam generation," as Spielman called it. "The 'Peace and Love' generation said there shouldn't be any restrictions on comportment…that anything you liked to do was considered acceptable." For Spielman, the issues are more complicated in today's world. His generation began to break down any rule of what is proper and improper. "There is no longer any shame. Nor is anything or anyone taught that *this is right* and *this is wrong*. We have a republic that does not have and thankfully does not sanction any state religion. But we always [at least] had a standard of language and behavior. In universities across the county, everyone is taught not to be judgmental. What America used to be was *E Pluribus Unum…From many: One*. That may remain our motto, but it is not in practice. We have, in effect, an abandonment of *E Pluribus Unum*."

Television reflects that change, the essential abandonment of what had been an American standard. While Spielman hasn't advocated for religion or conservative politics, he's "simply a witness to identifying the way things are." Today, the expanding cable and digital industries are not bound by the more stringent rules of the FCC, and he can't help but ponder the effect of entertainment that constantly exploits society's flaws: "We always knew that there were people who lived dreadful, seamy lives. We've always had impoverishment, crime, and antisocial behavior. But when you parade this as either entertainment or diversion night and day to a populace, you're going to get a societal result. I'm not blaming TV, but TV is simply reflective of that result."

Former child star and established actress Kathy Garver weighed in on the discussion. A working performer since her debut as a five-year-old slave in Cecil B. DeMille's 1956 feature film classic, *The Ten Commandments*, Garver went on to find TV fame as the elder teen sister, Cissy, to Anissa Jones and Johnny Whitaker as twins Buffy and Jody on *Family Affair*. Broadcast on CBS from 1966 to 1971, Brian Keith played their Uncle Bill, and Sebastian Cabot was British "manny," Mr. French. Along with Garver, only Whitaker is still alive. Keith committed suicide in 1997, Cabot died in 1977, and Jones fell victim to an accidental drug overdose in 1976.

On August 28th of that year, Jones attended a party at a friend's home in Oceanside, California, and ingested an extremely lethal dose of barbiturates, phencyclidine, cocaine, and methaqualone. Her boyfriend claimed to have checked in on her earlier, and all was well. But an hour later, a lifeless Jones was discovered by friends. After dressing her, they called the paramedics, but it was too late. The actress, just 18 years old, was declared dead by what the coroner had allegedly deciphered as one of the largest overdoses he had seen.

Garver knew all too well the ups and downs that fame and fortune can sometimes place on young contemporary talent from any era. At the time of Jones' passing, she said, "It's so tragic. As much as Anissa tried to dissociate herself from the little girl she played on [*Family Affair*], I still found her [to be] the same person. She and Buffy were the same wonderful person." Today, Garver added, "Anissa had it very difficult. But now you see Miley Cyrus and Lindsay Lohan, and all the new and upcoming stars on all the Disney TV shows, for example, and they have the fame a hundred-million-fold because of Facebook or Twitter. They can't wear a blouse or shirt that's incorrectly [matched] with the wrong color suit without it going worldwide. And placing that kind of pressure on a teen or a young person right when they are trying to develop their own identity and find who they are as human beings is very disturbing, from a psychological standpoint."

"Fortunately," she continued, "what Disney has started doing for their young stars is setting up sessions with a resident psychologist, helping them deal with the fame…the pressure…the publicity of being under the constant scrutiny of the public eye. It's a worthwhile and very necessary thing to do in our present culture. They take a teenager that's living a nice regular life when they're 13, who then does a series for three years, during which they want that young actor to remain looking 13 instead of their real age of 16. So, it's a very productive thing to have Disney organize any self-esteem session that can help their young performers deal with the many-times-overwhelming price of fame."

Sadly, Jones was not as blessed with such support while filming *Family Affair*. Instead, she had just turned nine years old upon starting the series, and Whitaker was only six. Five years later, when the series completed its original run, she was almost 14, but still donning pigtails and a little girl's dress, and carrying around Mrs. Beasley, Buffy's famous doll. "That really did a number on her psyche," Garver said. "Here she was trying to have a normal life, but playing an 8-year-old when she was really 14. It was very difficult for her to deal with, not only while we were doing the show, but when it ended. The experience jaded her. She never wanted to be in show business ever again from that point on."

Jones was offered the teen lead in *The Exorcist*, the 1973 feature film that made a star out of Linda Blair, who was eventually cast in the role of Regan, the young girl possessed by demons. But Anissa rejected the offer, clearly fighting demons of her own off-screen. "She wanted to be a normal kid," Garver said. "She wanted to go to the beach and hang out with her friends." Unfortunately, her friends led her to a seedy culture that killed her and devastated her fans and those closest to her, including Garver. "It was horrible what happened and unbelievably sad—and it still is. To this day, I miss Anissa—and always will."

To counter films like *The Exorcist* and all others that have appeared since on the big screen and TV, Disney and other youth-skewed networks like Nickelodeon are at least attempting to bring family-oriented shows to the modern viewer. More than any other network that creates and airs all-new programming, as opposed to screening only reruns of classic programs, The Hallmark Channel has worked diligently to showcase quality original shows in prime time. In doing so, the network has in recent years made every attempt to cover all bases, at the risk of isolating its core conservative audience.

In July 2020, Hallmark vowed to put more LGBTQ representation in its content following criticism that the movies lacked diversity. After the company was criticized online for pulling commercials including a lesbian wedding the year before, it not only reinstated the commercials but showed its first same-sex wedding in the movie *Wedding Every Weekend*.

On November 22, 2020, Hallmark, best known for its heartwarming Christmas TV-movies, premiered its first LGBTQ holiday film with a gay lead couple. Jonathan Bennett, of *Mean Girls* fame, and Brad Hardner played husbands who visit family during the festive season while awaiting adoptive news of their first child. "I'm proud of everyone at Hallmark Channel for making the holiday table bigger and more welcoming and warmer this year," said Bennett, who is gay in real life. The movie inspired him and his boyfriend, Jaymes Vaughn, to consider adopting a child themselves.

"Representation is important, but correct representation is more important, not just for viewers who may not interact [with] or accept LGBTQ people, but it's also important for LGBTQ people to see themselves in media," he said.

Years before *Wedding Every Weekend*, Hallmark aired, among many other uplifting original films and shows, *Signed, Sealed, Delivered* (created in 2014 by *Touched By An Angel's* Martha Williamson), *The Good Witch* (in production since 2008 and starring Catherine Bell), *Cedar Cove* (featuring Andie MacDowell since 2013), and daytime fare like *Home & Family* (a talk/lifestyle series on the air since 2012).

Besides traditional and digital networks, there are also other ways to enjoy new and classic family programming by way of the DVD and Blu-ray. Producer/director Danny Gold partnered with colleague Matthew Asner for Mod 3 Productions, which had produced the DVD release of Ed Spielman's *Kung Fu* series as well as other classic TV shows like *Growing Pains* (ABC, 1985–1992), *The Dukes of Hazzard* (CBS, 1979–1985), *CHiPs* (NBC, 1977–1983), and *The Mary Tyler Moore Show*, (CBS, 1970–1977), the latter of which featured the Emmy Award-winning actor Ed Asner, Matthew's father.

Classic television programs, in part, have the "awesome power of reflecting society, escapism, and personal aspirations," Gold said. "*The Mary Tyler Moore Show* reflected the burgeoning women's equal rights movement. Additionally, its storylines humorously centered on love, friendship, and camaraderie." In comparison, a series like *The Dukes of Hazzard* focused on family, friendship, and escapism. "Who wouldn't want to jump a car 200 feet across a ravine," he mused.

"*CHiPs* blended many social issues with a healthy dose of friendship," Gold added. "And what made *Growing Pains* so attractive to audiences comes down to two thematic elements—love and family. Family shows have always been the most popular and long-lasting on television. We all come from families and face issues on a daily basis. It is both from an escapist and cathartic view that audiences love to watch other families dealing with similar issues."

"TV shows that reflect social issues of the time give audiences perspective on their own feelings and often garner water-cooler discussions," Gold concluded. "Accordingly, shows that facilitate communication impact society in a positive way. As long as people talk—good things are possible."

PART 2
THE LEARNING CHANNELS

"It's a brand-new science called bionics…
where the biology of your own body controls electronics."
—Steve Austin, *The Six Million Dollar Man*
[Episode: "The Bionic Woman, Part 1" – 3/16/75)

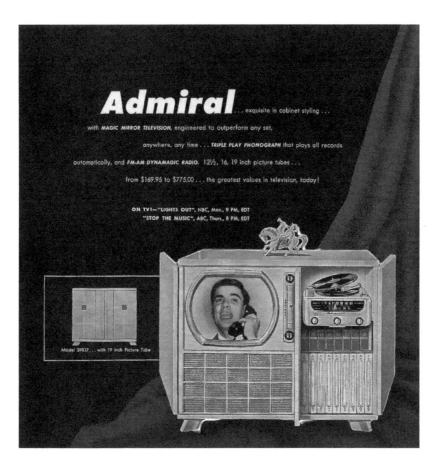

Nichelle Nichols blazed the way for female African-Americans on television
[Credit: Courtesy of Nichelle Nichols/Author's Collection]

Chapter 3

Classic television ignited Tom Zapiecki's creative spark.

The writer/producer "wanted to be a journalist because of *Lou Grant* and a D.J. because of *WKRP in Cincinnati*." The PBS documentary *The Natural History of the Water Closet* inspired him to make documentaries, which he does today.

Don Seaman is on the other end of the spectrum. As the Manager of Marketing Communications for the Television Bureau of Advertising (TVB), Seaman was responsible for promoting and raising awareness of the company and of local broadcast television's value propositions within the traditional and digital media industries. He was Vice President, Director of Communications Analysis for the Media Planning Group (MPG, which later merged with Havas), where he oversaw the agency's broadcast research department. During his tenure, he established MPG as a thought leader with much of the trade press. His insights have been published in magazines like *Ad Age, Adweek, Media Life, Broadcasting & Cable*, and *eMarketer*; in *The New York Times, The Huffington Post*, and *The New York Post*; on *Bloomberg Television*, and by many other local, national, and international media outlets. He has also worked with additional media and advertising agencies, including DraftFCB, Universal McCann, Media Edge: CIA, and NW Ayer, as well as the ABC and Lifetime television networks.

In a blog post at Jack Myers' www.MediaBizBloggers.com, Seaman cited words spoken by *Avengers* actor Don Cheadle at the *2013 Emmy Awards* regarding TV's culture-defining occurrences of November 1963 and February 1964. Namely, the assassination of John F. Kennedy and The Beatles were first seen on American TV in late 1963 on a broadcast of *The Tonight Show* with Jack Paar. Said Cheadle:

"Two emotionally charged events, forever linked in our memories. Fifty years later, they underscore the immediacy of TV and its tremendous impact on our society. The boxes are thinner, the screens are flatter and more portable, but television's power to engage, inform, and unite continues to have a profound purpose as we remember the past, celebrate the present, and anticipate our future."

In turn, Seaman named the Kennedy Assassination a seminal moment of the Television Age, one that marked the first time more Americans received their news from TV than from print, and an "event that proved television's unique ability to bring people together with sound and sight to share in milestone moments. Newspapers delivered information and interpretation—but television also provided emotion. We were now in the moment, not just reviewing it…People's relationship with news suddenly changed forever. And with it, television became more than just a novelty for entertainment. It became an essential part of American households."

The Beatles' historic appearance, Seaman continued, "…provided instant relief from our rock-bottom national despair…they reenergized the airwaves with joy and love, and a sense of fun…. In that one night, they reached down, held our hand, and made us all feel younger and happier again. As a television moment, the repercussions would be felt in many areas of society—and one could make an argument that this gave rise to youth marketing. The hysteria created by four 'Lads from Liverpool' may be the turning point of a demographic shift in American marketing. Suddenly, the housewives-in-aprons target [audience] seemed so very 'yesterday,' so very 1950s. We'd become a youth culture, almost overnight, as a TV audience 73 million strong changed us to our core…. But these two moments were just fixed points in our television landscape. They were huge boulders dropped in a large, calm body of water, which created ripples that still are being seen today."

It's been documented how the human body has served as a conduit for electric current and pulsation, a line of thinking provocatively addressed on television in an episode of the TV medical series *3 Lbs*, which aired on CBS in 2006. Stanley Tucci's fictional Dr. Douglas Hanson, which was based on a respected real-life neurosurgeon at New York Presbyterian Hospital, described the human brain as a wet cell battery or "wires in a box." Beyond the ironic reference to "television" as a "box," this explains why, for example, a light bulb may at times blow a fuse with a mere human's touch to switch off a lamp.

An amusing anecdote from one of TV's most beloved performers helps drive the point home.

Bewitched icon Elizabeth Montgomery once discussed her fondness for fellow actress Marion Lorne, who played bumbling sorceress Aunt Clara to Montgomery's famously-stable house-witch-with-a-twitch, Samantha Stephens. On a break one day at the Beverly Hills Hotel, Lorne excitedly phoned Montgomery. "Elizabeth…You must come to the hotel immediately!"

Startled and perplexed, Montgomery wondered, "Why?! What's wrong?!"

"Please!" Lorne insisted. "Just come over here—and hurry!"

Montgomery became frantic. Fortunately, she lived near the famed Beverly Hills spot, where she soon found herself forlorn at Lorne's door. Once inside the room, Elizabeth persisted, "What's the problem?!"

"Watch this," Marion replied and proceeded to wave her right arm and hand towards her television set, which immediately flickered on. She motioned and pointed a second time, and—*poof!*—the TV turned off! Montgomery stood silent and significantly stunned as Lorne repeated this bit of apparent real-life sorcery.

"Don't you see?!" Lorne exclaimed. "I really *can* do magic!"

Montgomery was not one to suffer fools gladly, and Lorne was no fool. She may have played one as Aunt Clara, but, like Montgomery, she was a revered and stage-trained actress who, then 86, was at best slightly confused (she died shortly thereafter). Montgomery eventually discovered that Lorne's bracelets somehow aligned with the frequency on the hotel's TV remote control device.

Science has long verified the electrical current that courses through the human conduit. Why wouldn't comparable currents cross or coordinate between the body electric and the TV machine each time an individual sits down to watch one of their favorite shows?

The potential for positive results is endless when it comes to television's link to society, at least when choosing to take the proverbial high road in viewing and producing quality programming. Is it possible for TV viewers to experience an energy surge or exchange with each random channel change? Does switching from a violent TV show or movie to a heart-warming, family-oriented movie, series, or special lend to or increase the viewers' positive state of mind? Can the audience members improve their mood by changing the channel from a drama to a comedy?

For decades, research conducted by Norman Cousins has provided scientific proof of terminally ill patients getting better with consistent and frequent prescriptions or doses of joyful entertainment if initially documented with feature films, as opposed to TV shows.

Cousins battled heart disease and arthritis and was an American political journalist, professor, and advocate for world peace. He served as an Adjunct Professor of Medical Humanities for the School of Medicine at the University of California, Los Angeles, where he researched the biochemistry of human emotions, which he believed were key to successfully battling illness. He authored several best-selling non-fiction books on the topic including *Anatomy of an Illness (As Perceived by the Patient): Reflections on Healing*, which was adapted into a 1984 TV-movie starring Ed Asner.

Cousins claimed he fought health challenges with extensive doses of Vitamin C; a positive attitude; healthy amounts of love, faith, and hope; and by watching classic comedy feature films starring The Marx Brothers. As he once said, "I made the joyous discovery that ten minutes of genuine belly laughter had an anesthetic effect and would give me at least two hours of pain-free sleep. When the pain-killing effect of the laughter wore off, we would switch on the motion picture projector again, and not infrequently, it would lead to another pain-free interval."

As reported by Yahoo News, the movies *Mrs. Doubtfire* (1993) and *The King's Speech* (2011) played into Cousins' theory and subsequent important roles in the lives of a few who watched them.

A real-life teacher in the United Kingdom utilized the speech therapy techniques chronicled in the Oscar-winning *The King's Speech* to help a student challenged with a persistent stammer. The experience was recorded for the documentary series *Educating Yorkshire*. Musharraf Asghar, then 16 years old, was preparing for his General Certificate of Secondary Education (GSCE) and was naturally concerned about the verbal portion of the English final exam, which was to count for 20% of his grade. He expressed how his stammering had been an issue for him for as long as he could remember. He was approximately 5 years old when he observed that others "started noticing it was a bit different to a normal stammer that goes away as people get older."

The speech impediment led to bullying at various benchmarks in his young life. With the exam soon upon Asghar, his English instructor, Mr. Burton, offered to help him rehearse speaking while listening to music, the same process that was employed by the real-life Lionel Logue, as portrayed by Geoffrey Rush, with George VI (Colin Firth) in *The King's Speech*.

In *Yorkshire's* final moments, Asghar delivers a speech in front of several fellow students while listening to music on his headphones. There are a few awkward moments, but his significantly-strengthened speaking patterns win over his peers. As explained in Britain's *The Guardian*, after the documentary aired, Asghar thought Burton was "a genius until he lent me *The King's Speech* afterward, and then I realized he just copied that other man!" Now in college, Asghar was pleased with being profiled in *Educating Yorkshire* and hoped it allowed others with a stammer the confidence to have "a go" at public speaking.

Mrs. Doubtfire, starring Robin Williams and Sally Field, provided teachable and lifesaving moments. For one, this film helped a seven-year-old little girl from Portland, Oregon, prevent her mother from choking to death.

Jennifer Thornton ingested a piece of sausage and soon experienced trouble breathing. By the gift of fate and maybe a few angels, her little daughter Amira came to the rescue. Amira was watching television when she heard her mother making strange sounds from the other room. Upon investigation, Amira saw her mom gasping for air and, with immediate poise, utilized the Heimlich maneuver. "I picked her up three times," Amira told a local TV station. "She spit the sausage out." It was then noted how Amira never enrolled in a first aid class. Instead, she learned how to do the Heimlich from watching *Mrs. Doubtfire…* on television.

The connection between the TV watcher and the TV monitor might be slightly more sophisticated than just the actual physically-electric or man-made electronic energy it remotely requires to change the channel or switch on or off the TV set. The mosaic of television's daily thread may reach far more extensively than any mainstream musical group, any presidential or minor event, or any disruption or activity of any kind throughout history.

"TV definitely influences people," Ed Spielman said. "There is no way that it could hold the standard of behavior, language, deportment, and citizenship when the rest of the society was having it eroded. Its underpinnings were being eroded in the educational system. TV is now simply reflective of societal norms. Nothing more."

In one episode of *Medical Center*, Dr. Joe Gannon, played by Chad Everett, cares for a former high-school teacher in the hospital. At one point, the teacher reminds him "not to split an infinitive," after which Gannon laughs and corrects himself. It was a significant moment for classic TV fans who may have not learned this concept in school.

Does this prove that the living room of television is more educational than the classroom of high school or college?

A few observations from Jan Hunt, M.Sc., may hold the answer. Hunt is the director of the National Child Project (NCP), a nonprofit organization, and the author of *The Natural Child: Parenting from the Heart* (New Society Publishers, 2001) and *A Gift for Baby* (Natural Child Project, 2009).

NCP's mission statement on www.NaturalChild.org reads as follows:

"Our vision is a world in which all children are treated with dignity, respect, understanding, and compassion. In such a world, every child can grow into adulthood with a generous capacity for love and trust. Our society has no more urgent task."

Hunt also published several articles online, including "Is *I Love Lucy* Educational?" in which she addressed a reader's poll in *USA Today* about legislation that would require a daily minimum of three hours of educational and informative TV. "One show that brought about disagreement among readers," she said, was *I Love Lucy*. A personal favorite of hers, the classic '50s sitcom introduced the mainstream television audience to the multi-talents of Lucille Ball. The charismatic redhead found stardom by way of her delightful and daffy portrayal of the eclectically dingy but darling housewife Lucy Ricardo on *I Love Lucy*, loosely based on a radio show in which she co-starred with Richard Denning.

In 1948, Ball took the leading radio role in *My Favorite Husband*, in which she played Liz Cugat (later changed to Cooper), the scatterbrained wife of a Midwestern banker. Two years later, CBS brought *Favorite* to television, which Ball conceded to do only if the network granted two main requests: Desi Arnaz, her real-life husband of Cuban descent, would have to play her on-screen spouse; and both she and Arnaz would retain all rights and creative control.

The network agreed, and Ball and Arnaz commenced work on what became the most successful and beloved situation comedy in television history.

Originally broadcast on CBS from 1951 to 1957, *I Love Lucy* was followed by three years of occasional one-hour specials titled *The Lucy-Desi Hour* and has aired every year since, first for nearly a decade on CBS and then in global syndication. After ending her run with Desi on *I Love Lucy* (they would divorce in 1960), Ball continued playing the Lucy character in one form or another in three more series: *The Lucy Show* (CBS, 1962–1968), *Here's Lucy* (CBS, 1968–1974), and *Life with Lucy* (ABC, 1986), and appeared in many TV specials and guest appearances, as well as feature films.

Before and after mugging it up as *Lucy*, Ball also sang, danced, and appeared in various dramatic roles—on the big screen and small. Off-screen, she was considered one of Hollywood's initial female executives, the last of which was served by her forceful, take-charge personality (which was at times somewhat off-putting to many a colleague, be they actor, writer, or director).

But it was with *I Love Lucy* that Ball first made mainstream media history, most notably because the show presented TV's first "mixed marriage" (an American-born woman and a Cuban-born man), but some adults who participated in the *USA Today* poll weren't all that impressed. As Hunt continued to point out, one older reader from Detroit said, "While some of life's valuable lessons may be included in shows designed primarily for entertainment, that does not qualify them as *educational*. Education can be fun, but it is a disciplined activity. *I Love Lucy* just doesn't fit the bill."

Other *USA Today* poll responders were children who believed that *Lucy* did serve an educational purpose by offering valuable lessons about the consequences of one's actions. "They saw Lucy Ricardo, whose escapades often backfire, as a sort of reverse role model, and the show as something of a morality play," said Hunt. "This is an intriguing perspective because Shakespeare's plays developed from comic characters in early morality plays, and his theatrical productions, written for audiences of a broad social background, were the popular entertainment of the day." As Hunt explained further, author-historian Frank Wadsworth noted in his *World Book* entry on Shakespeare, "Most of the Globe's [theatre] audience consisted of middle-class citizens, such as merchants and craftsmen and their wives. They went to the theater for the same reasons most people today go to the movies—to relax and to escape for a while from their cares."

"Shakespeare's plays were written with the intention of entertaining a mass audience, just as many TV sitcoms and dramas are written now," Hunt wrote. "At the time they were written, his plays were definitely *not* considered 'educational and informative'; nor would they have 'fit the bill' as a 'disciplined activity.' It was only from a later perspective that Shakespeare's plays were deemed 'educational.' In his day, there was even some criticism of Shakespeare as an actor-turned-writer, uneducated in traditional theatrical production. Had television been invented in Elizabethan times, it does not seem too far-fetched to imagine that 'Hamlet' would have been one of the first TV dramas, criticized for its violence and passion. Today, of course, Shakespeare's plays are considered a required part of a 'disciplined education,' with the unfortunate result of dissuading many students from enjoying the pleasures of his works."

"The determination of whether a production is 'educational' can change over time," Hunt continued. "Any show can provide 'educational and informative' material and food for thought on the thinking, fashions, roles, and lifestyles of its time. In fact, early shows like *I Love Lucy* are currently studied in university courses on American cultural history."

But is *I Love Lucy* educational in the ways mostly defined by the term? Hunt seemed to think so. As a writer on parenting issues, she was impressed with how parenting is presented on the show. Little Ricky, played by Richard Keith, a.k.a. Keith Thibodeaux, is "consistently treated with more love, kindness, and patience than is depicted in most current television families." From her point of view, nothing was more educational than that which "promotes and models empathic parenting skills," particularly as this pertinent topic was not included in the majority of curricula.

Hunt believed her son had learned a great deal from *I Love Lucy*, including what it takes to produce a quality television program, including skilled writers and talented actors who know how to improvise; how most "currently produced shows are more violent, less consistent in quality, and more poorly written than earlier shows…that persistence can bring about success…that smoking was common in the 1950s and not well understood.…that marital roles have changed over the decades… that an actor's personal life can be very different from the role he or she plays.…that if you look into history you can sometimes discover where social changes may have been introduced [such as the three episodes in which Little Ricky is permitted to join his parents in bed when he needed emotional support]…that even loving couples may not be able to sustain a marriage…[and]…on and on."

"Children know intuitively that *learning should be fun*," Hunt concluded. "With this definition, *I Love Lucy* certainly 'fits the bill' in our house. It may be that more people enjoyed Shakespeare's plays when they were told it was 'entertainment' than they do now that they are told it is 'educational.' Let us hope the same thing never happens to Lucy."

Given Hunt's perspective and beyond, TV shows of every genre throughout history have proven instructive and constructive.

Exhibit A is the majority of programming presented on the Public Broadcast System, a.k.a. PBS, which has defined itself as "educational television" since its inception.

PBS was founded by Hartford N. Gunn Jr. of WGBH-TV in Boston, Massachusetts, as the Corporation for Public Broadcasting on October 5, 1970, at which time acquired the several functions of its predecessor, National Educational Television (NET), which later merged with WNDT (of Newark, New Jersey) to become WNET (which, in 1973, merged with Educational Television Stations).

Unlike ABC, CBS, NBC, FOX, The CW, and others in which their affiliates give up portions of their local advertising airtime via barter for nationwide programming, PBS operates as a nonprofit organization, with its member stations paying fees for the shows acquired and distributed by the national organization. The network allows its affiliates to have more control in local scheduling than is granted by its more mainstream competition.

PBS has aired children's shows like *Sesame Street* or *The Electric Company*, or other series—for all ages—such as *The Joy of Painting*, which aired globally, and was hosted by Robert Norman "Bob" Ross (October 29, 1942–July 4, 1995), an American artist and teacher.

For a time in the 1970s, CBS screened PBS-like programming in the form of Saturday morning interstitials titled *In The News*, while ABC did the same with spots like *Multiplication Rock* and *Schoolhouse Rock* that aired between regular animated fare and live-action shows (such as the *Captain Marvel/Isis* hour on CBS, and *American Bandstand* on ABC). During the week, ABC aired its coveted *Afterschool Specials*, while CBS screened its equally-lauded *SchoolBreaks*, both of which showcased a combination of scripted and documentary programs with an academic slant. Such programming was joined in the evening by the likes of

[Credit: The Classic TV Preservation Society]

Marlo Thomas' award-winning, all-star special *Free to Be You and Me* (March 11, 1974), which was based on her book of the same name).

News and broadcast journalist/documentarian Linda Ellerbee later produced and hosted several similar specials for ABC and other networks like Nickelodeon. Before broadcast standards loosened (if not completely lost control), MTV (and other cable networks) aired similar specials or regular programming, such as early, less-edgy, less-brash editions of *The Real World*.

Prior to any of that, the original three broadcast networks (ABC, CBS, NBC) periodically aired teachable moments in the form of scripted TV shows that we were set in elementary, high school, college or university-level, or within the premise and/or actual physical confines of an education facility. *Our Miss Brooks, Mr. Peepers, Room 222, Welcome Back Kotter, Head of the Class, Saved by the Bell*, and *Boy Meets World* (the latter two of which were rebooted in recent years) each became examples of TV's mainstream strategic approach to becoming the very example of an educational tool.

When a TV show, scripted or otherwise, is defined as educational, the intention is clear. But when a mainstream series about education is presented within, for example, a comedy format, as with *Our Miss Brooks* and *Room 222*, the teaching principles are less defined.

In December 2013, *Classic Images* magazine published a profile of *Brooks* star Eve Arden that was based on writer James Bawden's various interviews with the actress which began in 1972. *Our Miss Brooks* was based on her radio show of the same name. "A lot of TV hits came from radio," Arden said. "*Father Knows Best, Life of Riley, Burns and Allen*. We'd get the new [TV] script on a Friday and do a rough block and, on Monday, more rehearsals…and then do it before a studio audience. Then on Tuesday, we'd film touch-ups. So, we did two episodes a week, which was heavy. Don't forget the order was for 39 half-hours—plus the radio show! I always thought the radio shows were better because listeners had to imagine so much."

In 1956, Arden brought *Brooks* one step further and transformed it into a feature film, which she called "a strange experience" that confounded her because the movie was produced when the TV show completed its original run. She felt the motion picture should have been made "when the series was at its peak." She also believed her TV show "wasn't a sitcom at all. It was more of a drama."

This was also the case with *Room 222*, a charming, innovative half-hour that was filmed like a movie, without a live audience or laugh track, mostly because it made every attempt to be real. Originally on ABC from 1969 to 1973, the show featured Lloyd Haynes and Denise Nichols as teachers Pete Dixon and Liz McIntyre, Karen Valentine as a novice instructor Alice Johnson, and Michael Constantine as Seymour Kaufman, the principal—each on faculty at the fictional Los Angeles high school Walt Whitman High. One of TV's first 30-minute dramedies, *Room 222* featured a stellar cast, and quality talent behind the scenes, including writers like James L. Brooks (who later penned and produced *The Mary Tyler Moore Show*), and directors such as Gene Reynolds (who in 1972 adapted the feature *M*A*S*H* for the small screen).

TV scribe Treva Silverman wrote two 16 episodes of *222*, including "First We'll Eat, Then We'll Strike" (10/22/69) and "The Exchange Teacher" (December 17, 1969). On "Strike," the teachers of Walt Whitman, led by Mr. Dixon, formally protest a proposed school bond that will cut what they believe are important educational programs at the school—a development that Mr. Kaufman is none too pleased about. In Silverman's second segment, an exchange teacher from England (Charmion King) mixes things up a bit at Walt Whitman with her unconventional teaching methods, which include random seating, no homework, and playing music by Simon & Garfunkel and The Beatles in class.

The cast of *Room 222* (from Top Left): Lloyd Haynes, Michael Constantine, Denise Nichols, and Karen Valentine *[Credit: The Classic TV Preservation Society]*

Silverman addressed how important it was to keep *Room 222* realistic, more relatable for the audience: "The story sessions were the first time I was invited to kind of dig down into myself and find grains of truth that could be expanded into a story. There was a lot of laughing in the story sessions where we would meet together and figure out what I was going to write about—and I could relax because I knew the script didn't have to be funny every minute. But what it had to be was authentic. No cartoon characters. No larger-than-life stuff. The challenge was in making sure each character was exactly who they should be."

Two years after ABC cancelled *Room 222*, the network premiered *Welcome Back, Kotter*. In 1977, entertainment journalist Peggy Herz chronicled the development of this half-hour school-geared series that was envisioned as a star vehicle for comedian Gabe Kaplan. Based on Kaplan's exploits from his high-school youth in Brooklyn, *Welcome Back* (the show's original abbreviated title) ends up making a superstar out of John Travolta, then just 23 years old. Kaplan portrayed teacher Gabe Kotter to a group of mischievous students nicknamed Sweathogs, who were led by Travolta's dim-but-dynamic Vinnie Barbarino.

As Travolta told Herz, "The kids are troublemakers but in a harmless way. They give their teacher a hard time. But there's never been a series on TV about a class like this. Kids are getting a bigger kick out of the show than anyone else."

Kaplan addressed how his real-life adventures contributed to *Back's* development, including his decision to leave school in his senior year, prior to graduation. He had a few happy school memories, but mainly it was "a pretty confusing time," he said. And while he is unsure of his aspirations, he was certain he would not attend college. "I saw nothing I wanted that I could get with a high-school diploma. I was missing some credits, so I wouldn't have graduated that year, anyway. What I really wanted to do was play baseball."

Kaplan's fellow students in his real-life high school were rated on a scale of one-through-five. "I was always in the fours. That was next to the dumbest. Once you tell a kid that, he stops trying."

Kaplan quit school when he was 17. Good at baseball though "not great," he tried out for minor league clubs in Florida and Texas. But he never made the cut. For four years, he pursued various vocations, but "mainly nothing," he admitted.

Had the young Master Kaplan been blessed with an experienced teacher like Mr. Kotter, the actor's life might have turned out differently. Instead, no one teacher took any particular interest in him. Periodically, he would be ushered aside by a seemingly-caring faculty member who'd wonder why he wasn't performing more productively. "Everything they said was fine," he recalled, but then he never received any follow-up support. "I never had a Mr. Kotter or anybody like him. I was really drifting during those years after I left school."

Anything could have happened to Kaplan. At that point, his chances of being happy and successful were slim to none. "I don't recommend what I did," he said. "It's better to stay in school."

The result: another teachable moment, proving how TV and reality sometimes cross-pollinate to set a good example.

Entertainment historian and archivist Rob Ray co-lectured for decades at the Long Beach Film Forum in California. He offered his academic insight into *Welcome Back, Kotter*, *Room 222*, and *Our Miss Brooks*, beginning with a reference to Travolta's comments that *Kotter* was the first show to display a rowdy class as regulars:

> "What Travolta says is largely true. The students on a show like *Leave It to Beaver* probably gave their teachers more trouble than even Miss Brooks got from her class. I've never seen much of *Our Miss Brooks* as a TV show and mainly know it from radio, but the Walter character [played by Richard Crenna, later cast as one of *The Real McCoys*] has a crush on Miss Brooks and I don't recall any other students having much to do on that show. As to *Room 222*, one of the students gives Miss Johnson [Karen Valentine] some trouble in the pilot and actually makes her cry. But after that, the students as a whole were respectful of the entire faculty on that show. They…weren't like the Sweathogs [of *Kotter*], that's for sure. *Room 222* was more realistic and explored contemporary teenage issues in a more relevant way."

Chapter 4

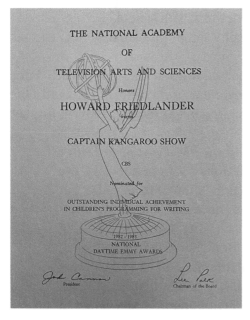

THE NATIONAL ACADEMY

OF

TELEVISION ARTS AND SCIENCES

Honors

HOWARD FRIEDLANDER

writer

CAPTAIN KANGAROO SHOW

CBS

Nominated for

OUTSTANDING INDIVIDUAL ACHIEVEMENT
IN CHILDREN'S PROGRAMMING FOR WRITING

1982-1983
NATIONAL
DAYTIME EMMY AWARDS

President

Chairman of the Board

[Credit: Courtesy of Howard Friedlander]

For many classic TV fans, the animated children's series *Rocky & Bullwinkle* contributed to their love for puns, irony, poetry and history. That's a significant amount of inspiration from just a TV cartoon show. But that series also had several smaller compartments of influence, all comedy-based. *Rocky & Bullwinkle* ignited many to research Jay Ward, one of the show's creator, who gave birth to its comedic style and content. However, some fans were more practical than others, and chose in their youth to watch programs like *Emergency* and *Adam-12*, inspiring some to join Emergency Medical Teams (EMT) or the police force.

In October 1977, *TV Guide* documented what remains an inescapable fact: children are a core sector of the television viewing public. Two-to five-year-old children typically spend approximately 30 hours a week in front of the traditional TV set-turned-monitor, while the six-to-11-year-old group kicks in at around 27 hours. With the onset of mobile devices, those numbers have assuredly increased.

How could such an enormous amount of any consistent activity not affect the human psyche and development, particularly a young mind?

Fortunately, through the years there's been a long line of life-affirming TV shows geared towards children, and/or that have included children in the cast. Some have featured adults interacting with puppets, such as *Kukla, Fran & Ollie* (NBC/ABC/PBS, 1948–1971), *Captain Kangaroo* (CBS, 1955–1992), *Mister Rogers' Neighborhood* (PBS, 1968–2001), *Sesame Street* (PBS, 1969–Present), and *The Muppets* (Syndicated, 1976–1981). Others have featured only puppets, or marionettes, as with *Thunderbirds* (via British airwaves ATV, 1965–1966). Others still featured adults appearing to be oversized puppets such as *Bozo The Clown* (Syndicated Franchise, 1956–1964), *Howdy Doody* (NBC/Syndicated, 1947–1960), *H.R. Pufnstuf* (ABC/Syndication, 1969–1978), and *Barney* (Syndicated, 1992–2010). Others still have paraded multi-talented youngsters singing, dancing, and acting with energetic aplomb as a party to *The Mickey Mouse Club* (ABC, 1955–1959), *The Electric Company* (PBS, 1971–1977), *Here Come the Double Deckers* (ABC, 1970–1972), and *Kids Incorporated* (NBC/Disney Channel, 1984–1993). Additional live-action shows appeared including ABC's *AfterSchool Specials* (1972–1997), and CBS's *SchoolBreak Specials* (1984–1996), and *PeeWee's Playhouse* (CBS, 1986–1991).

Along with the *Disneyland/The Wonderful World of Disney* (ABC, 1954–1992) series *The Mickey Mouse Club* was created via barter with ABC to loan money to help build the Disneyland Park in tandem with the Wrather Corporation. This company, headed by Jack Wrather (who wed former child actress Bonita Granville), also oversaw the *Lassie* TV show (from 1954–1971 on CBS, and in first-run syndication from then until 1974) as well as, for decades, the Disneyland Hotel. Starring Jimmy Dodd and Roy Williams, *The Mickey Mouse Club* introduced an energetic cast of young performers called "Mousketeers" who later found stardom of their own, including future '60s beach film icon and recording artist Annette Funicello, and Bobby Burgess, who later danced with Barbara Boylan, Cissy King, and Elaine Balden on *The Lawrence Welk Show*. The behind-the-scenes talent was top-notch, as well, including writers Stirling Silliphant, who later composed episodes of the acclaimed *Route 66* drama, as well as segments of *Alfred Hitchcock Presents* (CBS/NBC, 1955–1965), *Naked City* (ABC, 1958–1963), *Longstreet* (ABC, 1971–1972), and hit feature films like *The Poseidon Adventure* (1972), *The Towering Inferno* (1974), and *Circle of Iron* (1978), and TV-movies such as *Pearl* (1978) and *Fly Away Home* (1981).

Producer/editor Les Perkins was a creative director at The Walt Disney Company, which presented *The Mickey Mouse Club,* one of the first national network children's programs, with a young cast. "It was a *huge* hit," Perkins said. "Always concerned with high quality, Walt poured more money into the series than he made. But he knew it would pay off in ancillary sources of income [merchandise, publications] and also help promote his new Disneyland Park, all of which it did."

There were cost savings by extended reuses of the elaborate, daily opening production numbers, and similar repetitive elements. "The shows were pretty much divided into four segments/acts between commercial breaks," Perkins said. "You often didn't get any new program material until 15 minutes into the show." But young viewers didn't mind because "kids love repetition anyway," said Perkins. Disney staple Bill Walsh had just completed production on the hit TV- miniseries, *Davy Crockett* (1954), "another first," Perkins noted of the man who later supervised the company's successful feature films such as *Mary Poppins* (1964) and *The Love Bug* (1969).

There are also several books that profile *The Mickey Mouse Club*, including *The Mickey Mouse Scrapbook* by Keith Keller (Grosset & Dunlap, 1975), and *Walt, Mickey and Me* by Paul Petersen (Dell, 1977), a former Mouseketeer and co-star of *The Donna Reed Show*. Perkins speculates there may also be a moniker connection between the Mouseketeers and *The Three Mesquiteers*, the Republic Pictures western series of 51 films made from 1936 to 1943. "Ironically, the last cast-change in that series included *Mouse Club* host Jimmie Dodd. He was a Mesquiteer before he was a Mouseketeer!"

Adjunct to Bob Keeshan on *Captain Kangaroo* and Fred Rogers on *Mister Rogers' Neighborhood,* Shari Lewis was one of the most influential live-action performers in classic children's television. A ventriloquist, puppeteer, writer, musician, and popular children's and Emmy Award-winning TV show host from the 1960s to 1990s, Lewis was best known as the original puppeteer of Lamb Chop, a character first seen on *Kangaroo,* and later with a more formal debut on *Hi Mom*, a local New York morning show that aired from 1957 to 1963 on WRCA-TV (now WNBC-TV).

It all started in 1952 when Lewis and her unique skills won first prize on CBS' *Arthur Godfrey's Talent Scouts,* after which she hosted several New York children's programs, including NBC's studio-and-home audience participation series *Facts N'Fun* (July 5 to September 26, 1953, on WRCA-TV). She changed stations to WPIX where she replaced Ted Steele as host of the *Kartoon Klub* variety series, which morphed into *Shari & Her Friends*, then *Shariland*, then finally, *Hi Mom*.

From October 1, 1960, to September 28, 1963, Lewis starred in NBC's *The Shari Lewis Show,* her first national variety series, which replaced *The Howdy Doody Show*. From here she marketed a successful line of dolls based on her puppets and made occasional acting appearances on shows like *The Man from*

U.N.C.L.E. and *Love, American Style*. In 1968, she and then-husband, Jeremy Tarcher, co-penned "The Lights of Zetar," an episode of the original *Star Trek*. Nearly thirty years later, PBS contracted her for *Lamb Chop's Play-Along*, another Emmy-winning show, which aired from 1992 to 1997. She released the video *Lamb Chop's Special Chanukah* in 1996 (when it received the Parents' Choice award of the year), and later took the lead in the PBS hit series, *The Charlie Horse Music Pizza*, which was one of her last projects before her death in 1998. An accomplished musician, Lewis conducted major symphonies in America, Japan, and Canada. She wrote many books, created seventeen home videos, and when it came to children's programming, she, with Lamp Chop by her side (on her left hand), had some very strong opinions.

In 1993, Lewis and Lamb Chop appeared before Congress to testify in favor of protections for children's television. When Lamb Chop was granted permission to speak her passionate, well-informed, and vivid testimony made an indelible impression.

In December 1986, Lewis was interviewed by Steven Mitchell Schiffman for *TV Gold Magazine*, and talked about what she believed was the sad state of children's television—and again, she didn't mince words. "Children's television programming [had become] horrible…In the final analysis, TV for children nowadays is just awful!" Referring to the popular *Road Runner* animated series, in which the lead character frequently foils and plummets his nemesis Wile E. Coyote in violent ways, she said, "We treat our kids like they're dead from the neck up. And then we expect them to grow into intelligent human beings able to cope with the world around them." She also complained that TV at times presented too idealized a family life. "The problem arises," she said, "when children discover that life doesn't come in half-hour parcels with a happy ending at the end of each situation. It becomes distressing. I think that our commercial networks have let our kids down dreadfully!"

Lewis adhered to the belief that TV violence, in particular, de-sensitizes viewers of all ages. "It has been proven this past decade at a number of universities, such as Indiana and Penn," said Schiffman. Such facilities were forerunners in conducting experiments that proved that those who observed violence consistently, "even in short spurts of viewing" become complacent to it and allow it to transpire. This was also validated when researchers presented violent films to children and adults. "After the screenings, the two groups were then [placed] into situations where they were in positions to prevent violence from happening. The tests showed that the two groups went out of their way a great deal less to prevent it than the norm simply because they had viewed the violence. Violence seemingly lowers their accepted standards."

Lewis was well-aware that children were her key viewership, and how she designed her show to reflect positive values. As she told *TV Gold*, "I presented a picture…of characters who dealt with one another, sometimes competitively, but always lovingly. Personally, I think that a loving situation is inductive to nice relationships."

For Lewis, TV brought hope —at least in the '80s, when viewers were rediscovering the positive reinforcement that she had tried to present with Lamp Chop. There was a pent-up demand to have her kind of entertainment back on TV. Shortly after her *TV Gold* interview, nostalgic-oriented networks like Nick at Nite began airing classic TV shows in prime time for the first time since their original runs. "There has been a swing back of the pendulum," she said. "There has been an easing up of the need to be bold."

TV writer Larry Brody contributed to some of that swing. He wrote for everything from crime dramas like *Police Story* to medical shows such as *Diagnosis: Murder* and children's shows, including the animated *Star Trek* series. For Brody, "Television has been a cornerstone of American society since the late '40s when Jackie Gleason and Milton Berle became that postwar version of Must See TV. When I was a small child, television absolutely fascinated me. I couldn't read yet, and here was this box that brought everything I'd ever imagined to life right in front of my eyes…and then went beyond that to give me new things—people, places, stories—to daydream about…And, believe me, I was a very big daydreamer. Some people might say that television in that era brought families together…the old, 'huddled-together-in-front-of-the-little-screen' thing."

In Brody's case, it had the opposite effect. He enjoyed all the children's programs of the late '40s and early '50s and was even more enamored of the comedy shows for adults, such as *The Bob & Ray Show* (NBC, 1951–1953), and *Kukla, Fran & Ollie*. He was even a huge fan of Arthur Godfrey's TV shows for reasons he "can't fathom today." His parents had no interest in any of that, but they did watch some TV shows that aired after he was asleep. "My mother's main reason for letting me watch television was that I had a habit of wanting to eat the things pitchmen like *Howdy Doody* hustled. And since I was a skinny kid who, in her mind, never ate enough, she was glad to see something going into my mouth…even if it was Bosco [chocolate syrup]. But since I was one of those kids who, if I could, would watch television all day Saturday and Sunday [when there was an extensive block of children's programming], and my parents wished I would go outside and play more, TV definitely caused some intra-family conflict."

Bozo the Clown is also a noteworthy addition to the world of live children's shows. This series was technically more of a franchise marketed to and produced by various independent stations around the world and actually began as a recording album character for Capitol Records starring Pinto Colvig. In 1949, KTTV in Los Angeles started airing the first television edition, *Bozo's Circus*, featuring Colvig as Bozo with his blue-and-red costume, oversized red hair, and whiteface clown makeup. Larry Harmon, who portrayed Bozo for promotional appearances for Capitol, purchased the rights in 1956 when the series was syndicated to local markets.

Kukla, Fran and Ollie [Credit: The Classic TV Preservation Society]

The most notable performers to have played Bozo, aside from Colvig and Harmon, include Willard Scott (1959–1962), Frank Avruch (1966–1970s), Bob Bell (1960–1984), and Joey D'Auria (1984–2001). Bozo TV shows were also produced in other countries including Mexico, Thailand, Australia, Greece, and Brazil. Harmon, who died in 2008, had claimed that more than 200 actors portrayed the clown.

In either case, *Bozo the Clown*, in any of its incarnations, more than any live-action children's show in history, best represents the particular form of a classic variety show for kids that affected society in a way that only one such visual character could. Cultural-observing publishers Neil Strauss and Anthony Bozza expressed their affection for Harmon in particular in the foreword for *The Man Behind the Nose*, the performer's biography (which he co-authored with Thomas Scott McKenzie, and which was published in 2010 by Strauss/Bozza HarperCollins imprint, It Books). "He wasn't just a hero," the duo said of Harmon, "he was an icon."

As with millions of other viewers, Strauss and Bozza explained, they were raised with *Bozo the Clown*. Since Harmon's first performance as the character on television in 1958, and in ensuing years, they said he's "held a virtual media monopoly on clowndom." In this way, every famous clown including Ronald McDonald from the McDonald's food franchise, to Krusty the Clown, as voiced by *Frasier*'s Kelsey Grammer on TV's *The Simpsons,* would not have come into being without Harmon's initial influence. "With his flaming red wings of hair, bulbous red nose, enormous ruby smile, and machine-gun chuckle," they said Harmon's Bozo was not only the quintessential clown but one of the only adults on television who understood children. Harmon, they continued, wasn't condescending towards young viewers, and never expected them to behave maturely or coerced them into learning. "He simply was one of them," they decided. "And, for that, children loved him."

Approximately 15 years later, ABC's *AfterSchool Specials* took children's programming in a new, yet similar direction with scripted programming that slightly mirrored the network's very popular prime-time film series at the time, the *Tuesday* and *Wednesday Movie of the Weeks*. Said classic TV fan Randy Grimsley, "*The ABC AfterSchool Specials* were a great mix of entertainment and learning."

One early episode of this series, from 1969, titled simply, *J. T.*, has long held significance for fans through the decades. Here, Kevin Hooks played J. T. Gamble, a shy, withdrawn Harlem youngster who takes compassionate responsibility in caring for an old, one-eyed, badly injured alley cat shortly before Christmas. With any perusal of the episode's 40-plus fan reviews on www.imdb.com, it becomes abundantly clear just how special an impact this ABC *AfterSchool* segment made on its viewers.

In 2001, *TampaKirby* from Tampa, Florida, wrote, "I saw this movie when I was about 10 and it had a profound effect on me. Growing up in a white, middle-class neighborhood, I had very little exposure to people of different races and cultures. Seeing how a boy about the same age as I lived so differently prepared me in a small way in dealing with people from different backgrounds later in life."

In 2005, *Tgree-3* said, "[I] absolutely loved this film! I haven't seen it in 30 years but still remember the feelings it provoked…I wish they would show it on television again. [Instead, the] networks show so many horrid Christmas shows over and over again…."

Over at Slate.com, Marisa Meltzer acknowledged the significance of the ABC *AfterSchool Special* series in general in her essay from 2006, "My Dad Lives In A Downtown Hotel: The Subtle Brilliance of the *AfterSchool Special*":

"Anyone who grew up in the pre-Internet age is bound to remember the 4 p.m. showings of *AfterSchool Specials* on ABC. The melodramatic teen cautionary tales always contained an awesomely literal title—'She Drinks a Little' [alcoholic mom]…'My Other Mother' [foster parents], and 'Schoolboy Father' [teen pregnancy]—and a life lesson by the 44-minute mark."

"*AfterSchool Specials* dealt with plenty of hot topics," she said, "…including… bullies, inner beauty, stuttering, foster care, physical abuse, dropping out of school, death, racism, and disabilities. But they also explored lighter fare such as what would happen if you turned into a dog for a day, how to deal with curmudgeonly grandmothers, having a crush on your teacher, and how hard it is to anonymously write an advice column for the school newspaper…It's a much more realistic ending than the countless, neat teen-pregnancy plot lines of *Beverly Hills 90210*, *7th Heaven*, and *The OC*," all of which borrowed heavily from the series, Meltzer added.

"Decades later, they do feel dated, but they still seem relevant. Fitting in, peer pressure, drugs, family drama—those are problems for teenagers regardless of era. More often than not, teens in *AfterSchool Specials* made bad decisions, but they were treated as an essential part of growing up. Underlying all of Tahse's shows is an appealing faith that everything would eventually work out, both for his protagonists and viewers at home."

No TV format has had a larger impact on children than the animated series, images of which in recent years have blurred with adult content (for better and worse). The less intense, and more traditional *Batman and Robin* network cartoons of yore were replaced with the syndicated and edgier *Batman: The Animated Series*. Though the latter took its cue from the original, the darker comic book edition inspired the more violent feature films like *The Dark Knight*. Before *The Simpsons* waxed sardonic, there was the stilted but effective *Tom Terrific* segments of *Captain Kangaroo*, alongside more fully-drawn episodes of *The Flintstones*, *The Jetsons*, *Jonny Quest* (ABC/CBS/NBC, 1964–1981), *The Herculoids* (CBS, 1967–1969), various editions of *Scooby-Doo* (CBS/ABC/Syndication, 1969- Present), and *SuperFriends* (ABC, 1973–1986, and beyond).

ABC's original 1973 incarnation of *Super Friends* grouped uplifting editions of Superman, Batman, and Wonder Woman together as the Justice League, while NBC and Marvel screened *Spider-Man and His Amazing Friends*, featuring more textured characters from 1981 to 1983. This variation on Stan

Lee's webbed superhero (which he created in 1962) also featured Firestar and Ice Man, as well as guest appearances by other masterful mutants from the Marvel universe.

But Spiderman had always proved a popular presence on Saturday morning, first on ABC, from 1967 to 1970 with the original *Spider-Man* show (which opened with that pulsating musical theme). Multiple interpretations of the character have aired since, including Disney XD's *Ultimate Spider-Man*, which began in 2012 and featured the vocal prowess of teen star Drake Bell as Peter Parker.

Other classic Saturday morning cartoon favorites have included various network editions of *The Archies*, while ABC's lineup through most of the 1970s featured interstitials of *Multiplication Rock* and *Schoolhouse Rock*.

The subject matter of classic daytime children's television was similar to that of prime-time adult shows if naturally, not as in-depth. But certain daytime dialogue and images may have made their way past the network censors on the animated shows, simply because they featured non-live-action characters.

In recent years, Seth MacFarlane, the irreverent multi-hyphenate genius behind Fox-TV's *Family Guy* and *The Cleveland Show* animated shows, had planned to remake *The Flintstones*, which originally ran on ABC from 1960–1966. Produced by Hanna-Barbera studios (*Yogi Bear*, *Huckleberry Hound*, *Jonny Quest*, and *Scooby-Doo*), *The Flintstones* presented the pre-historic adventures of Fred and Wilma Flintstone, voiced by Alan Reed and Jean Vander Pyl, and their next-door neighbors, Barney and Betty Rubble, voiced by Mel Blanc and Bea Benaderet, and later, Gerry Johnson. Inspired by *The Honeymooners* (CBS, 1955–1971, in various formats), *The Flintstones*, with 166 episodes, was the longest-running primetime animated series before *The Simpsons* came along in 1989.

With MacFarlane's irreverent touch, his planned reboot of *The Flintstones*, which never saw the light of daytime or prime time, would have become a very different series from the original. The initial adventure of Fred and Wilma was masterful for its time.

One episode, "Little Bamm-Bamm," from October 3, 1963, is a particular standout with teachable moments across the board. Here, the Flintstones and the Rubbles discover the truth of what it means to be a parent as well as a friend. It's significant not only because it introduced the super-powered Bamm-Bamm to the series (presenting an additional element of fun-fantasy) but also because of how the tot is interposed into the program. The action takes place shortly after Wilma gives birth to Pebbles (which, in and of itself, is a milestone in the annals of small-screen animation). Because of the blessed event, Barney and Betty become even more frequent than usual visitors to their neighbors.

Fred becomes extremely frustrated with the situation. He doesn't feel he's spending enough quality time with his new daughter and, in a vile moment, he (who more times than not is slightly cranky), is incredibly rude to Betty with a derogatory remark about the Rubbles not having children. Betty runs away crying. Barney and Wilma are furious. Fred is morose. In a very poignant and real moment (for any hour of television, much less an animated half-hour geared towards children), Betty is next seen, sobbing, in the arms of her husband on a bench in their side yard. As Barney attempts to console his teary spouse, to near no-avail, the two of them look skyward and notice a shooting star. A wish is made.

The next day, Bamm-Bamm is abandoned at their door, and the Rubbles make every attempt to adopt the infant. The episode would be significant enough, such that the Rubbles actually adopt Bamm-Bamm, which marks the first time in animated history that cartoon characters gave time to foster children. But it's this segment's legitimate moments of emotion recited so believably well by the characters (and their voice-overs) that christens this episode as vintage and definitive.

Like any good series, animated or not, *The Flintstones* played to the logic it created. As with its live-action TV counterpart, *The Honeymooners*, Fred and Wilma's adventures invite us into a self-contained world and make the viewer feel welcomed. *The Flintstones*' Neanderthal ways remain ageless, mainly because of the intelligent, time-honored episodes like "Little Bamm-Bamm." [If anything, it would have been interesting to see just how Seth MacFarlane and his questionable humor would have held up to that kind of sophistication.]

In wake of *The Flintstones'* success, Hanna-Barbera created *The Jetsons*, which was sort of the flip side of the adventures of Fred and Wilma. Premiering in 1962 on ABC, and as the show's opening theme song suggested, *The Jetsons* invited you to "meet George Jetson…Jane, his wife…daughter Judy, his boy Elroy." The voiceovers provided included George O'Hanlon as George Jetson, Penny Singleton as Jane, Janet Waldo as Judy, Daws Butler as Elroy, Don Messick as Astro (the dog), and *Flintstones* vets Mel Blanc, as Mr. Spacely (George's boss), and Jean Vander Pyl as Rosie the Robot.

Whereas *The Flintstones* was based in the stone-age, *The Jetsons* took place in 2062—exactly one century into the future of its network debut. While *The Flintstones* enjoyed a healthy six-year original run, *The Jetsons* lasted just one season, if not for lack of trying; and even though Judy and Elroy may not be nearly as well-remembered as Pebbles and Bamm-Bamm, fifty-one new episodes of *The Jetsons* were syndicated between 1985 and 1987, an animated feature film premiered in 1990, and today the original singular season remains more popular than ever in reruns and on DVD.

The Paleo-Future blog (then published by *The Smithsonian*, and now aligned with Gizmodo.com) once referred to *The Jetsons* as "the single most important piece of 20th Century futurism…that helped define the future for so many Americans today."

In 2012, *The Hollywood Reporter* said the show "arrived at the height of the Space Race, as the United States and the Soviet Union jockeyed to make it to the moon first…On February 30, 1962, just seven months before *The Jetsons* arrived on TV, John Glenn became the first American to orbit the earth in the Friendship 7 space capsule…President Kennedy had promised to land a man on the moon in a speech to Congress on May 25, 1961."

The Jetsons debuted on ABC's Sunday night schedule at 7:30 PM opposite *The Wonderful World of Disney* on NBC and the live-action *Dennis the Menace* on CBS. *The Hollywood Reporter* documented *The Jetsons* as ABC's first color show, even though the majority of viewers at the time were still watching television on their black and white sets: "*The Jetsons'* future included flying cars that folded into briefcases, floating cities, video chat, an all-knowing computer called RUDI (short for Referential Universal Digital Indexer) and colonies on other planets…More influential than any particular prediction was the show's iconic Space Age look and feel, which both reflected trends and influenced them going forward."

In his blog MediaBizBloggers.com, Jack Myers once discussed how more contemporary animated fare like *SpongeBob* and *Rugrats*, which air on the children's network Nickelodeon—and whose viewership consists of young, bright "Internet Pioneers"—influences society in "the real 21st Century…our 21st Century," specifically with regard to that year's presidential election which granted Barack Obama his second term. "An awareness of Internet Pioneers' early television experiences can help us better understand their values, attitudes, and expectations today, including their voting decisions…and their future behaviors and consumption patterns. During their formative years, Nickelodeon had a strong influence on Internet Pioneers and many of their ideas, perspectives, sensibilities, and attitudes can be tracked to these early television viewing experiences. Nickelodeon programs dominate the list of shows that Internet Pioneers name as their favorites at age 12 or younger."

Chapter 5

Melissa Byers has served as an editor for digital content on Emmys.com, which is owned and operated by the Television Academy. A fan of *The Smothers Brothers Comedy Hour*, Myers said this show "informed my musical tastes, my political views, and honed my sense of humor. I told them once that they were responsible for the person I am today, and I'll stand by that."

In the history of classic television, musical-comedy variety shows like the *Smothers Brothers*, which originally aired on CBS from 1967 to 1969, are definite standout entries in the positive social impact category. In the '50s, '60s, and '70s, the format, at the height of its popularity,

The Carol Burnett Show was a group effort. From left: Tim Conway, Harvey Korman, Lyle Waggoner, and Vicki Lawrence, and Carol Burnett *[Credit: The Classic TV Preservation Society]*

included comedic skits and, for the most part, steered clear of the more controversial overtones that contributed to the early demise of the *Smothers Brothers Hour*. Irreverence later became par for the course with shows like *Saturday Night Live*, which debuted on NBC in 1975, while decades before, programs like *The Ernie Kovacs Show* pushed the limits and buttons of censors with outlandish segments.

In the early 1950s, NBC had a big hit with *Your Show of Shows*. The granddaddy of all variety shows, this series was a comedy showcase that featured a stellar cast including Sid Caesar, Imogene Coca, Carl Reiner (*The Dick Van Dyke Show*), and Howard Morris (*The Andy Griffith Show*). The writing team comprised a who's-who list of pre-fame talent: Woody Allen, Neil Simon, Mel Tolkin (*All in the Family*), and Larry Gelbart (*M*A*S*H*).

In 1954, NBC granted Caesar and Coca their separate series, and their producer Max Liebman his own showcase. But as author Gerard Jones expressed in his book, *Honey, I'm Home*, "…the chemistry was gone, and NBC got itself a triple failure. Network executives and producers were in part relieved by the decline of the comedy-variety shows. Their broad style of humor drew heat during the censorship debates; radio commentator Paul Harvey spoke for many critics when he complained of 'bawdy New York comedians imposing their taste on the other forty-seven states.'

Except for programs like *The Smothers Brothers Comedy Hour* (also on NBC, 1967–1970), the comedy-variety format became significantly tamer through the years with *The Ed Sullivan Show* (CBS, 1948–1971), *The Milton Berle Show* (NBC, ABC, 1948–1967), *The Jack Benny Show* (CBS, NBC, 1950–1965), *The Dinah Shore Show* (NBC, 1951–1957), *The Jackie Gleason Show* (CBS, 1952–1970), *The Red Skelton Show* (NBC, CBS, NBC, 1951–1971), *The Garry Moore Show* (CBS, 1958–1967), *The Andy Williams Show* (ABC, CBS, NBC, 1958–1971), *The Dean Martin Show* (NBC, 1965–1974), *The Carol Burnett Show* (CBS, 1967–1978), *The Flip Wilson Show* (NBC, 1970–1974), *The Sonny & Cher Comedy Hour* (CBS, 1971–1974), *Tony Orlando and Dawn* (CBS, 1974–1976), *Donny & Marie* (ABC, 1976–1979), *The Captain and Tennille* (ABC, 1976–1977), *Barbara Mandrell and the Mandrell Sisters* (NBC, 1980–1982), and others.

Even feature film and recording superstars like Frank Sinatra (ABC, 1957–1958), and Judy Garland (CBS, 1963–1964) tried their hands with the variety format while rotating hosts fronted *The Hollywood Palace* (ABC, 1964–1970), *The Kraft Music Hall* (NBC, 1967–1971), and *The Muppet Show* (Syndicated, 1976–1981). In the fall of 1975, ABC and Howard Cosell combined to create *Saturday Night Live with Howard Cosell* in prime time. At the same time, NBC delivered *Saturday Night Live* to weekend late-night, with its original edition of The Not Ready for Prime Time Players: Dan Aykroyd, John Belushi, Jane Curtin, Chevy Chase, Garrett Morris, Laraine Newman, and Gilda Radner.

After that, the comedy-variety format, which never set out to be anything but entertaining, was all but dead, if with a few noble attempts to revive it. Dolly Parton's lavish *Dolly* series gave it a shot on ABC in 1987 (a decade or so after she enjoyed a relatively successful syndicated musical series). In 1991, *In Living Color* on Fox introduced the world to Jim Carrey and dancer/vocalist Jennifer Lopez then hired as the show's main choreographer. In 2008, NBC and Rosie O'Donnell tested the evening waters with *Rosie Live!*—a one-shot hour-long musical-variety special. O'Donnell hosted a very popular syndicated daytime talk show from 1996 to 2008 and, for a short while after, was a slightly successful, if controversial co-host of ABC's *The View*. But as with Parton, the attempts at primetime variety failed particularly O'Donnell's show, which was simply too loud, too ornate, and plain too much on every level (just like her 2012 return to daytime talk on Oprah Winfrey's OWN network). The in-studio audience was oversized, and the intimacy, or at least the sense of intimacy, and pure likability brought forth by variety hours hosted by Carol Burnett and Dean Martin were nowhere to be seen. Mike Darnell, then-Fox president of alternative programming, told *The New York Times*, "The entire industry has been trying to figure out a way to bring back variety in some way."

In an article focused on the comedic aspects of the musical-variety show, Red Skelton shared his thoughts in the 1960-1961 issue of *Who's Who in Television and Radio*. He talked about the success of his show, which at that time, was entering its 10th season. "I don't know what it is about the number 10 that makes people sit and take notice," he mused. "Now that my show is starting its tenth year on television, I suddenly find myself pictured as some kind of oracle on the subject of comedy. There's a rumor that I've been quoted in wisdom."

"Well, ten years in television should qualify a comedian for something," he continued, "…even if it's only an eleventh year. But as far as analyzing my own durability is concerned, I'm afraid you won't find the answer here. I can only tell you my formula – you try to make people love you."

As for TV comedy in general, Skelton believed the public taste is something not to be examined. "You're too busy trying to please it to worry about what it is. I have about 600 routines I can do, yet I can't tell you why any of them are funny. It still surprises me when I hear people laughing at some of my stuff. I kind of think it surprises my sponsor, too."

"This much is true," Skelton went on to say, "…television comedy is better than it was in its early days. It's more refined, and a bigger percentage of your jokes get laughs, probably because we've learned what comes across on television and what doesn't. Even so, we come up with our share of clinkers. You can't win every time."

"In the years ahead," Skelton projected, "…I suppose there'll still be a place for a *Red Skelton*, because audiences will always need the laugh-with-a-tear that only clowns can bring. I don't want to discuss the prospects of other comedians, or types of comedy—I'm a clown, not a critic. And critics belong on the other side of the footlights."

In a contemporary interview, Arnie Kogen explained how he wrote skits for numerous classic variety hours, including those headlined by Burnett, Martin, the Osmonds, and others. He arrived in California in 1968 when "there were a zillion variety shows. Well, maybe not a zillion. There were 14. It seemed like a zillion. The Smothers Brothers had a variety show and Don Knotts and *Laugh-In* and Andy Williams and Red Skelton and Phyllis Diller. There were stars, sketches, musical production numbers, and dazzling celebrity guests. It was a great time for viewers and writers. I was fortunate enough to hook up with a few of the very best: *The Dean Martin Show, The Carol Burnett Show,* and *Donny & Marie.*"

The Osmonds, Kogen said, were "cute, fun, had the ice skaters, and their show was beautifully directed by Art Fisher, who had the *Sonny & Cher* [*Comedy Hour*]. Donny and Marie are still fun to watch in Vegas. Yes, the variety format has changed considerably since the 1960s and '70s. There's much less of it, and when you do see a variety show, it's much edgier, not nearly as classy, and less family-friendly. I guess it's sort of mirroring our society."

With yet another reference to Miley Cyrus's infamous TV performance of 2013, Kogen "put it this way…You didn't see a lot of twerking on the old *Don Knotts Show* or *The Phyllis Diller Show*. I think we're all mighty grateful for that."

The Dean Martin Show, Kogen said, "was one of the most entertaining variety shows ever. Dean was loose and easygoing. He had a great voice, great charm, and great style. And Dean was a very funny guy. Both [he] and Jerry Lewis had variety shows on NBC at the same time in the same year. Ironically enough, Dean opened his show with a monologue and Jerry opened his show with a song."

Kogen was "spoiled" by working on *The Carol Burnett Show*, which featured "great comedy performers," including Burnett, Harvey Korman, Tim Conway, and Vicki Lawrence. "The series was a writer's dream. If a sketch wasn't funny, the cast would make it funny. If a sketch was funny, they'd make it funnier." He did four seasons on the show, the first three of which the writers were nominated for an Emmy award and won each time. Winning the Emmy, he thought, was going to be "automatic," until his fourth year, when Burnett and company were up against the premiere year of *Saturday Night Live*.

While SNL may have become the new kid on the variety show block, the classic skits of the *Burnett Show*, including Conway's satiric newscast skit, which was later mirrored by Chevy Chase on SNL's Weekend Update, remain timeless—as do these notable Burnett skits, written by Kogen, which he recalled:

"The Pail": "I co-wrote this sketch with Ray Jessel. Carol plays a woman who regularly visits a therapist (Harvey). He discovers that one of her lingering problems is a traumatic moment in her past. When she was nine, a neighborhood sandbox bully stole her favorite pail. The therapist tells her she'll get over it. These things happen in life. Carol is obsessed and continues, 'But it was my favorite pail. This fat bully stole it and put a dent in it.' Harvey: 'Hold it. Was this pail blue? With a picture of Minnie Mouse?' 'Yes.' It turns out her lifelong problem was caused by her very own psychiatrist/therapist. Carol asks for her pail back. Harvey claims this is preposterous. It was many years ago. He doesn't have it. Carol threatens to tell the patients in his waiting room. He opens his desk drawer and produces the pail. A short while later he also returns her little shovel."

"The Fireman": "Tim Conway as the world's oldest fireman. Tim is always hysterical as 'the old man' never funnier than he was here. A wealthy Harvey discovers smoke in his mansion and calls the 'Sun City Fire Department.' Let's just say Tim was not speedy entering the premises. The sketch ended with Tim giving Harvey mouth-to-mouth resuscitation."

"The Invisible Man's Mother": "Carol is talking with other neighborhood women who are all bragging about their children. One's son is an attorney; another is a pediatrician. They ask Carol what her son does. She clams up and avoids the question. Turns out she is the mother of the 'Invisible Man.' Later, her son visits her. A mother-son talk ensues. Carol: 'Stand up straight when I'm talking to you.' Son: 'How do you know I'm not standing up straight?' Carol: 'A mother knows.'"

In the classic talk show era of the '60s and '70s, before the repulsion of Geraldo Rivera's broken nose antics on the once-popular *Geraldo!*—and the ignorance of the Jerry Springer-driven-type programming, there were only a chosen few chat-shows on the air, namely those hosted by Jack Paar, Steve Allen, Mike Douglas, Dick Cavett, Merv Griffin, and Dinah Shore to name a few.

Shore's Southern charm and sophistication left an indelible mark on the tube. Always pleasant on-screen, whether in character or as a TV talk show host to any number of her celebrity peers, Shore was equally welcomed by home viewers as an accessible, yet elegant presence. Following a successful run as a recording artist during the Big Band era of the '30s and '40s, Shore triumphantly turned toward the TV, first with *The Dinah Shore Show* (NBC, 1951-1956), then with numerous guest appearances (on sitcoms like *Here's Lucy* in the '60s), or via her daytime talk shows from the '70s: *Dinah's Place* and later *Dinah!* In her personal life, she was a trendsetter, on into her middle-age. Her December-May six-year-long relationship with actor Burt Reynolds transpired before the term *cougar* joined the vernacular to described relationships like Demi Moore's former marriage to the much younger Ashton Kutcher. Her charitable charms and organizations, implemented specifically with her Dinah Shore Golf Tournaments, became staples. But it was her presence on television that made the most impact.

The New York Times documented Shore's core appeal on February 25, 1994, shortly after she passed away from cancer. As reporter Stephen Holden explained, Dinah's charm and vitality made her one of the small screen's brightest stars. "Much more than her singing," Holden wrote, "…it was her personality—direct, unpretentious and enthusiastic—that made her into a symbolic Everywoman of the 1950s and '60s."

"I don't know how to be afraid of that old red-eye," the *Times* quoted Shore saying in reference to the TV camera. "It's one person to me. I don't visualize large numbers of people out there. I'm comfortable with it."

For an article she wrote for the 1960-1961 issue of *Who's Who in Television and Radio* titled "The Important Ingredient," Shore said, "Putting on any musical TV show…is tremendously complicated (and expensive!), involving the time and effort of many people."

Shore believed that confidence is "the one thing people must have in order to do their best" on television. "Self-confidence," she said, "…comes only after hard work, at least with me. If it appears that I am self-confident on the TV screen, it is only because we have rehearsed so carefully and so intensely that by the time we go on the air, I'm numb."

"I've always believed in positive thinking," Shore continued, "…what you want, you must earn. I have always tried to be a part of everything. Everything fascinates me. In school, I was in drama, glee club, on the school paper and swimming tream, and a cheerleader. Enthusiasm makes you work and play well and in turn, that gives you confidence in yourself."

"Shyness, to me, is a form of self-pity," she added. "It can be an agonizing state but it can be corrected. You must want to come out of your shell. You must realize that most 'popular' people, those who seem fairly to burst with self-confidence—constantly give a lot more than they take."

"I've never been what you might call a raving beauty," Shore concluded, "…but I learned early the basic rules of good grooming and correct dressing, and I tried not to deviate. It gives me the greatest boost to know that I look well, and feel comfortably, and as a result, I have enough confidence in my appearance to stop thinking about it. And that's what counts."

Veteran entertainment journalist, host, and producer Margaret Wendt worked with and befriended some of the biggest stars in Hollywood while being closely linked with the Creative Artists Agency (CAA). For Wendt, Shore wasn't as "perky," as for example, Gracie Allen, but she had that "great Southern accent and a beautiful speaking voice," which was unique to the mainstream TV audience in Los Angeles. "Then there was her wonderful singing voice, which just sort of pulled you in. The audience always couldn't wait to hear her sing that delightful song of hers at the end of her show: 'See the USA in Your Chevrolet.' And to this day, that song is remembered by anyone who is over 40."

Years later, that playful tune inspired Oprah Winfrey and her best friend Gayle King to do just that. They embarked on a road trip across America, which they chronicled on Oprah's heralded talk show of her own, facsimiles of which in one form or another now air on her OWN network.

Along with talk shows hosted by Oprah and Shore, there were those like the ones headed by Mike Douglas and Merv Griffin, both known also for their musical vocal talents. A former band-singer and short-lived TV game-show host, Griffin in particular is also known for creating two of the most popular game shows in TV history: *Wheel of Fortune* and *Jeopardy!* He was also once a media and real estate mogul and subsequent business rival to those such as Donald Trump. Steve Randisi, the author of, among other books, *The Merv Griffin Show: The Inside Story*, shared his insight into the life and career of the talk-show prince:

"Throughout his career as a talk-show host, Merv Griffin demonstrated a flair for innovation. From its inception in 1962, *The Merv Griffin Show* offered a sophisticated alternative to the soap operas, game shows, and reruns that dominated daytime television. Griffin successfully used the variety/talk format as a backdrop for serious discussion, ranging from the war on drugs to the war in Viet Nam. Among his major coups were interviews with the political heavyweights of the day: Bobby Kennedy, Dr. Martin Luther King, Jr., and Richard Nixon. Griffin's easy-going style made it possible for him to be controversial without being confrontational. But there was also a lighter side to Griffin. On his couch sat scores of showbiz legends such as fresh-faced newcomers George Carlin, Richard Pryor, and Lily Tomlin. Although Jack Paar is credited for creating the desk-and-sofa routine [on *The Tonight Show* in the '50s] it was Griffin who redefined the genre by introducing the 'theme show,' an entire episode devoted to one topic. Merv Griffin was a host who thrived on trying something new. And that may very well be the attribute that made him one of the greats."

In 1982, Griffin had experimented with an "educational" or "self-help" segment for his program which, unfortunately, failed—and was quickly dropped. "His show was 90 percent entertainment," Randisi said, "the balance being devoted to topical issues that hadn't been discussed in a daytime talk/variety format."

Direct education, therefore, does not always work with popular television shows, assuredly not within the talk/variety format of shows like Griffin's, or as with *The Mike Douglas Show* and *Dinah!* (as opposed to the more intellectual chat programs like those hosted by David Susskind, Tom Snyder, or Dick Cavett). While certain talk or variety shows such as *The Smothers Brothers Hour* (or *Rowan & Martin's Laugh-In* for that matter) were still at times platforms for mainstream political figures and topics that might not otherwise have been observed by middle America in such intimate ways, Merv, Mike, Dinah, et al, still offered vulgar-and-violent free programming that created a positive impact "outside the box," so to speak.

From 1980 to 1989, the syndicated *Hour Magazine* series followed the same path. This uplifting daily talk show was hosted by former actor Gary Collins, who made guest-star appearances on TV shows like *McMillan & Wife*. Collins, who died in October of 2012, had also taken the lead in weekly programs such as *The Wackiest Ship in the Army*, *Iron Horse*, and *The Sixth Sense*, heavily edited episodes of which were later syndicated as segments of Rod Serling's *Night Gallery* (and which should not be confused with the 1999 feature film also titled *The Sixth Sense.)* He was a likable, affable fellow and, under his careful supervision, *Hour Magazine* clearly became the predecessor to the beloved *Merv*-like-format. When Collins passed away, *The Los Angeles Times* called his show "a gentler version" of the genre that avoided some of the controversial topics tackled by *Phil Donahue, Geraldo,* and other tabloid programs. Shortly after *Hour Magazine* was canceled in 1989, Collins told *The Times*: "It seems that the viewing public and producers of [the tabloid-like talk shows] have tapped into this insatiable desire for stronger formats, stronger issues, stronger confrontations, a stronger example of subject matter and reality subject matter. And that was never *Hour Magazine*."

Collins described himself as "inquisitive, sensitive, caring, likable, non-confrontational," and said, "I don't think all television has to be on that hard edge…That's basically not a part of my character."

Emmy-award-winning TV writer/producer Dan Weaver was revered in the talk show realm. Weaver, who died much too young in 2017, had worked on both *Hour Magazine* and *Geraldo* as well as *Entertainment Tonight*, and the short-lived but heralded *Pat Sajak Show*. He offered his thoughts on how television talk shows have changed over the years, for better or for worse; and how he believed the more tranquil, less edgy edition of the format still has the potential to thrive and have a positive impact on its viewers:

"I greatly appreciated *Hour Magazine's* approach to news and entertainment. It was just good plain talk, and having the celebrity co-host brought out their humanistic qualities. When I worked on *Geraldo* one producer joked that he felt he needed to take a 'shower after every hour.' There was such a focus in the '80s and '90s on being provocative. I remember one show, stealing another show's guest who had taken out her own breast implants. It made for a major story for the talk show wars. The host who did the best at being edgy and yet smart was *Donahue*.

"While I have to admit that one of the topics I produced was 'Porn Stars and their Spouses,' we always looked for the important social issues of the day and wound up getting into a great discussion of HIV. *Oprah* carried the torch that Phil first flamed and thankfully it has burned brightly with shows like *The Ellen DeGeneres Show*, which proves time and time again that you can be kind and competitive," at least until recently.

As to working with Collins, Weaver said, "Gary was a gracious man both on and off camera. On my last day there I remember him helping me pack up my car with my belongings. He was as warm and caring behind the tube as he was in front of it. A favorite show of mine growing up with *The Sixth Sense*, and it was an honor to work with Gary and watch him use that sixth sense so often with his interviews. There is no question he helped pave the way for kinder, gentler talk."

Weaver then recalled a time when there were efforts to make *Hour* more provocative, by booking male strippers, sex experts, and the like. "Gary was not happy and it just didn't work," he said. "*Hour* was that warm cup of coffee you could turn to and get a glimpse of Hollywood, some great ideas on making life a little easier, and make an appointment to see a friend who was always gracious, fun, and loved doing what he was doing. Gary, you are missed."

And so is Weaver, especially in today's TV talk era, which includes CBS's *The Talk* and its predecessor, ABC's *The View*, which was created by veteran news journalist Barbara Walters. On the air for now almost 30 years, *The View*, as *Variety* once put it, "was never designed to be softball TV." Or as Walters once said, "We're not a puff show. We can be more opinionated."

Variety described *The View's* format as "a panel of women discussing topical issues, the morning headlines, relationship issues and gossipy matters in coffee-klatch style was inspired by the lively conversations Walters had with her daughter, Jackie. She recognized the importance of putting women of different backgrounds and generations together to offer perspectives on all manner of subjects. From the start, the energy of the program came from its ability to turn on a dime."

For those like Ed Spielman, Oprah Winfrey remains a formidable presence in the talk show realm, even though her long-running, original, ground-breaking series is no longer in production. "Oprah is leading in the most positive, visible way," he said. "She is showing things which have to do with the ennobling of human beings…the inherent worth of human beings. She should get some extraordinary gold medal for having done this throughout her career because she's an inherently spiritual person…who valiantly continues to make a contribution."

"How wonderful it would be if there were more people like her who are in a position to do a bit of what she does and ennoble people to recreate a societal standard," he continued. "When she's on the air you know there's something inspirational about your godly human quality…about your potential that she is going to address and when you finish watching her you will be all the better for it."

Although Winfrey's traditional talk format is now a part of history, along with those hosted by Dinah Shore, Merv Griffin, and Mike Douglas, her influential presence has at least remained and expanded with the Oprah Winfrey Network, otherwise known as OWN. Prior to OWN's debut in the spring of 2010, *New York Magazine* wondered, "Can Oprah, the channel, succeed without Oprah, the talk-show star?"

At first, it was dicey. OWN began without any strong visual presence from its owner, but Winfrey has since returned with several incarnations of her former TV self. On OWN, she's hosted *Oprah's Next Chapter*, *Master Class*, and *Where Are They Now?* Her lack of screen presence would have been counter-productive and cost-defective. As *New York Magazine* once put it, "Oprah's great gift is the way she can be at once a star and Everywoman. She contains multitudes: There is empathetic Oprah (commiserating with abuse survivors, the parents of autistic children, or the entire nation of South Africa), indignant Oprah (seething at James Frey over fabricating his memoir), fun-loving Oprah (road-tripping across America with best friend Gayle King), news-making Oprah (Tom Cruise), tabloid Oprah (her weight is up, it's down), mystical Oprah (*The Secret* [book] and its Law of Attraction [philosophy], suggesting you can get whatever you want if you just want it enough), and altruistic Oprah ('*Everybody gets a car!*')."

The traditional daytime and late-night talk show formats may be history (save for reruns or special DVD packages) while they both have to some extent merged with the variety show premise. In the early 1990s, Arsenio Hall, the first black mainstream talk-show host, brought it up a notch with an energetic late-night chat. Before his ousting due to alleged inappropriate behavior behind the scenes, PBS talk show host Tavis Smiley was frequently compared to Dick Cavett and Tom Snyder. Other chat titans over the years have included David Letterman, Wendy Williams, Larry King, Ellen DeGeneres, Drew Barrymore, Kelly Clarkson, Tamron Hall, and more. Barrymore and Clarkson, a Top 40 pop-music star, both have incorporated variety-show elements into their programs. DeGeneres expanded the format even further with game-show segments that gave birth to their own shows. In each case, when present and not in pandemic-mode, the audiences have been free to be as loud and obnoxious as possible, a development that Arsenio Hall ignited with his show.

In the end, Oprah Winfrey and Carol Burnett will most likely be remembered as true queens of the daytime talk and nighttime variety show worlds. The King of Late Night title will arguably remain with Johnny Carson, the third host of NBC's *The Tonight Show*, following Steve Allen, Jack Paar, and preceding Jay Leno, Conan O'Brien, who briefly held the spot before Leno returned a second time, and Jimmy Fallon, who replaced Leno in February 2014.

Writer/producer Dan Holm worked at NBC for decades in the Burbank, California, location. He was positioned in the promotions department, where, among other things, he created the famous "Must See TV" campaign associated with the network's '90s popular Thursday night lineup of *Cheers*, *Seinfeld*, etc. "No thorough discussion of classic television is truly complete without a nod to *The Tonight Show*," said Holm. "For generations, this venerable franchise has entertained, informed, enlightened, and even helped many of us, after a long day, nod off with a smile."

Holm's earliest personal TV memories involve his older brother Don, who would insist that Dan sit up with him and watch Steve Allen on *The Tonight Show*. For Dan, it was Allen's "unending talents and versatility that made each show an unpredictable adventure filled with wit, music, and tongue-in-cheek irreverence. He obviously loved what he was doing and my brother and I loved watching him do it. Here was a guy who broke the rules! Here was a guy who got *paid* to have fun! For a young boy in Racine, Wisconsin, the attraction was immediate and undeniable. Now *that* is the business to be in!"

A recurring highlight for Holm was when Allen would unexpectedly bring up the house lights and turn the camera on the audience, causing many to "scurry up the aisles," their faces covered as not to been seen on camera. "It was cold outside," Holm recalled, "…tickets were free and the *Tonight Show* studio was a great place to hide out in the dark for a while."

Holm also shared his strongest memory of subsequent *Tonight Show* host Jack Paar and that performer's "low-key demeanor and dry wit…A highlight for me is when he'd bring his baby lions onto the show."

"Then came Johnny Carson," Dan said. "Along with Carnac the Magnificent, the Matinee Lady, Ed McMahon's 'live' Alpo commercials, Tiny Tim's marriage to Miss Vicki, Doc Severinsen, and guests who never failed to bring their 'A' game, Johnny explored the potential of *The Tonight Show* and set the high-water mark for the franchise."

When Holm began working for NBC in 1990, one of his first assignments was to write and produce *Tonight Show* episodic promos. "What an honor! The show taped in the same building where I worked and I recall that often on the way to—or returning from—lunch at the NBC commissary, bands or performers would be rehearsing. Since the route back to the office went right past *The Tonight Show* studio, we'd often slip in, sit in the shadows, and watch the biggest names in entertainment perform and prepare."

A few years later, Holm also had "the privilege of attending the last *Tonight Show Starring Johnny Carson* with a live audience." He was "among the last of the audience let in the door and was seated *way* back in the far corner of the very last row."

In January 2014, Holm returned to NBC for freelance promotion assignments and was once more assigned to *The Tonight Show*, this time writing the episodic promo, along with editor Mike Dowell, for the last segment hosted by Jay Leno. "Having worked in television at local, studio, and network levels for many years, I can truly say that more than any other show or influence, my career is forever entwined with NBC and *The Tonight Show*."

Growing up, Holm was an ambitious, aspiring kid trying to carve out a career in TV. "*The Tonight Show* taught me that television can be fun," he said. "It *should* be fun. The degree to which the people in front of and behind the camera love what they're doing is the same degree to which the audience will appreciate and enjoy it. That same insight, that same spark that kept me up every night glued to the black and white box has driven my television career."

Today, Holm is a successful photographer, while the latest edition of *The Tonight Show* "starring" *Jimmy Fallon* (as opposed to just being "*with*" *Jay Leno*) more readily resembles NBC's *Saturday Night Live*. That's mostly because SNL's creator/producer Lorne Michaels supervises *Tonight*, which moved back to its original home city of New York, which has been *Saturday's* base. Johnny Carson will forever remain the "King of Late Night TV," but Fallon has held his own. Said TV writer Treva Silverman:

"It's the perfect time for Jimmy Fallon. Everyone is sick of what's going on—the divide in our country. The poor are getting trampled on: cut-off unemployment insurance…*Stop coddling those urban inner-city people*, some say. *Why do we need universal health care…What are we, Socialists? We have the best health care on Earth*, say the people who have never been any other place on Earth…*Make it a sacred mission to prevent gay marriage…it's a threat to the sanctity of marriage*, says the Bible-quoting husband who's sleeping with his assistant after-hours…The hatreds and the anxieties, neighbor despising neighbor… and along comes Jimmy Fallon, who loves life, loves what he's doing, a *what-you-see-is-what-you-get* guy with no hidden agenda…no axes to grind, doubling over with laughter when people say funny stuff, having the time of his life…all the while a sophisticated renaissance man, brilliant storyteller, dancer, singer, improviser, reminding you of a kid in a candy store of guests, stories, games, silliness—a ray of sunshine in this world. What a delight! Settle back and enjoy how things should be—an old-fashioned let's-all-have-fun atmosphere…Authenticity in a phony, selfish world."

Chapter 6

"Our name says it all."

So said the welcoming voiceover in many a Kraft Foods commercial during a number of TV specials and anthology shows sponsored by Kraft Foods including *Kraft Music Hall*, *Kraft Mystery Theatre*, *Kraft Suspense Theatre*, *Kraft Television Theatre*, sporadically airing on NBC throughout the '40s, '50s, '60s, '70s, and '80s. Similar anthology programs and campaigns were presented by ALCOA, the Aluminum Company of America, which funded *The Alcoa Hour* (NBC, 1955–1957), *The Alcoa Theatre* (NBC, 1957–1960), *Alcoa Presents: One Step Beyond* (ABC, 1959–1961), and *Alcoa Premiere*

Back in the day, families watched television together *[Credit: The Classic TV Preservation Society]*

(ABC, 1961–1963). The anthology category in particular also included, among others, *Armstrong Circle Theatre* (NBC/CBS, 1950–1963), and *Playhouse 90* (CBS, 1956–1961), the latter title of which signified its time-length in minutes. Each decorated the "Golden Era" of TV with dramatic content, within a variety of timeframes, and featured original scripts or plots based on short stories, novels or articles.

Some anthologies were narrated with audio only, while others featured a visual host that opened and closed each series on a periodic (*The Loretta Young Show*, NBC, 1953–1961) or semi-regular basis (*Robert Montgomery Presents*, NBC, 1950–1957). Others like *The Twilight Zone*, hosted by Rod Serling, or *Alfred Hitchcock Presents* and Boris Karloff's *Thriller* (NBC, 1960–1962) showcased the macabre or were sci-fi/fantasy-geared, presented within a 30- to 60-minute format. Still more, like *Route 66*, *The Fugitive* (ABC, 1963–1967), *Run for Your Life* (NBC, 1965–1968), or later, *Kung Fu* (ABC, 1972–1975) were anthologies cloaked in a one-hour or half-hour series format, featuring characters that drifted or traveled across the American threshold. The anthology format reconfigured throughout the '70s with series like *Police Story* (NBC, 1973–1978), and ABC's *Tuesday* and *Wednesday Movie of the Weeks* (1969–1976), which many times showcased films that were presented by the same production company (ABC Circle Films, for example).

The Fugitive and *Route 66* are two of the best clear-cut dramas that doubled as anthology shows. The former was created by Roy Huggins, produced by Quinn Martin, who presented a barrage of hit police/detective series in the 1960s and '70s, everything from *The FBI* to *Barnaby Jones*.

But *The Fugitive*, alongside *Route 66*, created and produced by Stirling Silliphant, who wrote most of the episodes, were standout series with superior scripts, at least in the first few seasons of each show. *The Fugitive* featured a singular star, in the form of David Janssen as Richard Kimble—a man on the run after being falsely accused of murder. *Route 66* starred George Maharis and Martin Milner (later of *Adam-12*) as free-spirited twentysomethings roaming the countryside in a '59 Corvette.

Both programs, essentially anthology shows, were innovative in their own way, with a positive message of some sort that pervaded each episode. Whereas a more defined anthology series like *The Twilight Zone* was hosted and/or narrated by a singular "real-life" voice or presence apart from the actual story, *The Fugitive* and *Route 66* actually inserted their main characters into the plotline from week to week.

On *66*, Maharis, the show's heartthrob, played Buz Murdock, streetwise and tough, and Milner was Tod Stiles, refined and rich enough to own that Corvette which drove them into one adventure after the next. Maharis was forced to leave the series due to developing pneumonia on the set. While the show carried on with Glenn Corbett as Tod's noble new traveling companion, Lincoln Case, it was never the same without Maharis.

Years after the *Route 66* ended, Maharis and Milner talked with *Corvette Quarterly* magazine about what it was like to work on the series, what made it unique, and how it offered the viewer a front-row seat to the country's panorama. Milner credited Silliphant and the show's producer Bert Leonard for having the courage to push the envelope regarding the scripts, most of which were penned by Silliphant. "Stirling always had a finger on the pulse of what was happening before the general public seemed to know about it," Milner said. "We did [an episode] on LSD called 'The Thin White Line,' when nobody really knew what LSD was. I had certainly never heard of it, but Stirling had. I think he was kind of in the vanguard on things like that. And Bert Leonard had the good sense to go along with him on those [decisions]…I thought it was wonderful. I thought we were breaking new ground. I was always very happy with the storylines on the show…The fact that we were pioneering a very innovative way to make television—to do it on the road, in the actual locations. We were doing something nobody else had ever done, and nobody really has done it since, either. But one of the sad things is that we weren't in color, because we were in so many beautiful spots [around the country], like being in Vermont in the fall when the leaves were changing."

For Maharis, playing Buz allowed him the opportunity to express a few personal beliefs, if from the character's perspective, "a philosophy of the way I believed this particular person lived his life." That was "important" for him to convey, as opposed to what "was going on in other shows."

Maharis' favorite episodes included "Even Stones Have Eyes," in which Buz is blinded, a development that allowed the actor to utilize his theatrical muscles more than his physical stamina. This "was always really a nice one for me," he said. "The Mud Nest" was also a personal best for Maharis, for personal reasons: his two brothers, Bob and Paul, performed in a story in which they played siblings in search of their mother.

Maharis was also fond of a core attribute of the series: every subsequent season he and Milner would get to drive a different shiny, new, high-end vehicle. "We never would explain how these poor kids had a brand-new Corvette every year," he mused, "but it was called 'dramatic license' and we left it at that."

Veteran TV writer Larry Brody worked on *Police Story*, an anthology series that aired on NBC in the '70s. *Route 66* aired while he was in high school. He watched a few episodes but "never got into it" because, contrary to his family's fears, he "had too much to do outside in the real world. My particular peer group—I was the drummer-leader of a very popular band that played all the school dances and such—did talk about the series quite a bit, but 99% of that conversation was about what a sensationally beautiful and fast car the heroes' Corvette was. I fell in love with it as well, and the first car I ever considered my own was a '59 Corvette that I bought for $1500 used when I was a sophomore in college. Unfortunately, it was white instead of red like the *Route 66* 'Vette, so it didn't give my shallow self the full satisfaction I'd hoped for.

"At the time, as an audience member just turning on the TV in order to see an interesting story and relax, I never noticed whether the stories featured the heroes and their problems or the guest cast and its particular tribulations, and neither did anyone else I knew. A TV show was a TV show, and as good as *Route 66* may have been, at the time it looked like the ultra-tough/ultra-cool kickass heroes I really wanted to see…and, I suppose, be."

In several episodes of *66*, many characters seek religious or spiritual counsel or are seen praying for help, in churches, temples, and the like. This transpired in at least two different instances in the first season. First, with an episode titled "Legacy for Lucia," in which Tod and Buz, now working in a small-town Oregon sawmill, aid a young woman (played by Arlene Martel, who would later portray Spock's intended bride in the famous "Amok Time" segment of the original *Star Trek*) recently arrived from Italy. An orphan of World War II, the woman journeyed to America to sell a legacy betrothed to her by a dead soldier in order to raise funds for her church. The issue at hand: the soldier had no possessions. In another episode, "The Strengthening Angels," the boys buzz through California in a rainstorm and encounter another female stranger, this time, nearly running her over. Played by Suzanne Pleshette ten years before she became Emily Hartley on *The Bob Newhart Show*, the woman seeks spiritual counsel. After giving her a ride to the next town they discover she's a fugitive with a murder rap. Despite the protests of the local authorities and community, and even the woman herself, Buz believes the situation is more complicated than it may appear.

The religious or spiritual angle or reference in these episodes, even in the most subtle way, is rarely seen in today's TV shows, and when it is, such a mention is not usually handled with respect or reverence. Brody explained why things were different in the days of *Route 66*:

"Although I didn't watch much *Route 66* during its day, many years afterward, I worked with Bert Leonard, who owned it, and Sam Manners, who was the *nuts-and-bolts* producer-production manager. They were proud of the fact that the show presented a more realistic view of human beings than most TV before, during, or since and were well aware that one of the ways it did that was by having characters who actually believed in something beyond the generic and material. Sam Manners, especially, made the point to me that back in the day, religion and its place in society wasn't as controversial as it has since become. It provoked neither angry letters nor kudos but just *was*. I think Sam mentioned that Leonard was always worried that they'd get network flak when he saw the church in a script, but they never did. Maybe Leonard was prescient because even a whisper of any specific religion drives network executives into a frenzy of fear today."

But to some extent, Brody was disillusioned by many of the classic TV shows on which he worked. That included the multi-award-winning *Police Story*, on NBC from 1973–1976 (and briefly resurrected by ABC in 1988), which Brody called the "*NYPD Blue* of its day." "We were never allowed to be as realistic as I thought we should be," he said. "On *Police Story*, for example, we were never allowed to show a character actually in bed with someone to whom he or she wasn't married unless, at some point later in the story, both members of the couple were punished for it in some way.

"*Police Story* was the best police series on television—ever. A genuine anthology in which different stars—most of them major—played different cops involved in different crimes every week, linked only by the fact that they were on the same mythological Southern California big city police department. The basis for all our episodes was, 'The cop works on the case, and the case works on the cop,' a concept which had never been done before and was later used pretty darn well on *Hill Street Blues*, *NYPD Blue*, and *Homicide: Life on the Street*. I'm frustrated as hell because these days *Police Story* is all but forgotten, as the others are also but to a lesser extent."

Several different divisions of the drama format have aired over the years. Those ranged from crime anthologies like *Police Story* to regular series like *Caine's Hundred* (starring Peter Mark Richman), in which Richman's Nicholas Caine was out to get the top one hundred criminals (which is exactly what Robert Kennedy said he would also do when he became Attorney General). Other crime-geared shows included *The Naked City* and *The Untouchables*, to programs with a journalistic bent like the syndicated *Deadline* anthology series from 1959, to the episodic *Lou Grant* show that ran on CBS from 1977 to 1982.

Deadline, a half-hour series, ran for two years and was hosted by actor Paul Stewart, who also performed in a few episodes. It was produced by the same team responsible for *Decoy*, another 30-minute syndicated anthology series, if based within a police format. This show ran for only one season, from 1957 to 1958, and starred Beverly Garland as an undercover policewoman. On *Deadline*, Stewart played himself and introduced stories in which he would periodically appear as different characters based on real-life newspaper crime articles of the day. A non-hosting but narrating Garland appeared every week as the same role amid different characters. Both *Deadline* and *Decoy* were groundbreaking, if low-budget entries, while the latter featured TV's first female law enforcement lead before *Honey West* of the '60s and *Police Woman* and *Charlie's Angels* of the '70s.

With Ed Asner in the lead, *Lou Grant* was the first one-hour drama to be spawned from a half-hour sitcom, *The Mary Tyler Moore Show*, which later saw its namesake taking the edgy lead as a tabloid editor in the short-lived CBS series *New York News*, which only lasted half a season in 1995.

A standout drama with a journalistic bent that was not given even half a chance to survive was NBC's *Gibbsville*, which lasted only one month in late 1976. Larry Brody worked on this show, which was based on short stories by John O'Hara, whom Brody called "a master of the genre in the 1940s. Every episode was an adaptation of one or more of his brilliant character pieces. It starred a newcomer named John Savage and Oscar winner Gig Young [who was for a time married to *Bewitched* actress Elizabeth Montgomery]. The show was canceled after only 3 episodes [aired], but we had to keep writing and shooting 10 more because of a large overseas sale. I think of *Gibbsville* as possibly the most artistically ambitious series in the history of TV and am thrilled to have been a part of it. Both the leads had terrible problems during the shoot. John Savage had been in a motorcycle accident that left him with total amnesia and was still fighting his way back to remember who he was. And Gig Young was suffering from what turned out to literally be terminal depression. [He killed his third wife and himself a few years later.] But they created art that was truly transcendent."

Chapter 7

While the late 1950s brought us criminal-and-journalistic dramatic flare like *Decoy* and *Deadline*, that period is best known for delivering a significant number of westerns. This very successful sub-genre of the TV drama format included traditional cowboy/*shoot-'em-up* action, while other entries could be defined as dramas that just so happened to be set in the Old West.

The Guns of Will Sonnett aired only two years on ABC (from 1967–1969) but was one of the more unique properties on the Western front for its time. The show starred curmudgeon-king Walter Brennan, who was by then an established actor of more than five decades. In the middle of Sonnett's run, *TV Guide* profiled the actor, who had three Oscars under his belt for supporting performances in *Come and Get It* (1936), *Kentucky* (1938), and *The Westerner* (1940), feature films that represented Hollywood when "happy-endings-no-matter-what" reached their peak. He also appeared in several silent movies, stayed relevant through sound pictures and worked through the 1930s and 1940s, and went on to star in three notable television shows: *The Real McCoys* (ABC/CBS, 1957–1963), *The Tycoon* (ABC, 1964–1965), and *The*

The original cast of TV's *Gunsmoke* (from left): Milburn Stone, Dennis Weaver, Amanda Blake, James Arness *[Credit: The Classic TV Preservation Society]*

Guns of Will Sonnett, in which he portrayed the title's lead character—a senior former cavalry scout who with his grandson Jeff (played by Dack Rambo), searches the Old West of the 1870s for the boy's father. "It's very lightweight," Brennan told *TV Guide*. "It isn't much, maybe, but it has a good moral it teaches young people."

One of those young people at the time was entertainment historian James Knuttel. He believed the show became popular because the history of the real Old West was still fairly recent by the time television became prominent in the late 1940s. There still remained those who, if not lived the experience of the original western era, at least remembered it. "If a man was 85 years old when *Gunsmoke* first aired in 1955, he would have been born in 1870 or late 1869. He would have been old enough to remember hearing first-hand about Custer's Last Stand and the murder of Wild Bill Hickok [both of which occurred in 1876], the gunfight at the O.K. Corral and the death of Billy the Kid [both 1881], and the death of Jesse James [1882]. And he would've been a grown man when Butch Cassidy and the Sundance Kid were leading their outlaw gang. So, he could relate to what he was seeing on the television."

For others, Knuttel said the Old West might have been something that original TV viewers may have heard about from their parents or grandparents. Or for people outside the United States, the history and mythology of the Old West are seen as the American equivalent to Nordic myths and the Robin Hood legends.

The Wild Wild West remains one of the most mythical westerns in TV history. Decades before *The Adventures of Brisco County Jr.* (which was inspired by *Wild,* and which ran for one season on FOX from 1993–1994) *West* was quite the nontraditional cowboy romp that premiered on CBS in 1965 and continued its original run until 1969. A unique mix of James Bond in the Old West, the show featured Robert Conrad as Secret Service agent James West, some years before his famous Eveready batteries commercials of the 1980s ("Knock it off my shoulder...I dare you"), and his second hit period series, *Baa-Baa Black Sheep* (NBC, 1976–1978), which was based in the 1940s.

As a child, Knuttel embraced what all of the show's fans appreciated: how *Wild* combined the basic elements of traditional westerns (six-shooters, horses, frontier towns) with secret agent gadgetry: the trick derringer up Jim West's sleeve or the knife in his boot. Also embraced were the show's appealing diabolical villains and their outlandish inventions; the numerous disguises adorned by Jim West's sidekick, Artemus Gordon (ingeniously portrayed by the late, great Ross Martin); and the action-packed sequences with Conrad (who performed most of his own stunts; Conrad was occasionally doubled by stuntman James George) as West blissfully and successfully taking on four or five opponents at one time (at least twice in one episode).

As an adult, Knuttel, like many, grew to appreciate the more aesthetic traits of the series. There was the superb art direction and costumes, and the stunning photography, which was clear-cut black and white in the first season and vivid color in the second, third, and fourth years. "The series looks great on DVD," Knuttel said, "but I think it cries out for a Blu-ray release," the more detailed delivery of which will more productively display the show's ethereal visual qualities.

Knuttel's other choice classic westerns include *Bonanza* ("Dan Blocker's Hoss was a favorite"), *Gunsmoke* ("I liked Ken Curtis as Festus the most, but James Arness as Matt Dillon loomed high"), *The Virginian* ("I remember Doug McClure as Trampas more than I do James Drury in the title role"), *Alias Smith and Jones* ("which was fun until Pete Duel's tragic death" by suicide), and *Bearcats,* an unusual and short-lived western series, unusual western set during World War I, with its lead heroes (Rod Taylor and Dennis Cole) traveling the country in a Stutz Bearcat automobile ("I loved that car").

Knuttel acquired the seventh season DVD release of *Wagon Train* and was also impressed with that series. As was Gene Roddenberry, during *Train's original-run* on NBC and ABC from 1957 to 1965. Roddenberry was inspired to create *Star Trek,* which NBC premiered in 1966, and which he later dubbed *Wagon Train to the Stars.*

Back on Earth, Knuttel was making fond memories with pre-school viewings of *The Roy Rogers Show* and *The Lone Ranger,* which he called "those thrilling days of yesteryear! TV Westerns often offered short morality plays with a clear distinction between the 'good guys' and the 'bad guys.'"

In like manner, there are two core forms of the genre.

One set was made primarily for children, such as *The Lone Ranger* and *The Roy Rogers Show,* along with *The Gene Autry Show, The Cisco Kid,* and *Hopalong Cassidy*—and locally-produced series like *Action in the Afternoon* (which aired in Philadelphia).

The next group was classified under the "adult" western—shows that were aimed at more mature viewers. Such programming began in 1955 with shows like *Gunsmoke* and *The Life and Legend of Wyatt Earp*, and continued in the next few years with, among others, *Cheyenne, Maverick, Wagon Train, Have Gun—Will Travel*, and *Bonanza*. Other TV westerns provided stepping stones for actors who became big-screen stars, such as James Garner via *Maverick*, Steve McQueen in *Wanted—Dead or Alive*, and Clint Eastwood by way of *Rawhide*.

Dale Robertson headlined several small-screen westerns, notably *Tales of Wells Fargo* (which was set in the 1870s-1880s, and which NBC originally screened from 1957 to 1962). Robertson, who died of lung cancer and pneumonia at 89 in 2013, was a veteran of feature film westerns like *Fighting Man of the Plains* (1949, with Randolph Scott) and *The Farmer Takes a Wife* (1953, with Betty Grable) before he came to play Jim Hardie, "the left-handed gun" on the *Tales of Wells Fargo* TV series. As Hardie, he protected stagecoaches from outlaws and Indians, safely guiding them to their destination (and allegedly conducting his own stunts).

An Oklahoma native and member of the Cowboy Hall of Fame, Robertson was born in Harrah, Ohio, where he grew up around horses. He served in World War II, where he was twice wounded in combat and won bronze and silver stars. He also was a professional boxer, which is when Hollywood talents scouts noticed his picture in a photography studio. He was tough as nails and a real-life hero off-screen, which only peppered and prepared him in spades to play heroic roles on screen.

Such parts included the gambler-turned-railroad tycoon Ben Calhoun in *Iron Horse* (ABC, 1966–1968), and when he took the contemporary cowboy lead as a Texas billionaire in *J.J. Starbuck* (NBC, 1987–1988), the latter of which was produced by Stephen J. Cannell (of NBC's *The Rockford Files* and *The A-Team*). He then continued to follow the modern-day wagon (and gravy!) train with recurring roles on primetime soaps like CBS' *Dallas* (1978–1991) and ABC's *Dynasty* (1981–1989), years before which he also portrayed semi-regular Western characters on shows like *Harts of the West* (1993–1994), or as host and narrator of the anthology series *Death Valley Days* (following Ronald Reagan and Robert Taylor).

Robertson utilized his Hollywood earnings to raise horses on the Haymaker Farms ranch that he constructed in Yukon, Oklahoma (just west of Oklahoma City). He owned 235 horses, five of which were world champions—and a title of which could have easily be applied to the man himself. That is to say, while some television viewers may have become interested in riding horses because they observed him or other actors do so in Westerns, Robertson actually was a cowboy before, during, and after he played one on TV (and the big screen).

Similar to stance and style to Robertson was actor Clint Walker, who died at 91 in 2018. As the star of *Cheyenne* on ABC (from 1955–1963), Walker also found fame via playing stoic Western characters. In the days after the Civil War, Walker's Cheyenne Brody was a tough guy looking for adventure, moseying along from job to job, be it as a ranch foreman, a wagon train trail scout, or even as a newly deputized lawman. As TV's first-hour long western, *Cheyenne* was a polished production that aired with other series under the umbrella banner of *Warner Bros. Presents*. Hosted by Gig Young (of future *Gibbsville* fame), *Warner Bros.* also presented shows like *Conflict* (1956–1957), and *Sugarfoot* (1957–1959).

In the fall of 2012, Walker and the Warner Bros. Studios commemorated *Cheyenne's* place in history during a two-day Retro Action-Adventure Thon at the Paley Center for Media in Beverly Hills, California. Susan King and *The Los Angeles Times* chronicled the event, which showcased a Warner Archive Collection DVD release of several classic TV shows. The festivities also granted fans the opportunity to tour "Television Out of the Box," an exhibition that featured memorabilia, costumes, props, photos, and sets spanning the last six decades of Warner Bros. Television, including original costumes from *Cheyenne*. Rene Reyes, then-director of public programs and festivals at the Paley Center, told King that *Cheyenne* "was pivotal in TV history because it really proved the hour-long Western could really succeed."

She described the actor as a "tall, ruggedly handsome former security guard and bouncer became an overnight sensation" who remained popular 60 years after *Cheyenne's* debut. Walker had his own website which helped to coordinate the global requests for his autograph and photograph—and as he clarified, those demands did not just come from original fans of the series, but new viewers. "I am getting crayon pictures from children of Cheyenne on a horse," he said. "I am also getting letters from 17-years-olds and younger people."

Another sector of the TV cowboy genre featured former film stars who settled on the small screen. Henry Fonda as *The Deputy*, George Montgomery in *Cimarron City*, Joel McCrea in *Wichita Town*, Dick Powell who hosted *Dick Powell's Zane Grey Theatre*, Ann Sheridan as the comedic lead in *Pistols 'n' Petticoats*, and perhaps most notable of all, Barbara Stanwyck, who ventured into *The Big Valley* (which originally aired on ABC from 1966–1971).

The Big Valley rode high in the saddle above the rest. Inspired by the popularity of NBC's *Bonanza* (1959–1973), *Valley* featured a close-knit wealthy Western family, but was superior to *Bonanza* in every way, with regard to storytelling, acting, and star quality.

Bonanza's clan was headed by widower-patriarch Ben Cartwright, portrayed by Lorne Greene (later of *Battlestar: Galactica*, and the short-lived detective series *Griff*; both on ABC in the late '70s). He was father to Little Joe, played Michael Landon (later of *Little House on the Prairie* and *Highway to Heaven*, both on NBC from the mid-'70s through the '80s), Dan Blocker (who died following the production of *Bonanza's* penultimate season), and Pernell Roberts (*Trapper John, M.D.*, CBS, 1979–1986).

Valley's brood was headed by widow-matriarch Victoria Barkley, played by Stanwyck. She, like Greene on *Bonanza*, had three sons: Richard Long, Peter Breck, and Lee Majors, the latter of whom was a brother from a different father. They were joined by sister Audra, played by Linda Evans, fresh from her big-screen debut in 1965's *Beach Blanket Bingo* (directed by William Asher of *I Love Lucy*, CBS, 1951–1957; *Bewitched*, ABC, 1964–1972), and a few decades prior to her long run as Krystle Carrington on ABC's *Dynasty* (1981-1989).

Long would later star in *Nanny & the Professor* (ABC, 1970–1971), though die shortly thereafter. Breck made sporadic guest appearances on various shows through the years. Majors would soon find super fame (from 1973–1979) as ABC's *The Six Million Dollar Man* (and husband to Farrah Fawcett), and later on that same network's *The Fall Guy* (1981–1986).

But back on *Big*, Lee, Long, Stanwyck, Breck, and Evans were an unstoppable family brood. The show's quality was sustained by stickler Stanwyck. Whereas *Bonanza* was an affable, albeit periodic frivolous romp, *The Big Valley* played it straight, many times introducing guest characters and plots in a more credible fashion. Unlike *Bonanza*, many of the guest characters on *Valley* were more textured, allowing the actors to perform with sincere poignancy, if within the sometimes-violent scope that reflected the Old West. The show's premium scripts and direction gave it a layered depth not seen since the early years of the *Gunsmoke* series (CBS, 1955–1975), with James Arness portraying Marshal Matt Dillon. Whereas *Gunsmoke* and *Bonanza* became too formulaic (and may have lasted one too many seasons, if not decades), *Valley*, with only four seasons, never out-stayed its welcome.

A premium production to the end, *Valley* balanced the lows and highs of drama, with a subtle measure of humor, without bordering on slapstick, to which *Bonanza* fell prey one too many times. From its pulsating opening theme music to its closing credits, *The Big Valley* delivered as a Western and as a family show.

One episode from the fourth season is a prime example of its quality.

In a story titled, "The Secret," which aired January 27, 1969, Simon Oakland (*Kolchak: The Night Stalker*, *Baretta*) guest stars as Adam Howard, a wealthy rancher and dear friend of the Barkley's who seeks them out because he suspects Jarrod (Richard Long) of having an affair with his wife (Nancy Malone). But it's the scenes between Adam and his young son David (Kelly Corcoran) that prove to be the segment's most moving, mostly because he's confused by his father's intense hatred, which goes against the very core of their family dynamic. In order to prevent irreparable damage (physically and emotionally), David, once thought timid by his dad, rides a harnessed horse for the first time and arrives in the nick of time, begging his father to turn toward God and away from his vengeful heart. Impressed with his son's newfound independence, courage, and sound spiritual faith, Adam relents and, in the end, father and son share a heartrending embrace.

Such moments separate *The Big Valley* from the other weekly Western packs of the day. The series had grand style and elegance, with warm-hearted integrity that earned its welcomed place in millions of homes. But did it have a positive effect on those who lived in those homes?

As fond as James Knuttel was and isof classic TV shows, in general, and Westerns in particular, he didn't recall "anything on television ever consciously" influenced him. "My moral character was undoubtedly shaped by my parents more than anything else." In other words, *The Wild Wild West* never made him want to become a secret agent. "Even as a child," he said, he knew that show "was a fantasy."

Fans and historians like Jim Knuttel continue to keep the spirit of classic television alive after TV writers and producers such as Ed Spielman first gave them life. Both have held the Western sector in reverence with a measure of nobility, especially Spielman.

When he was growing up, "Nobody ever killed anybody because they saw it on TV. But what you have today is a systemic erosion of American mythology. A lot of our belief system has been mythologized, and there was always mythology, but we had a standard. The fact is, when I was a kid, I ran around the street with a cap gun. Every kid had a cap gun because we had cowboy heroes, but you never saw *The Lone Ranger* [on ABC, 1949–1957] shoot anybody. He shot the gun out of the guy's hand. You never saw [film and TV stars] Gene Autry or Roy Rogers shoot anybody. They stood for 'truth, justice, and the American Way.' They were cowboy heroes and they were held to a standard. The reason—and since we've had the second amendment—there have always been guns in America, but thankfully, nobody ever went into a shopping mall or a schoolroom and killed anybody [as has been the unfortunate case recently]. What's happened is there's been a process of—along with the moral decline—there's been a process of dehumanization."

The fact that many in music videos, for example, "kill each other, carry guns, are vulgar, primitive… this is used as a kind of entertainment," he said. "When you do that, you're going to get a result. Why did Charlton Heston have to go into a Time Warner stockholders meeting and read lyrics to a cop killer rap thing and take them to task?" Spielman said it had to take a significant movie star like Heston to perform such a task, someone who became unpopular in Hollywood due to his more conservative views. "But you had a major corporation putting out stuff with cop killer lyrics. Some would call that 'artistic license.' It's not that, but if you don't say that it is, that means you're being judgmental. Does a person have a right to put out lyrics about killing cops? If you do that, you're going to get somebody killing a cop. To me, that's a very natural and devastating consequence."

Spielman also finds video games disconcerting. Those who play them "can push a button with their thumb, and learn to kill. They're animated people and the killing has nothing whatsoever to do with good guys and bad guys most of the time." When Spielman was growing up, he and his friends played with cap guns and argued over "who was going to be the good guy in the white and who was going to be the bad guy when we hid behind the bushes."

"The cap gun was simply an implement of justice," he said. "Nobody played with the cap gun just shooting and killing somebody; it wasn't in your mindset; it wasn't what you were taught and it wasn't what you saw on TV. When you say Gene [Autry] and Roy [Rogers], you knew who they were and what they stood for. The gun [as part of their fabricated Western character] was not a thing in itself. It went along with the rhinestone shirt. It was part of who they were [on screen]."

From the onset of literature, whether dating back to *The Three Musketeers* or beyond, Spielman said "there was always what you might call 'action-adventure.'" The classic story of Treasure Island, for one, "was full of action. But you knew who the pirates were, and you knew who the good guys were. That was how it was settled, through action or violence in classic literature."

These tales were then translated into film and television. "The way good triumphed over evil was exciting or entertaining." If an action-adventure film star like Errol Flynn was dueling a villain, he would have used a sword—or in the case of James Arness as Matt Dillon on *Gunsmoke,* there was a gun. "The *fast-draw* was mythology…never existed in the real Old West," Spielman said. "The leather gun-belt that Matt Dillon wore, the low-slung gun…none of that ever existed either. That was a purely Hollywood invention. But the gun was always an instrument of justice."

"Matt Dillon never shot or killed anybody intentionally," Spielman continued. "He had to do it as a lawman. The over-sensualizing…the titillation, the quality of the action became violence for its own sake. So today it doesn't matter if the reason for the action is for good or bad. It's the action, the violence itself, that's become the entertainment and when you do that, you get the miscreants and the people who have this bloodlust, because Hollywood has now created on the large and small screen violence for its own sake."

In Spielman's first big hit Western, *Kung Fu*, albeit an Eastern-Western, the show's protagonist, Kwai Chang Caine, never desired to maim anyone, much less kill them, as he did in the show's 90-minute pilot:

In the China of the 1880s, and shortly after Caine "graduates" from the sacred Shaolin Temple, he roams the Forbidden City, where he briefly reunites with the visually-impaired Master Po (played by Keye Luke), his favorite mystic mentor. Years before, the elderly teacher had affectionately called Caine "Grasshopper" because at their first meeting, Po, though blind, had sensed the insect at a pre-teen Caine's feet while the boy could not. Years later, as the two strolled through the Forbidden City, Po inadvertently crosses the path of the Emperor's arrogant, impatient nephew, who becomes annoyed with the senior's disability. The royal relative instructs one of his henchmen to slay Po. In a fit of rage that shames the entirety of his life-teachings, Caine grabs a spear and kills the Royal Nephew. As Po lay dying in Caine's arms, he instructs his cherished disciple to flee to America, where the Chinese Emperor sends an endless barrage of vigilantes to capture Caine.

Once the film turns into a series, subsequent episodes transpire in the American Old West, and Caine searches for the American half-brother he never knew. Through it all, he employs his ancient Shaolin wisdom (with visual flashbacks to China) and, when push comes to shove, his skillful martial arts to help, defend, and/or sooth conflicted souls and/or flatten angry cowboys. But he never used a gun, and he always felt severe remorse when he was forced to kill anyone. Caine never forgave himself for betraying his sacred vows after killing the Emperor's nephew; even after his beloved Master Po told him in a compassionate moment, "Sometimes you have to cut off a finger to save a hand."

"When you finished watching an episode of *Kung Fu*," Spielman said, "if I did my job right, you were better for it."

And he felt the same way with *Young Riders* and *Dead Man's Gun.* "I have never been ashamed of any show I ever put on TV or any book I wrote or anything else. Why? Because I always gave [the audience] what I wanted [to see]. Whatever I watch, I want to be better for seeing it, inspired if possible, maybe learn something, but more than anything, be a better human being. That's what I have always given an audience. In some small way, I like to think that I succeeded. I don't think anybody ever [committed a violent act] because of any show that I ever did."

The Young Riders featured regulars including future film stars Stephen Baldwin (brother to Alec, William, and Daniel) and Josh Brolin (son of James Brolin from *Marcus Welby, M.D.* and *Hotel*). As Spielman explained, the show was historically based and crossed decades. "It was about young kids who became Pony Express Riders." The actual want-ad read, "Wanted: Skinny young wiry fellows. Orphans preferred." Hired for only a year's time, they took an oath on a Bible that stated, "I, Pony Express, swear before the great living God, that I will not swear, use tobacco, etc."

Spielman utilized two historical characters for the series: the young William F. Cody (Baldwin), who was a real Pony Express Rider, and the young James Butler Hickok (Brolin), who was actually a wagon driver in the Pony Express but was upgraded to a rider for dramatic effect. The characters became the embodiment of what a young person could achieve, including one girl who masqueraded as a boy (Louise "Lou" McCloud, played by Yvonne Suhor). "They were people who had to make their way through life and hopefully you were inspired, you were entertained and got something out of their travels and their ultimate large and small victories. They were *you*," Spielman explained, referring to the viewer at home. "If they could survive *their* job," perhaps the audience member at home could "survive their day with the bad boss or a broken family or economic hardship."

Spielman has always sought to produce work that is inspirational and historically-based "so it rings true," he said. "It may be fiction, but it's filled" with references he believed the audiences intrinsically know. "It's not sci-fi. It feels real from the beginning."

"When [Cody] sees that horse that he wants to buy and its fifty dollars, and he doesn't have fifty cents, he goes into the ring against a professional prizefighter, where if he can stay for three minutes, he wins the money. He gets beaten half to death because he wants to buy that horse. So, he stays [in the ring]. He gets the fifty dollars. And he goes in all broken up and gives the guy the money for the horse, and [the audience loves] that guy. You know his relationship with that horse [will last] forever…He nearly died to get that horse. His sacrifice is [for] love of the animal."

The audience was inspired by Cody's actions and his sacrifice.

There was another female character on the show named Emma Shannon, played by Melissa Leo who, as Spielman described her, is "the mother to kids who have no mother." At one point in the series, she says of the riders, "They are not orphans while I'm around."

"These characters, without being preachy, showed the nobility of the human spirit," Spielman said. "My shows, whether it was *Kung Fu* or *The Young Riders*, displayed the nobility of the human spirit. I never had the bad guys win in the end in any [series episode] because you don't need me to do a show where good people lose."

In 1959, there were twenty-five Westerns on the air in the halcyon days of Warner Bros. Today, they are a rare breed because, as he explained, "the Western is the American morality play." The Western morphed from the days of Bronco Billy Anderson and *The Great Train Robbery* and these types of shows and films. No one ever wore a rhinestone shirt and played the guitar at sunset. Wild Bill Hickok carried two guns but not the average cowboy. He didn't have a fast draw. The cowboy and the Western were a mythological creation of Hollywood [with] some literary underpinnings. In its heyday in the '50s, the Western, Spielman said, "had a moral standard. The cowboy embodied courage and the value of an individual. This was a uniquely American thing, that the individual had value. If you look at what the political and social thrust was in Europe, it was essentially the collective. It was Socialism, Communism, and a more collective thing."

For Spielman, America represented "the unique value of an individual to stand up against any and all difficulties for the cause of good. In a judgmental America, you had Westerns because there's nothing more judgmental than a Western. There's good and evil, right and wrong, heroism and cowardice, life and death. You cheered for the good guy again and again and again whether it was Gene Autry, Hopalong Cassidy or Roy Rogers."

"The Western had to change societally," Spielman said, as with feature films like 1969's *The Wild Bunch*, directed by Sam Peckinpah. Here, the cowboy became the anti-hero. "There was *some* right and wrong and good and bad in Peckinpah's work."

Such was not the case with the Warner Bros. age of television Westerns, whether it was *Lawman* on ABC from 1958 to 1962 or *Gunsmoke* which, was the longest-running dramatic show in history, airing on CBS from 1955 to 1975). On these series, there was "always right and wrong," said Spielman. "Matt Dillon was the good guy. They even had the dance hall girl…Miss Kitty [Amanda Blake] would have been a common prostitute." Instead, she was a woman who the audience respected, "…even the fact that she worked in the dance hall," Spielman said.

But in that America of the Old West, circa the 1860s, "You defended a woman at the risk of your life or unto death. You defended the young kid…you defended the defenseless. It was the era of *The Lone Ranger*. That was its social and moral thrust for the life of the Western. It changed, and the violence itself became the entertainment."

With the demise of the Western came the close of the cowboy as the American hero. "We got rid of the hero," said Spielman.

In 2013, *The Lone Ranger*, which originally featured Clayton Moore, was rebooted for the big-screen starring Armie Hammer, with Johnny Depp as Tonto, the famous American Indian sidekick first interpreted by Jay Silverheels on TV. Depp's deft Tonto was very different from the series. Or as Spielman said, "I don't know of any kid who gets up in the morning and says: 'I want to be like Johnny Depp with the dead crow on his head.' We don't have the heroes today that we had in Hollywood and on TV in the beginning."

"One of the good things, naïve though it may be," he continued, "…was that if you were going to take a girl dancing on a date, you wanted to be like Fred Astaire. If you were a person who was poor, you wanted to dress and be polished like Cary Grant…those were your role models."

Or others like Frank Sinatra, who made his share of respectable motion pictures, many in which he performed with his popular "Rat Pack" of pals, including Dean Martin, Sammy Davis, Jr., Joey Bishop, and Peter Lawford. "Frank Sinatra as a kid was a plasterer's assistant," Spielman said. "He saw people go out to work every day in dirty old clothes." And many of his friends, with the exception of Lawford, were raised in humble beginnings, such as Martin who, as Spielman recalled, "was briefly a prizefighter…a poor kid," as were Davis and Bishop. But when they performed on stage, "the way they looked from head to toe… they presented themselves as the men they always wanted to be. That's how they appeared. They aspired to something." As opposed to contemporary performers who wear "torn jeans, sneakers, wrinkled shirts…it's very different. I'm not [just reminiscing] about the *good old days*…I'm talking about the fact that we had heroes and people who were role models."

Like the character of Caine on *Kung Fu*. "People wanted to be like him. They really did. [Same with] *The Young Riders* or any of my other shows…they were squarely in the tradition of being role models because of their standards, their moral judgments, what they [would] do and not do.

"The great thing about *Dead Man's Gun*," Spielman continued, "is that it was actually my brother, Howard Spielman's, idea. At the time, you can't sell a Western on TV and you can't sell an anthology like *Twilight Zone* without recurring characters because [the networks] won't buy them [anymore]. Thankfully because of Jerry Offsay who was then the head of Showtime [which aired the show, produced by MGM] and our partner was Henry Winkler ["The Fonz" on *Happy Days*] we succeeded."

"It was the first and only Western anthology since *Death Valley Days* which started [on syndicated TV] in 1952. So, it was really 'one for the books.' We did 41 one-hours…morality tales with double and triple twist endings and the only recurring character was a mythical gun, which was created by my friend and master gunsmith Terry Becker. That gun has my initials on it of all things. [Episodes] were a little bit like a combination between O. Henry [literary stories] and *Twilight Zone*. When you got the gun, you became like yourself only more so. The gun itself had a kind of a power to have people do odd things. It influenced them and not for the good. We had the variations of people in 41 one-hour shows who would do all this stuff. It was always the good guys win at the end. It was very much like O. Henry. They were morality tales and artfully crafted."

Producing such an ambitious series wasn't without its challenges. As Spielman recalled, the difficulty was this: "We built two Western movie towns in a place called Maple Ridge outside of Vancouver. We did this with our partner Larry Sugar in Canada. We had our own horses, our own guns, our own stock, two armorers, we had our own stagecoach. We had a complete Western production company like a throwback to the days of Republic. It was quite remarkable and great fun. We did this from 1996 till 1999. We won almost every award we went out for. We were nominated for Best Dramatic Series at the last Cable Ace Awards. We also were picked as one of the 12 best shows on the air by the *Orange County Register*. And *Dead Man's Gun* is still on all over the world."

Each of his shows have remained unique and unified by his participation.

"*Kung Fu* was a single character who is kind of like a wandering samurai in America. It was very much influenced by the films of Kurosawa. My idea was to take what I loved about the films of Kurosawa. That was very, very important to me. And again, I wasn't the first guy to do this because Walter Mirisch took the *Seven Samurai* and made one of the great Westerns of all time, *The Magnificent Seven,* by transposing it to an American understanding. I took what I loved about Kurosawa, knowing martial arts could be really very important, but it had to be adjusted for an American appetite and that's what *Kung Fu* was—the classical lonesome stranger who goes from place to place. As they said in the promos: 'No horse, no gun, no equal.'"

To gain interest in Caine's adventures, Spielman envisioned the great American canvas, almost like a space odyssey, where he could travel anywhere and meet anyone because America at that time was "so big and so constantly unexpected," Spielman said. "You could always do the unexpected and the interesting."

The Young Riders was a return to the classical Western which, like *Kung Fu,* there was "a vast American expanse," Spielman explained, "that I could create anything for them to meet, whether it was an Indian chief or somebody coming across in a wagon with a wheel broken. You could meet anybody out on The Plains. The good thing about *The Young Riders* was I could feature any one of my little repertory company of the riders or whatever in the episode that week and have the others being supporting players. You would literally never run out of material on a show like *The Young Riders* because it was an ensemble."

At its core, Dead Man's Gun, even with its Western motif "was profoundly a human story," Spielman said. "It presented very contemporary stories. The gun was literally a catalyst for human frailty and conflict, so they were intrinsically dramatic stories. You lead in and you saw somebody who had a particular human situation and once the gun was introduced, you knew everything was going to change."

For example, if the town drunk, "who everyone always laughed at, and who always wanted to be a gunfighter," Spielman said, "...what if he finds the gun and becomes a gunfighter? Or the abused wife? What if the gun comes into her hands?" Or as in an early episode about a photographer, written by Howard Friedlander, Spielman's writing partner on *Kung Fu*, the photographer realizes that wherever the gun is, there also is a picture. As such, he meanders around wherever the gun is and takes a picture, and knows the result will be remarkable.

"*Dead Man's Gun* was a delicious anomaly," Spielman said. "It lent itself to unique writing. We had masterful production with our partner Larry Sugar doing a lot of the heavy lifting in Canada. We had our wonderful Western company there. What is interesting is that the way we did it, we had one starring non-Canadian actor and the rest were supporting actors in Canada so that also was like a repertory company. It was great fun to do and they were very, very artfully crafted. They had to be because you literally were making a little mini-movie every week in seven days. You really had to know your stuff."

For an essay he wrote for the magazine *Who's Who in Television and Radio*, published at the onset of the 1960-1961 TV season, James Arness summed up nicely the reasons why Westerns succeed:

"The brief period on which today's Westerns are based is one of the great misunderstood eras of American history. In it the pioneers struggled to succeed against a hostile environment – as men always have and perhaps always will, but with one difference. Their environment happened to be unusually exciting and unusually romantic. Men pushed westward against big, wild land against fearful climates. The romance came in conquering these elemental obstacles – and in conquering other elemental men. Men banded together in common purpose against real things they could see and feel. Right and wrong were clearly defined, as rarely happened in any other time. In such times men could make their noblest achievements. Why would we not be affected by the story of these men? The story of the West will always be exciting, as long as it's told well and honestly."

Arness had often been asked why *Gunsmoke* was so popular. He believed it retained one strong characteristic that was shared by everyone at the network and all who worked on the show, the entire cast and crew: "*Gunsmoke* has a sincere and honest respect for that period in American history. Great care is taken not to violate the spirit of that classic time – what the real Old West stood for. All of us have the feeling, telling its story, that we are actually a part of it."

"That is the X factor in *Gunsmoke*," Arness concluded. "As long as one show has it, or some part of it, there will be Westerns – and they'll be popular."

Chapter 8

Westerns like *The Young Riders, Dead Man's Gun, The Big Valley, Bonanza,* and *Cheyenne* were sixty-minutes in length. But the genre was introduced on TV in half-hour increments with shows like *The Lone Ranger* (which began in 1949) followed by other series aimed at children like *The Gene Autry Show, The Roy Rogers Show, The Cisco Kid, Hopalong Cassidy,* and *Gunsmoke.*

Gunsmoke began on radio, debuted on CBS-TV in 1955, Gunsmoke expanded to an hour in 1961. It switched to color in 1966. After which it switched from a black-and-white format to color. Another half-hour Western, *The Rifleman,* aired on ABC from 1958 to 1963 and starred Chuck Connors as Lucas McCain, a widowed struggling rancher, and his young son, played by Johnny Crawford. Unlike *Gunsmoke, The Rifleman* remained in its original black-and-white, half-hour family-oriented format, while the adventures of Matt Dillon presented smarter, more mature, edgier, and at

The Andy Griffith Show, the ideal representation of retro rural television charm *[Credit: The Classic TV Preservation Society]*

times, very violent scripts, particularly in the show's first few years. But the episodes for both shows, and mostly all the Westerns that proceeded them, and a few that aired during and before, were, for the most part, presented as morality plays.

Beyond the core Western format, the half-hour rural-series materialized with comedies like *The Real McCoys, The Farmer's Daughter,* and *The Andy Griffith Show.* The latter of these debuted in 1960 and became one of TV's most iconic series of any genre. When its star died in 2012, President Barack Obama called him an "American Institution." Or as *The Los Angeles Times* once put it, "Andy Griffith was famous for playing hayseed characters full of homespun wisdom."

The popularity of the *Griffith Show* led CBS to add other bucolic-natured shows such as *Griffith* spin-offs *Gomer Pyle* and *Mayberry RFD,* as well as *Petticoat Junction* which fertilized *Green Acres.*

In December 1996, Breck Richardson, then of Arlington, Virginia, penned a letter to *Classic TV Magazine,* defining the term "spin-off," as well as clarifying what he called an "erroneous" report about *The Andy Griffith Show.* He explained how *Griffith,* which began life as a segment of *The Danny Thomas Show,* had for years been misidentified as the first spin-off in TV history. "This is a long-propagated myth," he wrote. "The fact is the idea for a spin-off had come about long before *The Griffith Show*," which he also referred to as "TAGS." Richardson continued:

"Several spin-offs preceded it, dating as far back as 1950. That was the year that *Beulah* debuted on ABC. Technically, *Beulah* was a radio spin-off, having sprung from *Fibber McGee and Molly* in 1945. So, the TV series was the television version of the radio spin-off, but with different actors in the title role. [The radio edition first starred Marlin Hurt, a Caucasian male, in the lead role, followed by Bob Corley, another Caucasian man, and then Hattie McDaniel; Ethel Waters took over the role on the TV version for the show's first two seasons, followed by Louise Beavers for the final year].

"In 1955, five years after *Beulah* came to television, *The Adventures of Champion* debuted. This was the first legitimate television spin-off: an actual television series that spun off from another television series, *The Gene Autry Show*. *The Adventures of Champion* is additionally unique in that the character that was spun-off from *The Gene Autry Show* was Gene Autry's horse, Champion. This, to my knowledge, is the only time the character upon which a spin-off was based, was an animal.

"In 1958 came the next television spin-off series, *Wanted: Dead or Alive*. This popular series had its beginnings in a manner similar to that of *The Andy Griffith Show*. Just as the pilot for TAGS [*The Andy Griffith Show*] had aired an episode of *The Danny Thomas Show*, the pilot for *Wanted: Dead or Alive* aired as an episode [in early 1958] of…*Trackdown* [which like *Wanted*, was a Western]. In the fall of 1959, *Law of the Plainsman*, whose pilot episode had aired earlier that year as an episode of *The Rifleman*, began a three-year run. And some might even consider *The Untouchables*, which debuted in 1959, a spin-off of the anthology series, *Westinghouse Desilu Playhouse* since *The Untouchables* first appeared as a two-part episode of that series in early 1959.

"On September 1960, the first sitcom spin-off, *Pete and Gladys*, which ran on CBS, premiered. This occurred two weeks before the October 3, 1960, CBS debut of *The Andy Griffith Show*. *Pete and Gladys* featured Harry Morgan reprising the role of Pete Porter, which he had played for five seasons [1954-1959] on the sitcom, *December Bride*. Verna Felton also reprised her *December Bride* role, Hilda Crocker, on *Pete and Gladys*.

"By the mid-1960s, the country-based situation comedy was firmly seeded in the vast field of television, if mostly because of *The Andy Griffith Show*. The popularity of *The Beverly Hillbillies*, *Petticoat Junction*, and *Green Acres* only increased, as they frequently cross-pollinated characters. By the early '70s, such programming was eradicated to make way for more sophisticated shows. Or as was once observed by actor Pat Buttram (who played Mr. Haney on *Green Acres*), "They canceled every show that had a tree in it."

While *Hillbillies* offered quaint insight to certain life priorities, and *Petticoat* presented one of TV's warmest families and settings (the small town of Hooterville, which also farmed *Acres*), it was *The Andy Griffith Show* that rose above the rest. As Richardson explained to *Classic TV Magazine*, this series was introduced as an episode of *The Danny Thomas Show*, titled "Andy of Mayberry."

Up until that point, Griffith—the performer—had risen to fame in feature films like *A Face in the Crowd* (1957) and *No Time for Sergeants* (1958), which was adapted from Broadway, along with co-star Knotts. The two actors then reteamed on *Griffith* as Sheriff Andy Taylor and his dedicated if dippy Deputy Barney Fife—team protectors of melancholy Mayberry, South Carolina. The show also starred Frances Bavier as Andy's endearing Aunt Bee and little Ronnie Howard as his loyal on-screen son Opie.

Additional cast members included: Floyd the Barber (Howard McNear), county clerk Howard Sprague (Jack Dodson), Helen Crump, Opie's teacher and Andy's steady girl (Aneta Corsaut); Thelma Lou (Betty Lynn), Barney's devoted gal (following Juanita—whom we never see), and cousins Goober (George Lindsey) and Gomer Pyle (Jim Nabors), who later joined the Marines (on that spin-off of his own). The second spin-off, *Mayberry, RFD*, featured Ken Berry (formerly of *F-Troop*) and was a sequel (and its parent series without Griffith, Knotts, and Howard).

But it is *Griffith* that remains preferred entertainment, and no wonder: each segment is a classic, exampled by these four standouts from the *Griffith* observatory:

- "Andy Saves Barney's Morale," in which Deputy Fife bumbles more than usual his flighty over-the-top legalities.
- "The Clubmen," in which Andy and Barney meet with the members of an exclusive private men's association, and only one of them is invited to join.
- "Mr. McBeevee," in which Andy is convinced that Opie's new friend is merely illusory.
- "Barney and the Cave Rescue," in which Barney leads a rescue attempt to save Andy and Helen, both of whom are snared in a rock-riddled cavern after an inner landslide.

"McBeevee" holds several heartrending moments, several between Andy and Opie, and one in which Andy professes to Barney and Aunt Bee, "I believe in Opie."

"Morale" and "Clubmen" display the true bond between Sheriff Taylor and Deputy Fife, which was the main relationship of the series. In each of these segments, Andy's diplomatic integrity and generous spirit of friendship and/or family shines bright. These episodes showcase high comedy, homespun appeal, and solid interaction between the main characters.

The same could be said of "Cave," which was directed by actor Richard Crenna, a former co-star of *The Real McCoys*, and one of the original choices for Darrin on *Bewitched*. Written by Harvey Bullock, "Cave" caters to several agreeable *Griffith* elements, with style and distinction. As the episode begins, Barney embarrasses by falsely accusing Mayberry's bank manager of pilfering. To help ease tensions, on a picnic, Barney, Thelma Lou, Andy, and Helen explore one of the boys' childhood stomping grounds: a spooky cave. A rockslide ensues. Andy and Helen are trapped. By the time they free themselves, Barney's arranged a mammoth rescue endeavor, involving two mean-spirited townsmen who had publicly humiliated him. Rather than risk further damage to Barney's self-esteem, Andy and Helen re-enter the cave and feign near-death. The rescue works and Barney is looked upon with monumental respect, and his character is restored.

"Cave" represents and solidifies the *Griffith* appeal with emotional, psychological, and even physical strength (Barney and the town's finest sweat through stone and elbow grease during the rescue). Andy's affection for Barney is taken to new heights, as he seeks Helen's help (mostly before, it was only Andy who saved face for Barney). Not only does this reinforce the bond between the two best friends, but it helps to cement (in more ways than one) Andy's relationship with Helen (as she proves her devotion to him by going the distance…back into the cave).

Other fine moments transpire near the end, when Thelma Lou shares her pride in Barney with Helen, who seconds the notion, in reference to Andy. All the while, Helen not once mentions that she and Andy never required the rescue, thus displaying her affection for Thelma Lou with Andy-like discretion and poise.

But one of the most telling, subtle scenes occurs mid-episode when Andy takes Helen home so she can change her dirty clothes, to which she reverts (when she and Andy learn of Barney's massive rescue maneuvers, via the radio). As Andy waits in her living room, decorated with doilies and big '60s furniture, a nostalgic, inner-home warmth seeps through the TV screen, and seemingly into our real-life parlors. With near-*Twilight-Zone*-like surrealism, it's as if we are transported into Helen's home to a simpler time, basking in the tranquil effects of that ol' Mayberry magic. This episode more than most succinctly combines Barney's loving lunacy and sincere courage; Andy's discretion, diplomacy, and sincere heroics; as well as Helen and Thelma Lou's prodigious support for the men in their lives. Despite the absence of Ronnie Howard's youthful intelligence as Opie, and the core exclusion of Frances Bavier's amiable Aunt Bee, "Barney and the Cave Rescue" shines in *Griffith* observatory as one of the show's finest half-hours, proving without the shadow of any doubt just how educational a popular primetime classic television show can actually be.

As classic TV books, websites, and fans have professed for ages, *The Andy Griffith Show* continues to have a positive lingering effect on its viewers, namely Jim Clark. For years, he has supervised *The Andy Griffith Show* Rerun Watchers Club, which has approximately 20,000 members, and an online newsletter called "The Bullet." As he told *The Los Angeles Times* in September 2010, the show's 50th Anniversary, *Griffith's* on-going appeal is due to its quality and unique nature. "Primarily, it's great storytelling," he said. "And wholesome—it's got lots of nostalgia."

"I think people want a nostalgic kind of show, and they don't have that on TV anymore," added Jessica Icenhour Roberts, Executive Director of the Mount Airy, N.C., Tourism Development Authority & Tourism Partnership of Surry County, where the Surry Arts Council operates the Andy Griffith Museum. Even she was shocked by the number of younger viewers familiar with the show. "Mayberry is the hook that brings people to Mount Airy," she said, "and will continue to be the hook for years to come."

Indeed. In 2009, a "Mayberry Days" event attracted about 20,000 visitors, which increased to 50,000 in 2010, and more in subsequent years. "Mayberry is going to be in Webster's dictionary someday," said Tanya Jones, executive director of the Surry Arts Council and one of those behind the Mayberry Days festivities. "Mayberry is iconic for gentle living," she told the *Times*.

Salvatore Amato, a radiology coordinator at a respected hospital in Western New York, has dealt with matters of the heart. Applicably, he has also been a fan of heartwarming nostalgic television. "I enjoyed many classic TV shows as a kid," he said, "from the laugh-out-loud comedy of *The Dick Van Dyke Show*, *The Carol Burnett Show*, and *All in the Family*, to the thrills of *The Twilight Zone*, *Mission: Impossible*, and *Hawaii Five-O*. But two shows always struck deeper for me than any others and truly affected my life: *Star Trek* and *The Andy Griffith Show*."

"The character of Sheriff Andy Taylor," in particular, Amato continued, "was as close to a perfect person as I can imagine. In retrospect, I can honestly say that no other fictional character's integrity has stood as a benchmark in my development as an adult as much as his. I watch the old episodes and realize how much Andy's strict but loving handling of his son Opie influenced me in raising my four children. His selfless efforts to save his bumbling deputy friend Barney Fife from embarrassment, and even to build him up beyond what he could accomplish himself, is an example that, if we all followed it, would make the world a different place. I've tried to pass these values on to my children."

After he was Opie on *The Andy Griffith Show*, the now-adult and Oscar-winning film director Ron Howard played another popular young TV character: Richie Cunningham on *Happy Days*, which aired on ABC from 1974 to 1984. In 1986, Howard reprised Opie in the NBC TV-movie *Return to Mayberry*, and last worked with Griffith during President Barack Obama's 2008 campaign for an online political comedy skit that streamed on the *Funny or Die* website. Shortly after Griffith died, Howard authored "Remembering Andy Griffith: A Life in Tune," a tribute published in *The Los Angeles Times*, in which he professed how his "TV dad taught me how to truly appreciate the work and the work of others." He more fully explained it like this:

"Andy Griffith entertained us for decades on stage, via our radios, sound systems, TVs, and up there on the silver screen. Comedy, drama, or music, he brought his love of performing to each creative undertaking. He was known for ending shows by looking directly at the audience and saying, 'I appreciate it, and good night.' Perhaps the greatest enduring lesson I learned from eight seasons of playing Andy's son, Opie, on the show was that he truly understood the meaning of those words, and he meant them, and there was value in that respect. At every turn, he demonstrated his honest respect for people and he never seemed to expect theirs in return, but wanted to earn it.

"He taught me a great deal through the examples he set and the approach to our work on the set. I learned about comedic timing, paying off characters in the third act of a storyline, and the equal values of both focused rehearsal and, at particular moments, of total chaotic spontaneity.

"I saw him lobby against jokes that were admittedly funny but that were at the expense of and undercut the long-term reliability of a character. I was fortunate to witness and even participate in thousands of minutely detailed creative problem-solving interactions with Andy always tirelessly engaged.

"He proved hour by hour, episode by episode, that creativity and neurotic angst were not inexorably linked. He led by example, and we demonstrated that a cast and company could play practical jokes on one another, laugh till they cried, and still get 12 pages of the script shot every day while producing a No. 1-rated show.

"And as I look back today, knowing that Andy's vision yielded a show that still airs daily all over the country and holds an absolutely unique place in the annals of its medium; I'm reminded of another lesson taught by example.

"Do all that, and don't forget to have as many laughs as you can along the way."

With that being said, Norman Lear's litany of groundbreaking series debuted in the 1970s, with topics, stories, dialogue, and characters considered taboo for the time and previously. But before that, bold steps were taken on television if just with casting, while stories about prejudice and racism, for example, would sneak through the back door of sci-fi/fantasy shows like *The Twilight Zone* (CBS, 1959-1965), *Star Trek* (NBC, 1966–1969) or *Bewitched* (ABC, 1964–1972), all of which presented morality plays in disguise.

For some viewers, such as graphic artist and classic TV fan Steve Reeser of Los Angeles, other shows like *The Beverly Hillbillies* (CBS, 1962–1971) and *Gilligan's Island* (CBS, 1964–1967), proved enriching on a similar level. Growing up in eastern Montana, Reeser was inspired by the settings depicted on *Hillbillies* and *Gilligan*. While such programs seemed exotic and the situations far-fetched, Reeser knew at a young age that they represented something original and timeless. "Although the setups of these shows start out as jokes," he said, "…their fish-out-of-water stories of societal juxtaposition presented some very good commentaries on social class, prejudice, and what it takes to overcome these differences. It was hilarious to watch the Clampetts turning the haughty culture of an upscale Beverly Hills neighborhood on its ear while demonstrating their bias for their own native homespun manners. And who isn't amused by the inhabitants of Gilligan's tropical isle, where people from different backgrounds are thrown together to develop a culture and micro-society of their own, using nothing more than their wits and what they've scavenged on the island? Although I'm still puzzling over how Mary Ann found the rest of the ingredients for her famous coconut cream pies."

Reeser has enjoyed world travels with his wife, Virginia, an established marketing writer. So, perhaps it was *Gilligan's Island* that led to an interest in learning and understanding more about foreign languages and cultures and visiting abroad for a year in a cultural exchange. "There are still a few shows on television today and in the recent past that comment on people's quirky habits and different backgrounds," he said, such as *Northern Exposure* (CBS, 1990–1995) and *The Big Bang Theory* (CBS, 2007-2019). "But nothing warms my heart more than hearing Buddy Ebsen [who played father Jed to Donna Douglas' Elly May Clampett on *Hillbillies*] exclaim in excitement, 'Weeeellll, doggies!'"

Who can say whether Gilligan or the Clampetts inspired Reeser to pack up his car and "*move to Beverlee*" (via the *Hillbillies* opening-theme). And while he's been enjoying life in sunny southern California for several years, he concluded, "I have yet to set sail on a three-hour cruise."

The cast of *Petticoat Junction*, which is considered one of the most bucolic-geared sitcoms in TV history (from bottom left): Linda Kaye Henning, Edgar Buchanan, Bea Benederet. [Credit: The Classic TV Preservation Society]

71

Chapter 9

Diahann Carroll starred in *Julia* [Credit: *The Classic TV Preservation Society*]

Diversity took a more serious turn on CBS in the 1960s when African-American actress Gail Fisher played Mike Connors' secretary Peggy on *Mannix*, shortly before Diahann Carroll would break all race and gender vocational barriers with her historic lead on the NBC sitcom *Julia*. Carroll not only presented TV's first black female character on a weekly basis, but she was a medical professional to boot, eons before such African-Americans and Asian-Americans became a regular presence on a dramatic series like ABC's *Grey's Anatomy* (which debuted in 2005).

African-American actor Ivan Dixon played Staff Sgt. Ivan Kinchloe on the CBS comedy, *Hogan's Heroes* (1965–1971). His career expanded beyond this sitcom, which he utilized as a platform for positive social impact. Active in the civil rights movement, Dixon, who died at age 78 in 2008, served as president of Negro Actors for Action. As he explained in *Reel Black Talk: A Sourcebook of 50 American Filmmakers* by Linda Allen and Spencer Moon, his political and organizing efforts "helped to integrate television."

Another time, he called television "the most powerful medium operating in the world today, and we must have access to it to discuss our problems and concerns." During his tenure on *Hogan's Heroes*, Dixon, along with Bill Cosby on *I Spy*, was one only a few African-American males on TV. Dixon reportedly left *Heroes* because he felt underutilized and considered other acting roles more definitive of his career. After his death, Dixon's daughter Doris Nomathande Dixon told *The Associated Press* that her father welcomed the attention he received by playing Kinchloe. "It was a pivotal role as well because there were not as many blacks in TV series at that time," she said. "He did have some personal issues with that role, but it also launched him into directing."

Dixon's talents as a director proved equally innovative as his acting skills. After receiving rave reviews for directing Maya Angelou and Cicely Tyson in a Los Angeles production of "The Blacks," Cosby encouraged Dixon to venture into television, and he complied. In the '70s and '80s, when it was still somewhat rare to see African-Americans behind the camera of feature films, Entertainment Weekly noted that Dixon inconspicuously directed numerous TV shows like *The Waltons*, *The Rockford Files*, *The Greatest American Hero,* and *Magnum, P.I.*

Dixon was born April 6, 1931, grew up in Harlem, and, in 1954, graduated with a degree in drama from North Carolina Central University (where the drama troupe is still titled the "Ivan Dixon Players").

In 1957, he made his Broadway debut in *The Cave Dwellers* and, a few years later, portrayed Nigerian student Joseph Asagai in the original 1959 Broadway production of *A Raisin in the Sun*. He reprised the Asagai role in the 1961 motion picture, co-starring Sidney Poitier, a lifelong friend, who had also appeared in the original stage rendition. "As a fellow actor, one had to be on one's toes; otherwise, he was quite likely to walk away with the scene," Poitier told *The Los Angeles Times* after Dixon passed away.

Dixon had steadfastly refused to play roles that he felt were stereotypical. In 1964, he starred in the civil rights movie drama *Nothing But A Man*. Long after its release, Dixon continued to view this film as an example of Hollywood's potential to accurately reflect black life. "He encouraged the making of more honest films," wrote one film critic for *The Los Angeles Times*. According to *Entertainment Weekly*, Dixon fans considered *Man* his best performance on-screen and called it "the supreme example of what he could do when he wasn't trapped in that prison camp."

In 1967, Dixon was Emmy-nominated for his lead performance in the CBS Playhouse drama *The Final War of Olly Winter*. A veteran of World War II, Winter was resolute to make Vietnam his last battle. As the TV production played out, and after his comrades were killed, Winter had to make his way to safety. The reviews for *Final* were safe and solid. *The New York Daily News* called it "a haunting, mordant work of infinite pathos, with a memorable virtuoso performance by Ivan Dixon."

In talking with *Newsday* in 1993, Dixon said, "Even among black directors today—and I'm not saying these guys haven't done good work—there is more concern with making movies that make money, that titillate and get people to the box office. And I think that is the kind of horror of black American life that we have accepted that struggle for the dollar instead of struggling for humanity. For honor."

Early television shows also rarely featured regular characters of Asian descent beyond the insulting subservient stereotypes, such as when Sammee Tong portrayed houseboy Peter Tong on *Bachelor Father* (CBS/NBC, 1957–1962), or when Victor Sen Yung played Hop Sing on *Bonanza* (NBC, 1959–1973). A few exceptions to this embarrassment transpired on *Star Trek*, when George Takei played Lt. Commander Sulu on *Star Trek*, or on the original *Hawaii Five-0* (CBS, 1968–1980), which more respectfully utilized the talents of Asian-American actors such as Kam Fong (who played Chin Ho) and Harry Endo (as Che Fong); or when Bruce Lee (a few years after playing Kato on *Green Hornet* (ABC, 1966–1967), and just prior to becoming a martial arts film legend) was cast as martial arts instructor Li Tsung to blind detective *Longstreet* (played by James Franciscus, ABC, 1971–1972).

It wasn't until *Kung Fu* debuted on ABC in the early '70s did Asian-American actors become a regular respectful presence on screen. Well-trained actors like Benson Fong, Mako, James Hong, and Victor Sen Yung himself were finally granted the opportunity to employ their skills in reverent roles. David Carradine, the show's lead, was not of Asian descent in real life, as was Kwai Chang Caine, who was Eurasian, half-American/half-Chinese). But the regular ensemble of *Kung Fu* thespians played non-stereotypical Asian characters for the first time in TV history. The show became the first television series to introduce Asian thought, creed and culture to the American mainstream in the most elegant and literate way—all of which transpired with the show's 90-minute pilot which premiered February 22, 1972—the year President Richard Nixon (though soon-to-be-disgraced via the Watergate scandal) was holding historic talks with China's Chairman Mao.

In 1975, Erik Estrada as Frank "Ponch" Poncherello on *CHiPs* became the first Latin actor to land a series lead since Desi Arnaz on *I Love Lucy*. On-screen, Estrada's pretty "Ponch" was frequently confronted by racism, which would show its ugly head in several episodes of the series. Around the same time, veteran Latin leading man Ricardo Montalban (who died in 2009) was making headway with his performance as the mysterious Mr. Roarke on TV's *Fantasy Island* (ABC, 1978–1984) years after his debut as the diabolical Khan in the 1967 "Space Seed" segment of the original *Star Trek*.

Playing Khan became a landmark performance for Montalban, who resuscitated the character 13 years later for the 1982 hit feature film sequel, *Star Trek II: The Wrath of Khan*. Twenty years after that film debuted, Paramount Studios presented in Hollywood a special 20th Anniversary screening of *The Wrath of Khan*, hosted by the film's director, Nicholas Meyer, featuring a special guest appearance by Montalban, who by then, was in a wheelchair. For years, many of his fans were unaware that he was fitted with an artificial leg. But by the time he attended this special event, his increased disability did not detract from his charisma and still potent ability to connect with his multitude of admirers. The press had documented his appearance as a monumental moment in entertainment history, one that will most likely never be repeated again, not in today's TV environment.

Beyond his *Trek* and *Fantasy* performances, Montalban made countless other appearances on the big screen and small, including a guest-shot on an episode of TV's *The Name of the Game*, which originally aired on NBC from 1968 to 1971. This series, one of the more unique entries in TV history, featured a rotating cast, like that of the network's original *Sunday Mystery Movie* wheel of shows (1971–1977, including *McMillan & Wife*, *Columbo*, and *McCloud*, among others). Unlike those showcased in the *Mystery* series, the revolving weekly characters on *Game* (which also happened to air on Sundays) were interlocked by a singular plot device: they worked alternately for a publishing firm in Los Angeles. A set number of characters were played by Robert Stack (post-*The Untouchables*), Gene Barry (post-*Burke's Law*), and Tony Franciosa (pre-*Matt Helm*).

Montalban appeared in one of the Stack segments called "Echo of a Nightmare," an average story (about a kidnapper freed from prison) that was outweighed by another one of Ricardo's above-average performances. Yet, his *Game* performance is noteworthy due to his stellar talents and his mere participation. While filming the *Game,* Montalban was approximately forty-something. Years later, when he was Mr. Roarke on *Fantasy Island* and returned to playing *Trek's* Khan (in *Wrath*), he was a senior citizen in his late 50s and early 60s. In addition to his Latino, disabled status, he was three times a minority, an assessment which now begs the questions:

Would such an actor find work today on television or in a feature film? And would any network or film studio hire a senior non-Caucasian with an artificial leg?

The answer, most likely and sadly, is probably not.

In the fall of 2013, NBC attempted to reboot Raymond Burr's post-*Perry Mason* series, *Ironside*, about a disabled police commissioner in a wheelchair. When Burr appeared in the original series (on NBC, 1968–1975), the awareness level of the disabled was low, and their air time was set aside mostly for one episode at a time on medical shows like *Marcus Welby, M.D.* (ABC, 1969–1976), or *Medical Center* (CBS, 1969–1976). More times than not, the disabled characters on these shows were portrayed by completely healthy actors. When NBC opted to remake *Ironside* in a more enlightened era, the peacock network rustled the feathers of the disabled community by not hiring a disabled performer in the lead. Instead, they cast the very robust Blair Underwood in the lead role. The casting of Underwood, who just so happens to be African-American, was a noble choice (making colorless by definition the lead character of *Ironside*), but the part should have been cast with a disabled performer (of ANY cultural heritage or background).

In the '80s, the same network wisely cast actress/comedian Geri Jewell, diagnosed with cerebral palsy, as a semi-regular on the sitcom, *The Facts of Life* (NBC, 1979–1988), a spin-off from its super hit *Diff'rent Strokes* (NBC, 1978–1986). Whereas *Diff'rent* was innovative in one way, casting the one-of-a-kind mega-talent of Gary Coleman, a young African-American as the adopted son (with Todd Bridges) to Caucasian (and former *Maude* regular) Conrad Bain's wealthy Mr. Drummond, the show's attempt to demarginalize racism paled in comparison to Jewell's appearances on *Facts*.

The remarkable actress, who first gained the national spotlight through guest-shots on The Carol Burnett Show, and later became a regular on shows like *The Young and the Restless* and *Deadline*, quickly won fans at home—and within Hollywood. For one, TV writing/producing legend Norman Lear praised Jewell's book, *I'm Walking as Straight As I Can: Transcending Disability in Hollywood and Beyond* (ECW Press, 2011), saying, "I haven't known a more inspirational life and talent…One of the true gems in my career is Geri Jewell."

After Jewell ended her run on *The Facts of Life* in the spring of 1984, it wasn't until the fall of 1989 that rival network ABC had the foresight to present another performer from the disabled community on a weekly *Life* series. *Life Goes On* featured the remarkable Chris Burke, who has Down syndrome, as Corky Thacher, the middle son of an average American family living in the suburbs of Chicago. As with Jewell on *Facts*, *Life Goes On* presented Corky not as a young teen with a disability but, as show creator/executive producer Michael Braverman said in late 1993 (shortly after the series completed its ABC run), as a teen who "just so happens to have Down syndrome."

No weekly drama so uniquely, directly, or fully addressed the topic of prejudice more than

Life Goes On, which, interestingly enough, might also be classified as a dramedy. Originally broadcast from 1989 until 1993, *Life* was a one-hour drama with comedic overtones, at least in its first two seasons, when it was more focused on the daily challenges faced by the Thacher family, led by parents Drew and Libby (Bill Smitrovich and Patti LuPone), whose middle child Corky had his own particular struggles. What contributed so very much to the show's likability factor was the straightforward manner with which it addressed the subjects of Down syndrome and disability. The TV viewer responded to the program's peerless flavor, and presentation. The producers respected its subject manner (as well as the audience), by not insulting or talking "down" to them. Burke himself said in 1993, "I don't have Down syndrome I have 'Up' syndrome!" That's the kind of positive spirit the young actor brought to the series which connected directly with the American public on several levels.

When Drew and Libby thought Corky was out of line, they reprimanded him, as would any responsible parent towards a misbehaved child. If this was any other family TV show or any other TV show about a family, such interaction would be par for the course. But *Life* was never like any other TV show. Corky was presented as a regular high-school student dealing with the challenges of adolescence, compounded by additional challenges that are not usually experienced by the average teen. He had a younger sister named Becca (Kellie Martin), and an older sister named Paige (first played by Monique Lanier then Tracey Needham). Tommy Puett rounded out the initial cast as Tyler Benchfield, the apple of Becca's eye, the jock with a heart—and a brother of his own with Down. Chad Lowe was added to the series in the third season in his Emmy-winning role as Jesse McKenna, who is HIV-positive, a diagnosis that later developed into full-blown AIDS.

Down syndrome and AIDS: traits unusual for weekly characters on television, a medium infamously circumspect of figures that viewers found surprising. In the fall of 1991, the year Lowe's Jesse joined the show, basketball superstar Magic Johnson revealed in real life that he was HIV-positive. This was not a case of life imitating art but simply a parallel incident. After *Life Goes On* was on the air, Michael Braverman interviewed small focus groups and discovered that many teens thought AIDS could be contracted through casual interaction; he set out to dispel that ignorance, as well as the scorn aimed at those like Burke. Once pegged a failure by some, *Life* instead sprung eternal. Once misunderstood, those with Down syndrome and AIDS—as well as those of other minority groups and/or with other disabilities—were now perceived more clearly because of the show.

In 1989, Chad Hoffman, then-vice president of ABC Drama Programming, explained how *Life* came about: "We wanted to do a show about a working-class family which I thought, at the time, did not really have a voice on television. We wanted to prove that this family could overcome the daily obstacles of life. And into that situation, we thought to add an extraordinary circumstance; that being a child with Down. We asked ourselves, 'What would it be like for this person to function in the mainstream of society?' and 'What would it be like for the family?'"

"The decision we made," Hoffman said, "…was that Corky was not going to be treated as a special child. Yes, he was a child who was born into certain circumstances, and it was a struggle, but we didn't want to do 'poor Corky' shows."

Expanding on his assessment from 1993, Braverman offered his personal inspiration in creating *Life*: "The show was not about a family with a son who has Down syndrome. The show was about a family with a son who happens to have Down syndrome. I have a nephew who happens to have Down syndrome, but that doesn't define who he is. And with *Life Goes On*, I wanted to create a legacy for him to reflect upon. I wanted to create a world where it didn't matter if people were different. And that was the whole point of *Life Goes On*."

Although it finished its original run over twenty years ago, *Life* still goes on in syndication and DVD sales. It continues to inspire viewers and reach beyond the realm of average entertainment with superior production values and credible, yet compelling stories, each delivered with a sincere dedication to presenting "good" television—a philosophy that was carried through for its entire four-year run.

In the show's final season, Corky marries Amanda, a woman (portrayed by Amanda Friedman) who also has Down syndrome. Like any other newlywed couple, he complained about her cooking, and she was interested in romance. In its last episode, Libby, with Drew, Becca, and Paige in silent agreement, tells her son, "The world is a better place because of you, Corky."

On every level, *Life* lives on to say more than just "I'm okay, you're okay." Instead, it affirms: "I'm great and so are you, and although we may be unique unto each other, together aren't we grand." A positive life-fulfilling television legacy if there ever was one. While shows like *Ironside* and *Longstreet* at least introduced disabled characters to the mainstream, courageous performers like Ricardo Montalban, Geri Jewell, and Chris Burke beat the odds of their disabilities and became a success on screen and in real life for themselves, the mainstream home viewers, and the disabled community on every level.

Vince Staskel, challenged by cerebral palsy, is a producer of Able Pathways Media and an advocate for disabled performers. Jewell, Burke, and television, in its most positive form, have inspired him in both his personal life and career. "As a person-with-a-disability, it was very significant for me seeing performers who looked like me on television shows as I got older. I really identified with Geri Jewell on the *Facts of Life*. This was very affirming to me. Here was a very attractive young woman with the same disability as me. She not only had the talent but the self-confidence to be a comedian and an actress. She was the first person-with-a-disability to have a recurring role on a network series. I was surely hooked on the entertainment industry after enjoying her performances. Another significant occurrence for me was seeing Chris Burke become the first disabled person to co-star on a television series. These were groundbreaking events for the disabled community. Now I was even more determined to pursue a career in the media."

"It is extremely important for children with disabilities to see people like themselves on television and in film," Staskel continued. "These portrayals create positive role models and extend tremendous opportunities for them to be part of an accepting and inclusive worldview…These television shows gave the disabled community a foundation to build even more creative opportunities for real-life situations to be aired…and, most importantly, to be performed by real-life actors-with-disabilities."

Into this equality mix, historic strides were made by performers like Ellen DeGeneres and her ABC sitcom *Ellen*, originally titled *These Friends of Mine* (ABC, 1994–1998). In one episode from the show's later seasons, Ellen Morgan, the character she played, revealed her true sexuality: gay. That same year, *Time Magazine* featured a cover story on DeGeneres, who admitted the same thing with the headline, "Yep—I'm gay."

The season after *Ellen* left the air, *Will & Grace* debuted on NBC (1998–2005), and became the first series to feature weekly gay characters already out of the closet, twenty years after the network made a noble attempt to feature a character that was assumed to be gay; and played by Tony Randall in *Love, Sidney* (1981–1983). Before that, there were straight characters played by actors who were thought to be gay, such as Paul Lynde portraying the eccentric Uncle Arthur on *Bewitched*.

All of those classic shows, in one way or another, broke ground for contemporary sitcoms like *Modern Family* (ABC, 2009-Present), which defines family as the unconditional love shared by individuals who care for one another as human beings, despite any differences there may be in age, race, or sexuality.

PART 3
THE FAMILY UNIT

"…some things which may seem too simple, or unimportant, or even just downright plain…those things are really every bit as important and every bit as beautiful as the most magnificent things in the whole world."
—John-Boy Walton, *The Waltons*
(Episode: "The Air Mail Man" – 12/13/73)

The cast of *The Waltons* (from top right): Michael Learned, Richard Thomas, Ralph Waite, Ellen Corby, Will Geer, Kami Cotler, David L. Harper, Jon Walmsley, Judy Norton Taylor, Eric Scott, Mary McDonough *[Credit: The Classic TV Preservation Society]*

Chapter 10

In the early years of television, many programs like *The Andy Griffith Show* may have been filmed, broadcast, and received in black and white on small-dimension black-and-white TV sets, but they were permeated with colorful, textured, and multi-dimensional characters. Family shows such as *Father Knows Best*, *The Donna Reed Show*, *Leave It to Beaver*, and *My Three Sons* were classified as purely sentimental and accused of lacking depth regarding story and character development. But the majority of their characters interacted on very real terms in very realistic stories honestly presented within the context of their time.

Father Knows Best and several more black-and-white shows sprang from radio, including other comedies like *The Adventures of Ozzie and Harriet*, *I Love Lucy*, and *Our Miss Brooks*, as well as dramatic programs including TV's first major western hit *Gunsmoke*, and the legal series *Perry Mason*. Such transference provided a solid foundation for building visual counterparts from a long and previously-established rich and fertile field of storytelling and character development.

On both the radio and TV editions of *Father Knows Best*, Robert Young played stable insurance salesman Jim Anderson. The radio edition of the show was broadcast from August 25, 1949, to November 19, 1953, and featured a "question mark" (?) at the end of its title, denoting if indeed the patriarch possessed the correct amount of wisdom to run a household. When the series migrated to television, the question mark was dropped, as were these performers who played Young's wife and family: June Whitley and Jean Vander Pyl (Wilma, from *The Flintstones*) shared the role of Margaret Anderson, Jim's wife, while Rhoda Williams played the eldest daughter Betty (a.k.a "Princess"), Ted Donaldson was Jim Anderson, Jr. ("Bud"), and Norma Jean Nilsson played little Kathy ("Kitten").

In the television format, Margaret was portrayed by Jane Wyatt (whose initial pathway to fame stemmed from roles in feature films like 1937's *Lost Horizon*), while the children were played by Elinor Donahue, Billy Gray, and Lauren Chapin. Whereas the radio rendition was slightly silly, after the first season or so, the revised TV format morphed into more of a family drama with comedic overtones. The Andersons enjoyed many a joyful meal together, but their life, as presented in the TV series, was no picnic. Jim and Margaret became angry and impatient with one another and frequently upset with and disappointed in their children. In the episode "Margaret Wins a Car," premiering December 1, 1958, Mrs. Anderson purchases a raffle ticket to help a local orphanage and wins the grand prize: a brand-new vehicle. When publicity photos of her are plastered around town (in their fictional, if generic Springfield, USA), Margaret is taken to task for not giving more attention to the orphanage. She donates her new car to a local children's center, which angers her offspring at home. Astounded by their self-absorption, she lets them have it. In one of the more startling moments in the series, Margaret berates Princess, Bud, and Kitten and utters a different nickname for the entire group: She actually calls them "brats"!

On *The Donna Reed Show*, the feature film female lead of classics like *It's A Wonderful Life* (1946) transferred to the small screen as a character who fully embraced being a housewife and mother. She adored her husband (played by Carl Betz) and children (Shelley Fabares, Paul Petersen, and, later, playing an adopted younger sister, Patty Petersen—Paul's real-life sibling). Still, she'd not skip a beat to correct them if they misbehaved.

As patriarch Steven Douglas on *My Three Sons,* Fred MacMurray portrayed one of TV's first widowed parents, with an amiable but firm hand in raising his trio of young boys (Tim Considine, Don Grady, and Stanley Livingston; later, Barry Livingston—Stanley's real-life brother—joined the cast after Considine exited).

As Ward and June Cleaver on *Leave It to Beaver*, Hugh Beaumont and Barbara Billingsley raised their two young sons (Tony Dow as older brother Wally, and Jerry Mathers as "The Beaver") with a close but respectful eye, allowing each the proper amount of space for personal growth deserving a human being of any age. *Leave It to Beaver* remains one of the most mature-geared family sitcoms in history, despite a narrative that sprang from the perspective of its youngest child.

The Adventures of Ozzie and Harriet showcased real-life married couple Ozzie and Harriet Nelson, arguably the king and queen of classic TV parentage. They raised their two sons, Ricky and David Nelson (their real offspring off-camera) with a sound, spiritual hand, each playing a version of themselves. In each case, *Father*, *Reed*, *Sons*, *Beaver*, and *Ozzie and Harriet* were all too often unfairly and harshly misjudged and incorrectly labeled as syrupy shows. The episodes for *Father Knows Best,* in particular, were solid.

Billy Gray, who played Bud on *Best*, credited executive producer Eugene B. Rodney, and director Peter Tewksbury, who helmed the majority of the episodes for the show's last four seasons, was responsible for all that:

"[Rodney] hired the writers and went over every script with a fine-tooth comb. Not one word got into a script that didn't pass his oversight. There wasn't any ad-libbing or improvising on the set. All the words were written down. I tried to change some verbiage from time to time. It soon became very apparent that that was a fool's errand. You say the words and don't worry about it. There were some 'goshes' and 'oh, gees,' and stuff like that that I didn't think were timely or appropriate. This is in the era when the vernacular included 'crazy' and hip talk. I remember not being able to say 'crazy' because it would offend the mentally ill…[Tewksbury] was just remarkable! I don't think I ever worked with a better director. He was just phenomenal as far as having a good eye, knowing when it was working or not. When it wasn't working, he would be able to suggest things that would help it work. He was just incredibly talented. I think a huge amount of the show realistic-ness (if that's a word) comes from his stewardship of the whole deal."

Robert Young had his say in which creative direction the show would move and be sustained. As a business partner with Rodney, he was a silent executive producer on the series, which was transferred from radio, not only with a new cast…but also with a slight change in the title. Gray said the original title of the show was *Father Knows Best*—with a question mark at the end, as in *Father Knows Best?* Kent Cigarettes, one of the show's sponsors, was not that excited about using a question mark and wanted to drop it from the title. Robert Young argued to keep it, but had his objection been solidified, Kent would not have sponsored the show. As Gray explained it, the question mark quandary "turned to be a deal-breaker. That was the only sponsor that had a time slot available they could just slip right into. It wasn't a very good time slot…10:00…it didn't last very long. At least it was vailablee. So, [Young] compromised to get the show on the air. He acquiesced to leaving the question mark off."

Young was adamant about retaining the question mark because it added texture to the show and its lead character. Gray said: "[Young] felt that you should question authority. You shouldn't just defer to a person in power. He was ahead of his time. Not that he wanted the father to be a buffoon. But he wanted him to be vulnerable…not the absolute be-all-and-end-all…I liken it to, 'To thine own self be true!' It's what he's saying there with that question mark. It was his concept. He originated the whole thing. This wasn't something he just moved into. He and Rodney came up with the entire idea. And if he had been allowed to, he would have kept the question mark."

Gray believed *Father Knows Best* produced "some really wonderful episodes. No question about it. The writing was superior…the direction was superior, and the production was superior. How are you are going to miss in a situation like that?"

Each episode had a moral lesson, many of which were embraced by Gray's Bud Anderson. In one segment later in the fifth season, "Bud and the Debutante" (April 13, 1959), Bud dates a wealthy girl. They go to dinner, and when the meal proves too expensive for his wallet, she hands him the cash under the table to cover the bill and to save him further embarrassment in front of the waiter. "It was an incredible opportunity to push the edges of being a kid and all of the circumstances that come with that," said Gray of episodes like "Debutante." "It really did give an opportunity that you rarely get [as an actor at the time]. I was incredibly lucky to be involved with a show of that kind of consequence."

Elinor Donahue played Gray's older sister Betty on *Best* and later, Sheriff Andy Taylor's girlfriend, Ellie, on the first season of *The Andy Griffith Show*. She offered her thoughts on the long-lasting and positive impact of *Father Knows Best*. "Besides the show being 'funny,'" Donahue observed, people have periodically approached her and said, "I didn't have a particularly good life, but by watching your show every week I could pattern myself after the Andersons. When I grew up, they were the kind of family I wanted to have."

"Anytime a person can have a good belly laugh," she said, "they feel happier and healthier, and that happier person passes their feelings onto others. So [in that case], yes—that would be a positive influence I would think."

While filming *Father Knows Best*, Donahue married CBS-turned-Screen-Gems-TV executive Harry Ackerman. Together, they had four sons, including Peter Ackerman, who today is a married Methodist minister with a family of his own. When asked to describe the relationship between television and society and/or what role he believed TV has played in the development of the American family, Peter began his reply with a few questions of his own:

"Which came first, the chicken or the egg? Did television emulate the positive potential of society and family, or did society and families try to raise the bar and live up to what was presented? Perhaps this was a time where both elements worked hand in hand. For instance, the show my mother co-starred on, *Father Knows Best*, presents a snapshot that informs us today of what the American Family of the day aspired to be like. Yet, I know from meeting people, after they learn who my mother is, they say to me something like: 'Oh, my family tried so hard to be like hers on television, and I wanted to be so good like her…but I could never make it.' Others share how much they admire me, and they truly believe that because of who my parents were, our homes must have been as perfect as those in a '50s television show. Though I am always happy to say that we enjoyed a loving household together, we were like any other family in the real world. Comments from people about trying to emulate my mother's television family prove to me that the show, whether the producers intended to do so or not, affected how families tried to live."

As to his mother's first series, Peter said, "FKB was the kind of show where you knew you were going to laugh, you might shed a tear, but you always knew there would be a wise resolution in the end. I was not born when [the show was in production], but my older brother Brian was. Though my dad adopted him later, Brian was the son of our mother's first husband [Richard Smith] to whom she was married during a portion of the time of FKB. Columbia Television still being under the strong hand of the studio system was able to hide this from the press. Yet there is one episode where Betty has to compete in a track meet and go to prom all within an hour of each other ["Betty the Track Star," April 5, 1957]. If you look at the cut of the prom dress and the extra huge runner's shirt on her, especially when she briefly turns sideways, you can see the telltale 'baby bump.' I am not sure what '50s folks would have done if they knew Betty was pregnant [even though Donahue in real life was married]. Today, they would just write it into the show!"

It took Peter a few years, but he finally met all of the *Best* cast members except Robert Young. "One thing I always did for my mom was to help her go over her lines. She would tell me what she was trying to do with her reading and/or how exactly they had to be read, and I would read the other character's parts. I got to play everybody else in almost every show she did in the 1970s! Anyway, I was off from school and was going to do this with her and Jane Wyatt on the set of one of the FKB reunion specials [videotaped by NBC in 1977]. Unfortunately, Mom came home and told me that it was not going to happen. I later heard her tell my dad that Mr. Young had a bit of a fit over another cast member who brought their child to the set that day. My mother explained him off diplomatically and true—Mr. Young was a professional, and worked like one, and wanted a professional atmosphere on the set."

Such integrity exemplifies the mentality presented on *Father Knows Best*, a show that Peter believed "illustrated what the American Family could be like, she emulated the standard to which people could try to attain. This reminds me of my dad's shows as well; they showed us who we could try to be if we lived out our better natures. Instead, today, in television there is so much that presents humor as dumbed down."

Not to mention, lacking charm and humanity, both of which could have easily doubled as Harry Ackerman's middle name.

As with other "behind the scenes" classic TV icons Bill Persky, Sam Denoff, Norman Lear, and Garry Marshall, Harry Ackerman's legacy remains an integral part of television history, with regard to family shows, specifically this list of hits connected with Screen Gems: *Bachelor Father, Dennis the Menace, Leave It to Beaver* (the first season), *Hazel, Gidget, Wackiest Ship in the Army, Mr. Deeds Goes To Town, Bewitched, Love on A Rooftop, The Flying Nun*, and *Temperatures Rising* (the first season).

Peter Ackerman shares more personal insight into his father's influential life and career, a few aspects of which were clarified after reading *Team of Rivals: The Political Genius of Abraham Lincoln* by Doris Kerns Goodwin (Simon and Schuster, 2006). Peter was fascinated with how effortlessly those in Lincoln's time left their homeland and families, heading elsewhere, usually west, to create their own lives. Such was the case with his father who a fan and collector of Lincoln artifacts. Ackerman was not one to openly share much about his past, but Peter recalled asking questions as a youth, and getting answers, mostly because his family lived under one roof. "My dad, perhaps, like all of us, wanted to keep the apple polished and thus it was rare to hear of anything negative about his [childhood]."

But one day, Harry and son were alone at the Ackerman home watching a movie, while Donahue was performing in a play in Canada. It was then Harry told Peter about the time he was just a boy and ran away from home in Albany, New York, to the Big Apple. Not knowing what to do, and not really having anywhere to go, young Harry escaped the hustle and bustle of Broadway and beyond, and into a movie house showing of 1929's *The Cocoanuts*, the first big-screen misadventure of the Marx Brothers. After that, he became involved with, as he told Peter, "the wrong crowd," and eventually returned to Albany. "Perhaps there is an exciting story in there," Peter said, "but my dad probably did not share his wrong turns in life, as not to give us, his children, any ideas of our own!"

Eventually, Harry attended Dartmouth University, majored in English, and had early aspirations to act, performing in a few college productions, and on radio. After graduating in 1935, he eventually settled on a vocation behind the scenes. He went into advertising at one of the large agencies in New York, "possibly Ogilvy & Mather," Peter said, and somehow and eventually segued into radio for CBS. After becoming the Vice President in Charge of West Coast Programming and reporting directly to William Paley, the president of CBS, Harry "had to move," Peter said, and settled in Los Angeles.

In 1939, Harry married Mary Shipp, and they adopted two children named Steven and Susan. They soon divorced, and those children were grown and living on their own by the time Harry married Donahue in 1962. In the home Peter grew up in there were four brothers, the oldest being Brian, Donahue's son from a previous marriage, who was adopted by Harry. Peter was the first biological child of his father's second marriage and was followed by his younger brothers James and Chris. He's proud that his godfather, director Edward Buzzell, was best friends with those like George Burns, and guided two Marx Brothers films and one *Thin Man* movie. But it is his brother Chris "who has the bragging rights. *His* godparents were *Bewitched* director Bill Asher and his then-wife, Elizabeth Montgomery. And I remember being at Chris' baptism when even the priest asked if Liz would wiggle her nose!"

Harry was "a good father [who] emulated the kind of dad that was a product of the shows of the classic television era," Peter said. "He was loving, wise, warm, and respectful." While growing up, Peter was comfortable living at home. "I was the last of all my brothers to leave," he said. "I was trying to be an actor, working in a restaurant, and without rent to pay, was saving money in the bank. Most parents would just lay down the law with their 22-year-old who had the means to live on his own. Instead, my dad invited me to lunch so that we could 'have a chat about some things.'"

It was after their meal and casual discussion that Harry turned to Peter and said, "The reason I asked us to get together here was so that I could talk to you about your living arrangements at home." Ackerman and son then negotiated a timeline where Peter could comfortably remain at home while looking for an apartment, as well as how the father was willing to financially help him through that kind of transition. "I know this sounds like a business meeting over lunch," Peter said, "but there was love, respect for me and my feelings and fears, and lots of warmth [that day and always]."

It's important to clarify and document just how key a role Harry Ackerman played in the history of classic television, with specific regard to the creation of the television sitcom format, which was generated during his executive/creative affiliation with CBS and the network's massive hit: *I Love Lucy*. It's hard for Peter to describe his father's role today, "where any production company and studio throws out the title Vice President like teenagers do Frisbees on a sunny day in the park," but in his Harry's time at CBS, the title of Vice President was reserved for the actual individual in that position. "He was a true second in command and reported to CBS President William Paley. I am told that my dad was groomed as Paley's successor when the television giant retired, but my father wanted to produce his own projects instead."

Part of Ackerman's job with CBS was to acquire and adapt creative properties into television shows. He would mine the network's radio list, including his friend Eve Arden's show, *Our Miss Brooks*, which he helped transfer to TV, as well as Lucille Ball's radio show, *My Favorite Husband*, which became TV's *I Love Lucy* (with Ball's real-life husband Desi Arnaz replacing Richard Denning as Lucy's on-screen spouse upon her request). "As many biographies of Lucy will detail," Peter said, "my father was instrumental in getting these projects through the idea phase and finally into production."

"I love my dad's involvement with that show," he added, "but because he was the network Vice President he did not get any screen credit. Yet, there is still one episode where he sits on camera at a table with the show's producer Jess Oppenheimer as they play agents sitting at a table in the club who are present to catch Ricky's show [which, to no surprise, the Lucy character has inserted herself in]. And there is another episode where Lucy throws out a line that says something like 'telephone the Ackermans and tell them...' and that is sort of special."

An important contribution that Peter will never try hard to battle was his father's role in helping to create the three-camera process on *I Love Lucy* that is still used today. As he recalled in detail:

"Al Simon took sole credit...Jess Oppenheimer took sole credit...William Paley took sole credit... and so did Desi Arnaz. In a brief outline of what my dad thought might one day be developed into a book, he wrote that the creation of the three-camera work was done collaboratively. The reason that they needed this is well known…it was determined that Lucy worked better in front of a live audience and thus they had to find a way to film her in one take, catching various angles at once. Having been involved in the *Amos 'n' Andy* show where they had apparently also used dual cameras at times, as well as game shows (which Al Simon had worked on) my dad, Al, Jess, Desi, and probably others, worked together to make this happen. I am biased, but when you think of it, the idea of this technique presented multiple challenges. The performer still needed to be able to connect to the live people and not be merely surrounded by cameras. The audience had to be able to see what was going on, not just the backs of camera persons. Sound folks and lighting folks as well needed to navigate within the same space. No one person could adequately look at all these elements and/or solve all of them. It was a puzzle that took many voices and seeing how my father always worked as a collaborative person. I am convinced that what my dad wrote was true. No one person 'invented' the three-camera technique. It was collaborative, and he was involved."

Beyond the technical genius that Harry Ackerman contributed to American TV, he was simply in tune with the mainstream audience. Or as Peter told it, "My dad gelled with the times. He knew that family-friendly, fun shows were enjoyed by people and that was the kind of shows he made."

Unfortunately, once the mid-'70s arrived, Ackerman was out of work for over a decade, during a time when shows like *All in the Family* were, as Peter conveyed, "just not the type of product that my father created. They were edgier, darker comedies, and not fit for the whole family. Now in his 60s, my dad was passed over for many opportunities because the developing norm was to hire young, untried, hip, hotshots."

Such practices, combined with Ackerman's inability to adjust to the television viewing family who, as Peter explained, "were not separating themselves from the campfire and were watching television apart, in separate rooms," compromised the executive's employment status. "Thankfully in the early '80s when *The Cosby Show* brought back the television family who everyone in the household could watch, as well as a new respect for the 'old-timers', allowed him to have one more shot before his death and he was able to executive produce *The New Gidget* for the two years it was on the air, as well as some other specials and TV movies."

In bringing his type of programming to the air, Ackerman utilized a specific creative process in selecting and developing product. As Peter reiterates, his father was "a collaborator" who, for example, "worked with Bill Asher and his wife Elizabeth Montgomery on creating *Bewitched*. Bill and Liz had a couple of ideas, whereas my dad had some and when shuffled together they became the show. Though the show was not a TV version of the [1942] film *I Married a Witch*, I recall my dad mentioning that he thought that there was something that could be developed with the idea of a witch living a normal life with a mortal."

The Ashers introduced Ackerman to *The Fun Couple*, a series idea they had in mind about an automobile mechanic engaged to a wealthy debutante. But as Peter recalled, the elements of both his father's concept and that of the Asher's were "brought together and *Bewitched* was born. Of course, neither of those mentioned [above] gets credit for creating the show. I am unclear if this is true, but someone in the know once told me that my father wrote down the Bewitched we know, but since he was not a member of the Writer's Guild, the union would not allow a non-Guild member to create the show, so Sol Saks was hired, given the notes from which he fleshed out a script, and then awarded the 'Created by' credit. I have no idea if this is fully true and I expect that Mr. Saks probably had some significant contributions as well."

Besides *Bewitched*, Ackerman continued to develop other TV projects. For example, he briefly worked for William Hanna and Joseph Barbera, the animated-television team otherwise known as Hanna-Barbera, who was responsible for mega-hits like *The Flintstones* and *Scooby-Doo*. They also tried to break into the live-action primetime market, while their creative roster consisted of Saturday morning cartoons. "Then Dad brought home all kinds of comic books from Marvel Comics who were working with Hanna-Barbera to produce shows," Peter said. "Versions of *The Incredible Hulk, Spiderman,* and more were floated as ideas that my dad tried to get produced [before live-action versions of these were done with other production companies]. My dad might also get an idea from a book [as was the case with *The Flying Nun,* which was based on *The Fifteenth Pelican* by Tere Rios] or an article. We had a lot of books in the house growing up, and in many, I would find his familiar felt tip pen underling a comment or bracketing a paragraph along with a note 'good idea for a Sally Field series,' or something [to that effect]."

It was Ackerman who discovered, tested, cast, and mentored Field during *Gidget,* her first series before *The Flying Nun,* both of which were produced at Screen Gems for ABC. As Peter recalled, there was "a huge evening party" that transpired at his parents' home, and he and his brothers were allowed to be present, along with "Rams football players, an African explorer, actors, and actresses and the like," including Field. Upon her exit from the party, Ackerman lifted little Peter in his arms so the boy could bid a proper goodnight to the actress who was by then filming *The Flying Nun.*

Harry asked Peter if he recognized Sally, and the quiet and shy child nodded. The father then prodded further, "Who?" Peter thought of her character's name on *Nun,* and enthusiastically replied, "Sister Bertrille!"

The response earned him "a hearty laugh from all who were gathered around, and I've tried to nurture my ability to make people laugh since."

"I have heard good things about Ms. Field commenting positively about my dad in some documentary interviews," he added, "but I do not think he was alive to hear those comments, which is a shame."

Born in the early '60s, Peter is not old enough to recall original network runs of some of his father's

earliest shows, like *Bachelor Father,* which he had not seen until recently, *Dennis the Menace* CBS, 1959–1963), or *Hazel* (NBC/CBS). But years later, Peter moved next door to actress Jeannie Russell who played Margaret, Dennis's little TV neighbor. "When I moved away from home and into my first apartment and discovered that her mother was my next-door neighbor! Small world! Through Jeannie, at an autograph show, I got to meet Jay North. I have seen shows and documentaries where I heard Jay talked negatively about the *Dennis* producers in general, but when I [met] him, and Jeannie introduced me as *Executive Producer Harry Ackerman's son,* Jay could not have been kinder."

"Packed away somewhere," Peter added, "I have a cartoon by *Hazel* cartoonist Ted Key that he gave to my parents as a gift at hearing the news of my birth. The caption reads something like *I hear the baby looks like…*and there in the bundle is Hazel's face!"

His father also produced the first season of *Leave It to Beaver* and was respected by the show's entire cast, all of whom Peter eventually met, except for Hugh Beaumont, who played Beaver's father Ward. The rest of the show's actors appeared in a cereal commercial Peter worked on as a production assistant in the late '80s.

Peter also met the cast members of other Ackerman shows like *Bewitched, The Flying Nun, Temperatures Rising,* and *The New Gidget.*

Elizabeth Montgomery as Samantha on *Bewitched* was one of TV's first independent women *[Credit: The Classic TV Preservation Society]*

The *Bewitched* set is the one Peter visited the most often. "I loved *Auntie Liz* as we Ackerman boys called her. She was wonderful. She was bright, loving, pixie-like, and 'alive.' I always remember her with a slightly crooked smile on her face and a glint in her eye; she truly was like an aunt to me. Bill [Asher, her husband] was great as well, a little louder than the rest of the room when he came in, but again he positively amped up the atmosphere when he was around. I will never forget, after their divorce, he still came over to our house on Christmas, and as a gift that year, he gave me my first collection of the original 'Sherlock Holmes' books, which introduced me to that detective, and a lifelong love of mystery stories."

"During the time of the show, our families were close. Bill Asher and Liz and their kids [Will, Robert, and Rebecca] came over to our house all the time. Bill and Dad would place wagers of football games and sometimes we'd all get into a limo and head to Rams games. Sometimes it was just the guys as my mom and Liz stayed home together, perhaps with some of the younger kids in the house. Fun times they were. Auntie Liz *would* wiggle her nose for us if asked, and never denied the request."

He also shared memories of Montgomery when dressed as Serena, Samantha's feisty twin cousin. "She played the trick she would on anyone and pretended that she was not Liz, and I believed her. That, and two different signed pictures on the wall in my dad's office, one from Liz and one from Serena, made me think that Liz and Serena were two different actresses!"

Additionally, Peter spent significant time on the set of *Temperatures Rising*, which aired on ABC from 1972 to 1974. Initially starring James Whitmore and Cleavon Little, the series was retitled *The New Temperatures Rising Show*, with Paul Lynde replacing Whitmore after the network canceled his *Paul Lynde Show*. As Peter recalled, "Bill (a.k.a. Uncle Bill) Asher worked with my dad on *Temperatures Rising*, directing only, I believe. Cleavon Little was really nice and I only recall meeting James Whitmore when I worked with him. There was a Christmas episode where the hospital staff had a party for the kids in the Children's Ward and all the crew's family including my brothers and I were cast as those kids. I remember that being a fun day, though I was placed in a hospital bed and when reaching for the gift being extended to me by another actor, I leaned on the hospital bed railing which was not locked and thus it went immediately downward and I did a somersault out of the bed, over and onto the floor. It was not the first time that some bonehead move of mine would cause a director to yell 'Cut!' but I think that was the first!"

Temperatures Rising and *The Paul Lynde Show* were the last episodic television shows executive produced by Ackerman for quite some time. The *Lynde Show* was canceled after its first season, and Ackerman left *Temperatures Rising* after the freshman year. In doing so, *Rising* lost its charm. Peter called this "an example of the lynchpin of television changing. Watch the first season of *Temperatures Rising* and you see a 'typical Harry Ackerman half-hour comedy' that could be enjoyed by the whole family." In the second year of *Rising*, the show became "edgy, cruel and somewhat ugly and dramatic in its presentation, even though it was a comedy," Peter said. Perhaps the network and producers "were going for a *M*A*S*H* kind of thing," but it did not work, and the show was soon canceled. "You could study those two seasons, and see how television comedy changed, and not always for the better obviously."

Some of Peter's fondest memories transpired one week on the set of *The Paul Lynde Show*. The series was filmed before a live audience on a Friday, and Peter had attended the rehearsals for an episode from Tuesday through Friday. He was there for every run-through and the segment's filming. Besides the regular cast, guest stars that week included a very young, pre-Oscar-winning Jodie Foster, as well as the married comedy team of Jerry Stiller and Anne Meara, who played the parented heads of a hippie commune. Peter's older brother Brian befriended Foster that Monday, the only day Peter was not present, the two sat, "coloring together." When Peter arrived on-set the next day, he sat near Foster but was quiet and shy. "I only stole some glances at her and she at me," he said.

In addition to his father, this was the first time Peter had the chance to see Bill Asher at work directing a three-camera show. "Perhaps under different stresses, I saw him in an unfavorable light," Peter said. That Tuesday morning, Asher was guiding a run-through with Lynde, Elizabeth Allen, who portrayed his wife, and 14-year-old actress Pamelyn Ferdin, who played Paul's daughter. "Pamelyn was a wonderful girl and very talented," Peter recalled. Besides voicing the Lucy character on a few of the *Peanuts* animated holidays specials, Ferdin also had a part in the *Lassie* television series, among many other roles. "I really got to see my dad at work on this episode," Peter said.

"On Tuesday afternoon, he arrived for the producers' run-through and I sat next to him and watched him take notes. He went out afterward and spoke to the prop guy to find out how he was able to get a spear gun to spear into a suitcase in the pool and not miss (thus not calling for multiple retakes). I remember him going to Bill and asking him to direct one of the co-stars of the show to change his delivery of a particular line because what should come off as frustrated was being presented by the actor as violently angry. After all, this was a comedy! Sure enough, I was present on Wednesday morning and watched as Bill delivered the note to the actor, and the inflection was changed, for the better.

"Mostly it was repetition, and I can still repeat lines from the show. 'How is the rat race going, Paul?' his wife [played by Elizabeth Allen] asks, as he replies, 'The rats are winning.' The other Lynde line that I still say is the response he gave 'I'll see you later!', which was, "Not if I see you first!"

Twelve years later, *The New Gidget* was born, starring Caryn Richman, William Schallert, and Sydney Penny. For Peter, this show, like his weeklong experience on *The Paul Lynde Show*, "was a joy to be a part of in so many ways." His father was finally employed again as the executive producer of the 1985 TV-movie, *Gidget's Summer Reunion*, which eventually served as the pilot for *The New Gidget*. At this time in Peter's life, he was acting, and after an auditioning for this updated *Gidget*, he was given a small part, playing Darryl, one of the two surfers (the other played by Vince Van Patten) who now ruled the beach. "I think I had one short line every fifteen minutes of the two-hour TV-movie," Peter mused. "I was actually farmed out to casting for one week to read with some of the actresses who were up for the part of playing Gidget's niece [before Sydney Penny was cast in the role], and they actually considered me for the niece's love interest based on this, but appropriately cast me in a smaller role."

Peter later appeared on the show, usually in very small parts with a line or two like, "Hey, Marge—you wanna dance?" "I was in my mid-twenties, but looked younger," he said. "Caryn Richman who played the now-adult Gidget was great. One of the nicest people you could meet, and a true professional. At the time, she and I were in the same acting class [run by former child actor Darryl Hickman of *Dobie Gillis* fame], and that added to the enjoyment for me; to be able to see her putting to use what we learned in class into her character and performance. I do not know why she is not working more."

"Another great actor and all-around good guy was Dean Butler, who played Jeff 'Moondoggie' Griffin—now Gidget's husband," Peter said. "I did not know Sydney well, though I recall having a scene or two with her when I was on the show. Bill Schallert was a hoot. He was always cast in warm, wise, friendly dad /uncle roles but, in reality, he loved playing against that television version of himself by telling the dirtiest jokes one could imagine when the camera was not rolling! That is not to say he was not a great actor; he was. I heard from someone that during the filming of a scene between him and my mother, who guest-starred on one episode, that between them they would slightly alter their line deliveries with each shot, keeping their interaction so fresh and interesting that the crew was apparently transfixed watching these two pros act."

As to the production team, Peter said *The New Gidget* set crew was "a family, which I tended to notice about [all] the crew members on my dad's shows. If you were not respectful, or nice, you found yourself on another crew. I remember acting on one episode and one of the new makeup persons was quite nasty and spoke behind the backs of actors once they left her chair. The head of the department got word of this, and she was gone the next day. In comparison, *Scarecrow and Mrs. King* [CBS, 1983–1987] was filming at a nearby stage, and their crew could not have been more miserable, some of them actually begging to trade places with *The New Gidget* crew!"

Knowing the type of person his father was, it does not surprise Peter that this attitude of camaraderie and respect was lived out by the crew as well. After his dad died, and he got into television production, Peter worked with and for various producers and he then saw how "good and kind behavior or mean and backstabbing elements rolled down the line and would be emulated by the cast and crew." When he later worked as an assistant to one of the producers on a hit show that he chooses not to name, "there was this competition from the some of the producers about who could get 'more stuff/party invitations' out of their association with the series, and one actually stated to my boss that he wanted to be 'feared' by the production office staff."

Having seen his father at work, and having worked in production offices Peter knows how easy it is to be feared. "What is more difficult," he said, "is emulating a behavior of sharing and respect and getting folks to replicate that with others." Sadly, he ended up working on shows that had more of the negative types, which prompted him to "prayerfully rethink my vocation and leave show business before it chewed me up and spit me out. Luckily, I have happy memories, like the two weeks I spent at my dad's side on *The New Gidget.*"

Following back surgery (circa 1980), Harry Ackerman was not able to drive, so Peter became his driver. On breaks from his waiter job at Hamburger Hamlet in Sherman Oaks, he shuttled his father around to sets, scoring sessions, casting sessions, and more. "I saw my dad as a man who respected others, and gave them the room to do the jobs that they were hired to do, and brought them collaboratively into the conversation for decisions when appropriate. It was during this time that he showed me the wonderful jewel that is the business that goes on behind the camera, and soon after I gave up acting and began looking for production gigs. After he died [in 1991], I coincidentally got my first job in television production, which led to working for about ten years in television production at Warner Bros. on various shows and departments. This remained...until I was called into ordained ministry, but that is another story!"

Does he believe that classic television shows like those of his father's have had a positive influence on society?

"Yes, for the most part. My dad's shows were pretty much about nice people, who tried to do good, though they made mistakes," which he defined as "an important ingredient for any television comedy." His father's shows were more for entertainment purposes, but "they were about likable people who tried their best and learned from their mistakes. For the viewing public his shows were clean. For a time in our society when the television was the modern campfire around which the family gathered for a story or two before retiring for the evening, my father's shows like *Leave It to Beaver, Gidget, Bewitched,* and *The Flying Nun,* and more were clean entertainment offered to all ages. This is not to say that they are trite, because my dad and others proved that with clean entertainment and likable characters you could challenge some of the prevailing thoughts about the times."

"For instance," he continued, "...there is at least one episode of *Bewitched* that artfully tackles racism without getting ugly ["Sisters at Heart," 12/24/70]. For me this is an example where issues were presented to families around their television campfires in nonthreatening ways which might have led to positive discussions; thus, I see this type of show as a positive influence on society."

Peter's favorite quote about his father hails from one of the many books on Lucille Ball: *Lucille: The Life of Lucille Ball* (Hecate Publishing, 2013) by Kathleen Brady, who on page 182 of the hardcover writes: "[Harry Ackerman] was that rare corporate individual who believed that ushers were as worthy of his notice as executives."

"My dad was not out there to have a statue built of himself for people to worship," Peter said. "But instead, who knew he was a part of projects that included the work and talents of many persons, and he respected that, and most importantly them."

Peter's second favorite quote about Harry Ackerman "would have warmed my dad's heart." It can be found on the dedication page to a mystery novel titled *Happiness is Often Deadly* (Brendan Books, 1992) by Roy Gilligan who in part wrote, "Harry did what few people seem to be able to accomplish these days. He produced shows about nice people, who seemed to be able to get along without a lot of emotional hang-ups. Most Hollywood people nowadays would call 'em fairy tales. But what's wrong with having the nice people win once in a while. Harry was a truly nice guy."

Chapter 11

Because Lisa Mateas "loved TV so much" while growing up, she would phone local TV stations to ask scheduling questions, particularly about *Star Trek*. "One time in high school I hung up and said to myself, 'There's a job where you get to talk to people about *Star Trek*?! I have to do that for a living.' So, I went into television programming and worked in it for many years. TV became my career...my hobby and passion and very important to me!"

It's that kind of passion that drove the marketing behind the resurgence of retro television networks like Nick at Nite in the late 1980s and early 1990s. So much so, Dick Van Dyke was officially christened Nick at Nite's Chairman of the Board in 1989.

A multi-faceted star of stage and screen, Van

The cast of *The Dick Van Dyke Show* at the TV Land Awards decades after the show originally aired on CBS. From left: Larry Mathews, Dick Van Dyke, Rose Marie, Mary Tyler Moore, Carl Reiner *[Credit: Courtesy of David Van Deusen/The Walnut Times. All rights reserved]*

Dyke has starred in Broadway musicals like *Bye Bye Birdie*, as well as the 1963 film version, and more movies such as *Mary Poppins* (1964), and *Chitty Chitty Bang Bang* (1968), among others. But he is best known for two hit TV series, *The Dick Van Dyke Show* (CBS, 1961–1966) and *Diagnosis: Murder* (CBS, 1993–2001).

Van Dyke got his start on TV as a comedian and then comedy show host in New Orleans with NBC affiliate WDSU-TV. His first national network appearance was in 1954 on the talent show *Chance of a Lifetime*. After that, he made guest appearances on *The Phil Silvers Show* (CBS, during the 1957–1958 season), *The Pat Boone Chevy Showroom* (ABC, 1957–1960), and *The Polly Bergen Show* (NBC, 1957–1958), among others. An Army friend-turned-CBS executive then recommended him to the network, which resulted in a seven-year contract. After anchoring a CBS morning show, he found himself the star of his own primetime sitcom. Originally envisioned as a star vehicle for its creator Carl Reiner, a former supporting player from Sid Caesar's *Your Show of Shows* variety hour, CBS liked the series concept, but not the leading man. So, after failing as the star of his own pilot, Reiner replaced himself with Van Dyke, and *The Dick Van Dyke Show* was born.

In Hollywood and across America, this innovative family series has long been considered one of classic TV's best and most sophisticated sitcoms. Filmed in black and white, *The Dick Van Dyke Show's* appeal rested with the high-wattage abilities of its star who sang, danced, acted, mimed, and did it all with perfect aplomb, alongside the equally versatile Mary Tyler Moore as his TV wife. As married love-birds Rob and Laura Petrie, Van Dyke and Moore portrayed the ideal parents to their only child, son Ritchie (Larry Matthews). Rob's job was as a comedy writer for the fictional TV variety hour starring Alan Brady (played to annoying perfection by Reiner) while Laura was content as a stay-at-home mom with a mind of her own.

To this day, couples of all cultures, classes, genders, and denominations watch *The Dick Van Dyke Show* and feel gleeful. With each viewing of the Petries' comic adventures (in syndicated reruns or on DVD), an attractive, happy upper-middle-class couple is presented. He has a great job. She enjoys being a housewife and mother. Though they sometimes behave silly, that just means they're not perfect, like the rest of us. Modern viewers, like original watchers, find it difficult to reject Van Dyke's handsome Mr. Petrie, a refined, respected, and well-established husband and father fashion staple with a good job. He's the guy who's a little kid at heart, unafraid to admit that he doesn't have a workroom that's seething with machismo, courageous enough to reveal that he's always wanted to be Perry Mason or an operative for the FBI. He's in touch with his feminine side, that is, his wife, his prettier better half; the one to whom he's not embarrassed to divulge emotions or make admissions of physical inferiority (Laura once flipped a drunk in a bar in self-defense while Rob flipped out).

Laura is cultivated, sophisticated, and, like her later twin-TV-counterpart Mary Richards (on *The Mary Tyler Moore Show*), she "can turn the world on with her smile." With her elegant intelligence and sometimes (but not too often) subtle irreverence, her appeal to the viewers was nothing less than magnetic. With her stylish capri slacks and Jackie Kennedy hair, Laura established a model trend in the fashionable '60s in apparel and demeanor. She and Rob were the first self-effacing hipsters of the television age. They made it okay to laugh at oneself. For them, humor was an attractive trait instead of an inopportune burden.

The friends and co-workers of the Petries also showcased significant milestone character developments for the time. Rob's co-writers on *The Alan Brady Show* included Buddy Sorrell, played by the late, great Morey Amsterdam ("the human joke machine"), and Sally Rogers, portrayed by lifelong performer Rose Marie with rapid-fire comic timing. Rose Marie had known Morey since Vaudeville, and, on the *Van Dyke Show*, their chemistry as Buddy and Sally was nothing less than spot-on. Buddy was the first real character of the Jewish faith to have ever been presented on a mainstream television situation comedy; Sally was one of the first professional female career women on a TV show and actually considered "one of the guys." Even when behaving "ladylike," she waxed dimensional. She didn't just cry; she dealt with her tears. Sally both explored and embraced her inability to find true love and was more than a survivor. She had her own apartment, was a member of a male-dominated workforce, and was independent. She, not Buddy, was the true threat to the hen-pecked *Alan Brady Show* producer Mel Cooley (played with great sportsmanship by also-gone Richard Deacon (who later replaced Roger C. Carmel on the CBS 1967–1969 sitcom, *The Mothers-in-Law*).

At home, Rob and Laura lived next door to dentist Jerry Helper, played by Jerry Paris, who also directed several episodes (and later, *Here's Lucy*, *The Odd Couple*, and *Happy Days*, among other sitcoms). Alongside Jerry was his meddlesome though caring wife Millie (Ann Morgan Guilbert, who later played Fran Drescher's grandmother on CBS' *The Nanny*). Around his in-home dental chair, Jerry was a sincere and trusting professional. Once across the fence with Rob, he would let loose and get silly. Like all *Van Dyke* characters, Dr. Helper adapted to his situation. He wasn't always a dentist or ever a neighbor. He wasn't always serious or constantly laughing. He was a little of everything, the good with the bad, all the time, again, just like the rest of us.

The Dick Van Dyke Show was ahead of its time in the execution and display of three-dimensional characters; misled 21st Century viewers may think they're watching a contemporary sitcom filmed in black and white. As with any cultural masterpiece, albeit TV classic, *The Dick Van Dyke Show's* appeal rests with its stoic period representation, social influence, and timeless appreciation of non-insulting, marriage-encouraging, friendship-bonding, and work-ethic-inducing scripts.

Just ask Rita Kocis. Today, she's a happily-married mother, grandmother and career woman who's employed as a global program quality manager for a Fortune 500 company. *The Van Dyke Show* originally aired during a more challenging period in her life, around the time she moved in with her grandparents after her mother and father divorced. "I loved to watch *The Dick Van Dyke Show*," she said, "...to see how a 'traditional' family lived together. Having both parents in the house and every little disagreement ending in a big hug and kiss is how I imagined life would be had my parents stayed together. It's how I imagined my life would be when I got married. And although that's not the reality for most people, *The Dick Van Dyke Show*, along with other shows like *Leave It to Beaver*, set the bar for me. Those shows were all I needed to stay focused on family and marriage, and I always kept them in the forefront of every decision I made and how we lived our life as a family…and I still do that. I have married daughters of my own that thank me every day for the kind of morals I instilled in them. And really, shows like *The Dick Van Dyke Show* helped me along that path…to never throw in the towel, even when things get rough. The show taught me how marriage can work, if you stay in the game, and not give up too soon like so many families unfortunately do."

Writing partners Bill Persky and Sam Denoff (who passed away in 2011) had teamed for decades on some of TV's most masterful television treasures. For example, they created *That Girl* and wrote several segments of the *Van Dyke Show*. Persky recalled his and Denoff's early days in New York, how they became involved with the series, discusses a few of the pertinent elements that made the show click, and touches upon one particularly popular "black and white" episode of *Van Dyke*:

"Sam and I had written a Christmas show for radio in New York, when we were signed by George Shapiro, a young agent from the William Morris Agency who had just left the mailroom, went on to discover Andy Kaufman…and who is Jerry Seinfeld's manager. We were his first clients—and he started getting us jobs writing for night club comedians in the '50s because that's what you did back then to get started in the business. And we wrote for a lot of nondescript comedians who were never heard from again."

In 1959, Shapiro transferred to California to represent *The Steve Allen Show*, on which he promised writing gigs for Persky and Denoff. Shapiro submitted a significant amount of their material to Allen's show, which would be produced by Bill Dana, who, along with Denoff, had been a page for NBC—a position which Persky had long desired himself but never attained. "They wouldn't hire me," he said somewhat wistfully, "and it was then the biggest disappointment in my life."

Persky and Denoff then followed Shapiro west to California where, as Persky relayed, the team experienced "ups and downs…failures and successes." Soon, they landed a job that "everybody wanted… to write for the *Van Dyke* show which, at the time, had been on the air for two years. We wrote a sample or spec script, which is what everybody used to do back then. That's how you got noticed. Today, you can't do that for legal reasons."

Carl Reiner embraced their writing style. Persky called their initial spec "kind of stupid," but Reiner invited them to flesh out a story that became an episode titled, "That's My Boy??"—the first entry for the show's 1963–64 season. In this segment, and with help from the show's periodic trademark "flashbacks," Rob tells visitors about the time Laura gave birth to Ritchie and how he thought the hospital switched babies by mistake. By the end of the episode, such is not the case, as evidenced if anything by the "hysterical" reaction of the studio audience, which Persky said delivered one of the largest and longest laughs in the show's history.

In September 2013, five decades after "That's My Boy??" premiered, writer Neil Genzlinger explained it all in *The New York Times*. "Amid the watershed year of 1963," he wrote, the episode "perhaps nudged the needle of social change toward integration and inclusiveness," and became "worth revisiting as a then-and-now study in how television effects transformation."

The moment in question was the episode's climactic scene when Rob opened the front door of his home in New Rochelle and welcomed Mr. and Mrs. Peters, the parents of the infant who Rob believed was truly his and Laura's. Yet since the Peterses were an African-American couple (played by Mimi Dillard and Greg Morris, just prior to his regular role in *Mission: Impossible*), their "appearance" at Rob's door immediately disproved his "wrong baby" theory. The hospital's administration had indeed at some point interchanged "Petrie" with "Peters," sending a few flowers to the wrong room, and so forth, but that was the extent of the confusion.

"Today," wrote Genzlinger, "TV seems to push various envelopes with a vengeance, often clumsily so, trying for shock value in a world that is increasingly hard to shock. You have to admire the bravery and the unwillingness to tolerate any barrier, whether it be the one against gay characters or characters with disabilities or unsettling subjects like rape and child abuse. But you also sometimes are left mourning the lack of subtlety and art. A half-century ago television was generally not nearly as brave or inclusive. The 1950s, with the medium still experimenting, had seen some ambitious programs like the series *Playhouse 90*, but by the early 1960s, especially on the sitcom side, things had become pretty tame. The audience was not expecting to be jostled out of its comfort zone, and ['That's My Boy??'] gave *The Dick Van Dyke Show* the opportunity to be slyly, hilariously subversive in its Season 3 premiere."

"It's difficult today to appreciate the jolt this expertly rendered joke must have sent through white America," Genzlinger continued. "If the March on Washington a month earlier had put race on top of the national agenda, 'That's My Boy??' perhaps gently inserted it into the living rooms of suburbia. The Petries' New Rochelle had essentially been an all-white world for its first two seasons. Now here was a new idea: middle-class blacks, having a baby just a few hospital rooms away from America's most prominent and whitest sitcom couple."

"So white was the Petries' world," he continued, "…that the moment when the Peterses walk through the door was a comic payoff that had been building not only for the whole episode but also for the life of the series. The most subversive bit in 'That's My Boy??,' though, is sometimes forgotten. It occurs after the flashback, when Rob tells his dinner guests that, now that the boys who were babies in his story are in school together, the Peterses' child earns straight A's while his son, Ritchie, is mediocrity incarnate."

"I still think we got the wrong kid," Rob said.

Mary Tyler Moore recalled in a previous interview that a few cast members were nervous about the episode and the studio audience's potential reaction. As Reiner told Genzlinger in a phone interview, "They were worried that it might be racist, that black people would be upset…That was an unusual thing for them to be worried about."

While Reiner was more concerned with, as Genzlinger put it, "the guardians of taste who policed his scripts," he was so pleased with the episode he couldn't wait for it to air. "I knew it was something very, very special," he said.

As to that final remark from Rob about Ritchie's intelligence, Reiner was "very proud that in the gag I got that little dig in that their kid was in the top of the class and Ritchie was in the bottom."

"That gag was the real victory," Genzlinger also noted before offering this conclusion:

"Perhaps it's piling a lot onto one episode of a mild-mannered sitcom to say that it helped change attitudes about race, but this was a time when television altered the landscape with small steps rather than big, brash statements. That impact wasn't always beneficial, of course. *The Dick Van Dyke Show* was, in the fall of 1963, the No. 3 show in the country. At the top was *The Beverly Hillbillies*, whose backwoods stereotypes about "poor mountaineers" (to invoke its theme song) are still with us.

"But it's worth noting that doors would soon begin opening. In three years, Mr. Morris [who died in 1996] would become one of the first black actors in a major role on TV when he was cast as Barney Collier, the electronics expert, on *Mission: Impossible*. [The breakthroughs of Bill Cosby on *I Spy* and Ivan Dixon on *Hogan's Heroes* preceded Morris by a year.] Television shows would eventually grow more willing to shake things up with bold strokes like Sammy Davis, Jr.'s kiss on the cheek of Carroll O'Connor's Archie Bunker in 1972 and *Murphy Brown's* single-woman pregnancy in 1991…Today almost anything goes, often replacing the slyness of 'That's My Boy??' with a sort of desperation."

"That's My Boy??" was based partially in truth. Prior to writing the episode, Bill Persky had a similar experience: when his wife gave birth to their daughter, the hospital had delivered the wrong meal and flowers to her room. Thus, the plot was born for "That's My Boy??" for which Persky has two favorite if simple lines. The first occurs after Laura has had it with Rob's "wrong baby" beliefs, and he tells her, "Laura—I think it would be best if you went to your room."

"It's not a joke…it's just a statement, and what he said was just so stupid," Persky recalled with, well…a laugh.

The writer's other favorite line from "Boy" occurs when Rob tells his neighbor, "Jerry—I live in a house without a safe place."

Another of Persky's favorite *Van Dyke* episodes is "The Case of the Pillow," which originally aired on February 17, 1965. Here, Rob and Laura find themselves in small-claims court as plaintiffs against a defendant who they accuse of selling them faulty bedroom pillows that have an unappealing chicken feather odor. Like "That's My Boy??" the "Pillow" case was based on one of Persky's real-life experiences:

Shortly after he and his wife married, they moved into an apartment in Forest Hills, which was soon visited by a man selling pillows from his car. The newlyweds purchased the pillows and, that first night, were unable to sleep because the pillows smelled like ducks (which became chickens on the *Van Dyke Show*). So, Bill phones the salesman, who returns to the Persky residence, where he disclaims their assessment. "Well," Bill insisted, "my wife thinks otherwise." At this point, the salesman exits, and returns with *his* wife, who agrees with him: the pillows do not smell like ducks. "So, I guess it's two against two," he told Persky, who replied, "This isn't a contest. We only bought pillows."

Persky then reaches out to his new neighbors, all of whom he never met, and invite each of them, one by one, to test the feathers, so to speak, to keep their nose if not to the grindstone but to his new bedroom pillows. The minute any neighbor steps into the Persky abode, a pillow is placed in their face, and they are instructed to "smell this."

In explaining how this comical, if frustrating, real-life incident became a misadventure of Rob and Laura Petrie, Persky laughed and said, "That's the great thing about writing for shows like *Dick Van Dyke*…you wrote about things that actually happened to you, and that's not how it works on new shows today. [Contemporary TV writers and producers] ask themselves, 'What would be stupid? What would be dirty? What would be sexy?' And then they write that. But they don't write from their personal experience. And everything I've ever written has had something to do with something I lived through." Or it was at the very least relatable to the audience.

Exhibit C: another episode from *The Dick Van Dyke Show*: "The Lady and The Baby Sitter," which premiered October 7, 1964. For Persky, "Lady" is "the worst episode" that he and Sam Denoff "ever wrote for that show," but it still presents one of the most fan-beloved moments of the series. This time, Rob and Laura are faced with Ritchie's 17-year-old boy babysitter (played by Eddie Hodges), who has a crush on her. At one point, Rob and Laura discuss how to deal with the boy's infatuation while having chocolate cake. When Laura serves the dessert without milk, Rob complains. It has nothing at all to do with the main plotline, but it's a simple relatable moment to which the audience still responds. Fans of the show still approach Persky and say, "I love the milk-cake episode."

"So, that was the fun of *The Dick Van Dyke Show,*" he added. "It gave the audience something they identified with…the kind of a mild precursor to the type of humor that was later presented on *Seinfeld*… the little incidental stuff."

Referring back to classic sitcoms that were filmed in black and white like and before *Van Dyke,* Persky agreed with *Father Knows Best* star Billy Gray who believed that shows like *Best* and *Leave It to Beaver* created an idealized vision of the family, which, like *Happy Days,* later presented an idealized perception of teenage life. "But at least those shows looked nice, and made the audience feel like they wanted to have the kind of life that was portrayed on those shows."

For some viewers, Persky said shows like *Father Knows Best* in particular "caused anxiety…because, even though real families didn't function that way, they aspired to do so." He remembered when even his own writing partner Sam Denoff disagreed with his wife over this very topic. Mrs. Denoff complained, "Why can't we be like *Father Knows Best*?" Perksy himself was compelled to step in and say, "Bernice— nobody's family is like *Father Knows Best.* If people were like *Father Knows Best,* they sit and watch one another and not the show."

Sadly, Sam and Bernice Denoff divorced in 1964, during the original super success of Rob and Laura's wedded blissful misadventures on *The Dick Van Dyke Show,* which Persky described as "a show that will never die. New people discover it all the time. I've lectured a lot at schools and taught a few courses, and I've introduced students to the show, and they become huge fans. First of all, it's funny. Dick was the consummate comedian and performer. Funny doesn't change…a guy who slipped on a banana peel while they were building the pyramids, even if he was whipping people and then slipped on the banana peel, they'd still laugh. And if Bernie Madoff [a former stockbroker, financier, and investor who was convicted of fraud] slipped on a banana peel while he was taken out in handcuffs, people would laugh…because it's the humanity behind a story that makes it funny."

Besides Dick Van Dyke's optimum family man Rob Petrie, and in addition to the tranquil genius of Harry Ackerman and his particular brand of happy family comedies, several other forms of family-oriented programming came into play namely, the dramedy—a particular genre that's not so easily defined.

There are half-hour sitcoms like Ackerman's *Bachelor Father* (starring John Forsythe), half-hour dramas with fathers like *The Rifleman,* and one-hour dramas with dads like *Little House on the Prairie.* There are half-hour comedies like *Reba,* which feature dramatic elements and divorced fathers. There are one-hour dramas with comedy like *The Rockford Files* (with James Garner playing opposite as his dad), and *Diagnosis Murder* (in which Van Dyke performed with his real-life offspring Barry as on-screen father and son). There are one-hour comedies with drama and no dads like *Moonlighting* and half-hour dramas with comedy like *Flipper* (which featured more widowed fathers).

The term "dramedy" may be applied to each of these formats and several more (with and without fathers). But mostly the dramedy was at least introduced to the viewer as half-hour comedy with dramatic elements, when such shows were filmed like a movie with a single camera, instead of filmed or videotaped with several cameras, a laugh track or in front of a live studio audience.

In the late 1980s, NBC aired one such dramedy titled *Buffalo Bill,* which starred Dabney Coleman as a self-absorbed single man. The series failed to catch on not because it was a dramedy, but mostly because the main character was unlikable. Usually, it doesn't matter whether or not a supporting or guest character in any kind of television series is likable. But when a lead character is unlikable, specifically, in a comedy—as was the case with Coleman's Bill, the series does not have a strong chance at success.

Shortly after *Buffalo Bill* left the air John Ritter, formerly of ABC's *Three's Company* farcical-fame, returned to the network with the half-hour dramedy called *Hooperman* in which he played a young single police detective. Produced by Steven Bochco (*Hill Street Blues*), *Hooperman* featured Ritter's likable lead, but it faltered mostly because it was simply ahead of its time.

Both *Hooperman* and *Buffalo Bill* were noble attempts at a unique format, but they failed to find an audience. At the time, the viewer was becoming reacquainted with the traditional sitcom format that Bill Cosby returned to TV with NBC, prestige, high ratings, and *The Bill Cosby Show* in the fall of 1984. Not a dramedy by design and or by name, as the genre had not yet been defined, this Cosby entry took itself relatively seriously and became the first half-hour comedy to feature a non-stereotypical married professional African-American male (just as Cosby had done with the one-hour drama and *I Spy* in 1966).

The Cosby Show is not to be confused with the 1969–1971 short-lived half-hour series called *The Bill Cosby Show*, which could be defined as a dramedy. Here, Bill portrayed bachelor Chet Kincaid, a Los Angeles high-school physical education teacher with a good heart. The show was an intelligent character study that delivered presented realistic situations and lasted two seasons. On *The Cosby Show* of 1984, Bill played a successful physician opposite Phylicia Rashad as an equally successful attorney, and there was little doubt that any of their children (including the only son played by Malcolm-Jamal Warner) would not be one day attending college. After *The Cosby Show* ended on NBC in 1992, the actor-comedian came back to weekly TV with the marginally-successful and very traditional sitcom called simply *Cosby* which aired on CBS from 1996 to 2000 (and which was seemingly videotaped in front of a studio audience).

There was also *The New Bill Cosby Show*, on which Bill played himself (by then a father in real life) on a variety series that CBS aired from 1972 to 1973—one decade after John Forsythe ended his run on *Bachelor Father* in 1962.

In 1969, the same year Cosby played a single nice guy on his innovative *Bill Cosby Show* on NBC, Forsythe returned to TV as a widowed father who takes his three children to live in Italy on CBS' *To Rome With Love*. In many ways, *Rome* was a European take on *Family Affair*, which began in 1966 with a laugh track—an element that was phased out of production as the series finished its original CBS run in 1971 as dramedy.

As previously explained, on *Affair* Brian Keith played bachelor Bill Davis, who adopted his teen niece, Cissy, portrayed by Kathy Garver, and her two younger twin siblings, Buffy and Jody, played by Anissa Jones and Johnny Whitaker. Sebastian Cabot, formerly of the crime drama *Checkmate* (CBS, 1960–1962), was cast as the persnickety British housekeeper Mr. French (who made a guest appearance on *To Rome With Love*, in the episode "Roman Affair," airing 10/6/70).

Garver talked about what worked on *Family Affair*, detailing its innovative and realistic premise, and how it affected the home-viewer in several positive ways:

"The audience always thought *Family Affair* was a poignant series, and fondly remembers it in one of three ways: 1] It was TV's first dysfunctional family. We didn't have a mom and a dad, but we had Uncle Bill. 2] It was the first half-hour family show to be filmed in color and 3] It followed a classic literary format that was used on *I Love Lucy* before it and *Laverne & Shirley* after: *Start out with a problem which becomes more complicated, followed by the climax and the denouement.*"

As with *I Love Lucy* and *Laverne & Shirley*, Garver said the audience for *Family Affair* "knew what to expect so they weren't startled. They could get into the emotions of the characters and what was happening with those characters and not wonder, *well...why are we back on the street, that problem was solved, so why are we doing this?* [The audience] didn't have to worry about the show's structure. It was just there, and they could easily become involved and follow the story, and some of those stories didn't always have a happy ending."

For example, the holiday episode "Christmas Came a Little Early," which originally aired on November 11, 1968, and "Mr. Osaki's Tree," first broadcast on January 22, 1970. In "Little Early," Buffy is devastated by the severe illness and subsequent death of her little friend named Eve (played by Eve Plumb, future Jan Brady on *The Brady Bunch*). Eve dies before seeing Christmas, and Buffy asks Uncle Bill why it had to happen that way. In "Tree," Mr. Osaki (Teru Shimada), the family's elderly Japanese friend, gifts Jody with a bonsai tree that the young boy believes is somehow spiritually linked to the old man. As the tree becomes ill, so does Mr. Osaki. When his health improves, the tree blooms. Both stories were not the usual fare for family comedies in the '60s, but the Osaki tale has a happier ending and one which Garver said in perspective "has a really wonderful analogy."

"Many episodes of the show explored and investigated what was really important in life," she added, even when certain developing circumstances challenged the family's core bond. "What we really tried to do with the show is to prove that family members need each other. You see some shows today, and everybody's insulting and yelling at each other and putting each other down. *Is that the way any of us want to live? Is that something one looks to for guidance? Is television or art a reflection of society or is society a reflection of television?* That's always been a kind of chicken-and-the-egg question."

"I would describe *Family Affair* as comfort food," she continued. "Sometimes it was like eating ice cream, and occasionally biting down on a nut in English Toffee. And I don't think it was *fluff* just because it was about love or because the stories were meaningful."

Another important character, unusual as it was, was Mrs. Beasley, Buffy's inanimate doll. Garver goes on to explain just how much an impact this inanimate object had on the audience in general, and one celebrity viewer in particular, actress Laura Dern, with whom she appeared in the 1996 feature film, *The Siege of Ruby Ridge*: "Laura told me that when her parents [actors Bruce Dern and Diane Ladd] were divorcing, "The only thing that comforted her was a Mrs. Beasley doll that she had and looked at because that doll was so loved by Anissa as Buffy on *Family Affair*. People cared about that doll, even though it was a figure outside of reality. Actually, even more people identified with it because it was nebulous…like how everyone loved E.T. [from the 1982 feature film, *E.T.: The Extra-Terrestrial*]. Maybe a lot of people feel like an outsider. They can identify with Mrs. Beasley without being overly concerned. They could give it a lot of love, and they knew for certain that it was loved."

As Garver goes on to explain, Buffy lost the doll. "The entire story was about Mrs. Beasley," she said. "She hurt her arm, and she had to go to the hospital. So, we all had to fix her up, and again, give care to this kind of nebulous being," for the sake of Buffy and her perception of the doll.

With moments like those, and what turned out to be Mr. Osaki's miraculous recovery, Garver said, "There's been harsh criticism of *Family Affair*, with some calling it fantasy, and that *people really don't live like that.*"

"Maybe they don't," Garver concluded, "but, in my estimation, they *can.*"

But it was in the fall of 1969 when ABC premiered *Room 222*, and another series half-hour dramedy before it would be defined as such: *The Courtship of Eddie's Father*, which starred Bill Bixby as Tom Corbett, a widowed father to his young son Eddie, played by Brandon Cruz. They were helped along by the family housekeeper, Mrs. Livingston, who was played by Miyoshi Umeki. Based on the 1963 feature film of the same name, which just so happened to have featured performers from other classic TV family programs (Brian Keith of *Family Affair* and Ron Howard from *The Andy Griffith Show*), the small screen *Courtship* was the first show to involve an Asian female character in a regular capacity, and the first to co-star a young Latino actor in the form of Cruz.

Before he began his *Courtship*, Bixby, who died of prostate cancer in 1993, was best known as the adopted human "nephew" of Ray Walston's alien Uncle Martin in CBS' *My Favorite Martian* (1963–1966). After *Eddie*, he played the lead in NBC's *The Magician* (NBC, 1973–1974) and later Dr. Bruce Banner in heralded CBS-TV-edition of *The Incredible Hulk* (which co-starred Lou Ferrigno from 1978–1982).

As was explained by *Miami Herald* reporter Steve Rothaus in November 2012, when the first season of the show was released on DVD, Bixby lived a tragic later life. His 6-year-old son died suddenly in 1981, and his ex-wife, actress Brenda Benet, shot and killed herself shortly thereafter. Wed twice more, Bixby learned of his cancer in 1991 and died two years later at age 59. Shortly before his passing, he took to task the tabloid press for publicizing the details of his terminal disorder.

Today, Cruz is pushing 60. When the show's pilot began production in 1968, he was only 5½. Though he has not received residuals from *Father*, Cruz promoted the DVD to help keep alive the memory of his former senior co-star, with whom he shared a father-son-like bond. "That show is going to bring Bill back to a lot of people's forethoughts," Cruz told the *Herald*. "The Emmys [never recognized] him. He [never received] an award for lifetime achievement. That sucks."

Cruz, a father of two, had retired from acting years ago and formed a punk-rock band called *Dead Kennedys*. He went "underground" and, like another former child star, Johnny Whitaker, who played Jodie of *Family Affair*, became a drug-and-alcohol rehab counselor. Anissa Jones, Whitaker's TV twin sister Buffy on *Affair*, died of a drug overdose in 1976, and both he, Cruz, and other former child stars were affected by the passing of their young peer. Determined to move forward with every success, Cruz has learned to also cherish the past; to help ensure, for one, that Bixby receives a star on the Hollywood Walk of Fame in Los Angeles. Bixby, Cruz, *and the fans of Eddie's Father* have been waiting years for that to happen.

In 1996, *Classic TV Magazine* heard as much from one of its dedicated readers. In a letter to the periodical, D. Henderson of Mission Viejo, California, called *Courtship* his "favorite show" and "family dramedy," and pleaded:

"Can someone please use their influence to return this show to television? Our society is lacking wholesome programming, and I believe that *The Courtship of Eddie's Father* would be encouraging to dysfunctional and functional families alike. We need families to stick together through thick and thin, plus keep their happy humor. Please do what you can. I'd love to have my kids grow up with this wonderful moralistic program."

The article, "The Son Also Rises," published by *Classic TV Magazine* that same year, explained how Brandon's Eddie was dedicated to finding a second wife for Bixby's Tom Corbett (who, in 2004, *TV Guide* ranked as #15 on its list of "50 Greatest TV Dads of All Time"). None of the women Eddie selected for his dad ever panned out, but the lessons learned through various prospects were worth the experience as far as he—and the home audience—was concerned. Through it all, the show's opening and closing conversations between father and son remained grade-A and accented with the melodic theme song, "Best Friend" (written and performed by the musical genius of Harry Nilsson).

Working on the show affected Cruz, more than any other individual associated with the series, behind or in front of the camera, mainly because of the actor's impressionable young age. Up until *Father*, Brandon's only major acting role was that of Toto in a stage version of *The Wizard of Oz*, in which he "crawled out and growled," he said.

Cruz also watched a lot of television, especially *The Rifleman* Western which, as previously noted, featured Chuck Connors as Lucas McCain, a widowed father to a young son named Mark, who was played by Johnny Crawford. Not without significant irony, this half-hour show, though not a dramedy, is most similar to *Courtship*. In watching *The Rifleman* with his parents close by, Cruz would persistently point to Crawford and say, "I want to do that [act]. I want to be Mark [and star on a TV show]."

Cruz, who lived with his family in Oxnard, California, a town sixty miles north of Los Angeles, bugged his parents enough that they brought him to a general audition in LA. With his mother expecting her fourth child, and his dad and two other siblings in the car, it was a huge trek to the big city. The Cruz clan met with less than professional casting directors, who videotaped and photographed Brandon's image and told his parents, "Okay, okay. We'll find your kid an agent." As Cruz recalled, the entire operation "was a total rip-off. It doesn't exist anymore. It was a scam thing, where you pay these people all this money, and they say they'll get you jobs."

Fortunately, from the wicked, rose the virtuous.

Soon after, an authentic casting director named Gary Shaffer was working with *Courtship* producer and co-star James Komack (who later guided *Welcome Back, Kotter*). Shaffer contacted Brandon's parents, who sent their son on an audition for a commercial gig that he failed to win.

From defeat, rose mastery—when the opportunity to read for *Courtship* materialized. Shaffer thought Cruz was too young, as the young actor had just entered kindergarten. "I could count pretty high," Cruz remembered. "I knew the alphabet, but I couldn't read very well."

No matter. Shaffer was willing to take a chance and reconnected with Brandon's parents. But by this time, the Cruz controllers were now against their son's acting aspirations and, to protect him from any repeat trauma (as when he failed to get that commercial), they refused to haul him back to LA for yet another Hollywood screen test.

Brandon's grandparents felt differently and drove him to the tryout, which transpired at an MGM Studios auditorium in Culver City, California, where *Courtship* later filmed. Present in the room were Bixby and Komack, along with approximately 300 other young performers each interested in winning the show's child-lead. When Brandon's name was finally called, he approached Bixby and Komack, and simply said, "Hi." He was then instructed to walk away, turn, and say the line, "Daddy, I love you."

Brandon did so and, shortly thereafter, began shooting the show's pilot episode, the early rehearsals for which Bixby sat his new co-star down and said, "Okay, do you know your lines?"

Cruz was like, "Uh?"

"Well, you can't read," Bixby continued. "And you don't know how to act, so I'll just say *this*, and then you say *that*, and then I'll say this, and then you say that."

Upon hearing some of the initial dialogue, Brandon looked at Bixby "kind of funny" and said, point-blank, "I don't talk like that. Kids wouldn't say that."

Bixby gazed at the writers gathered in the room, glanced back to Cruz, and said, "Okay. I guess 30-year-olds writing for a 6-year-old isn't going to work. So, you tell me how you would say these lines, and then we'll roll the cameras."

As the actual first season began, rehearsals continued in the same way, and Bixby interplayed with Brandon's natural reactions. By around the fourth episode, as Cruz recalled in 1996, "somebody decided it was time to teach Brandon how to act. And acting was something that Bill hated. He liked reacting."

Bixby once more sat Brandon down and said, "I want you to react to me, normally, just as a kid, just as you are. I know this is an unusual situation, but just react to me, the real person, not the character I'm playing."

"And the rest," Cruz said, "…was *The Courtship of Eddie's Father* as you saw it."

As it turned out, a substantial amount of the filmed conversations between Eddie and his father were observed as genuine—because that's exactly what they were. The articulations stemmed from the real-life discussions and relationship that had developed off camera between Cruz and Bixby.

Unfortunately, Brandon's parents were divorced around the time he began the show's first year. "They were not getting along," he revealed. "So, my relationship with Bill became that of a kind of surrogate dad. Although Bill was a bachelor, and I wouldn't say that he was incredibly comfortable around kids, in the beginning, he and I hit it off quite well. I would spend weekends at his place, and he'd get used to me. He lived in Malibu, and I would play at the beach. What you saw on screen was pretty much how Bill and I got along off screen. We were very close."

Brandon's relationship with his real father was distant due to the divorce. "I didn't get to see him all the time," he said. "And every aunt, uncle, cousin who was over 18 wanted to bring me to the set just so they could meet Bill Bixby."

In that 2012 interview with *The Miami Herald*, Cruz referenced another classic TV show in further describing his real-life brood. "My family wasn't [like] Ozzie and Harriet…My mom was a free-spirited woman, [and] my dad was a bartender in a rowdy bar."

Bixby, Brandon's TV-dad, picked up the slack. "Bill stabilized things when he could," Cruz said. Besides Bixby, Brandon did not have what has become for most children (in and outside of the entertainment industry) the luxury of two adult family members properly monitoring his life, let alone just one full-time dad. "Bill was the most consistent positive figure around me," he said in 1996.

So much so that the two actors stayed in touch until Bixby's demise in 1993. "I had lunch with him one month before he passed away," Cruz told *Classic TV Magazine*. "And I probably would have called him again if I hadn't been working on a movie [as a location manager] in Santa Barbara the day before he died. Had Bill lived, he would have gone back to work [as director of the NBC sitcom *Blossom*] the following Monday. He was that way. He was a fantastic human being, a fighter, compassionate, and a true professional who refused to slow down."

Bill Bixby was a person from whom a once young lad-turned-dad-himself conceived how to be a good "best friend"—on-screen and off. As Cruz relayed to *The Miami Herald* in 2012, "Bill was a tough [s.o.b.]," and Brandon named his son, Lincoln Bixby (who's now pushing 30), after his former co-star. "[Bill is] always with me," said Cruz. He taught me a lot of stuff and showed me some pretty amazing things."

Brandon Cruz became a living example of how a classic TV show can not only have a positive impact on its audience but on the very stars that brings it to life. As he concluded to *Classic TV Magazine* of his total experience in performing on *The Courtship of Eddie's Father*, "I learned how to never give up, to do my job, to be good to myself, and to take care of my son."

Chapter 12

Marlo Thomas and Ted Bessell as Ann Marie and Don Hollinger remain one of TV's devoted couples on *That Girl* [Credit: Courtesy of Marlo Thomas]

Several female-driven classic shows also made their mark on television, helping to clear the path in particular for the single professional woman, each displaying a liberated soul that inspired millions of young women to make it on their own in the working world.

Eve Arden was *Our Miss Brooks*, which conveyed the life of a teacher/lecturer on CBS from 1952 to 1956. Gale Storm portrayed the strong un-silent type in two hit sitcoms: *My Little Margie* (CBS/NBC, 1952–1955) and *The Gale Storm Show* (CBS/ABC, 1956–1960); as did Ann Sothern in *Private Secretary* (CBS/NBC, 1953–1957) and on *The Ann Sothern Show* (CBS, 1958–1961).

Marlo Thomas later hit the pavement—and pay dirt—as aspiring actress Ann Marie on *That Girl* (ABC, 1966–1971), which cleared the way for *The Mary Tyler Moore Show* (CBS, 1970–1977), in which America's most-beloved TV sweetheart played Mary Richards, who became the medium's first regular female producer/journalist character. The Richards role inspired TV's very real, single, independent female persona of all time: Oprah Winfrey. Besides *The Andy Griffith Show*, which Winfrey has long-professed as her favorite classic TV series, it was the *Tyler Moore* show that influenced the queen of all-media to get into television in the first place.

After *Mary Tyler Moore*, the intelligent, self-sufficient female persona showed up on *One Day at a Time*, which featured Bonnie Franklin as Ann Romano, TV's first divorced working mom. Franklin's *Time* followed Vivian Vance's divorced non-working Viv on *The Lucy Show* (CBS, 1962–1968), and appeared one year before Linda Lavin's widowed working mom on *Alice* (CBS, 1976–1985), and thirteen seasons prior to Candice Bergen's very-Mary-Richards-like role on *Murphy Brown* (CBS, 1988–1998, on which Bergen later played a single unmarried mom). In the last decade or so, the female characters on shows like *Sex and the City* (HBO, 1998–2005) and *Girls* (Showtime, 2012-Present) are just single, period (and extremely self-absorbed).

Had it not been for early female TV roles like those interpreted by Arden, Storm or Sothern, there may never have been a Marlo, Mary, or a Murphy. All three pre-*That Girl* stars showcased a certain physical allure but also retained a specific intellectual and independent spirit that proved appealing to both men and women. TV pioneers Sothern and Storm in particular led the charge for single women in the workplace, holding glamorous if not particularly remunerative jobs in sophisticated surroundings.

Back when Marlo's Ms. Marie and Moore's Ms. Richards were still in grade school, Sothern's charming character, Camille "Susie" MacNamara was proudly single even if she was always on the hunt for a handsome prince to "take her away from all this" (a '50s cliché that all successful career women would give up their glamorous jobs and stay home if the right man came along and proposed marriage). Sothern's Susie was somewhat similar to Doris Day's Doris Martin in the season two format of Day's ever-evolving, format-changing *Doris Day Show* (CBS, 1968–1973). Susie had no children, had never been married, but Don Porter (father to Sally Field on TV's *Gidget*) played her boss, Mr. Sands, and Ann Tyrrell was her co-conspirator, Vi, in roles similar to those played by McLean Stevenson and Rose Marie (and later Jackie Joseph and John Dehner) on the *Day Show*. Unfortunately, after a money dispute with producer Jack Chertok, Ann bolted *Secretary* in 1957, returning to TV the following year with *The Ann Sothern Show*, playing a guest relations manager at a glamorous New York hotel. This show failed to click with the audience, and, with a quick format revision to boost ratings, Porter returned by Sothern's side as her boss, as did Tyrrell as a co-worker.

Beyond these most memorable TV roles, Sothern had a vast and varied career, similar to that of good friend and fellow-small-screen-trailblazer Lucille Ball. While unlike Lucy, Ann found a measure of stardom on Broadway in the early 1930s before transferring to the big screen in Hollywood. By then, she and Ball both worked periodically for Columbia and RKO studios before securing their pull with MGM. In 1934 at RKO (which was later acquired by Lucy and then-husband Desi Arnaz), Sothern introduced the classic song "Let's Fall in Love" in the movie of the same name. But her film career was largely limited to a succession of B pictures, and again, like Lucy, was sometimes referred to as the "Queen of the B's."

Sothern, Lucy, and other female performers like Eve Arden were drawn to television, following success in radio. Each was charismatic, regal and bold, on-screen and off. Sothern lacked Lucy's knack for slapstick but had a sarcastic wit and delivery similar to Arden. After her second sitcom was canceled, Sothern returned to movies, if as supporting characters, in dramas like *The Best Man* and *Lady In A Cage* (both released in 1964). She then went back to TV with guest spots on *The Lucy Show* (as the pseudo-sophisticated Countess Framboise, a.k.a. Rosie Harrigan). In the fall of 1965, Sothern took the lead in a "star vehicle": the notorious short-lived sitcom, *My Mother the Car*, in which she was heard, but not seen. Here, she played Jerry Van Dyke's deceased mother whose soul embodies that of a 1928 Porter classic automobile. While not the disaster its ridiculous premise would seem to indicate, the show still wasted her talents and conked out halfway down the road of its first and only season.

In the late '60s and early '70s, Sothern made guest TV appearances on *Family Affair*, *The Virginian*, *The Girl from U.N.C.L.E.*, *Love American Style*, and a few installments of ABC's *Movie-of-the-Week*. In the next decade, and sometime after she semi-retired (due to her persistent health issues), she performed on the big screen once more in a small but memorable role in 1987's *The Whales of August*, supporting screen legends Lillian Gish and Bette Davis. With Whales, which would be her final role on screen, Southern, who was Canadian, received her only American Oscar nomination after nearly 60 years in the business.

Veteran TV producer and journalist Margaret Wendt began her professional career in association with Creative Artists Agency. She recalled seeing Sothern's photo during a special excursion to Idaho that was sponsored by CAA. "She'd be skiing down the slopes with all these big movie stars, like Robert Montgomery. She had a tiny waist and a big ol' behind—and she always wore those dresses that fit her waist just perfectly. She was the closest thing to Marilyn Monroe that television was ever going to get."

Similarly, Marlo Thomas and Mary Tyler Moore became the small-screen editions of motion picture legends like Barbara Stanwyck, pre-TV's *The Big Valley i*n 1966, who made their initial mark on the big screen with fiercely independent film characters. Stanwyck portrayed an evangelist in *The Miracle Woman* (1931), the lead in *Annie Oakley* (1935), and a newspaper reporter in *Meet John Doe* (1941), among other take-charge movie roles.

Future TV star Eve Arden also appeared on the big screen, if in supporting roles. Many times, she was the wise-cracking career woman that sacrificed a happy home life with a man for an office environment where she could toss off snappy dialogue to older men like Adolphe Menjou.

Then Arden moved to television, alongside Sothern, and Gale Storm, and later Thomas and Moore, defining a generation of single working women. Each helped the other with every step of the way, carrying television the mainstream torch that was ignited by the big-screen female stars before them. Moore had always credited Thomas for paving the way for female empowerment on TV. "Mary always said that Marlo opened the door that she walked through," recalled Bill Persky. "There would have been no Mary Richards had there not been an Ann Marie. It's like Marlo was the dynamite that cleared the playing field for Mary."

After Persky and writing partner Sam Denoff completed their substantial contributions to *The Dick Van Dyke Show* on CBS, which introduced that network's future *Mary Tyler Moore Show* star as TV wife to its namesake, they created *That Girl* for ABC. *Girl* featured Marlo's Ann Marie, an early twentysomething who leaves behind the comfort and security of her childhood home in Upstate, New York to pursue her theatrical dreams in New York. "*That Girl*," said, Perksy, "…changed an entire generation of young women. And there are women around today in their 50s and 60s who tell me how that show changed their lives."

The *Moore Show* had more restrictions. "Mary wasn't allowed to be divorced," Persky said, because her single status "was all very vague…either her husband died or she broke up with her boyfriend or something like that. As Ann Marie, she was excited and refused to take no for answer. She wanted something more from life as a woman. And then there was Mary…who was really just this transitory woman who was on the way to something but wasn't quite there yet. She had a job that was exciting that she might not have had five years earlier."

In the magazine *The 100 Most Influential People Who Never Lived* Moore talked about her experience with Mary Richards. At a very early age, she knew what she wanted to do with her life. But it wasn't until years later when she began developing *The Mary Tyler Moor Show* that she realized that Richards was "the person I wanted to be…She navigated opposing personalities with charm and wit, she was fair in her relationships, she found excitement and joy in every aspect of her life, and she wasn't afraid to show vulnerability. Mary Richards had effortless ease and likability that drew people to her, even won over the tough but lovable Lou Grant [Ed Asner], her boss. She had…spunk [a reference to the famous interplay between Richards and Lou upon their first meeting, when he tells her, "You've got spunk! I *hate* spunk!"].

When the show began production in the summer of 1970, Moore knew that Richards was "special." What she didn't expect was how many women across America would also embrace the character. "In 1970, there weren't many women like her. She was unapologetically interested in her career and found fulfillment in her life, without a husband or children. We weren't trying to change the tide, but Mary did make some waves. Behind her perfectly coifed hair, enviable wardrobe, and near-perfect demeanor was a woman who wanted more for herself and was going to try her best to get it. Suddenly, Mary was part of a shift in our culture: she had a life many women aspired to have. She sparked conversations about glass ceilings and opened the door for women."

Since the show's debut, Moore said she encountered "hundreds if not thousands" of women who have told her that they dreamt of living like Mary Richards: moving to Minneapolis, working at a TV station there, and tossing their hat in the air (as did Moore as Richards in the show's famed opening credit sequence). "It's lovely to see she has brought to many as much joy as she brought me," Moore relayed. "I'm humbled to have played such an iconic character [that] has had an impact not only in the world of television but also in the lives of those who hold a special place in their hearts for Mary Richards."

TV writer Treva Silverman contributed several scripts to both *That Girl* and *The Mary Tyler Moore Show*, and once more shares her keen insight into what it was like to work on a hit series which, this time for her was the *Tyler Moore Show*, an assignment that she called "a dream come true." Silverman's perceptions prove especially valuable with regard to the Moore series because she was one of the first female television writers of her generation:

"I sought the best in myself, the most honest in myself, because [show creators/producers James L. Brooks and Allan Burns] had set the bar so high I wanted to reach higher and higher. You got spoiled writing for this series because it was what writing for a series should be, but rarely is. This was because of the generosity of Jim and Allan. No, *we're-in-charge-here* attitude…the goal was to make the best episode, and best series, that could be made. I was invited to write the series very early on. Jim made it clear to me that he wanted me to contribute as many episodes as I wanted even before I sat down and wrote.

"At first, I felt a sense of security—he knew my work well and I didn't feel I had to prove myself… which, of course, led to a feeling that I'm terrific and can do no wrong, which of course led to a feeling of *Oh, no…suppose I fail.* But it being a given that you're insecure to begin with…and I speak for myself, and also for most writers I know…I ended up working extremely well knowing that I was trusted. I felt I was—pardon the cliché…*home.* I got so involved writing my first episode that I think it was nearly a third over the length. Jim and Allan's characters were so beautifully drawn, it was hard to resist writing them and writing them—their voices were so clear.

"Later on, when Ed. Weinberger came on board and wrote so many episodes that were just wonderful, we all became sort of a family unit. Working with Ed. was odd. He and I didn't have that much in common as people, but we worked extremely well together. I loved the group—working with Allan was a pleasure—the nicest guy in the whole world, so accepting and brilliant—and working with Jim, when he would go into what we all call his 'trance'—when lines of dialogue would come out of his mouth like— who is it—the Oracle of Delphi—in this case not predicting the future, but predicting future lines…lines that would get laughs weeks later with the studio audience.

"Now, you have to remember, this was way before the Writers Room of today. The method was first you'd meet with Jim and Allan and figure out the story. Sometimes it would be something that Jim and Allan had thought of—it could be just maybe a thread of an idea—like—*Hey, Val lost weight over the hiatus, and we want you to write that episode.* (From that remark, Val won the Emmy that year. Jeez, those guys are brilliant.) So, let's take that remark—and then we'd move on.

"We would hammer out the story together—it would often take a whole week (of short meetings) until we got it where we wanted it. Then I would go home and write out a scene-by-scene, beat-by-beat couple of pages. I never felt secure with a scene until I could get at least two lines of dialogue that I liked—a confidence-builder in me that the scene could work. I approached each scene—like most comedy writers—with a how do I get into this scene attitude. Each scene has to have an angle that you kind of felt would make it be funny. Often in these story meetings, Allan would throw in a phrase that would make me laugh and I'd know the scene would work, or the Delphic Oracle would do a run of dialogue—but I had to, absolutely had to, have an angle before I would write out the beat-by-beat. Then I'd drop the sheets of paper off and it'd most likely get approved, and I'd begin writing."

Something additionally amazing then transpired in Silverman's own life and career; how she, as a female writer, inspired the subsequent lives and careers of other female writers. As she concluded:

"I'm always grateful and overwhelmed these days when a younger woman writer tells me that she was influenced by the fact that a woman was writing the show, and that I was the first woman to win an Emmy for a comedy episode.

"I never, ever in my wildest dreams imagined that actual living people would be influenced by what I was doing. I was too busy fighting for my life out there—had to do well, had to do well, because, well, there just wasn't any choice. I was inching my way along, word by word, line by line, speech by speech, had to do well, had to do well, and my only thoughts were about making my scripts better and better. Hearing about myself from an entirely different point of view—women I'd never met who said that it gave them hope—it's so satisfying and makes me feel wonderful."

A decade after both *The Mary Tyler Moore Show* and *That Girl* were no longer in production, CBS debuted *Kate & Allie*, 100 episodes of which were directed by Bill Persky. This show paired former NBC stars *McMillan & Wife* co-lead Susan Saint James and *Saturday Night Live* regular Jane Curtin (now ready for prime time) as two divorced women with children sharing the same household.

Persky measured the threads that lined the most popular single-female-driven shows from 1965 to 1985: "*That Girl* and *Kate & Allie* are the bookends, and in the middle is Mary. And then it just exploded after that. When Ann got a clogged sink on *That Girl*, she called her father. When Mary had a plumbing problem on *The Mary Tyler Moore Show* she called the plumber. When their washing machine didn't work on *Kate & Allie*, they tried to fix it themselves and flooded the apartment. They then called the plumber, and Kate had an affair with him for eight episodes. And then, of course, after that was *Murphy Brown* who did whatever the hell she wanted [in personal relationships]. And then with *Friends* (NBC, 1995–2006), [the situation] just loosened up more and more. But those shows still did it with style because it was part of their makeup."

After that, Persky said, the story objective became looking for opportunities to have sex and that was the main motivation for the characters. "In other words," today's TV characters aren't "alive for any other reason except to have sexual encounters."

While *That Girl* remains "very special" to Persky, he's also quite fond of *Kate & Allie*, "in its own way, even more so. That [show] was a very personal experience for me. I was a single father at that point. I had got custody of my 12-year-old daughter when she was really in trouble on a lot of levels. And so, I raised her myself. And that was the *modus operandi* or one of the themes in *Kate & Allie*…raising a kid as both father and mother or in their case both father and father…because the fathers were there but not really as strong figures."

Persky, like Treva Silverman, became living proof that classic television shows have a positive impact, even on those who are making them; for it was in the making *Kate & Allie* that his personal life was directly influenced and vice-versa.

And while the top rank of superstardom always seemed just outside the reach for someone like Ann Sothern, the actress still had a long and generally successful career. She was a bright star who made every production she performed in (even *My Mother the Car*) that much brighter by her participation. Along with Gale Storm, Eve Arden, Marlo Thomas, Mary Tyler Moore, Susan Saint James, and Jane Curtin, Sothern left her mark on television in every possible, positive way and helped clear the playing field for the single professional working woman – on and off television.

Chapter 13

Domestic life has been portrayed in classic television shows since the days of *I Love Lucy,* which, in a recent *TV Guide* poll, was voted one of the Top Five Favorite TV Shows of all time (along with *Star Trek, Batman, The Twilight Zone,* and *Gilligan's Island*). While *Lucy* also became one of the first shows on TV to showcase an inter-racial marriage (Lucy was a red-haired American woman in love with a Cuban-born man), the (somewhat) blissful state of marriage was showcased on other television series, such as comedies like *I Married Joan* (NBC, 1952–1955), which starred veteran performer Joan Davis and Jim Backus (*Gilligan's Island* and *Mr. Magoo*); *The Honeymooners* (CBS, 1955–1956), and *The Bob Newhart Show* (CBS, 1972–1978); and mystery dramas like *Mr. and Mrs. North* (CBS/NBC, 1952–1954), *McMillan & Wife* (NBC, 1971–1977), *Hart to Hart* (ABC, 1979–1984), and additional categories, and sub-categories of every genre.

David Birney and Meredith Baxter played opposites who attracted each other on *Bridget Loves Bernie* [Credit: *The Classic TV Preservation Society]*

Bridget Loves Bernie, more than any other comedy, was above and beyond one of the best one-season-only series featuring a married couple. Briefly airing on CBS from the fall of 1972 to the spring of 1973, *Bridget Loves Bernie* (BLB) made its mark. Jaime Weinman addressed the evolution of BLB in the "1970s Fun Flops" online essay from *This Was Television,* September 25, 2013, published on www.thiswastv.com.

Along with *The Paul Lynde Show* and *Temperatures Rising,* BLB was one of the last new TV shows produced by the Screen Gems sector of Columbia. With BLB in particular, Weinman said the studio decided to "stick with its usual way of making shows" but updated the subject matter. The series was created by Bernard Slade, a former contributor to shows like *My Living Doll* and *Bewitched,* who later found fame with "Same Time, Next Year" on Broadway. It was about a young newlywed couple played by David Birney and Meredith Baxter (who later married in real life). He was Jewish, and she was Irish-Catholic, and the show, as Weinman put it, addressed the "culture-clash" conflicts that resulted when "his family meets hers. This was the premise of the play *Abie's Irish Rose,* a Broadway show that became the biggest hit of the '20s even though the critics hated it."

As Weinman explained, "Columbia was presumably hoping that the premise was still critic-proof, and they were also hoping that this was a 'with-it' enough idea to sell in the new sitcom environment."

Indeed, it was. The show became a hit, sandwiched between *All in the Family* and *The Mary Tyler Moore Show* on Saturday nights. Unfortunately, BLB, which Weinman compared to a "non-magical *Bewitched*," due to its "mixed-marriage" premise, created issues for a few Jewish and Catholic organizations that objected to its general presentation, and it was replaced by *M*A*S*H* the following year.

This was a sad development on several fronts, as the opportunity was missed to utilize a television comedy as a platform for unity among those of different heritage.

Here Come the Brides sang a completely different tune, earmarked by its joyful opening theme music ("The bluest skies we've ever seen are in Seattle"). Airing Friday nights on ABC from 1968 to 1970, this gentle one-hour series was loosely based on the 1954 motion picture *Seven Brides for Seven Brothers* (which itself somewhat stemmed from Stephen Vincent Benet's story "The Sobbin' Women"). With gentle scripts and strong leading performances by Robert Brown, Bobby Sherman, David Soul, Joan Blondell, Susan Tolsky, and Bridget Hanley (married to classic TV director E.W. Swackhamer from 1969 to his death in 1994), *Here Come the Brides* balanced romance, family values, and adventure. Set in Seattle, Washington, during the post-American Civil War, *Here Come the Brides* was one of television's first hour-dramedies. The series lasted only two seasons but made a lasting impression on the audience.

Chronicling the adventures of a logging-working group of men and the husband-hunting single women who were sent to them, the show's premise may have seemed risqué, but its scripts and sentiment were nothing more than earnestly displayed with a sweet moral week after week.

The same year *Here Come the Brides* debuted on ABC, *The Doris Day Show* premiered on CBS and ran a much healthier five seasons. Movie-turned-TV-star Day played a widow named Doris Martin in this comedy of which one episode directly guided a young female audience member towards wedded bliss. Day did not fully or critically discuss the sitcom in her book, *Doris Day Her Own Story* by A.E. Hotchner—as told by Day (William Morrow and Company, 1976), but she came close with a poignant recollection about that one special life-changing segment. In "The Fashion Show," which originally aired October 26, 1970, Day's Martin wore a bridal gown and, in doing so, tendered the soul of that unique female fan.

After "The Fashion Show" aired, the actress received a letter from the woman who was brought to tears after watching the episode. As Day explained it, the young lady was to be married five months later, and "so badly" desired a replica of the gown Day adorned on the show. She asked Day to please reveal the name of the store that sold the garment so she could purchase one just like it. "I want to look like you looked," she told Day.

Instead of filling the woman's request, Day did her one better. The performer with the reputable big heart remained true to form. After consulting with her costumer and fitter, she went to work on the actual gown utilized in "The Fashion Show" and made it "even more attractive." From there, her design team gathered yards of tulle, which Day said made "a beautiful headpiece decorated with lilies of the valley and little orange blossoms."

"It was a darling wedding dress," Day went on to say, one she then had sent on a sentimental journey of sorts, to be delivered to the young bride-to-be with "good wishes for her happy marriage."

Months later, the dress long forgotten, Doris received a second heartrending letter from the newlywed along with a photo of herself at her wedding in the wish-fulfilling attire that was now her own. As Doris continued to divulge with dignity, the young woman, now married, looked "so pretty...so radiant with happiness...so much the bride."

"It was very touching," the actress said. She even shed a few tears of happiness for "that sweet, anonymous girl."

Day thought to herself, "That's what it's all about, isn't it? That's really what it's all about."

In other words, bringing joy just to one fan through her work—specifically on a weekly TV show—is rewarding beyond measure or compare. "God knows I'm not one of the awesome beauties, like Elizabeth Taylor, who epitomizes the words 'movie star,'" Days decided with her trademark modesty. "What I am is the truck driver's delight. People on the street always call me Doris. That's just the way I want it. We are family, my audience, and I, and that's why I especially liked performing in a series that brought me into the living room every week. I think that's where I belong, as one of the family."

Parents have utilized television as a babysitter for years, more productively in the medium's early days than recently. Sadly, violence and vulgarity dominate contemporary airwaves. On one too many occasions, if not constantly, TV's modern moms and dads are made to be the fool while obnoxious, wise-cracking, incorrigible children run the households.

In 1947, the DuMont Network aired *Your Television Babysitter*, a series that rallied for more respect between all family members. Geared toward entertaining children while parents focused on household chores, *Your Television Babysitter* also happened to be one of the first shows to employ Hal Cooper as a writer/producer. Cooper would later direct two episodes of the sophisticated *Dick Van Dyke Show* and a few segments of *The Brady Bunch*, among other family sitcoms like *Gimme a Break* and sitcoms with families like *Maude*. Such programming featured relatively respectful mutual family members that were loving mothers and fathers and children who knew their place; as did other TV classics from the '50s, '60s, '70s, and '80s, like *I Remember Mama*, *The Goldbergs*, *Ozzie and Harriet*, *Make Room for Daddy*, *Petticoat Junction*, *Good Times*, *Little House on the Prairie*, *Family*, *Life Goes On*, and more.

Two series, in particular, are the cream of the crop from this field: *The Partridge Family* (ABC, 1970–1974) and *The Brady Bunch* (ABC, 1969–1974), each of which remain prime examples of the ideal TV household. Though periodically criticized by some as being too perfect, like *Father Knows Best* and others before and after their debut, these two shows broke new ground on several fronts, while offering "comfort food television" along the way. These shows and the personalities of their inclusive characters still sparkle with a fresh appeal and a surreal quality that transcends television time and space.

Barry Williams played Greg Brady on *The Brady Bunch* and several of its sequels *[Credit: Courtesy of Barry Williams]*

For many viewers, *The Brady Bunch* was also considered a fantasy, but that didn't stop it from becoming an all-encompassing phenomenon. Originally broadcast on ABC from the fall of 1969 to the spring of 1973, *The Brady Bunch* (created by executive producer Sherwood Schwartz—fresh off of *Gilligan's Island*) was transmitted and translated over the decades into syndicated reruns; with retrospectives and remakes on additional networks (CBS and NBC); for the big screen and small; with DVD releases; on the live stage or the printed page; and online.

First, there was the animated sequel, *The Brady Kids* (ABC, 1973), followed by *The Brady Bunch Variety Hour* (ABC, 1976), which gave birth to *The Brady Girls Get Married* (NBC, 1981), which led to *The Brady Brides* (NBC, 1981), on into *A Very Brady Christmas* (1988), which morphed into the more serious-minded entry called *The Bradys* (1990), followed a few years later by the first feature film, *The Brady Bunch Movie* (1995), the subsequent big-screener *A Very Brady Sequel* (1996), then straight-to-video with *The Brady Bunch in the White House*; in addition to other incarnations.

So, what's the near-miraculous appeal of this increasingly popular and ever-expanding media-family franchise that made superstar names of Florence Henderson (as matriarch Carol Brady) and Robert Reed (father Mike Brady); the former child-actors-turned-icons Barry Williams (Greg), Maureen McCormick (Marcia), Christopher Knight (Peter), Eve Plumb (Jan), Mike Lookinland (Bobby), Susan Olsen (Cindy), and Ann B. Davis as the lovable housekeeper Alice.

The core of its appeal is nothing less than vast, particularly if viewed through childlike eyes. Adults who grew up with the original show during its initial run find themselves transported back in time with each rerun viewing and observe, "What if I was a child again? What would I think if I saw *The Brady Bunch* through yesterday's eyes?" Any young TV viewer from today would be hooked upon being suddenly startled by a thin white line that streams across their monitor, have it transform into a visual of an extremely welcoming woman with a pretty smile, only to have three similarly facial-clad young lasses appear to the left of the screen; followed on the other side of the screen by a pleasantly handsome man and his three charming young sons, all of which transpires as a bouncing, happy music with story-telling lyrics plays in the background.

Any viewer of any age is mesmerized by the colors in the Brady kitchen alone, all orange and blue, as the original series presented the perfect home setting with amiable if at times conflicted personalities dealing with the daily challenges of family life wrapped up within a thirty-minute time-frame. Watching *The Brady Bunch* is like watching a living cartoon, in the most surreal way. What more could any child want? What more could any adult want than to view life through a kaleidoscope of lovingkindness that resolved all conflict? Who wouldn't want to experience that feeling again and again, in as many ways as possible, in as many formats as feasible?

Even *The Brady Bunch Variety Hour*, which was unduly criticized by some (who also probably secretly adored it), holds valid appeal. The *Variety* show debuted two years after the original *Bunch* sitcom was canceled, and many Brady fans were ecstatic. The original cast, sans Eve Plumb (who was replaced by an eager Jan played by Geri Reischl), were all there, singing and dancing their Brady hearts out. They weren't billed as Florence, Robert, Barry, and Maureen, and so forth. Instead, it was Carol, Mike, Greg, and Marcia, etc., who were given the reins.

Years later, *A Very Brady Christmas* (with a new Cindy, portrayed by Jennifer Runyon) became the highest-rated TV-movie of 1988, which inspired the 1990 *thirtysomething*-like, more dramatic-geared weekly series, *The Bradys* (with Susan Olsen back as Cindy, but with Marcia now played by Leah Ayres) and so on into Brady-infinity. Again, there was something surreal about it all, and there most likely always will be.

The same could also be said for *The Partridge Family* which, starting in the fall of 1970, followed *The Brady Bunch* on ABC Friday nights at 8:30 PM for four hit seasons.

Like the Bradys, *The Partridge Family* fast became one of America's favorite TV families. Even Emmy-award-winning actor Bryan Cranston has named the show important in his life. Crantson began his career with guest spots on *Seinfeld* and went on to star in *Malcolm in the Middle* and *Breaking Bad*. In a recent interview with *The Los Angeles Times* to promote his new Showtime series, *Your Honor*, he explained how classic TV has affected his life and career—beyond the obvious ways.

In 2003, David Cassidy, star of ABC's 1970s musical sitcom, *The Partridge Family*, made a guest appearance on *Malcolm in the Middle*. In the episode called "Vegas," which Cranston directed, Cassidy played a self-absorbed singer. "But David was a sweetheart," said Cranston, who was and remains a *Partridge Family* fan. To prove it, every December he makes sure to nestle in his backyard pear tree an autographed photo of Cassidy, which he's called "a puzzlement to visitors during Christmastime." But the annual Partridge in the pear tree placement has long paid homage to both Cassidy and Cranston's classic TV family lineage.

For years, that photo has made Cranston smile and feel safe and secure. Many from his and every generation have worshipped *The Partridge Family*.

Viewers consistently enjoyed the singing family (inspired by The Cowsills real-life musical group), which made a superstar of Cassidy, the biological son of actor Jack Cassidy and Evelyn Ward, and step-son to Shirley Jones, who was cast as David's TV mom on the show. Joining David as his small-screen siblings on the show were Susan Dey, Danny Bonaduce, Suzanne Crough, and Jeremy Gelbwaks, who was replaced in the second season by Brian Forster. Dave Madden rounded out the cast as Reuben Kincaid, the band's manager. Created by *Bridget Loves Bernie's* Bernard Slade, *The Partridge Family* was nominated for five Golden Globes and even a Grammy.

The series was also revolutionary to some extent, as it was the first television series to feature a single mom who also had a career. As the show's lead actress revealed in her best-selling memoir, *Shirley Jones*, the woman who played Mrs. Partridge actually first rejected an offer to play Mrs. Brady on *The Brady Bunch*, deeming that role too subservient. "While the idea of playing the mother in *The Brady Bunch* was initially attractive to me," she wrote, "I turned it down because I didn't want to be the mother taking the roast out of the oven and not doing much else."

She had no doubts at all about portraying Shirley Partridge, mostly because the character "was destined to become the first working mother on TV" and she loved the script, and also because working on the series would allow her to be "an almost full-time mom and raise her own, real-life children."

Somewhat more realistic than *The Brady Bunch*, with somewhat more sophisticated scripts, *The Partridge Family* was the last of its kind. As Jaime Weinman so succinctly explained in "This Was Television," the show was produced by Columbia/Screen Gems which had several hit shows on the primetime schedule throughout the '60s and early '70s, including *The Donna Reed Show, Dennis the Menace, Hazel, Bewitched, I Dream of Jeannie, Gidget, The Monkees, and The Flying Nun*, while they distributed *The Flintstones*. "The Screen Gems style was the essence of the old Hollywood B-movie style applied to TV sitcoms…make 'em fast, make 'em professional, and don't get too topical and ruin the show's shelf-life.

"Screen Gems shows all used the same pool of sets and crew members, and they all had a certain charm and lighthearted wit…They also seemed to be a little more progressive than most studios about hiring women as comedy writers. Barbara Avedon, Ruth Brooks Flippen, and Treva Silverman were among those who wrote a lot of scripts for them. 1960s sitcoms were where we went to escape from the times, and no one was better at providing that kind of escape than Screen Gems."

As Weinman went on to assess, by the third and fourth seasons of *The Partridge Family*, Screen Gems attempted to "make a comeback after a tough break: the struggling Columbia had sold off a lot of its studio space, forcing Screen Gems to rent space from Warner Bros. Most of Screen Gems' shows had been canceled," including studio comedies like *The Partridge Family*. "While big studios

dominated the expensive field of scripted drama, comedies had come along that were cheaper than studio shows and more popular: by using videotape and never leaving the soundstage, the four-camera *All in the Family* could be produced for a lot less than a Screen Gems show. And much as people grew tired of the four-camera sitcom format in the 2000s, audiences, and critics by 1972 had [become weary of the] single camera comedy, which as today was the format of choice for film studios."

In her memoir, Shirley Jones addressed the demise of *The Partridge Family* which she thought was premature and made her sad. "If it hadn't been canceled," she said, "I would have been happy to carry on playing Shirley Partridge for another four years. For me and all the rest of the cast, this was the end of an era."

Chapter 14

Carroll O'Connor played Archie Bunker on *All in the Family* [Credit: Author's Collection]

"I am very glad that there were these 'bold shows' like *All in the Family* and *Maude*. It is well known that they loosened the reins...that they got us away from the pure saccharin that so many of the [older] shows seemingly reflected."

So said children's TV star and advocate Shari Lewis to *TV Guide* in 1986.

The irony of course, in contemporary time, is that programs like *All in the Family* and *Maude* both produced by the prolific Norman Lear, are certified class programs with heated topics and dialogue that most likely would not be allowed if produced today, with regard to various name-calling and bullying that was presented to a lesser or fuller extent by the very liberal, multi-married Democrat Maude Findlay or the ultra-conservative Republican Archie Bunker.

It's quite a conundrum all the way around, almost as if the rise and fall and rise again of quality programming were taking place simultaneously.

The Dick Van Dyke Show may have been one of the first shows to explore the more serious issues like prejudice or the pre-women's liberation movement in a comedic way, but other series would later take Laura Petrie's independent spirit or Sally Rogers' working girl mentality to the next level. *That Girl* paved the way for the women's lib view that was cemented by the time *The Mary Tyler Moore Show* hit its stride in the early '70s, and racism and other reflective issues of the day were then more frothily explored by Lear via his hit parade of sitcoms.

Lear has long been regarded as one of the medium's top influential producers when it comes to comedy. His "reality-based" scripted shows (as opposed to what later came to be known as unscripted "reality shows") are documented as some of TV's most popular and prolific series, beginning with *All in the Family* and *Maude*, followed by *Good Times*, and *The Jeffersons*, all on CBS, along with *One Day At A Time* and NBC's *Sanford & Son*. Each of these programs, videotaped in front of a live audience, stretched the boundaries of what would eventually and unfortunately later transform into vulgar programming.

Before that happened, the family of characters from *All in the Family*, *Maude*, and the rest of Lear's best engaged in credible conversations circumventing timely, realistic topics beyond prejudice, including abortion, homosexuality, divorce, and more. If it was controversial in the '70s, and the early '80s, one of Lear's shows was sure to address it.

Family, for one, presented Carroll O'Connor as the bigoted Archie Bunker, and Jean Stapleton as his long-suffering, angelic, if scatterbrained wife Edith. The eclectic Sherman Hemsley was the white-man-taunting George Jefferson who on *The Jeffersons* was paired with Louise, his long-suffering, angelic, more clear-thinking wife played by Isabel Sanford. As former neighbors to the Bunkers in Queens, New York, George and Louise (a.k.a. "Weezie") "moved on up to the East Side" of Manhattan, where his dry-cleaning business expanded. Never one to mince words, George always had issues with Archie's ignorance, and understandably so. Once upon a better life, his own lack of couth became spastically evident, especially when his son Lionel (alternately played by unrelated Michael Evans and Damon Evans, the former of whom went on create *Good Times*) fell in love with girlfriend Jenny (Berlinda Tolbert), the biracial daughter of her interracial parents (Franklin Cover and Roxie Roker, real-life mom to music genius Lenny Kravitz).

Unfortunately, for some viewers, Archie and George were heroes. A few audience members, both black and white, delighted in the dual ignorance of what they watched on *All in the Family* and *The Jeffersons*. Other, more enlightened, fans of the shows better appreciated the multi-talents of O'Connor and Hemsley and their ability to create such unlikable characters with such likable (and multi-award-winning) performances.

Hemsley said his TV's alter-massive-ego George Jefferson was "pompous and feisty." In a 2003 interview for the Archive of American Television, he said playing George "was really hard… because—rude, I don't like to be that way. But it was the character. I had to do it. I had to be true to the character. If I was to pull back something, then it just wouldn't work."

Work, it did. When Hemsley succumbed to lung cancer in 2012, approximately 150 people attended his memorial service at the Cielo Vista Church in El Paso, Texas. Mourners were amused by the random clips from *The Jeffersons* that were screened during the service displaying Sherman as George, feisty and bigoted as ever. "He helped us to laugh, gave us an opportunity to forget the troubles, the stresses of life," El Paso Police Department Chaplain Sam Faraone said during the eulogy.

At the same time, shows like *The Jeffersons* and *Maude* not only helped us forget our troubles but also, in many ways, reflected those troubles—sometimes, as writer Amanda Marcotte observed in a manner that might be deemed objectionable today. In May 2009, shortly after the death of Bea Arthur, *Maude's* lead,

Isabel Sanford and Sherman Hemsley were a perfect mis-match on *The Jeffersons* [Credit: The Classic TV Preservation Society]

Marcotte penned the essay, "No Cop-Outs: 37 Years Ago, *Maude* Got the Abortion Experience Right," which was published on the RH Reality Check website.

"Watching '70s-era sitcoms when you're used to a steady diet of 21st Century sitcoms is a disconcerting experience," Marcotte wrote. "Old-fashioned ingredients like the three-camera sound stage set-up, the laugh track, and the three extra minutes of programming (instead of commercials) distinguish the experience from watching something like *30 Rock* or *The Office*. But what really shocks is the humor. A character with a new and unwanted pregnancy might tell her husband, as he makes a drink, 'Make mine a double. I'm drinking for two now.' No matter how edgy sitcoms are supposed to be in our century, I doubt anyone would dare put that joke onscreen these days."

"Of course," she clarified, "barely anyone would dare make a joke like that back then either... Envelope-pushing went to another level with *Maude*," which in 1972, aired a two-part episode titled "Maude's Dilemma," in which Arthur's leading lady of liberty opts to terminate an unintended pregnancy. As Marcotte explained, Maude lived in New York State, where abortion was legal in 1972. "You'd think that something that happens to over a million women a year would merit more than one portrayal in the 37 years since Maude terminated her pregnancy, but in [the world of TV], abortion is rarer than coffee shop employees who can afford enormous Manhattan apartments."

For Marcotte, it's hard to watch this episode of *Maude* today "without a pang of remorse about how no portrayal of abortion on TV since has been as realistic and sympathetic. (And funny!) It's not that Maude doesn't struggle with her decision to abort, but the reasons given in the show are refreshingly realistic. Maude isn't suddenly struck by waves of guilt for supporting abortion rights or being sexual. She's...uneasy because growing up in the mid-20th century, she thinks of abortion in terms of illegal abortion–sleazy, unsafe, and criminal."

That issue is resolved when Maude's daughter, Carol, as played by Adrienne Barbeau, compares attaining a legal abortion to, as Marcotte put it, "getting a cavity filled in terms of cost and safety... It's shocking how different this is than most subsequent portrayals of abortion. Maude isn't broken or pathetic. She doesn't need outrageous extenuating circumstances to 'deserve' her abortion–she's treated with the respect accorded an adult who has every right to decide her own fate. The sanctity of her marriage and her privacy alone justifies her decision. They even take some time to send up the cult of motherhood and suggest that not every woman enjoys being surrounded by children at all times. But nor is it suggested that Maude's unwillingness to be a mother at this point in her life means she was a bad mother at the time she did want it."

"In other words," Marcotte concluded, "...this episode of *Maude* was grounded more in a realistic understanding of people's actual lives than any show dealing with the abortion choice has been since. Abortion is presented as a sensible option for women dealing with unwanted pregnancy, which is exactly how many women experience it.

"Too bad TV writers since have been afraid to tell this basic truth."

It was also Arthur's Emmy-winning authentic performance as Maude that lent to the show's credibility. Producer/journalist Margaret Wendt weighed in: "I loved Bea Arthur. She was the best comedienne ever. I don't care who else was on her show, or no matter what anybody else did, she was the star. The only thing I didn't like were those long damn long jackets she'd wear. To this day, if I happen to wear anything long, I call myself Maude."

While it's lead actress may have lacked a fashion sense, *Maude* ran on CBS until the spring of 1978 and will forever be remembered for its courageous comedy and trademark lines like, "God'll get you for that!"

That line, among others, was stated with that spot-on deadpan delivery utilized by the multi-talented, liberal-minded, outspoken, courageous, gravel-voiced actress as the multi-married, liberal-minded, outspoken, courageous, gravel-voiced Maude Findlay character.

Until she later brought a kinder, gentler, and more fashionably-dressed persona to the small screen in the guise of divorced substitute teacher Dorothy Zbornak on *The Golden Girls* (NBC, 1985–1993), Arthur's *Maude* magnetism reigned supreme. Not your average female TV presence by any stretch of the imagination, Arthur's appeal as Maude continued to shine beyond what may have otherwise been considered by the mainstream to be a dark, intimidating unattractive presence. Instead, Arthur's somewhat androgynous charisma (which didn't stop late-night talk show host Jimmy Kimmel from purchasing a nude portrait of the actress in 2012) sprang purely from her raw, crisp, and verbose talent and very soul.

A highly-skilled Broadway actress and singer before and after her television popularity, Arthur won the Tony Award for Best Featured Actress in a Musical for her performance as Vera Charles in the original 1966 stage cast edition of *Mame*, a role she reprised in the 1974 feature film edition that starred Lucille Ball.

In 1999, Arthur told a reporter about three main influences in her career: *Your Show of Shows* legend Sid Caesar taught her "the outrageous," method acting maestro Lee Strasberg instructed her in the theatrical ways of what she described as "reality" acting, and Lotte Lenya who (as the original stage star of *The Three Penny Opera*) Arthur "adored" taught her "economy."

Each of these influences helps to shape and form the compelling persona that Arthur packaged into what became Maude Findlay, who made her initial big impression with just one small guest-spot on Lear's *All in the Family*, in an episode titled "Cousin Maude's Visit," in which she was introduced as a cousin to Jean Stapleton's Edith Bunker who was wed to bigot Bunker (as played by O'Connor).

Lear talked with *Entertainment Weekly* in 2009, shortly after Arthur's demise. He recalled first seeing her in the off-Broadway show *Three to Get Ready*: "The stage was dark, and she came out in the highest of heels and dressed to kill. She leaned against a street light and sang a torch song called 'Garbage'; it was about some guy who had treated her like garbage. It's a big song, and every time she hit the word '*garbage*,' there was a laugh attack in the audience. I never forgot that. We became great friends and worked together a number of times, and then came ['Cousin Maude's Visit']."

During the segment's premiere airing, December 11, 1971, Lear received a phone call from then CBS executive Fred Silverman, who told him, "That woman has got to have a series of her own."

Big and brash, Arthur instilled into *Maude* (the character and the TV series) a unique, if loud, female honesty that had never before been seen on television. Come Tuesday nights at 8 p.m., while the kids watched Ron Howard's Richie Cunningham and Henry Winkler's The Fonz on *Happy Days*, more mature audiences were drawn to *Maude's* more adult content.

Arthur's TV status was secured. "There was no doubt this was a television star," Lear told *Entertainment Weekly*. "Bea was the last one to take anything like that for granted. She never saw herself that way. But those of us working with her knew we were working with a golden comedic touch."

"Working with Bea was fantastic," Adrienne Barbeau said. "At the time, never having done a series, I took so much for granted, and it wasn't until years later that I realized how blessed we all were to have her as our star. She was the utmost professional, incredibly giving, and always putting the quality of the show above all else. The first one in the rehearsal hall, the last to leave, the first one to have her lines word perfect, and the first one to suggest that a joke might be better served by one of the other actors at the expense of her own lines."

Entertainment Weekly writer Ken Tucker concluded in 2009:

"Because we live in a pop culture that thrives on parody and irreverence, Bea Arthur existed in the popular imagination during her final years as the punch line to jokes about her deep voice and her Amazonian stature…Whether playing a character or being herself—she was a delightfully clever, articulate, self-deprecating guest on talk and variety shows—Arthur allowed you to both identify with her and to admire her. There was a lot to admire."

The same could be said for *Good Times*, Lear's series that was spawned from *Maude*. After only two years playing the Findlays' housekeeper Florida Evans on *Maude*, Esther Rolle was granted the lead in her own series, which also starred John Amos (formerly Gordy the WJM weatherman on *The Mary Tyler Moore Show*), as loving parents to three children: Bern Nadette Stanis, Ralph Carter and JimmieWalker as J.J. "Dynomite" Evans.

Whereas the adult and young viewers once were divided nicely into two viewing groups of *Maude* and *Happy Days*, by the time *Good Times* hit the air in 1974, ABC's one-two punch of *Days* and *Laverne & Shirley* now had a formidable opponent. But what proved so appealing for all age groups in the audience was how strong a spiritual presence Florida was as the female head of her family and the head of the family (after John Amos left following a contract dispute with Lear). On many occasions, "God" came into play, and the Evans family was frequently seen praying at the dinner table, the likes of which had not been seen since the days of *Father Knows Best* in the late '50s and early '60s.

Following *Good Times*, Lear had a single-mom's family field day with *One Day a Time*, an off-beat short-lived series called *Sunday Dinner* (CBS, June-July 1991) with a pre-*Lois & Clark* Teri Hatcher playing a character who talked to God—*every* week), and *704 Hauser* (CBS, April-May 1994), in which an African-American family moved into Archie Bunker's former house from *All in the Family*. Both *Dinner* and *Hauser* were noble attempts (the latter even co-starred John Amos, who had left *Good Times*). But the only success story was *One Day at a Time*, which starred Bonnie Franklin as Ann Romano, who became TV's first divorced single mom (to two children: played by Mackenzie Phillips and Valerie Bertinelli).

While one era ended, another began…with *The Waltons*, various editions of which have been worshipped by fans for decades in much the same and yet different ways than *The Partridge Family* or *The Brady Bunch*.

Tapped from the genius mind of literary giant Earl Hamner, Jr., *The Waltons* was based on his true-to-life experiences growing up during the Great Depression in Schuyler, Virginia, a small company town at the foot of the Blue Ridge Mountains. The genesis of the TV series commenced with his classic novel *Spencer's Mountain*, which in 1963 was adapted as a feature film starring Henry Fonda, Maureen O'Hara and James MacArthur (*Hawaii Five-0*, CBS, 1968–1980) as Clayboy, the precursor to John-Boy, as played so thoroughly by Richard Thomas on *The Waltons*.

The big-screen *Spencer's* was a hit but a bit too peppy and bright. It somehow missed the mark as it glossed over Hamner's down-home down-sized realistic vision, which was more clarified with *The Homecoming* TV-movie. Adjustably intimate and better suited for the small screen, the *Spencer's*-turned-*Waltons-Homecoming* TV-movie was originally conceived as only a Christmas special. When its ratings measured off the hook, CBS immediately ordered it to series. Patricia Neal and Andrew Duggan stepped into the parental figures played by Fonda and O'Hara in *Spencer's Mountain*. They were then joined by Thomas, Judy Norton-Taylor (as Mary Ellen Walton), Mary McDonough (Erin), Kami Cotler (Elizabeth), Jon Walmsley (Jason), and David W. Harper (Jim-Bob).

When the *Homecoming* TV-film became the *Waltons* weekly series, Michael Learned and Ralph Waite took over for Neal and Duggan as parents John and Olivia Walton, Will Geer replaced Edgar Bergen (father of Candice Bergen, star of *Murphy Brown*) as the Grandfather Zeb Walton, while Ellen Corby was retained as the Grandmother Esther Walton—as were all the young actors playing the children, the middle of who was the fresh-faced 12-year-old Eric Scott.

Scott's sparked freckles and bright-red hair caught the eye of *Homecoming* casting directors who believed that he, Thomas, and the rest of their young thespian peers looked enough like a family to cast them as a group.

A superior production on every level, *The Waltons* was real. Set in the Depression era of the late 1930s, it was blessed with premium talent, behind and in front of the camera in every aspect of production, from Emmy-winning performances delivered by Thomas, Learned, Waite, Geer, and Corby, to the also-award-winning tender but crisp writing and directing. As previously mentioned, a few members of the cast appeared on *The Today Show* in 2011 to commemorate *The Homecoming's* 40th anniversary. Declared Learned to *Today* host Matt Lauer, "Those who call our show too saccharine simply don't watch it."

"It was funny," Scott recalled, "…because when we'd read certain reviews that said we were too schmaltzy or a little too sweet, we just never thought that was the case. I mean, there'd be scenes where John Walton (the father played by Waite) would lose his patience and yell at the kids whether it was right or wrong. So, I disagreed with the critics back then."

As well he should have. Truth be told, the Walton characters, like the *Father Knows Best* characters years before them, interacted authentically. They laughed, cried, and became angry with one another, as in any actual family. But at their core was the love that held them together with a happy steady strength in poor tough times. With so solid a premise, it would be surprising for any associated actor, much less an alignment of young actors, to not walk away from such a creative environment without an indestructible moral structure.

Scott sensed something special was in creation, though no one envisioned the series would become so popular. "We all knew what we were making was quality," he said. "And I always felt that the production values of our show were very strong. We knew when we were making it that each episode was going to stand on its own. But we had no idea that it would be as timeless as it's become today."

The timeless appeal of *The Waltons* is attributed to many reasons. Each episode was like a little movie, with a beginning, middle, and an end, unlike contemporary television shows that feature convoluted arc storylines or guest characters who linger throughout the entire season. "Today," Scott explained, "there is more a soap-opera mentality. But on *The Waltons*, we'd introduce a character and in 48 minutes of production, you got to know that character, and there would be resolution with that character."

Upon recently viewing a few episodes, Scott was "amazed," especially with performances by Thomas, Waite, and Learned. "They were so strong, with regard to character development," he said. In their interacting with fellow cast members, Scott said, "Michael and Ralph listened so well," which is one of the most respectful gestures an actor could convey while working in a scene. "And Richard, of course," who played John-Boy, "was always a stunning person to be around."

As Scott continued to recall, Thomas took great strides to "care for us." If any of the younger *Waltons* cast members felt a particular line of dialogue was incongruent with their TV counterparts, Thomas would make certain the scripts were altered to maintain the integrity of each performance and the show in general. "If he felt there was a character flaw," he said, "or if something wasn't progressing smoothly or was inconsistent with any character, he'd address it. He made sure that John-Boy and all the other characters were covered. I would talk with him, make suggestions about my character, and the script would be changed. In many ways, Richard really was our big brother," on and off camera.

Thomas, as did Waite (who passed away in 2014), had directed a few episodes. "Ralph had that energy," said Scott. "He'd walk on the set, and he'd have all these different ideas that he wanted to do. He was amazing. He would usually get a script a few days before the rest of us, and when I say he worked on it…I mean he worked on it." As Eric saw it, Thomas was "an actor's director, just like Ralph. He allowed the technical side to just flow organically. And I cherished his insight. He was the driving force on our show, and he had an incredible influence on it. And when he had the opportunity to direct, he brought along the same kind of gusto. He had ideas and knew our characters as well as we did. Our characters were very much like each of our personalities, and he knew those personalities well. Because we had such a large cast, the producers recognized early who we were as individuals and set out to incorporate traits from our real lives into our characters."

With Ben Walton, Scott's character, "they saw him as a little bit of a wise-ass that could get into a little bit of trouble once in a while. But he also had a business sense. He was intelligent but emotional. And that was more or less taken from me," Scott acknowledged. And though Thomas' lead character of John-Boy—the alter ego of the show's mastermind Earl Hamner—received top billing, Scott said, "We didn't have prima donnas on our show. We were a troupe all the way."

That team spirit included Hamner. "I had never worked with a producer/writer like we did with Earl," Scott relayed. "It was like having an in-house writer on the set. Between him and Richard, we all always felt that there was someone to talk to. They looked through each script (as if) with [magnifying] glasses. Every word was under the microscope." With this kind of patience in production, the result was a quality product, "and it showed."

By contemporary standards, each 48-minute episode of *The Waltons* equals approximately 15 minutes in production time. "We took the time to develop characters, to let the characters and the actors find their way," Scott said. "Nowadays, it's all about quick editing and the seven-second approach to watching a show."

Another *Waltons* co-worker who served as somewhat of a mentor for Scott was Ellen Corby who played Grandma Walton, even after she suffered a stroke that disabled her speech. "All you had to do was look at those eyes of hers," Scott observed, "and how she conveyed so much without even saying a word. She had that little bit of spicy energy, and she saw that same vim and vigor in me, and she encouraged me to 'Go for it! Go out there and do it! Add to it.'"

The Waltons set provided a mutual support system that proved beneficial for the castand the home audience. As far as Scott can tell, the series was and remains popular for two main reasons: (1) Viewers relate to it and/or (2) Viewers aspire to relate to it. He explained: "When I talk to people that grew up watching it within my generation, I think they are connecting it back to the wonderful time they had growing up in the '60s and the '70s. So, I think that nostalgia is probably part of the attraction now. And remember, too, because it was based in the 1930s, it was nostalgic even then (when it debuted in the '70s)."

"But, it's interesting," he added, "because when we were doing the show, I didn't think about the effect it had on anything. We were just working. It was a production. I looked at it from an acting standpoint or learned from it from a post-production standpoint. It was all very technical for me. I didn't look at it as entertaining or consider if the public was enjoying it. I could never control any of that. And we would never change what we were doing to appease others. We just did what we felt was right for the show and with each script, and we honored that." In turn, fans continue to honor the show.

"People approach me," Scott continued, "and tell me of the impact that the show had on them growing up, how it changed their lives…that they raised their kids according to what they learned on the show… how they named their children after our characters. These are all like wonderful residuals for the effort and energy we put into doing the show. It's all love. It's a gift."

With The Waltons' popularity, additional one-hour family shows appeared on television, including NBC's *Little House on the Prairie* (1974–1983). Like *The Waltons*, *Little House*, which was produced by TV legend Michael Landon (formerly of NBC's *Bonanza*/1959–1973 and later *Highway to Heaven*/1983–1989), was a period piece, based on real-life experiences, specifically those of Laura Ingalls and the memories she shared in the monumental books of the same title. "Michael Landon was brilliant," Scott said. "I loved his work on *Little House, Highway to Heaven,* and *Bonanza*. He really knew how to entertain." But even though *House* was set in the 1880s, Scott believed "some of the dialogue was very contemporary," and he respected Landon's choice to go that route. "But I don't feel the development of his characters had the same amount of layers that we did on *The Waltons*. His show was wonderful entertainment, and parents could sit down and watch it with their kids, who absolutely loved it. And for that it was great. But on *The Waltons*, I always felt we were making an adult show and that kids could enjoy it as well."

As when Oscar-winning actress Sissy Spacek appeared in a few episodes playing Sarah Jane Simmons, a somewhat disgruntled friend of the Walton children. In one segment, it was suggested that her character was pregnant out of wedlock. "It was just two little lines," Scott recalled, and such subtle references may or may not have been picked up on by a 10- or 12-year-old viewer. "But for adults, that was a commentary on the times. So, our show had a great deal of depth, and that was one of its strengths. The stories were just terrific."

Most of the stories from the show's early years stemmed from the creativity and real-life memories of Earl Hamner. Other scripts were ignited by the equally gifted minds of writers like John Furia, who had previously worked on shows like *The Twilight Zone* (CBS, 1959–1965) and *Kung Fu* (ABC, 1972–1975), the latter for which had shared sets for the 1973 feature film remake of *Lost Horizon* (on which the young

Walton actors frequently played). In direct opposition to what became the unwritten "no hugging/no learning" rule later set down by *Seinfeld* (NBC, 1990–1998), the Walton characters frequently embraced one another, literally and figuratively. The characters had issues with one another, but by the given episode's end tag, those issues were resolved. Both *The Waltons* and their viewers were comforted and, as Scott sustains, "That's what TV shows are supposed to do. That's what life is supposed to do. We all lose our patience or perspective from time to time, and conflict arises. But as long as there is an apology that's appropriate, then great—that's what life is all about. I mean, we shouldn't all be on such pedestals that we can't be human."

In the fall of 2012, the Ebell Theatre in Los Angeles hosted a Waltons 40th Anniversary that celebrated the show, which featured the money-poor, but love-rich rural Virginia Depression-era family. The guests of honor included Earl Hamner, Jr. (ageless as ever in voice, down-to-earth demeanor, and appearance), Ralph Waite, Judy Norton-Taylor, Mary McDonough, Kami Cotler, Jon Walmsley, Eric Scott, and David Harper, and Joe Conley, who played Ike Godsey, the genial proprietor of the Walton's Mountain general store.

Will Geer and Ellen Corby, both of whom had by then passed away, were sorely missed, as were Richard Thomas and Michael Learned, each of whom was unable to attend the event due to prior engagements. But a cavalcade of classic TV stars attended the event, including (but not limited to): *The Jeffersons* star Marla Gibbs and her latter-day *227* co-star Hal Williams, who was a semi-regular guest star on *The Waltons*, as was Richard Hatch (who later starred on the original *Battlestar: Galactica* after replacing Michael Douglas on *The Streets of San Francisco*), Stephen Collins (*7th Heaven*), Gerald McRaney (*Simon & Simon, Major Dad, Promised Land*, the latter on which Richard Thomas played his younger wayward brother); Jonathan Frakes (William Riker from *Star Trek: The Next Generation*), among many other retroactive actors who came along for the fun ride (including Charlotte Rae, best known as Mrs. Garrett from *The Facts of Life*).

An especially touching tribute to those actors no longer with us included recollections of Geer and Corby, as well as the late, great Cleavon Little and John Ritter (son of cowboy movie legend Tex Ritter). Little had appeared in *The Homecoming* pilot and subsequent *Waltons* episodes and went on to star in a TV show of his own, *Temperatures Rising* (Cleavon Little had appeared in several films prior to *Blazing Saddles*.) Before playing the playfully womanizing Jack Tripper on TV's *Three's Company*, Ritter portrayed *The Waltons'* Reverend Fordwick, a role he once described as his favorite dramatic part.

The Ebell Theatre festivities served as a fund-raiser, headed by Waltons alumni Kami Cotler who, after earning an education degree in Social Sciences at the University of California, went on to her first teaching job that, coincidentally, took her to a small rural Virginia school in the Blue Ridge Mountains, much like the fictional one her Elizabeth Walton character attended on the show.

In 2001, Cotler returned to California, where she began teaching 9th grade at the Environmental Charter High School. In 2004 the raven-haired epitome of grace accepted the job as co-director of the Ocean Charter School, a position held until 2007 when she started her own educational consulting business. A past board member of the American Montessori Society, Cotler currently serves as the founding principal of L.A.'s Environmental Charter Middle School, the education facility that is the beneficiary of *The Waltons* Ebell event.

Other members of *The Waltons* cast remain just as active: Judy Norton-Taylor continues acting and also directs and sings (which she proved with a lovely performance at the Anniversary while poignant clips of the show were displayed on dual screens on either side of the theatre). Mary McDonough, too, continues to act and is a producer/director and best-selling author (her book, *Lessons from The Mountain: What I Learned from Erin Walton*, details with telling insight—and great humor—the image and health challenges she faced growing up in Hollywood). Jon Walmsley is a successful session musician for various TV shows (including ABC Family's *Secret Life of the American Teenager*). Eric Scott owns the renowned

Michael Learned played Olivia Walton on *The Waltons* and several of its sequels *[Credit: Photography by Bill Dow/Courtesy of Harlan Boll[*

Chase Messenger Service in Los Angeles and occasionally acts. David Harper is contemplating a return to acting and is also interested in writing (he delivered at the Anniversary a moving speech about his experience of working on *The Waltons*). Before passing away at 88 in 2013, Ralph Waite continued to work regularly (as with roles like playing Mark Harmon's father on the CBS-TV hit *NCIS*), while the effervescent Michael Learned and equally-talented Richard Thomas are always performing somewhere on stage or screen.

As any true fan of *The Waltons* comprehends, the show stands in TV history as one of the most realistic fictional family portraits the medium has ever produced. Again, *The Waltons* were real people who loved one another, but organically so, within the believable context of their situations and the development of their particular relationships. Many series episodes dealt with serious issues beyond its general time-period Depression-era premise, such as the *Hindenburg*, book-burning, and racism. The show's best episodes dealt more with the smaller stories, the personal nuances between the main characters, and the various "visitors" to Walton's Mountain (which was a character in and of itself), all of whom journeyed in and out of the Waltons' lives, each the better for meeting John-Boy and his loving brood.

The on-screen visitors, along with the off-screen home viewers, were seemingly "saved" by the richly-developed Walton characters and eloquent storylines presented on the show. It's almost as if the Waltons became a family of superheroes who swooped in to save the day, minus all the horns and whistles. Instead, it showcased kindness and how it helped heal whatever conflicts may have arisen within the family. As then-*TV Guide* front-man William Keck noted at the Ebell Theatre 40th Anniversary event, "We need more shows like *The Waltons* on television today."

That wish almost came true with Earl Hamner at the helm. Hamner had told the Anniversary audience that he's developing a new wine-country family TV show that sounded like a cross between *The Waltons* and *Falcon Crest*, the nighttime soap he created for CBS in the 1980s. But a short time later, Hamner passed away.

But his adventures of television's favorite Depression-era Virginia heroes live on, in reruns and DVD, employing their superpowers of lovingkindness to heal the given situation at hand. *The Waltons…* the characters—and the actors who portrayed them—as well as the behind-the-scenes creative team brought each character to life (and light) with every one of their wise words, sentiments, images, and compassionate ways.

Chapter 15

The Waltons continued its unique one-hour popularity for CBS, and years after half-hour '80s dramedies like NBC's *Buffalo Bill* and ABC's *Hooperman* failed, more traditional and better executed 30-minute family shows succeeded, mostly on ABC. To name a few: *Happy Days* (1973–1983) and its spin-off *Laverne & Shirley* (both produced by Garry Marshall), and the dramedies *Doogie Houser, M.D.* (1989–1993) and *The Wonder Years* (1988–1993).

Nearly twenty years after *Family Affair*'s end *Wonder* and *Doogie*, starring a pre-king-of-all-media Neil Patrick Harris (*How I Met Your Mother*), became two of the most successful dramedies of all time, at least within the half-hour format. But while *Doogie* was somewhat of a fantasy (about a pubescent genius physician), in reality, off-screen, the show almost single-handedly increased sales for personal computers, as Dr. Houser made weekly entries to his electronic diary.

The Wonder Years' effect was no less profound, as it became one of the most realistic shows to air in any decade. A period piece like *Happy Days*, which though broadcast in the '70s and set in the '50s (that grew into the '60s), *The Wonder Years*, which aired in the '80s and into the '90s, was premised in the '60s (and on into the '70s). Despite it all, *Happy Days* and *The Wonder Years* were similar shows. Their given decades weren't all that happy or wonderful from a historic standpoint; each era was littered with its share of international wars, revolts, and other conflicts, political, personal, global, sexual, and generational. But as TV writer Bill Persky previously suggested about *Happy Days*, the same could be said about *The Wonder Years*: Each show presented at the very least an idealized view of American life.

Happy Days has for years been incorrectly identified and documented as a spin-off from George Lucas' 1973 hit motion picture, *American Graffiti*, which just so happened to feature *Days* lead Ron

Anson Williams played Potsie and Don Most played Ralph Malph on *Happy Days* [Credit: Courtesy of Harlan Boll]

Howard (along with Cindy Williams, future star of *Laverne & Shirley*). *Happy Days* began as an unsold pilot called *New Family in Town*, which was reworked into the *Love, American Style* segment called "Love and the Television Set." This segment's title was changed to "Love and the Happy Days" for syndication. Here, the family of Howard's teenaged and freckle-faced Richie Cunningham purchased, appropriately enough, their first television set—a development that leads Richie and his best friend Potsie (Anson Williams) to assume the newfangled contraption would somehow contribute to their luck with the ladies.

Fresh off ABC's short-lived dramedy *The Smith Family* (Henry Fonda's slightly ahead of or past its time half-hour, depending on the perspective) and long-gone from *The Andy Griffith Show*, Howard's earnest portrayal of Richie had winning appeal, enough to convince ABC to greenlight the show. It took a few years, most likely influenced by *Graffiti's* popularity, but the *Days* weekly entry finally debuted on January 15, 1974, with Howard and Williams returning to their *American Style*-like roles. In the series edition, they were joined by veteran performers Tom Bosley and Marion Ross as Richie's parents, Mr. and Mrs. C. (Harold Gould played Mr. Cunningham in the pilot); Donny Most was wise-cracking teen Ralph Malph, and Gavan O'Herlihy (1974) and Randolph Roberts (1974–1975) shared the role of Richie's very tall but soon never-to-be-seen-again older brother Chuck (portrayed by Ric Carrott in the *Love, American Style* segment). Erin Moran rounded out the cast as Richie's little sister, Joanie, who later fell in love with Scott Baio's Chachi Arcola.

Chachi was a mini-version of what became the show's resident high-school hood and dropout, a main, motorcycle-driving force named Arthur Fonzarelli, a.k.a. The Fonz and Fonzie—portrayed with Emmy-winning bravado by Henry Winkler. While Chachi frequently and loosely voiced his approval of a pretty girl, mostly Joanie, with the catchphrase, "Wa-wa-wa!" the idolization of that colloquialism merely echoed that of Fonzie's even more popular "Aaaay!"—an equally loose locution that usually accompanied a "thumbs-up" motion with either one or two hands.

Other expressions like "Sit on it!" and "You're such a Potsie!" resulted from *Happy Days*, which began as an elegant half-hour sitcom, filmed like a movie, and minus a studio audience. By the show's third season, Winkler's Fonzie supplanted original show lead Howard, who had so perfectly interpreted the innocence of youth as *everyboy* Richie. Once Fonzie-mania began to soar, the show started filming in front of a live audience. *Happy Days* writer Marty Nadler compared the developing relationship between Richie and Fonzie, their interlocking chemistry and individual magnetism, and how format changes catapulted the show's success:

"What made Richie and Fonzie appealing was that they were opposite of each other. Richie was like the nerdish-type guy that really wasn't sophisticated around women, and Fonzie was the tough guy [who was]. But Fonzie had a heart and he also recognized that Richie was a good guy. Then, at one point, the network started to receive all kinds of fan mail for Fonzie. In the beginning, he only had minimal lines for every episode, but all the kids [in the audience] were writing in and saying, 'Who is this guy in the leather jacket? We like him!'"

ABC called a meeting with Garry Marshall, older brother to actress Penny Marshall, who would later star (with Cindy Williams) on his *Days* spin-off *Laverne & Shirley*, and who had a supporting role in his TV adaptation of *The Odd Couple* (all of which aired on ABC). As Nadler recalled, the network execs told Garry they wanted to change the show's title to *Fonzie's Happy Days*, and have most of the stories focus on The Fonz. Nadler said Garry was none too pleased with the suggestions. "They don't understand that Amos doesn't work without Andy," Marshall said, "and basically you need both Fonzie and Richie to make the show work."

As Nadler went on to explain, Marshall then offered ABC an ultimatum as a question: "Who's going to produce the show—because I'm taking Ronnie (Howard) over to NBC and do [another] show right away." To which an ABC rep swiftly replied, "Oh, no—*Happy Days* is a *good* title!"

"And from there," Nadler added, "…they worked it out to have Richie and his family become family to Fonzie," who eventually moved into a room above the Cunninghams' garage.

In his essay, *"Happy Days* Became One of the Biggest Hits On TV by Selling Its Soul,"* published on www.avclub.com, pop-culture journalist Todd VanDerWerff claimed "Garry Marshall faced a dilemma in the second season of *Happy Days.*" At first, the series attempted to "honestly depict a wistful look back at adolescence (Marshall told *The Associated Press* in 2004 that it was his 'artistic period')." It had become "a minor Nielsen hit in its first season, but it was sinking like a stone, falling out of the Top 30 and toward certain cancellation. He had one last shot at making the series a success, though it would destroy almost everything he'd set out to create. What he came up with was almost terminally dumb, but it made the show one of the biggest hits in television history, one of the ultimate case stories TV fans can point to when it comes to art versus commerce. Marshall and the show's other producers took a charming little single-camera comedy about the trials of growing up and made it a loud, kid-friendly, multi-camera comedy more about gimmicks than intelligent storytelling or nuanced characters. And it worked."

For Marty Nadler, that transpired on several levels, particularly, with regard to some very positive feedback from the audience of the literary kind. He said television has always "played a great role in American society because it is one of the great native mediums," and cited *Happy Days* as a prime example. "We did an episode in which The Fonz went out and applied for a library card. As a result, 50,000 kids went out and got library cards."

The episode, "Hard Cover" (also known as "Fonzie Gets His Library Card"), originally aired on September 27, 1977, and centered around Richie attending the local college, where he and Fonzie visit the campus library to meet girls. It was then The Fonz decided to apply for the card that sparked a 500% nationwide increase in library card requests in real life. While the episode became historic for both Fonzie and Richie (who that day met his future wife, Lori Beth Allen, played by Lynda Goodfriend), Nadler in real life deciphered how his own personal history was integrated into episodes he penned not only *Happy Days* but for *Laverne & Shirley* and *The Odd Couple.*

Like *Kung Fu* creator Ed Spielman, Nadler grew up in the Bronx, watching and being inspired by "a lot of television." For Nadler, that meant watching various musical-variety hours hosted by Milton Berle, and Jerry Lewis, and sitcoms like *Make Room for Daddy* (a.k.a. *The Danny Thomas Show*, ABC/CBS, 1953–1965). By the time he was 8, Nadler, who was also an actor and did stand-up comedy, decided he wanted to be in the entertainment industry, particularly the comedy sector. Looking back, "one of the greatest thrills" of his life was later standing on the *Happy Days* sound stage at Paramount Studios, "giving notes to Danny Thomas" for the episode, "Grandpa's Visit" (1/3/1978), in which he played Richie Cunningham's grandfather.

While working on *Days*, Nadler also began adapting many of his own real-life stories for a few of the show's segments, some of which, unfortunately, were never filmed. "We completed one script about gangs that was never used on the show. It was based on my memories of growing with gangs in my neighborhood."

With other real-life and fictional stories from each creative individual on the series including of course Garry Marshall, Nadler's memories and talent contributed to the success of *Happy Days.* The show became a TV classic that proved educational for impressionable young viewers in one of the most fundamental ways. As Marshall himself once concluded of the "Library Card" segment, in particular, "Our characters have identities and powers all their own, and a couple of lines from Richie or Fonzie can alter the thinking of millions of kids."

In another sense, *The Wonder Years* may have served a similar purpose.

Chapter 16

[Credit: *The Classic TV Preservation Society*]

The original edition of *The Wonder Years*, recently rebooted on ABC, premiered on that network in January 1988 as a five-part miniseries and ran its original course until 1993. As little Kevin Arnold, the wiser-than-his-years Fred Savage took us back to the '60s (and ensuing '70s) with psychologically-nutritious precision.

Many baby boomers, in particular, remember the episode in which his hippie sister, Karen, played by Olivia d'Abo, painted his pants with flowers. Many older female siblings did the same to their younger brothers. Or when Kevin kissed longtime first love Winnie Cooper (portrayed by Danica McKellar) in the woods in the first episode, reminding viewers of their own real-life first kiss.

The audience enjoyed the series so much because it reminded them of the many aspects and memories of their own lives. Everyone had a best friend like Paul Pfeiffer (played by Josh Saviano). Mostly everyone had a father like Kevin's dad, Jack (Dan Lauria) who made uncompromising career choices or who was frustrated with his life in some way. But that didn't stop them from loving their parents any more than it stopped Kevin from loving his father. Also, there to comfort Kevin was his understanding mom (and Jack's caring wife) Norma (Alley Mills), who eased everyone's troubles. And who hasn't been confronted by a trouble-making nemesis like Wayne (Jason Hervey) for a mean-spirited older brother or neighborhood bully?

Fortunately, good always wins out over bad behavior.

At least that's the way it played out on *The Wonder Years*. Every time Kevin's life seems to go awry, somewhere, by the 29th minute, he became all the richer for it. What doesn't kill him makes him stronger and all that stuff—stuff of which was so skillfully interwoven into the sound narrative on the show (compliments of skilled voiceover work from actor Daniel Stern as the adult Kevin).

So "How Does *The Wonder Years* Hold Up?" all these years after its debut? Steve Heisler, blogger for *The Huffington Post*, wondered the same thing with a so-named post from August 8, 2012. After rewatching all 114 episodes of the series available on Netflix, Heisler decided, "there's nothing particularly odd or dated about it. Even without HD, it still looks pretty good—plenty of sweeping shots of Jack Arnold's furniture shop or Karen's college hippie den—and is pretty historically accurate to the sixties. Plus, it's a period piece, so I reveled in the lack of bad eighties haircuts and references to Bo

Jackson's thriving NFL/MLB career. Though *The Wonder Years* was made to represent a specific period in history, it's universal enough not to show its age."

"Like Kevin Arnold," Heisler continued, "I grew up in a similar, quintessential 'Anytown USA' suburb. But as *The Wonder Years* points out, there's a story in each of those identical homes—hundreds of them. Revisiting *The Wonder Years* reminded me that we're all from *somewhere* and that even though I might think stories from my childhood are boring or unspectacular, there's gotta be someone who finds them interesting, universal, maybe even…*Wonder*-ful."

Numerous classic shows have celebrated friendship one way or the other, between all kinds of characters, defined as "just friends," engaged couples, longtime husband and wives, male buddies, female pals; in various formats of programming, as well; everything from half-hour comedies to one-hour dramas. There were basic female friendships, as was the case between Lucy and Ethel on *I Love Lucy*, a bond that was more or less later duplicated by *Laverne & Shirley* (pratfall comedy and all), and with added sophistication as on *Kate & Allie*.

Other pals in comparison were presented on shows like *The Life and Times of Dobie Gillis, The Patty Duke Show, Gilligan's Island, The Odd Couple, Happy Days, Three's Company, Alice, Taxi, The Golden Girls*, and in more recent years, *How I Met Your Mother, The Big Bang Theory*, and *Curb Your Enthusiasm*. There was the not-fully-appreciated sitcom from the '80s titled *Bosom Buddies*, which featured a pre-Oscar-winning Tom Hanks and Peter Scolari, who would soon find his perfect TV niche on *Newhart* and in the short-lived *Honey, I Shrunk the Kids* (the TV edition of the same-named 1989 feature film). Even crime-dramas had their share of pairings: *Dragnet, Adam-12, The Mod Squad, CHiPs, Starsky & Hutch, Charlie's Angels, Tenspeed and Brown Shoe, Hardcastle and McCormick, Remington Steele, Moonlighting*, all the way up to contemporary entries like *Psych* and *Rizzoli & Isles*, among others.

In this age of social media, the kinship between all peoples has become a cornerstone in every relationship, personal and professional. Being friends has expanded into and been identified within, among other arenas, the workplace (between co-workers and employer/employee relations), and at home. At the same time, the traditional family has extended past the husband/wife, parents/children/siblings category with parent-like types (Mom's boyfriend, Dad's girlfriend), ex-spouses, step-siblings, adopted children, gay and lesbian companions, and people forced to cohabit for no other reason but economics.

The work environment is different, especially when any relationship is played out between employee and employer, or even just co-workers. On television, this association was originally presented in the early seasons of *Cheers* (NBC, 1982–1993), Shelley Long was waitress Diane Chambers who had a love-hate-love-goodbye relationship with Ted Danson's former-baseball player-turned-bartender Sam Malone.

Sam and Diane began as friends (kind of), only to have their association become nothing but a long, strong, complicated romantic and physical affair. He was the aggressor, but she came around, if after much resistance. Their sexual tension came to a head with their historic confrontation ("Are you as turned on as I am?") which set the bar, so to speak, for all hot-and-heavy liaisons to follow (such as Bruce Willis and Cybill Shepherd's love-fest as David and Maddie on *Moonlighting*).

In more recent years, the work-born relationship, as that between Jim Halpert (John Krasinski) and Pam Beesly (Jenna Fischer) on *The Office* (NBC, 2005–2013) elevated to new heights (above their cubicles).

Either way, the questions become manifold: Are these relationships ethical in general, whether they transpire on-screen or off and, if on-screen; are they productive, helpful, and instructive to the audience at home; are they appropriate?

In February of 2014, *Entrepreneur Magazine* helped to provide the answers. Writer John Patrick Pullen described Sam and Diane's relationship as a business owner who makes advances ("some rejected, some accepted, some enjoyed") to an employee, creating a periodically challenging work-place. The "verdict" was this: "Extremely inappropriate. It doesn't matter whether it's accepted or not accepted. It's inappropriate to put the staffer in that position, just because of the differential positions of power."

Pullen then explained how Jim and Pam's relationship on *The Office* blossomed into "more"—outside the work environment. "They try to keep it a secret, but people have their suspicions." The verdict this time: "They should go to their supervisor and [Human Resources Representative] to let them know about the relationship. It sounds like it is leading to gossip—it could lead to a distraction."

Distraction, of course, is what television entertainment, in its ideal and purest form, is supposed to be all about. Whether or not that translates as productive for the home viewer is debatable. If anything, the supposition for debate is at least healthy minded and helps to define where any core friendship may lead, be it just lifelong pals or to eternal wedded bliss.

One of the more interesting TV displays of a modern and complicated friendship occurred on the relatively new classic show called *Reba*, which first aired on The WB from 2002 to 2007. This series, which remains popular in syndication on networks like CMT, Country Music Television, starred country music superstar Reba McEntire as Reba Hart, a divorced Texas soccer mom of three children: 17-year-old Cheyenne (Joanna Garcia Swisher), who marries Van Montgomery (played with rambunctious enthusiasm by Steve Howey) after he gets her pregnant; the tranquil and ever-wise seven-year-old Jake (Mitch Holleman), and Kyra (portrayed by the scene-stealing Scarlett Pomers (formerly of *Star Trek: Voyager* and *That's Life*).

This show was unique because of the friendship retained between Reba, her ex-husband Brock Hart, likably interpreted by Christopher Rich (formerly of *Murphy Brown* and a short-lived but ingenious fantasy-comedy *The Charmings*), and his new wife Barbra Jean, played to the hilt by Melissa Peterman (who somehow managed to cross-pollinate Gomer Pyle with Georgette of *The Mary Tyler Moore Show*). Peterman made Barbra Jean so appealing, even Reba came to call her friend and was almost made to forget that she was "the other woman."

The combined household premise was a winning aspect of the show, as were the several additional traits that its lead star brought to the series.

First and foremost, there is McEntire, widely known for her compassionate and caring nature, who utilized for years her celebrity for the greater good of charities. In 1991, she was devastated by the loss of her band manager and six band members in a horrific small plane accident, of which she was the only survivor (and paid tribute to colleagues with the subsequent hit album, *For My Broken Heart*). She heralded a new age of talent representation by having her real-life second husband (Narvel Blackstock) manage her career. She also remains an inspiration to her peers, having won a number of industry accolades, and cheers (a pre-superstar Faith Hill once shouted at a McEntire concert, "I love you, Reba McEntire!")

Her musical talents, combined with her uplifting personality, and that colorful Annie Oakley hair (she once starred in a Broadway revival of *Annie Get Your Gun*), the country-singing icon simply becomes unstoppable, as she continues to perform (and write!) her own songs, while her TV show, no matter how times the episodes are rerun (which is a lot!), clobbers the competition in any period that it airs.

Reba—the show—presented the contemporary family comedy in 2002 before a show even like *Modern Family* added its own spin in 2009. The characters on *Reba* interacted just like real people. Like their dramatic country cousins, *The Waltons*, the Harts of *Reba* actually got mad at each other, forgave one another, moved on, and dealt with it. From the rousing theme song ("I'm A Survivor," written and performed by McEntire of course) to its crisp writing, directing, and acting, *Reba* rocks.

The issues in *Reba's* family are real: unplanned teen pregnancy, childhood sweethearts divorce after years of bliss, and teen angst—each experienced, on one level or the other, by McEntire's Reba Hart—who holds the brood's brouhaha together, on equal relative standing with Carol Brady, Shirley Partridge, or June Cleaver.

The audience came to know, love, and befriend Reba because the characters became knowable, loveable, and friendly…as individuals and to each other.

Another relatively new classic TV show helped to define the new complicated friendships of the modern age in a very playful and witty way: *Friends*, which enjoyed a long original run on NBC (1994–2004), and included a mishmash of six young twentysomethings, some of whom became friends, remained friends or got married.

As with any quality product, there has to be a pre-set strategy for success and, in the case of *Friends*, that strategy was this: the storylines were always equaled divided among its young, talented six-member cast—Jennifer Aniston as Rachel Green, Courteney Cox as Monica Geller, Lisa Kudrow as Phoebe Buffay, Matt LeBlanc as Joey Tribbiani, Matthew Perry as Chandler Bing, and David Schwimmer as Ross Geller.

Each of the *Friends* characters was uniquely defined with specific dialogue and traits if all executed within a frenetic, yet controlled pace and, quite simply, brilliant performances. The group began as a close-knit sextet of New York singles who periodically overdosed on conversations and coffee at the Central Perk gathering hole. Monica was the neat-freak; Ross was her on-the-rebound older brother; Phoebe, a spacey-but-adorable-cadet; Rachel, Monica's rich-girl roomie; and across-the-hall were neighbors Joey, an aspiring actor, and Chandler, an acerbic office worker.

The characters evolved over the years and showcased just how challenging (and humorous) it can be to sustain any kind of friendship. Each was unattached, romantically, while Ross retained his elementary-school crush on the semi-oblivious Rachel, who left her groom at the altar. She and Ross eventually hook up, then separate, get married, get divorced, have a child, and then marry (and only true fans can understand the dynamics of those developments). Monica and Chandler eventually fall in love and wed. Joey has a brief fling with Rachel (while she and Ross are "on a break"), and at points flirts ever so slightly with the possibility of a romantic liaison with Phoebe, while all six pals date a ton of significant others in between.

There were also the gang's relationships with parents, co-workers, and additional friends, all of which presented various new challenges, yet never dissolved the core bond between the basically-cheery group of six originals; and there's something to be said for that. Early on in the show's first season, each of the *Friends* actors offered some defining thoughts on their own and fellow cast of characters:

Cox called Monica "the most normal" of the group. "She has her quirks. She's compulsive, but she's the voice of reason."

Schwimmer said his Ross was "…the '90s Guy, struggling with old-fashioned values in a contemporary world," while Cox said of Schwimmer's alter ego: "It's always nice to have a vulnerable character—girls love that stuff—and that's Ross."

Added Perry of Schwimmer in real life, "He's got this quality I admire and hate at the same time. I admire it because nobody else has that hurt-guy style, and I hate it because every single woman on the face of the planet wants him."

Early on, Schwimmer said he didn't want the *Friends* focus to shift to his (or any other) character. "That would be the downfall of the show," he intoned. "All of us signed up to do an ensemble" (and made millions of dollars with an all-or-nothing-stick-together deal).

In addition to Phoebe, Kudrow also portrayed Ursula, Phoebe's twin sister (an air-headed waitress who also offered double-duty on NBC's *Mad About You*). But of her main *Friends* façade, she said, "She's not stupid. She just has a different point of reference for everything."

Aniston, who created a sensation with her alter ego's rave hairstyle, The Rachel), once described her on-screen *Friends* persona as "…not bitchy," but "spoiled…She knows no other life."

LeBlanc once described his girl-crazy Joey as "…honest…a result of his cloudy perception of the world"; and Perry called Chandler "…the guy everybody thinks will do really well with women, but he thinks too much and says the wrong thing." So once more success, on-screen or off, comes down to bringing something unique to the table in a way that contributes to a bigger picture. The *Friends* cast members respected one another off-set, as did their characters on-screen. The result: chemistry that led to a hit series and the highest good for all concerned: well-played characters, strong friendships off-screen, and laughs with a little insight on the side for the viewers at home.

Like all well-made shows, *Friends* will continue to pal around with the audience for years to come either in syndicated reruns or via DVD. Viewers will forever feast on the immutable essence and image of friendship while enjoying a hearty, healthy, and a very happy dose of friendly humor.

Will there ever be a *Friends* reunion, as was orchestrated as a TV-movie for example, with the original cast members (save for Tina Louise) of *Gilligan's Island*?

Courteney Cox originally thought "probably not."

In April 2014, Cox appeared on *The Late Show with David Letterman*, saying she attempted to coordinate one such reunion over the years but to no avail. But the *Friends* reunion finally did transpire in 2020 a special on HBO Max.

Chapter 17

Like *Friends*, *Seinfeld* celebrated pals, if maybe with less joy. Debuting in the summer of 1989, under the title, *The Seinfeld Chronicles*, *Seinfeld* was based on the real-life adventures of stand-up comedian Jerry Seinfeld. Along with co-creator and good friend Larry David, Jerry served as co-executive producer on the series, which also starred Jason Alexander (as George Constanza, Larry David in disguise), Julia Louis-Dreyfus as Elaine Benes (Jerry's former girlfriend and now one of the guys), and Michael Richards as Cosmo Kramer, Jerry's manic next-door neighbor.

The "show about nothing" means something to millions of fans *[Credit: The Classic TV Preservation Society]*

The series ran 9 years on NBC following *Friends* and prior to *Cheers* during the network's "Must See" Thursday night campaign (created by Dan Holm) and before the later seasons became littered with characters, the first three or four years produced nothing but some of the finest half-hours of comedy ever made for television. Known to some as "a show about nothing," with unlikable characters, *Seinfeld* was the likable performances of the actors—particularly—the charismatic and charming lead and his self-deprecating smile—that outshined the unlikable antics of Jerry, George, Kramer, and Elaine.

There was Jerry's smirky appeal when he was confronted by the *Dragnet*-like librarian named Lt. Bookman (the Emmy-winning Philip Baker Hall) in search of a long-overdue "Tropic of Cancer" book in the episode "The Library." There was the Jerry who gave the rude rental car reservationist a deserved hard time in "The Alternate Side" yet still allowed the viewer to bond with him in this all-too-familiar position. "I think I know why we have reservations," the clerk said in her defense after giving away Jerry's car. "I don't think you do," he replied as the voice of Everyguy, with a witty tone, a twinkle in his eye, and sharpness (not the overt sarcasm that later took over his form).

In the early years of the series, the actors performed in character, in an otherwise staged but realistic situation. They'd speak the lines we all dreamed of saying to ill-mannered workers at any front desk; and they did so with style, not with the mean-spiritedness that later overwhelmed the characters—and their performers. But again, when *Seinfeld* was good, it was great—and instructive.

In its formative years, the series was commended by various interest groups for its frank perspective on life—a viewpoint they believed contributed to the mainstream acceptance of their particular religion, creed, philosophical belief, or race in a psychologically-nutritious, self-deprecating, almost—*almost*—humble manner.

What would the hipsters of the self-effacing 1990s have done if not for the chronicles of Jerry, the real-life word-wit, and his erratic band of pals? More than likely, they would have been substantially less hip and self-effacing, and less diverse. *Seinfeld* rang in a freshly cool decade of television parody with class and distinction, initiating a new "Golden Era" of television. It detached itself from the rules of typical TV humor, subtracted the situation from situation comedy, and brought to the living room viewer an extraordinary sense of humor, truth, and dare. Never a contrived plot to establish in its early years, never a syrupy moral lesson in a tidy 30 minutes, the first few years of *Seinfeld* helped us laugh through subway muggings, missing rent-a-car reservations, rude waiters, bad dates, and just plain bad luck. It refused to ignore touchy subjects, and instead, hit them straight on.

The series was the first comedy to address and hire the handicapped and various minorities in honest roles, minus the usual preachy storylines. It chose not to mangle social issues or ills but to inject a well-needed breath of fresh laugh into topics such as dwarfism, death, mental illness, contraception, and personal hygiene. In each instance, intolerance and ignorance stuck out like sore thumbs.

In one episode, "The Lip Reader," Jerry befriended a woman who was deaf, a character played by the Oscar-winning actress Marlee Matlin (*Children of a Lesser God*, 1986), who is deaf. Upon their first meeting, he thought she was continually ignoring him. He became frustrated and finally belted out, "What are you? Deaf?" To which she replied, "Bingo!" with forthright, unaffected confidence. In the end, it was Jerry who was shown to be impaired—with a severe lack of sensitivity (a personality quirk for which each regular cast member of *Seinfeld* was tastefully, if frequently, taken to task—in the early years of the show). There was the time George ludicrously decided, on impulse alone, that he didn't have enough chums of African-American lineage. But it was hard not to notice his imbecility.

In its infancy, *Seinfeld* was accused of being "too Jewish" or lacking a regular minority character (even after it becomes clear that George is of Italian-American descent). But whatever it might have lacked in a regular capacity, the show made up for in cultural guest-appearances and social-issue-oriented plots; and it allowed us to recognize and amend our imperfections; to rise above them with sophistication, style, and sincere, non-debasing merriment.

With its unequaled comic home delivery, *Seinfeld* like Norman Cousins expressed with the Marx Brothers films, prescribes a perspicuous memorandum: Laughter *is* the best medicine. With its satiric dose of reality, *Seinfeld* appropriately needled us, refused to insult our viewer intelligence, permitted us to accentuate the positive, ignore our differences, to concentrate on what makes us the same (we all like to laugh, right?), and gave diversity and pretty much every other social issue or concern on television a healthy shot in the funny bone.

Joining *Seinfeld* and *Friends* for more than a few Thursday nights was *Frasier* (NBC, 1993–2004), a spin-off of *Cheers* that bested its parentage in quality, execution, and staying power.

In the comparative history of classic TV, *Frasier* is party, also, to a group of shows that were radio-oriented in some way, whereas many TV shows first began on radio (*Burns and Allen, Perry Mason, Gunsmoke, Ozzie and Harriet,* and *Father Knows Best)*. Other programs, in addition to *Frasier*, were actually premised in the world of radio, including *Good Morning, World* (CBS, 1967–1968), *WKRP in Cincinnati* (CBS, 1978–1982), and *NewsRadio* (NBC, 1995–1999).

The Jack Benny Show (CBS/NBC, 1950–1964) was unique to the radio-TV crossover. In the radio edition of the series, he played himself with plots that dealt with the trials and tribulations of producing a weekly radio show. On the TV version, he played himself again, but this time the stories centered around the trials and tribulations of putting on a weekly television program.

Good Morning, World was a noble attempt from series creator Carl Reiner upon completing *The Dick Van Dyke Show* which it emulated in a few ways. Whereas the latter was based around a television variety show (hosted by Reiner as the egotistical Alan Brady), the former featured newcomer Joby Baker and the always energetic Ronnie Schell as "Lewis and Clarke," two early morning DJs at a small radio station in

L.A. owned by the obnoxious Roland B. Hutton, Jr. (played by the ever-capable Billy De Wolfe). Schell's Lewis was the freewheeling bachelor, and Baker's Clarke was the Rob Petrie-type married to Linda, his own Laura Petrie waiting for him at home. A pre-*Laugh-In* Goldie Hawn offered standout support as Sandy, the next-door neighbor reminiscent of Ann Morgan Guilbert's Millie Helper from the *Van Dyke* series.

World had a winning shot at the gold cup of quality, but alas, its ratings told a different story. In addition to various personal health challenges of cast member Julie Parrish, the series also faced other struggles, from a creative standpoint. As such, *Good Morning, World* lasted only one season.

WKRP in Cincinnati, on the other hand, had better luck. It also was connected to the Van Dyke sitcom in a way: It was produced by MTM, the production company headed by Mary Tyler Moore, who played Laura Petrie. Set at a struggling fictional radio station in Cincinnati, Ohio, *WKRP* was based upon show creator Hugh Wilson's experiences working in advertising sales at Top 40 radio station WQXI-AM in Atlanta. Several of the characters and even some of the episodes (such as the first season segment, "Turkeys Away") were drawn from real people and events at WQXI. The cast included Gary Sandy, Howard Hesseman, Tim Reid, Jan Smithers, Richard Sanders, and Frank Bonner, and Gordon Jump (the Maytag repairman in TV commercials), and Loni Anderson, who rode the pin-up TV star parade blazed by Farrah Fawcett and Suzanne Somers. Hughes and Reid would later partner on the critically-acclaimed but short-lived *Frank's Place* (CBS, 1987–1988), which was party to the dramedy revolution of the '80s.

Before that show aired, *WKRP* picked up the slack with a style that was all its own. As TV historians Tim Brooks and Earle Marsh have pointed out, like most MTM productions, *WKRP's* humor stemmed more from "running gags based on the known predilections and quirks of each character, rather than from outlandish plots or racy situations since the show has a realistic setting."

The series won a Humanitas Prize and received 10 Emmy Award nominations, including three for Outstanding Comedy Series. Andy Ackerman, who later produced and directed the later seasons of *Seinfeld*, won an Emmy Award for Videotape Editing in *WKRP's* third season.

Both bright and glib *NewsRadio* was created by executive producer Paul Simms, featured an optimum cast led by Phil Hartman, Dave Foley, and Andy Dick and a musical theme tune composed by musical vet Mike Post (who composed openings for shows like *The Rockford Files* and *Magnum, P.I.*, as well as MTM's *L.A. Law* and *Hill Street Blues*). *NewsRadio* was a combination of quirky characters and plots that many times reflected real-life events happening across popular culture. But as the Brooks and Marsh team once noted, the show's third and fourth season finales "took the absurdity to the extreme, setting the characters in outer space and aboard the Titanic."

The show sunk in the ratings and never saw a fifth season.

Frasier, for many, not only registers as the best of the radio-geared sitcoms but the last great sitcom ever to be produced. As with Norman Lear's hit comedies from the '70s, *All in the Family* and *Maude*, *Frasier*, originally airing on NBC from 1993 to 2004, was presented as short 30-minute plays. The stories were concise; the characterizations, rich; the dialogue, dense; the acting, staging and sets, impeccable. As Dr. Frasier Crane, Kelsey Grammer delivered a multi-Emmy-winning performance for twenty consecutive years, first on *Cheers* and then on the spin-off. Grammer's Crane, the psychiatrist with issues of his own, became the first comedic character to be portrayed by one actor over a continuous two-decade span, if on two different series. (James Arness and Milburn Stone portrayed their TV alter egos, Marshal Matt Dillon and Doc Adams, for twenty straight years on *Gunsmoke*, a dramatic show; Amanda Blake left her role as Miss Kitty in the 19th year).

Though Bob Newhart's Bob Hartley was a psychologist and not a psychiatrist, *Frasier* was a latter-day *Bob Newhart Show*. Both shows displayed a generous number of colorful characters with emotional and psychological eccentricities, which Frasier displayed in full-throttle. David Hyde Pierce was Dr. Niles Crane, Frasier's even more neurotic brother who shared his profession; John Mahoney played their father, Martin Crane, an ex-cop who was wounded on the job; Jane Leeves was Daphne Moon, Martin's physical therapist (whom Niles secretly adored for years then finally married); Peri Gilpin played Roz Doyle, Frasier's radio talk show producer and confidante; and Moose was Eddie, Martin's beloved dog (a Jack Russell terrier who died two years after *Frasier* ended its original run, though Eddie/Moose did not appear in the show's last season).

The result? *Frasier* helped open the mainstream acceptance of therapy for everyday life, while Grammer found himself responding in a life-affirming manner off-screen by playing Dr. Crane. In January 1994, mid-season of *Frasier's* first year on the air, the actor gave an interview to *USA Weekend* magazine. "I think of [the Frasier character] as my alter ego," he said. "He's a part of me that I've really never had a chance to express. I'm not overly fastidious...I'm an old surfer dude...So I would explore all those feelings that I wouldn't usually have sitting down listening to an opera [like the *Frasier* show] rather than listening to rock and roll."

"The idea of therapy isn't as foreign to the world as it once was," he continued, explaining how he recently dined with a real-life psychiatrist and director James Burrows, who had helmed several episodes of *Frasier* (as well as *Cheers*, which he also co-created). Grammer recalled how Burrows asked the psychiatrist if he felt the character of Frasier had made a positive impact on the psychiatric profession. The psychiatrist believed that it did because he felt both the character and the show allowed those in his line of work an opportunity to take themselves less seriously. Grammer then referenced "a wonderful line written by W.H. Auden on the death of Sigmund Freud," the father of modern psychiatry: "Here is another one of those people who was trying to do the world some good." "We're all doing that," Grammer concluded. "That's what I'm trying to do. If I die and somebody says, 'He tried to do the world some good'...I'll be happy."

Fortunately, Grammer is still with us, and his TV persona Dr. Frasier Crane will always be around as long as there is a television screen of some sort. So, assuredly, happiness will ensue at least on some level forever.

Joining later classics like *Frasier* is *The King of Queens*, which initially aired on CBS from 1998 to 2007. Stand-up comedian Kevin James was cast as Doug Heffernan, an everyman blue-collar-working character from *Queens* in the vein of Jackie Gleason's Ralph Kramden from *The Honeymooners* (CBS, which was set in Brooklyn). They even had very similar jobs, if somewhat different kinds of wives: Kramden drove a city bus, and Doug navigated a mail/packing service delivery truck for a UPS/FedEx-like company. Gleason's *Honeymooner* love-life partner was Alice, a "stay-at-home-engineer," originally played by Audrey Meadows (and in later incarnations by Sheila MacRae). James' TV wife was a career woman named Carrie Heffernan portrayed by the dynamic Leah Remini.

Doug and Carrie became TV's new generation couple while continuing the legacy established by Ralph and Alice. Like Ralph, Doug had specific waistline issues. At the same time, both characters proved their "inner" appeal could outweigh their physical appearance, becoming attractive to women who, on average, are usually drawn to more machismo types. That was the case even more so with regard to Carrie. While Alice on *The Honeymooners* was as strong-willed and strong-minded as Carrie, the latter had an independent edge that had developed on TV—and in real life—since the days of *The Honeymooners*.

Carrie's interest, devotion, and true love for Doug was refreshing. By the *King of Queens'* debut, television shows, comedy, and drama were littered with too-perfect-looking characters, which romanticized the notion that only traditionally handsome men or beautiful women fell in love. *Queens* could have easily gone the typical TV route, making both leads perfect-looking or at least equal in size, as was the case when Roseanne Barr and John Goodman played man-and-wife on ABC's *Roseanne*, from the late '80s and early '90s, or as with CBS's very contemporary new comedy *Mike & Molly*.

Queens was far from trite. James was brilliant as Doug, a mishmash performance of modern-mayhem Gleason and jazzy comic timing, and a "man in trouble" sensibility (which is at the heart of all true comedy). Beside him was the smart and sassy Remini, who whipped off one-liners faster than Estelle Getty on *The Golden Girls*. How could a relatively-upscale woman like Carrie fall for a regular guy like Doug? For the same reason that a beautiful witch like Samantha fell for a mere mortal like Darrin on *Bewitched*. It was true love, mixed in with workable chemistry between the two leads, their combined likability, and funny scripts. In November 2004, at the onset of *King's* seventh season, Sid Smith of *The Chicago Tribune* observed, "Comedian Kevin James as stalwart delivery driver Doug is well-matched by the willful moxie of Leah Remini as wife Carrie…angst here is sharp but never too discomforting. [In the sixth season], for instance, the couple dealt with the difficulties of living on one income, but the humor remains light, goofy, and giddily idiotic."

Smith then compared *Queens* to what he viewed as the similar blue-collar show, *Everybody Loves Raymond*, on which James made appearances as a Doug-like character. That series, he said, "is really more about its daffy menagerie of characters than the woes of a particular economic stratum…James and Remini are so married to their roles…that they breeze through" their performances with "solid instincts, easy believability, and the familiarity of next-door neighbors."

Joining the two *King* leads in supporting roles were Doug's pals: Victor Williams as Deacon Palmer, Patton Oswalt as Spence Olchin, and Gary Valentine (James' real-life brother) as cousin Danny Heffernan. Periodic appearances were made by former talk-show queen Ricki Lake as Doug's sister Stephanie, and guest stars like Lou Ferrigno, formerly of TV's '70s hit hero show, *The Incredible Hulk*. Playing a heightened version of himself, Ferrigno displayed his comedic muscles which proved equal to his beefcake stature, while other regular stellar support was delivered by Nicole Sullivan as Holly Shumpert, who Doug and Carrie hired as dog-sitter for her father, Arthur Spooner, played with stellar annoyance by Jerry Stiller.

Stiller, the real-life father to actor Ben Stiller, had previously made his sitcom-dad mark late in life as Mr. Costanza, father to Jason Alexander's George on *Seinfeld*. Decades prior, Jerry Stiller performed with his wife, Ann Meara (Ben's mother), their popular live comedy act, which led to several TV guest spots throughout the '60s and '70s, and later, Meara's semi-regular appearances on *King* alongside her husband.

Stiller as Arthur Spooner, in particular, was an especially appealing aspect of the *King of Queens*, as his involvement in Doug and Carrie's lives was realistically presented the component characters of the sandwich generation. Doug wasn't too crazy about the idea, but Carrie invited her father, a senior citizen on a fixed income, to come to live with them. Many viewers identified with the situation as people started living longer, and the senior population began to increase. Senior apartments and community centers across the country were expanding their social functions to include and/or reflect many of the activities that Arthur enjoyed on-screen (bingo, holiday dances, day trips, etc.).

Chapter 18

The cast of *Murder, She Wrote* (from left): Ron Masak, Angela Lansbury, Louis Herthum, and William Windom
[Credit: Courtesy of Louis Herthum]

Prior to the more trendsetting mature adventures, the senior set was represented on television with other comedies like *December Bride* (CBS, 1954–1961) and *Hazel* (NBC/CBS, 1961–1966), as well as with mysteries, dramas, lawyer, doctor and detective shows, including *The Snoop Sisters* (NBC, 1973–1974), *Matlock* (NBC, 1986–1995), *Diagnosis: Murder* (CBS, 1993–2001), and *Barnaby Jones* (CBS, 1973–1980), which featured former *Beverly Hillbillies* star Buddy Ebsen as a former private eye who returns from retirement to avenge his son's murder. His secretary, Betty Jones, also his daughter-in-law, was played by Lee Meriwether, a former Miss America who appeared in *The Time Tunnel* (ABC, 1966–1967), and in the feature film edition of *Batman* (ABC, 1966–1969), playing Catwoman (portrayed on the series by Julie Newmar and Eartha Kitt).

Writer Larry Brody worked on Ebsen's show and, as he recalled, "Our nickname in the office for *Barnaby Jones* was 'Foxy Grandpa.' Grandpa, a.k.a. Buddy Ebsen, was a natural presence onscreen. It was far from the most ambitious of TV series, but a hell of a lot of fun. And our boss, the legendary Quinn Martin, always had our back."

Martin was the consummate professional who was dedicated to a quality product, which meant holding in high regard the cast and crew of each of his productions. Distinguished actor Peter Mark Richman, who has made over one hundred television appearances since the medium's golden and subsequent classic eras, on everything from *Playhouse 90* to *Dynasty*, recalled working for Martin on several of his shows, including Barnaby Jones, as well as *Cannon*, *The Streets of San Francisco*, and the 1970 TV-movie, *The House on Greenapple Road*, in which he co-starred with Janet Leigh. "I was, thankfully, one of the actors on his list that that performed on his shows. I did one of the first shows he produced. It was an episode with Margaret O'Brien and me. He just liked my work. All of his shows were extremely popular. He had the formula for success."

And *Barnaby Jones* was party to that success. Martin treated that show and leading man, Ebsen, with kid gloves, even when others connected with the show took the gloves off and came out fighting. Ebsen explained it in his autobiography, *The Other Side of Oz* (Donovan Publishing, 1993):

Come 1971, two developments significantly changed the course of his career. One hour of CBS programming was canceled, and the network needed to fill that space. Around the same time, Ebsen was hired as a guest star on another Quinn Martin crime-drama *Cannon* (CBS, 1971–1976), which starred William Conrad.

One day, Ebsen's agent, Jimmy McHugh, visited the set of the 1972 TV-movie, *Terror at 39,000 Feet*, which featured his client among the cast. McHugh pulled Ebsen aside, told him that Fred Silverman, then head of CBS programming, wanted to cast the actor in a series lead, instead of just a guest on *Cannon*. McHugh said something to the effect of, "Silverman wants thirteen episodes—now!"

The initial *Cannon* segment had Barnaby emerging from retirement to avenge his son's murder with Cannon's assistance. From there, Jones would commence a new career as a private detective. As Ebsen recalled, this first take on the *Cannon* show was "structured as a possible spin-off, but it was a spin-off before exposure. A bold gamble. It was one more private-eye story in a saturated market." Even the episode's director, Walter Grauman, one of Martin's favorite directors since *The Untouchables* days, had his doubts if the audience would "buy" into the idea. "I don't know," Grauman told Ebsen, "[*Barnaby Jones*] has…every cliché, every gimmick that's ever been used on any other [private eye] show. There's nothing new in it. I don't know why anyone would want to watch it. Except for one thing…People like you."

TV viewers not only liked Ebsen and "bought" him as *Barnaby*, but also they loved him in the role. The premiere episode clobbered in the ratings the TV debut of *Lawrence of Arabia*, David Lean's epic feature film from 1962, and the show went on to become a massive hit—even as critics from the press and within the network itself conveyed their reservations. As Ebsen explained in his book, CBS executive Fred Silverman invited him for a drink during an affiliates' meeting at the Beverly Hills Hotel at the start of the show's third year. Silverman congratulated Ebsen on what he felt was the surprising success of the series, and then, fixing him a drink "with a meaningful stare," the CBS suit raised his glass and said, "Enjoy this year."

In other words, Silverman thought *Barnaby's* third year would be the show's last. But his words belayed the truth of what actually transpired: Ebsen not only went on to "enjoy a third year," but "a fourth, and a fifth and a sixth and seventh and even an eighth," and on into the residuals he received from syndicated reruns.

Barnaby Jones became the first hit drama and action-adventure series to feature a senior citizen. *Marcus Welby, M.D.* (ABC, 1969–1976) was about a senior physician, and *Owen Marshall, Counselor at Law* (ABC, 1971–1974) was about a senior attorney, but *Barnaby Jones* was TV's first older good cop! What's more, he was an older good cop with family values: he didn't even drink alcohol—but rather, milk. "It wasn't as though [*Barnaby*] disapproved of people who drink alcohol," said Ebsen, "it was just that he liked milk. It became his trademark."

One year, on hiatus from filming, Ebsen went sailing off the West Coast of Florida, visited a small restaurant in Pensacola, and was approached by a young waitress with a big smile who automatically brought him a glass of milk. "It was a win-win situation," Ebsen recalled. "She enjoyed the gag. I enjoyed the milk—plus the recognition."

In January 1973, when *Barnaby Jones* ignited the second part of at least his television career, the comedic senior television community was represented by Lucille Ball and Gale Gordon on *Here's Lucy*, which was in the midst of its fifth season on CBS. A reworking of Ball's previous sitcom, *The Lucy Show* (CBS, 1962–1968), *Here's Lucy* allowed the renowned red-head more air-time with her long-time sidekick Gordon (also transplanted from *The Lucy Show*).

For over twenty years, cinema, television, and *Lucy* historian Rob Ray hosted the Long Beach Film Forum in Long Beach, California, a weekly event that catered mostly to that area's senior community. Ball and Gordon worked well together for several reasons. "They had a long history together," Ray said. "They trusted one another's instincts and their own comedy styles complemented the others'. They first worked together on radio in the late 1930s on *The Wonder Show*, starring Jack Haley. Afterward, Gale went on to become one of the most sought-after radio performers throughout the 1940s, usually playing pompous blowhards and authority figures on such popular shows as *Fibber McGee and Molly* and its spinoff, *The Great Gildersleeve*."

The producers of Ball's radio show, *My Favorite Husband*, were seeking to cast the role of Mr. Atterbury, her husband's boss and Gordon was a natural choice. "Lucy played Liz Cooper, the scatterbrained wife of banker George Cooper," Ray said. "With Bea Benaderet playing Gale's wife, Iris, and Richard Denning playing Lucy's husband, George, the foursome gradually developed the same chemistry that later endeared audiences to the Lucy and Ricky Ricardo [Ball and her real-life husband Desi Arnaz], and Fred and Ethel Mertz [William Frawley and Vivian Vance] and on TV's *I Love Lucy*." When *I Love Lucy* was in development, Gordon was Ball's first choice to play Fred Mertz, "but he wasn't available. However, Gale did make two guest appearances that first year playing Ricky's boss, Mr. Littlefield, a role clearly modeled after Mr. Atterbury."

"Lucy loved working with Gale and trusted his instincts," Ray continued. "When she returned to the situation comedy format in the 1960s after divorcing Desi Arnaz, she immediately requested Gale for the role of pompous banker, Theodore J. Mooney." But once more, Gordon wasn't available. "He had been quickly cast as Mr. Wilson on *Dennis the Menace* (CBS, 1959–1963) following the unexpected death of Joseph Kearns. However, when he suddenly became available the following season, she grabbed him and he stayed with her for the remainder of her comedy career. Their comedy styles complemented one another. Lucy needed a strong male authority figure to play off of, someone who could be the foil of many of her outlandish schemes and could react accordingly. And Gale was the one of the best reactive actors in the business, a master of the slow burn (a facial expression of exasperation performed very slowly and deliberately) and the delayed take (where the character waits a beat or two or three before reacting strongly). Lucy, as an actor, could anticipate how Gale would react and feed into that anticipation to great comedy effect."

In the midst of it all, "audiences sensed that the two, though usually adversaries onscreen, had a great fondness for one another off-screen. They felt the comedy bond between the two and relished it."

That became the case when Ball and Gordon re-bonded on her short-lived return to weekly comedy in *Life with Lucy*, which aired on ABC September to November in 1986. This final series of Ball's was edged on by the success of her highly-rated TV-movie, *Stone Pillow* (CBS, 1985, a dramatic role, in which she played a homeless woman). It was attacked by the critics for being "too old-fashioned," but had it been given a chance, *Life with Lucy*, like any new series with potential (and with Ball and Gordon as its co-stars, this show definitely had potential), it would have found its voice and rhythm. But ABC, after giving Ball the farm, abandoned her during the drought.

None of that detracted from the fact that she and Gordon, as superior senior talents, gave their all on *Life with Lucy*, *Here's Lucy*, *The Lucy Show*, or any other time they performed with one another. "After working together, off and on, for nearly fifty years," Ray said, "it's not surprising that these two became a much-beloved comedy team. Lucy was perhaps unique in that she was partnered to great success with three people throughout her illustrious television career: Desi Arnaz, Vivian Vance, and Gale Gordon."

With regard to *Life with Lucy* in particular, had the show debuted a few years later, around the fall of 1989, it may have had a better chance at survival. By that time, the baby-booming generation who grew up with *The Lucy Show*, *Here's Lucy*, and the classic reruns of *I Love Lucy*, had become the primary consumer. Networks like super-station TBS and Nick at Nite (the evening edition of Nickelodeon) were frequently airing reruns of many classic TV shows, while viewers were embracing nostalgia like never before. As *Life with Lucy* continued, even with a brief run, it was becoming more an ensemble show; performers like Audrey Meadows (*The Honeymooners*) were added to the cast (as Ball's sister). Such a development allowed for less slapstick comedy, which was productive on several levels. First, it was unsafe for senior actors (even professionals like Ball and Gordon) to perform slapstick, and second, a larger repertoire of actors added a sense of contemporary flair—as was presented on shows like *The Golden Girls*, which NBC originally aired from 1985 to 1993.

Producers of *The Golden Girls*, which not only featured senior actors but progressive plots and storylines (which advocated for minority groups, and various charitable and social causes) had considered adding Ball to the cast, alongside Bea Arthur, Rue McClanahan, Betty White, and Estelle Getty. While such a development never transpired, it never hindered the success of the show, which was an instant success. As senior media analyst Ray observes, that popularity "took many in the industry by surprise because its focus was women over 'a certain age, precisely NOT the demographic eagerly sought out by advertisers" [everyone but McClanahan was over sixty]. But it was a target audience that had long been neglected by television and when the creative talents had focused on senior citizens in the past (in everything from *December Bride* to *Marcus Welby, M.D.*) they made sure to surround the older folks with young people for contrast."

"*The Golden Girls* may have been the first show in which the entire cast of regulars was over fifty," Ray added. "There was no pandering to the youth market. And audiences, young and old, were enchanted and charmed by the years (and years) of professional talent and experience on display. Seniors could relate, middle-aged folks were offered hope that their own forthcoming golden years could be invigorating, and younger viewers weren't turned off because the characters were instantly relatable to all ages. Dorothy [Arthur] was the ringleader of the foursome, the sane voice of wisdom amid the wackiness of the others. Rose [White] was the naïve one who exuded innocence and unconditional love for all. Blanche [McClanahan] was a borderline nymphomaniac but played for laughs. And Sophia [Getty], the oldest, was the outspoken sage who had no internal editor [due to a stroke]. These were all folks we knew in our own lives, regardless of age."

"In short," Ray concluded, "the show did not aim for any particular demographic and, as a result, it appealed to virtually all. Apparently, the lessons that the success of *The Golden Girls* gave the television industry need to be re-taught to each generation. For the Hollywood of today should once again take note and learn."

During and after its original run on NBC, *The Golden Girls* became so popular, it inspired two spin-offs: *The Golden Palace* (CBS, 1992–1993) and *Empty Nest* (NBC, 1988–1995). *Palace*, following the *Girls* cancellation (by way of Arthur's decision to end the series), was a continuation of the original show (minus Arthur's participation, and featuring Cheech Marin and future movie star Don Cheadle), while *Nest*, starring Richard Mulligan (late of ABC's 70s sitcom *Soap*, created by both *Goldens'* Susan Harris) aired on NBC during from three years before *Girls* began to two years following its demise. Television writer Arnie Kogen worked on several classics of the small screen, including *Empty Nest*, on which he now shares his insight:

"Richard Mulligan was an exceptional actor and, in this series, was a very positive role model. Mulligan portrayed Harry Weston, a widower, a caring pediatrician, and a dedicated father to his two nutsy twentysomething daughters, Barbara [Kristy McNichol] and Carol [Dinah Manoff]. The show was created by Susan Harris and was a very successful sitcom from the Witt-Thomas-Harris group [WTH]. But it wasn't the *most* successful. WTH also brought us *The Golden Girls*, one of the five best pilots I've ever read. *Golden Girls* was also created by Susan Harris. Here's the way it went down: Susan would write a brilliant pilot, follow up with a few incredible scripts to get the series rolling, and then move on (to collect royalties in the Larry David/Warren Buffett range). I think it was comedy writer David Lloyd who had the line about Susan. He said her credit should read: 'Show Written Created and Abandoned by Susan Harris.'"

One of Kogen's favorite *Nest* eggs was "The Mentor": "Harry (Richard Mulligan) has an idol and mentor who he reveres and respects. That veteran doctor is played by Danny Thomas. Turns out the doctor is 'losing it.' He's older now and can't perform the way he used to. Harry is torn about confronting his idol and telling him. This was Danny Thomas's last appearance on television. He was nominated for an Emmy for this episode."

Kogen compared both *Nest* and *Golden* to *Murder, She Wrote*, another long-running senior-oriented series, this one airing on CBS from 1983–1995, and starring only one leading lady: Angela Lansbury as the famous, fictional writer/mystery sleuth Jessica Fletcher: "*Empty Nest* was not a 'water-cooler show.' When America went to work the following morning, you didn't hear a lot of 'Hey, did you catch *Empty Nest* last night?' It was not a show with a lot of buzz, but it had a solid cast, strong writing staff, and entertained viewers for many seasons. I always had the feeling that *Empty Nest* was sort of in the shadow of *The Golden Girls*. Same network [NBC], same production company [Witt-Thomas-Harris]. But *Golden Girls* was a funnier show. *Empty Nest* was not particularly geared for seniors the way *Golden Girls* or *Murder* was. *Empty Nest* was more of a family show the way that *Father Knows Best* was 30 years earlier."

"I knew this much," he added with particular regard to *Murder, She Wrote*, "…If there was a murder committed in a small town with picturesque homes and picket fences and a beautiful seashore setting then Jessica Fletcher would be the one to solve that crime. If there was a brutal barroom stabbing in the South Bronx, I don't think I'd be calling her in. Sipowicz [Dennis Franz] of *NYPD Blue* [ABC, 1993–2005] would be my guy."

"All in all," Kogen said, "It's probably true that all three shows [*Golden, Empty, Murder*] contributed, each in their own way, to the positive self-image of seniors."

Before *Murder, She Wrote* was published on TV, sleuthing—in any medium—had largely been the domain of middle-aged, sexless men: Sherlock Holmes, Philo Vance, and Agatha Christie's Hercule Poirot. Finally, Dame Christie broke this mold with her elderly sleuth, Miss Marple, a literary role brought to the big screen in a series of films with the delightful Margaret Rutherford (and, in 1980's *The Mirror Crack'd from Side to Side*, with Lansbury).

The writing in *Murder, She Wrote* was expert, but the success of the series in no small measure is due to the charm of its leading lady. It should have come as no surprise that the British-born Lansbury achieved her greatest success as she approached the age of sixty, for, in her younger years, Hollywood really didn't know what to do with her, constantly casting her in roles the belied her actual youth. She garnered Oscar nominations for her first two roles while still in her teens, playing cockney tarts: a maid in 1944's *Gaslight* and a doomed music hall singer in 1945's *The Picture of Dorian Gray*. At 20, in 1946's *The Harvey Girls*, she played a cynical dance-hall hostess reminiscent of *Gunsmoke*'s Miss Kitty. At 22, she played a worldly newspaper magnate who tries to get her lover elected President of the United States in Frank Capra's *State of the Union*. And at 36, in a startling change of pace, she unforgettably played the monstrous mother of 33-year-old Laurence Harvey in *The Manchurian Candidate*. In between were innumerable supporting roles of middle-aged dowagers, seamstresses, and mothers.

True stardom eluded her until in her forties when she went to Broadway. Her turn as irrepressible Auntie Mame in Jerry Herman's musical of *Mame* finally brought her long-overdue notice. But Hollywood, ever-obsessed with youth, took no notice. Disney gave her the leading role as a middle-aged apprentice witch in 1971's *Bedknobs and Broomsticks* after Julie Andrews turned it down, but the film was not considered a success. The stages of London and New York beckoned once again with a revival of *Gypsy* and great acclaim in Sondheim's grizzly musical, *Sweeney Todd*.

Then arrived *Murder, She Wrote* at a time when she badly needed a career boost. Finally, she was the right age for the role. It was as if her entire career was pointing her toward Jessica Fletcher.

Seldom were star and role so perfectly mated. Jean Stapleton had ended her run as Edith Bunker by having the character die on *All in the Family*. Shortly after, CBS invited her to play Jessica Fletcher, but she rejected the offer. Lansbury brought a mature authority and maternal warmth that endeared her Jessica Fletcher to millions. It may have been the least taxing role in her career, but sometimes that's the way a career works out. Audiences often don't remember and usually don't cherish the challenging roles.

Media historian Rob Ray said, "Don't think that playing Jessica Fletcher was too easy. It's actually a difficult role to pull off—unless you have the unmistakable professionalism of an Angela Lansbury. Jessica Fletcher was genuine, kind, but no pushover, firm when she needed to be, but always warm and almost friendly even when fingering the killer. It's not easy to pull that off successfully, without falling into corn."

In the final analysis, it was the perfect melding of a true star with a role that fitted her like a glove. Like Raymond Burr and Perry Mason, James Arness and Matt Dillon, Elizabeth Montgomery and Samantha Stephens, Angela and Jessica were just meant to be.

PART 4
ENERGY FIELDS

"All life is sacred."
—Master Kan, *Kung Fu*
(Episode: "An For An Eye" – 2/25/1973)

David Carradine with Key Luke on *Kung Fu* [*Credit: Author's Collection*]

it along a little…' and 'My late husband, Ephraim Levi used to say that money, you should pardon the expression, is like manure. It isn't worth a thing unless it's spread around encouraging things to grow.'"

Such "fourth-wall-break" techniques then made it to television by way of George Burns who starred with his wife Gracie Allen on their benchmark *Burns and Allen Show*, which began in Vaudeville and then radio before TV. "Burns constantly commented on the action and sometimes even turned on the television set and invited us to join him to see what schemes the other characters were secretly devising elsewhere," Ray said.

Twenty years later, *The Jimmy Stewart Show* (NBC, 1970–1971) utilized a similar and confusing gimmick. Stewart introduced each episode as Jimmy Stewart, talking directly into the camera—from the actual set of the series; the credits would roll, and then the first fabricated scene would begin, and Stewart as the character named Professor James K. Howard would offer a second introduction. "Too many intros were provided by too many people, however true and false they'd be," said Ray.

The "Strange" technique was at least more successfully and cleverly presented in the '80s on ABC's mystery-detective series, *Moonlighting*, when the characters David Addison and Maddie Hayes, played by Bruce Willis and Cybill Shepherd consistently winked and mused with the audience, many times even bringing the home viewer in on their conversations. By this time, TV watchers were a hipper crowd, and other shows, of every genre, beyond mystery tales, started following the template. It became so common that the general viewing audience bought into the concept but rare enough so that the notion was still novel and cute.

The 1976 TV edition of *Ellery Queen* may have had a good idea that was simply not well executed, ahead of its time, or both, while fellow mystery shows of that time better utilized other innovative concepts, if not in such a self-conscious manner: namely, *McMillan & Wife*, which debuted on NBC in 1971.

Sharing the *NBC Sunday Night Mystery* spot with monthly installments of Levinson/Link's *Columbo* and Dennis Weaver as *McCloud* among other mystery two-hour movie-series, *McMillan & Wife* featured former movie star Rock Hudson, then 46, as Stuart "Mac" McMillan, a lawyer turned police commissioner in San Francisco. Susan Saint James, also popular on the big screen (in films like 1968's *The Trouble with Angels*) played Sally, Mac's much younger spouse by at least by twenty years. It was an unusual romantic pairing for TV, as Mac could have easily been mistaken as father to Sally who, if not young enough to actually be his daughter, was nearly aged so. So, while such older-men/younger women and older women/younger men scenarios are pervasive in today's world (on and off the big and small screens), having such a twosome on TV in the early '70s was ground-breaking.

Mac and Sally's age difference became a nonissue.

The chemistry and delightful dialogue between Hudson and Saint James were spot-on. Not every fortysomething man looked like Rock Hudson, and not every twentysomething female looked like Saint James, but they gelled on screen, and the show worked. Their characters knew each other intimately, could read each other's thoughts, and see through each other's schemes as they tried to stay one step ahead of whatever killer was on the loose this time. Joining them in the witty banter was John Schuck's bemused Sgt. Enright as the audience's surrogate and as more gentle comedy relief, and the nosy housekeeper, Mildred, played by the indefatigable Nancy Walker (who frequently switched networks while also playing Rhoda's mother for CBS on *The Mary Tyler Moore Show*).

Each episode contained a few violent scenes but not like today's crime-and-mystery dramas, which frequently focus on gore and horrific images. Instead, *McMillan & Wife* concentrated on character interplay and just plain fun. Characters would be murdered, and mysteries would be created, but the main plot was almost secondary to the characterization and performances by Hudson, Saint James, Schuck, and Walker. Once more, Rob Ray offered his keen insight:

"In 1970, the year before *McMillan & Wife* made its debut, the film industry was going through one of the most tumultuous changes in its history. Youth and relevance were in and middle-aged stars who had ruled the box office throughout the 1950s and early '60s were given notice that the times were changing. Hudson, along with so many of his contemporaries, sensed that it was time to follow his fan-base, which was staying home and watching television. On the big screen, the name Rock Hudson was becoming passé, a relic of fifties Westerns and some old Doris Day comedies. But to the world of TV, the name Rock Hudson still meant movie star! The time had come to make the move. And Hudson found the perfect property to do so with *McMillan & Wife*.

"The story of a San Francisco police chief who solves murders himself rather than rely on his underlings and who had a young, sexy wife with an insatiable urge to help him [and, like *Perry Mason* and *Ellery Queen*] had its genesis in novels, namely in Dashiell Hammett's classic sleuthing couple, Nick and Nora Charles. In Hammett's initial work, *The Thin Man*, and in a series of six films produced by MGM from 1934 until 1948, Nick and Nora worked as a team, a sometimes reluctant one on Nick's part. William Powell and Myrna Loy achieved cinematic immortality in the roles. A TV adaptation in the fifties with Peter Lawford and Phyllis Kirk didn't click, proving that properties like this have to have that perfect chemistry. Rock Hudson and Susan Saint James had it."

Mac and Sally were not far removed from being newlyweds, and like Nick and Nora, they enjoyed a healthy sex life, as their on-screen foreplay was evident throughout the series (and most productive in the fourth season, when Sally became pregnant—as did James; though once the actress delivered her baby in real life, Sally and Mac's child was never mentioned or seen again). They made sleuthing *fun*, almost as if it was sexual foreplay itself.

Mac and Sally's chemistry was so crucial to the show's success that, when it was altered, in the sixth and final season (1976–1977), *McMillan & Wife* fell apart…literally. Nancy Walker, for thirty years playing comedy relief on stage, screen, and television, left after finally being granted her own series contract (with ABC, on which her two shows failed), while her housekeeping role in the Hudson/James series was replaced by a mugging Martha Raye as her sister. John Schuck's work brought him to the attention of casting agents, and he also left (if, like Walker, to do another failed ABC series, this one called *Holmes & YoYo*). But most importantly, Susan Saint James exited over a contract dispute, and Sally was killed off, along with the character's unseen newborn son. Audiences could not accept such a downer of a change, particularly as they had watched Sally carrying the couple's son to term throughout the preceding years. The ratings plummeted in the one last season version titled simply *McMillan*, in which Rock Hudson starred alone, proving that chemistry is sometimes everything.

While *Hart to Hart* ten years later filled the gap left by *McMillan & Wife*, and while NBC resurrected the *Perry Mason* series for a number of reunion movies, other mystery shows before and after filled in the blanks, such as *Diagnosis Murder*, *Mystery Woman*, and *The Hardy Boys/Nancy Drew Mysteries* (ABC, 1977–1979), the latter of which starred Parker Stevenson and Shaun Cassidy, step-brother of David (and son of Shirley Jones and Jack Cassidy), and Pamela Sue Martin, to be replaced by Janet Louise Johnson. (Sidenote: Martin later played the first Fallon on *Dynasty*, where she later replaced by Emma Samms of *General Hospital* fame.)

Writer and voiceover artist Roger Hyman, who grew up with Shaun, offered his thoughts on how the more popular *Hardy Boys* segments made a positive impact on young viewers, potentially inspiring them to do more reading of both the original "Hardy Boys" and "Nancy Drew" novels, as many such contemporary cross-media literary and TV and film adaptations do today:

"Both Shaun and Parker were clean-cut, stunning to look at, and demographically perfect for the show. They had no 'issues' that would speak otherwise. They were an aspirational pair that got teens glued to the TV. There was no talk of drugs or violence—just a real all-American family show. The books were hugely popular and this made sense on many levels to do. The stories portrayed on screen were paintby-numbers perfect, so it engaged the viewers to read. It's very much akin to the 'Harry Potter' series to pre-teens of today. My niece was reading the books at age 7 or 8 because she fell in love with the movies and characters. It was the same thing with *The Hardy Boys*. The imagery and involvement on the screen brings everything to life, and the result is wholeheartedly engaging."

Also, too, whereas *Murder, She Wrote* provided a "thinking hero" for the senior set of mystery story lovers, *The Hardy Boys/Nancy Drew Mysteries* did the same for the teen set. Or as Hyman said it, "anything positive that can bring print to life is a good thing. But it has to be done right, of course."

The Hardy Boys did get it right, even though Hyman believed it wasn't the show, "per se," that was popular, but rather a combination of factors. For example, it was the *showrunners* who contacted Cassidy's managers who convinced him to do the series "that made it into the hit it became," Hyman clarified. "At the time, Shaun was the biggest singing teen sensation and filled arenas worldwide with screaming teen girls. And this was a 'synergy' move to get him to branch out and see how much money could be made from his talents. Shaun could have hated acting and wanted out, although he did do many TV movies. Eventually, he gravitated to working behind the camera [as a producer of hit shows like *Picket Fences*, CBS, 1992–1996]."

Hardy Boys heartthrob Parker Stevenson offered his keen insight into the show's success, and how it increased and encouraged the readership of its young viewers many of whom began to devour the original novels—a development that might not have transpired had the show not made its way to ABC:

"*The Hardy Boys* had a successful 3-year run because it was FUN. Yes, there was a built-in audience because of the long publishing history of the original books but the TV series…had a light-hearted charm. [The TV series] benefited from the audience's interest in solving each episode's mystery, the phenomena of Shaun's successful musical career, and Universal Television/Pro Art's successful merchandising campaign that drove viewership back to the show and back to the original book series. ABC succeeded in turning a charmingly innocent American classic into a ratings success and in the process revitalized the publishing success of the original book series."

The ABC television editions of the original *Hardy Boys* and *Nancy Drew* mysteries were the last of their breed, filled with style and intrigue, a rarely fine execution for its time of a property based on an established work. *McMillan & Wife*, *Columbo*, and *Murder, She Wrote* may have fascinated more senior watchers a few years before and later, but *The Hardy Boys*, for one, granted younger viewers their first mainstream weekly TV mystery hit with a certain "Disney-esque" flair. An early edition of the series was even produced and broadcast during Walt Disney's *Mickey Mouse Club* from 1957 to 1959. The '70s ABC adaptation modernized the concept with flair, like all classic TV mystery shows, and unlike today's mystery (and horror) TV and film productions, managed to exclude overtly-violent images and vulgar dialogue.

Chapter 20

Mysteries, Westerns, variety shows, and family series were the rage in the early days of television. But other genres would follow suit including medical-based shows. *Ben Casey*, *Dr. Kildare*, and *Marcus Welby, M.D.* would make their rounds alongside attorneys like *Perry Mason* who made their case. A mystery-legal hybrid, in particular, *Mason* debuted on CBS in the fall of 1957 and exited its court proceedings by the fall of 1966.

Additional lawyer shows took their bow as *The Defenders* (CBS, 1961–1965), *Judd for the Defense* (ABC, 1967–1969), *Owen Marshall, Counselor at Law* (ABC, 1971–1974), *L.A. Law* (NBC, 1986–1994), *Law and Order* (NBC, 1990-Present), and *Boston Legal* (ABC, 2004–2008). But none would have the impact of the original *Mason* series that featured Raymond Burr as the discerning, serious but empathetic lead; Barbara Hale as Perry's trusted assistant Della Street; William Hopper (son of famed Hollywood gossip legend Hedda Hopper) as detective Paul Drake; and William Talman as Hamilton Burger, the flabbergasted district attorney whom Mason always clobbered in court. Also in the cast: Ray Collins, Wesley Lau, and Richard Anderson (Oscar Goldman from *The Six Million Dollar Man* and *The Bionic Woman*) as various law enforcement characters through the years.

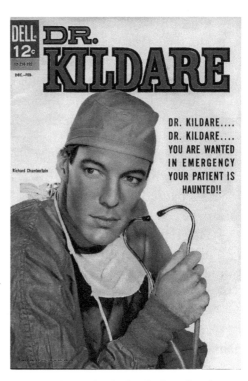

As *Dr. Kildare*, Richard Chamberlain played one of TV's top professionals *[Credit: Author's Collection]*

Mason was based on a series of best-selling mystery novels created by attorney Erle Stanley Gardner, which were adapted on CBS radio from 1943 to 1955, but with soap-opera elements. When the radio show transitioned into the Burr TV series, the soap-opera slant was shelved. But in 1956, two years before the TV series premiered, the original radio format was transplanted to the TV daytime serial, *The Edge of Night* (complete with the PM radio production staff and most of the cast, who were given new character names), where it remained until December 1984.

In the fall of 1973, seven years after CBS-TV canceled Burr's series, the network premiered *The New Perry Mason*, which featured an all-new cast: Monte Markham played Perry, Sharon Acker was Della Street, Albert Stratton was Paul Drake, Dane Clark was Lt. Tragg, and former B-movie star Harry

Guardino playing Hamilton Burger. This incarnation lasted only one season, while a little over ten years later, Burr and Hale reunited as their famous roles in the 1985 hit TV-movie *Perry Mason Returns* (this time for NBC), which also featured Hale's real-life son William Katt as Paul Drake, Jr. (by this time, both William Hopper and William Talman had passed away). The *Returns* film was so successful it led to an entire series of TV-movies that lasted even after Burr himself passed away.

Barbara Hale recalled how it all began:

"Erle Stanley Gardner and the show's publicity department started placing our photos of Della and Perry on the back covers of his books, which were filled with short stories that *Cosmopolitan Magazine* published for months before we started the show. So, we had a built-in audience before we ever made it to the air."

Hale was reluctant to do a television series. She was married with children and more interested in being a stay-at-home mom. But her friend, Gail Patrick—one of the show's producers—convinced her otherwise. "I didn't think the show would be a hit," Hale said, "but lo and behold—the viewers fell in love with it, and some nine years later, we were still cranking out episodes."

Two decades later, she was performing in even more episodes, via the reunion movie sequels, which aired ten years after Burr completed his second series (the original *Ironside*, NBC, 1967–1975). She was now not only reunited with Burr but, for the first time, found herself working with her son, William Katt—as Paul Drake, Jr., the latter of which, as she explained, happened quite by coincidence. "Dean Hargrove, the producer, told me they wanted to give the show a different spin…to reach a younger demographic. Our dear friends Billy Talman and Billy Hopper were now gone, so we needed someone to take their place. And one of those replacements would be Paul Drake's son which, ultimately, too… helped us connect with younger viewers."

Little did she know that Hargrove already had chosen her very own real-life offspring to play Drake, Jr. "So, who is the young man that you chose to play Paul's son?" she asked.

"A young blond kid," Hargrove responded. "He's been doing some show about a hero or something."

Hale paused and, in referring to ABC's then most recent new limited-run shows, asked, "Do you mean *The Greatest American Hero*?"

"Yes," Hargrove replied. "I've been trying to reach him, but I don't want to go through his agent."

"Just stop right there," Hale said, as Hargrove sat transfixed "…and let me tell you a story: I know this young man quite well."

Even more surprised, Hargrove wondered, "How?!"

"I changed his diapers," she replied.

Hargrove remained stunned. Although Hale's husband was actor Bill Williams, that was only his stage name. His real name was William Cameron Oliver Katt, which meant he was William Katt's father. "And with that," Hale said, "…we all went on to do the reunion movies. It was wonderful having Billy with us."

But then ABC wanted the young Katt back for more episodes of *The Greatest American Hero*. So, he decided to leave the *Mason* movies. At which point, Billy Moses, who Hale called "a very sweet actor," came aboard as Perry's new detective. "After that, my dear Raymond passed away," Hale said, "and we did three more movies. But it just wasn't the same without him." In the scripts, it was never mentioned that Perry died "or anything like that," Hale said. "It was just explained that he was on vacation," while the rest of the characters utilized his office and acquired other cases. "The ratings were still high," she said, "but of course we all missed Raymond. He was the heart and soul of the show."

In retrospect, it is still the original *Perry Mason* series that stands out. Written, directed, and performed with precision, the show remains gripping to this day. Perry never lost a case, except for once—later in the series, when that verdict was then reversed. The chemistry between the main four actors, Burr, Hale, Hopper, and Talman was solid. Over time, and especially in the show's later years, the audience came to observe and understand the respect between not only the characters on the show—but between the actors who played them.

Burr created a "family atmosphere" on the set, Hale said, and that transferred to the screen when the cameras began to roll. There was no gratuitous violence in the series. Instead, the series catered to the intellect. Burr's Mason was intelligent but compassionate—and always fair and honest. His objective for each case was justice and the truth—and not just based on technicalities. But on the heart—which is why it remains so popular today. A "classic," in every sense of the word, the show proved inspirational to many viewers, some of whom were inspired by Hale's performance as Della Street—one of TV's first single professional women. As Hale remembered, "I received so much fan mail from young ladies who were trying to decide what to do with their lives. This is when young women were just beginning to become more interested in their careers than finding husbands. It was when they started to think more about their vocations. And I cannot tell you the number of letters I received that said things like, 'We're so pleased with your show…' and how it inspired some women to become lawyers themselves"…or at least to work for one because, as Hale further revealed, "They were all in love with Raymond, and they wanted to study [law] in order to work for someone just like Perry Mason."

Exhibit A: In May of 2009, *The New York Times* profiled Sonia Sotomayor, the newest nominee to the U.S. Supreme Court, a 54-year-old federal appellate court judge who grew up in a housing project in the South Bronx, the oldest child of a couple from Puerto Rico who spoke no English. Winning a scholarship to Princeton University and graduating from Yale Law School, where she was editor of *The Law Review*, Sotomayor has bipartisan credentials. She was appointed to the federal district court by a Republican president, George H.W. Bush, and elevated to the appellate court by a Democratic president, then Bill Clinton, and, then too Sotomayor (the first Latina on the court), was then-President Barack Obama's selection for Supreme Court justice.

What proved most intriguing to *Times* reporter Johanna Neuman was how Sotomayor decided on her vocation: She grew up poor, suffered from the onset of childhood diabetes, was raised by a widowed mother, and spoke no English until after her father died when she was 9 years old. From there, Sotomayor drew her inspiration from reading "Nancy Drew" detective stories and watching *Perry Mason* on TV. It was one episode, in particular, that stood out: when prosecutor Hamilton Burger (Talman) was overruled by the judge. At that moment, Sotomayor decided that the judge was the most important person in the courtroom. As she told *The New York Times* in 1992, "I thought, 'What a wonderful occupation to have.' And I made the quantum leap: If that was the prosecutor's job, then the guy who made the decision to dismiss the case was the judge. That was what I was going to be."

With that said, next to attorneys, the most popular professional career choice presented on television takes places within the medical field.

We all know the commercial. "I'm not a doctor. I just play one on TV." That's been the case for many actors best known for portraying physicians on television's most prominent medical shows through the years—everything from *Dr. Kildare* and *Ben Casey* to *Marcus Welby, M.D.* to *ER* and *House*.

Kildare and *Casey* were the first TV doctors to make an impact on the home viewer, both premiering in the fall of 1961.

On NBC's *Kildare*, Richard Chamberlain portrayed the dashing (first name, James) young lead doctor who set hearts afire, on-screen and off. In his book, *Cult TV* John Javna called Kildare "every mother's dream and every girl's desire," as he fought nobly to "save human lives every week." By his side as a mentor: the much-older Dr. Leonard Gillespie, played by Raymond Massey. President John F. Kennedy was inaugurated in 1961 and, as Javna said, a new era of politics, and a fresh spirit of "optimism and idealism" was delivered to America, encouraging the country's youth to "get involved…make a difference" and to create life-changing interest groups and organizations like the Peace Corps.

Dr. Kildare was "the first bona fide TV hero of the '60s," Javna said, someone who represented the "best hopes" of this new generation. "Young, intelligent, committed, the evil he fought was disease. His weapons were a good education and a willingness to care about people. Teenagers loved him [more than 2 million watched him every week]. His popularity also reflected the growing esteem in which doctors were being held. America was turning to science for salvation, and doctors were the new gods."

The silver-tongued Kildare became so popular that Chamberlain received more fan mail than silver screen legend Clark Gable and three times as much as Vince Edwards and his character Dr. Ben *Casey*. Chamberlain also had a hit record with a lyric-based edition of the show's theme, while his likeness was spread across a *Kildare* comic book that sold more than 500,000 copies in six months. The show's adventures were also popular abroad, even behind the Iron Curtain, where the Polish Communist Party rescheduled its weekly meetings to Thursday from Wednesday when all eyes were glued to *Kildare*.

On ABC's *Ben Casey*, Vince Edwards played the straightforward, yet unconventional lead neurosurgeon at County General Hospital. Edwards was more rugged in appearance and less classically-handsome than Chamberlain but like Kildare, Casey had a mentor. Sam Jaffe played Dr. David Zorba, whose voiceover, "Man, woman, birth, death, infinity," opened every episode. "Casey wasn't just a doctor—he was a macho doctor," Javna said. "His shirt was always open, revealing a thick mat of chest hair. He didn't respect authority, and he didn't kowtow to anyone. The only man who could talk to him was the wise old grandfatherly Dr. Zorba."

Casey and *Kildare* aired almost exactly during the same period. *Casey* debuted a month after *Kildare* and was canceled 5 months earlier. Thirty-two million people watched *Casey* every week, and Edwards became as big a sex symbol as Chamberlain. Both inspired paraphernalia such as pins that said things like, "Doctor Kildare is A Doll" and "I've Got A Case on Ben Casey." There were competing board games such as "The *Ben Casey, M.D.* Game—The Drama of Life in A Big Metropolitan Hospital" and "*Dr. Kildare*: Medical Game for the Young." As with *Kildare*, the Casey theme song became a hit record, sung by Valjean (a pop artist of the day, and someone other than the show's star, as when Chamberlain recorded a rendition of *Kildare's* theme). The main difference is that Casey had a shirt named after him...a replica of that which he adorned on a weekly basis.

Javna, for one, doubted whether *Casey* would have found an audience, had not *Kildare* been along for the ride. "But you really can't separate them," he said. "They were always thought of by viewers as a single unit. Together, they were the most visible manifestation of an early '60s phenomenon—the emergence of doctors as media heroes."

A much different—and older—kind of TV doctor opened their practice a few seasons following the demise of the *Casey/Kildare* shows. Nine years after finishing his historic Emmy-winning run as Jim Anderson on *Father Knows Best* (the last two seasons of which aired during the Edwards/Chamberlin double-header), Robert Young returned to the small screen as the title character in another Emmy-winning performance in ABC's hit medical drama, *Marcus Welby, M.D.*, which aired from 1969–1976). Co-starring James Brolin as his young, motorcycle-driving associated Dr. Steve Kiley, and Elena Verdugo as their receptionist and trusted nurse Consuelo Lopez, Young's Welby became television's favorite doctor, the kind of physician that everyone wants to be treated by—just as viewers had formerly envisioned him to be everyone's ideal dad on *Father Knows Best*.

Like *The Bold Ones* on NBC (1969–1973) and, to a lesser extent, *Medical Center* on CBS (1969–1976), *Marcus Welby*, at times melodramatic, made every effort to be as realistic as possible in the presentation and portrayal of medical professionals, their treatment of and advice to patients (which ranged from young leukemia victims played by Barry Williams of *The Brady Bunch* to Lindsay Wagner who later became *The Bionic Woman*). To further ensure authenticity, the show's producers even went as far as to hire members of the American Academy of Family Physicians to serve as technical advisers (who reviewed every script for medical accuracy).

Whether *Welby* reflected reality or influenced it, the series reminded us all how truly rewarding a vocation the medical profession can be if, as with any career choice, conducted with respect and dignity for the highest good of all those concerned. As a physician who knew all his patients by name—and who actually made house calls—Young's Marcus Welby filled an increasingly rarefied niche in the medical field—on-screen, and off.

Beyond *Welby*, that niche was periodically filled, at least on TV, by various kindly and dedicated doctors and nurses over the years, in both the drama and comedy category; namely, *Trapper John, M.D.* This show was a semi-sequel to the 1972–1983 CBS show *M*A*S*H* which, due to its setting during the Korean War, was more a military-based series, than a medical show, if too, more a drama, than a comedy show. After exiting the role of the serious-minded oldest brother Adam Cartwright on *Bonanza* in 1965, Pernell Roberts went on to portray the now-more serious-minded Trapper John character once played by Wayne Rogers in the first few seasons of *M*A*S*H*, and originally portrayed by Elliott Gould in the 1970 feature film of the same name that spawned the series.

Co-starring with Roberts on *Trapper John, M.D.* was Gregory Harrison as Dr. George "Gonzo" Gates, a kind of free-spirited, hipper version of James Brolin's Dr. Kiley on *Welby*, and similar to the more unconventional Trapper persona from both the small- and big-screen editions of *M*A*S*H*. The show also featured Mary McCarty and Christopher Norris as loyal hospital nurses, and Charles Siebert as the stuffy Dr. Stanley Riverside II (a seemingly-semi-cross between the stilted characters played by Larry Linville and David Ogden Stiers on *M*A*S*H*).

Adding to the irony: after Rogers left *M*A*S*H* (to be replaced by Mike Farrell as a new character named B.J. Hunnicutt), he returned to CBS as yet another doctor—in *House Calls*, a throw-back 1979–1982 half-hour comedy based on the 1978 feature film of the same title starring Walter Matthau and Glenda Jackson. The TV *Calls* was filmed like a movie if with a by-then-unpopular laugh track (in place of what might have been a more successful studio audience format). *Calls* co-starred Lynn Redgrave (in Jackson's role) and a pre-*Cagney & Lacey* Sharon Gless (who had replaced a post-*M*A*S*H* Loretta Swit as Cagney once the *Cagney & Lacey* TV-movie pilot film went to series).

A little over two decades later, from 2004 to 2012 on FOX, another *House* moved into the neighborhood of doctor-based shows. Here, British actor Hugh Laurie played Dr. Gregory House, a relatively off-kilter, cynical medical genius of a curmudgeon who specializes in solving medical mysteries that mystify his peers. The *House* character was based on Sherlock Holmes, whose persona was inspired by real-life 19th Century Scottish doctor Joseph Bell who, like Dr. Gregory, utilized deductive reasoning as a diagnostic method.

Like Holmes has for centuries, *House* proved enriching for its followers, as had *Ben Casey*, *Dr. Kildare*, and *Marcus Welby, M.D.* But *House* went a few steps further in answer to a call. The show once influenced real-life doctors at a German clinic who were able to save the life of a 55-year-old man with a serious condition that confounded his physicians. For a year, the patient was challenged by a range of worsening symptoms. His heart started failing; his sight and hearing deteriorated; he suffered from acid reflux, swollen lymph nodes, and a baffling fever. The outlook was not good.

In 2012, the patient was referred to Marburg's Centre for Undiagnosed and Rare Diseases. In researching his medical history, the team found a past that was uneventful… apart from a double hip replacement. In focusing on this detail, they recalled a seventh-season segment of *House,* which addressed a similar situation. The real-life medical team began to suspect cobalt poisoning, a result of a suspected defective prosthetic hip implant. Scans and blood tests confirmed that suspicion and the patient soon had his metal prosthesis replaced by a ceramic one. "Shortly after the hip replacement, the patient's [blood] cobalt and chromium concentrations decreased and the patient stabilized and recovered slightly," the case report said.

By July of 2013, 14 months after the surgery, the patient's heart function improved to 40 percent, and his fever and acid reflex were nonexistent. With his hearing and vision returned only slightly, the patient had by then received a defibrillator to aid his damaged heart. "It was helpful for me that I was aware about the cobalt problems thanks to Dr. House," team leader Juergen Schaefer said at the time while noting other diagnostic tools were also brought into play. "All this demonstrates nicely that well-performed entertainment is not only able to entertain and educate, but also to save lives."

Schaefer was a fan of *House* and had referenced in his lectures, certain episodes of the show that were based on real cases, "to attract my students' attention for rare or unusual diseases." Nicknamed the "German Dr. House" by students, colleagues, and the media, Schaefer said his center had by then treated at least five other patients with cobalt poisoning, although with less severe symptoms. "There must be more awareness to the potential side effects of metal implants in humans," he noted.

Either way, such awareness was increased because an actor wasn't really a doctor—but just played one on TV, not only brilliantly—but effectively.

Chapter 21

The Armed Forces have been represented on television in many different incarnations including both dramatic and comedic shows. In the drama department, there was *Combat* (ABC, 1962–1967), *JAG* (CBS, 1995–2005), *NCIS* (CBS, 2003-Present), and *Army Wives* (Lifetime, 2007–2014), while the war comedy category dates back to *The Phil Silvers Show/ Sgt. Bilko* (CBS, 1955–1959), *McHale's Navy* (CBS, 1962–1966), *Gomer Pyle, USMC* (CBS, 1964–1969), *Hogan's Heroes* (CBS, 1965–1971), and *M*A*S*H*, the latter of which remains TV's most popular military-geared series, if with a medical slant.

[Credit: The Classic TV Preservation Society]

The show's special two-and-half-hour finale from the spring of 1983 proved as much. Titled, "Goodbye, Farewell, and Amen," this segment remains the highest-rated TV show episode ever documented.

"We wanted the series to say that war is destructive, wasteful, and stupid—and [that] there are better ways to solve problems."

So told *M*A*S*H* producer/director Gene Reynolds to author Peggy Herz in her book, *All About M*A*S*H* (Scholastic, 1975). Reynolds, who had worked on *Room 222*, and later *Touched by An Angel*, had partnered with writer Larry Gelbart (responsible for feature films like 1982's *Tootsie*) to develop and produce CBS-TV's *M*A*S*H*. The show's title took its name from Mobile Army Surgical Hospital and centered on a medical war unit called the 4077th—stationed in Korea during the Korean War. Like *222* before it, *M*A*S*H* was a half-hour dramedy, with a laugh-track (which *222* did not have) at least in its first few seasons. Three years after it debuted in 1972, the series became less humor-bound (but no less tragic in premise). Its original competition was long-running hit shows like *The FBI* on ABC, and *The Wonderful World of Disney* on NBC and, by the end of its initial year, *M*A*S*H* ranked at number 46 in the Nielsen ratings.

But CBS remained loyal to the series. For the show's second season, the network scheduled it on Saturday night, following its mega-hit *All in the Family*. The result: by the end of that year, *M*A*S*H* became a bona fide hit (if at the sacrifice of *Bridget Loves Bernie* which it replaced).

The show began as a novel by Richard Hooker, published in 1968, and adapted into a hit feature film in 1970 starring Donald Sutherland and Elliott Gould as unconventional doctors Hawkeye Pierce and Trapper John—characters later played by Alan Alda and Wayne Rogers in the small-screen edition. Also in the TV edition: McLean Stevenson as Col. Henry Blake; Loretta Swit as Margaret "Hot Lips" Houlihan;

Larry Linville as her stuffed-shirt lover, Major Frank Burns; Jamie Farr as the gender-bending Corporal Klinger; William Christopher as Father Mulcahy; and Gary Burghoff as naïve but daring Radar (the only casting carried over from the motion picture).

But there were roadblocks to the TV version. Herz said the language and "antics" of the medical personnel depicted may have been acceptable for adults in a movie theatre, but the standards of practices of television at the time were much more restrictive than motion picture codes. "The movie was probably the funniest film of the year," she wrote, but it was also "the bloodiest…The operating scenes were ghastly, and they were meant to be. If there's one thing that turns TV executives pale, it's the sight of too much blood on the home screen." [That was then, and not now, where blood and gore are the mainstays on today's primetime shows like *The Walking Dead* or *Breaking Bad*].

But Alda wasn't certain he wanted in on the show or any TV series, especially a comedy about war. As Reynolds told Herz, "[Alan] wanted to know our point of view. His concern was that the show should not glorify war or make it appear romantic. He wanted the humanity of the doctors to be emphasized." After reading the pilot script and meeting with Reynolds and Gelbart, Alda agreed to appear on *M*A*S*H*, because of its unique point of view on war. "It was probably the best television script I'd ever seen. But before agreeing to do it, I needed some assurance that they would show war as it really was. I didn't want to get into a fun-and-games war without meaning or content or reality. But I didn't have to worry. Larry and Gene had the same idea."

Reynolds said the series was a "good example of theatre of the absurd…the whole effort of these doctors [played by Alda, Rogers, etc.] is fruitless. They repair lives that are then sent back [into combat] to be destroyed…We show war for what it is—tragedy. That doesn't mean that people in the situation don't behave in very amusing ways. They use humor as a defense mechanism. If the sum total of the show were to say that war is fun—that would be wrong."

Herz agreed. *M*A*S*H* owed its success to several factors. "Brilliant writing, directing and acting… made it hilariously funny…[with]…a constant barrage of one-line jokes." Yet, with all of its "irreverence," there was also "a lot of heart…an undercurrent of caring. There is no moralizing or sermonizing—yet it is probably the most moral show on TV."

Alda threw himself into the role of Hawkeye, the core voice in the series. He enjoyed the character's candid outlook and verbiage, and straight-out moxie, and described him as possessing "some kind of caring at heart. It's a nice role to play. [He] steps out and takes over—and that rubs off on me. I always find that certain elements of the characters I play accrue to me. That's a way of growth."

As the series progressed, Alda became increasingly satisfied with what he called a "deepening" in the episodes. "We tried to make [them] more interesting by going deeper into the characters and the situations. We don't make war funny on *M*A*S*H*. We show the effects of war. People get hurt. In one episode, a guy died on the operating table. That's unusual for a comedy show—or even a medical show. We're not trying to get gruesome, but we want the show to be more real." For him, the show's humor arose from how the characters responded to war, which he called "a hurtful thing. I was in ROTC in college and was a second lieutenant in the reserves. I was on active duty [for] six months, but I didn't have to kill anybody. I was very disturbed by the whole experience."

"Basically," he decided, "any play, especially comedy, must be based on real people. We're trying to see all these characters as real people."

In some instances, the show's realism was overwhelming, as when the producers decided to kill off one of its main characters, namely, Colonel Henry Blake, played by the beloved McLean Stevenson, who would never again find success in series television. After leaving *M*A*S*H* on CBS, he signed with NBC for *The McLean Stevenson Show* (1976–1977), and *Hello, Larry* (1979–1980), a spin-off of the network's very popular *Diff'rent Strokes* (NBC/ABC, 1978–1986, which made a star out of the young dynamo Gary Coleman). Both programs failed miserably and lacked the cache and depth of even *Strokes*, which made frequent noble attempts to deal with social issues (as with the two-part episode, "The Bicycle Man," which dealt with child molestation), and *M*A*S*H*, which ran 11 seasons on CBS.

Alda felt the series outlived the controversy of the Vietnam War that inspired it, suggesting to Herz, "Perhaps that's a good sign, that a nation could laugh at itself even under those pressures; and it is certainly a good sign that the show could outlive the war. The setting was Korea in the 1950s, but there were few viewers who made the connection to the newer combat taking place in the heart of Southeast Asia. While in reality many of the circumstances were different, Korea was a substantial nation with a history of unity. Vietnam was not. The people of Korea supported our effort [but] in Vietnam there was division."

As *TV Gold Magazine* so expertly expressed in December 1986, "The armies of North Korea made no bones about it being a war between regular forces. In Vietnam for much of the war, North Vietnam pretended it wasn't involved. But the surface details were much the same. There was killing and casualties…there wasn't enough time or supplies or anything else, for that matter, to handle the incoming wounded…living conditions were very poor…and patients often died, needlessly. The doctors, used to a high standard of living and a very good income, couldn't quite believe the way they had to live and what they had to do. This high-pressure situation led to a mad release of energy in very funny waves [on *M*A*S*H*]. Each one of the characters was a unique individual, and stories would come to center around each of them.

"Even when the cast changed partway…when Henry Blake [Stevenson] gave way to Sherman Potter [Harry Morgan], and Trapper John [Rogers] was replaced by Captain B.J. Hunnicutt [Mike Farrell], things remained much the same. That is to say, hilariously funny but with a message that touched… the core of…humanity. Only after…Radar [Burghoff] and the stuffed-shirt foil for the acerbic Captains [Burns played by Linville] did the series begin to show its age and slowly lose its cutting edge. The type of humor changed and the essence was lost. Inertia kept it going but within a couple of seasons, it was all over. And besides, the country had changed. The circumstances that gave rise to the series no longer existed. The point of view of most [of] its potential audience had shifted. And perhaps most tellingly, those who had begun to watch *M*A*S*H* as potential-draftees in their late teens were now parents rapidly approaching the magic age of 30. The times had indeed changed and the show had come to the end of its long course."

CBS may have produced two sequels, *Trapper John, M.D.*, and *AfterM*A*S*H*, but neither approached the social impact of the original. *Trapper John* may have found a measure of success, brought back Pernell Roberts (gone too long from weekly TV since his days as elder brother Adam Cartwright on *Bonanza*), and made a star out of Gregory Harrison (who played Trapper's young associate), but *AfterMASH* (with Morgan, Farr, and Christopher) went the way of *Hello Larry*. There was also an unsold pilot called *W*A*L*T*E*R* with Gary Burghoff. Bill Bixby directed it. CBS aired it in 1984 as a special in the Eastern and Central time zones. In the Mountain and Pacific zones, it was pre-empted by the Democratic National Convention.

Chapter 22

Michael Douglas starred with Karl Malden on *The Streets of San Francisco*, one of Quinn Martin's more superior police/detective dramas [Credit: *The Classic TV Preservation Society*]

There's a memorable scene in an early episode of *Seinfeld* ("The Limo," 2/26/92), in which Jerry and George are held captive by Neo-Nazis in a moving black limousine. In planning their escape, George turns to Jerry and suggests opening the car door, rolling out alongside the road and down a passing hill into a ditch.

In utter astonishment, Jerry looks back at George and says, "Who are you—*Mannix*?!" It's one of the funniest moments in the entire episode, if not the series. It was just one line, but it's those one-liners that *Seinfeld* (the series, the character, and the actor) conveyed so well. At the same time, this episode of the show represents just how much TV detectives and police shows have permeated pop-culture.

If that isn't convincing enough of how pervasive and influential television cops have been on society—in a good TV parallel universe kind of way, there's this following comment shared by the Associated Press from Los Angeles Chief of Police Charlie Beck about *Adam-12* and its star Martin Milner, shortly after the actor died in 2015:

"*Adam-12* and Martin Milner embodied the spirit of the LAPD to millions of viewers. His depiction of a professional and tough yet compassionate cop led to thousands of men and women applying to become LAPD officers, including me. Godspeed Martin. You will live forever in our hearts."

Next to Quinn Martin's *The Untouchables* (ABC, 1959–1963), *Mannix* (CBS, 1967–1975) is considered the second most violent crime drama in early TV history. Fortunately, it also remains one of the best produced, with solid storylines and daring casting. As private detective Joe Mannix, Mike Connors became the first actor of Armenian descent to star in a weekly American TV show. Gail Fisher played his secretary Peggy Fair, a role that earned her an Emmy, making her the first African-American actress to win the award in the drama category (Diahann Carroll was the initial comedy victor for *Julia*).

Created by Richard Levinson and William Link (*Columbo, Murder, She Wrote*) and developed by executive producer Bruce Geller (*The Fugitive, Mission: Impossible*), *Mannix* was also the last series produced by Desilu Productions (headed by Lucille Ball).

But there's an extensive list of classic TV crime dramas and even a few crime comedies.

In the serious sector, there was *Mr. and Mrs. North*, (CBS/NBC, 1952–1954), *Highway Patrol* (Syndicated, 1955–1959), *Naked City* (ABC, 1958–1963), *M Squad* (NBC, 1957–1960), *Richard Diamond, Private Detective* (CBS/NBC, 1957–1960), *77 Sunset Strip* (ABC, 1958–1964), *Bourbon Street Beat* (ABC, 1959–1960), *Hawaiian Eye* (ABC, 1959–1963), the two NBC editions of *Dragnet* (1951–1959/1967–1970), *Adam-12* (NBC, 1968–1975), *The Mod Squad* (ABC, 1968–1973), *The Rookies* (ABC, 1970), *CHiPs* (NBC, 1977–1983), *McMillan & Wife* (NBC, 1971–1977), *The Streets of San Francisco* (ABC, 1972–1977), *Cannon* (CBS, 1971–1976), *Kojak* (CBS, 1973–1978), *Starsky & Hutch* (ABC, 1975–1979), *Charlie's Angels* (ABC, 1976–1981), *SWAT* (ABC, 1975–1976), *Hill Street Blues* (NBC, 1981–1987), *Remington Steele* (NBC, 1982–1987), *Moonlighting* (ABC, 1985–1989), *NYPD Blue* (ABC, 1993–2005), the original *Law & Order* (NBC, 1990–2010), the original *CSI* (CBS, 2000-Present), and others.

The lighter side of police work was showcased on half-hour comedies like *Car 54, Where Are You* (NBC, 1961–1963) and *Barney Miller* (ABC, 1974–1982) and the extremely short-lived but highly-innovative *Police Squad* (ABC, 1982), which inspired a list of hit feature films. *Miller* is frequently acknowledged for its realistic portrayal of New York's finest, but *Car 54* made its mark with a pre-*Munsters* dual bill of Fred Gwynn and Al Lewis, along with Joe E. Ross, as Gwynn's police car partner. The show presented legitimate police work within a comedic format and cast actor Nipsey Russell as a non-stereotypical Officer Dave Anderson who is not defined by his African-American heritage, which is never even mentioned.

Another innovative classic TV crime show also happens to be a half-hour; but this time it's a drama called *Peter Gunn* (NBC/ABC, 1958–1961). This series featured Craig Stevens as a tall, dark, and suave private detective who dates Lola Albright's sensual nightclub singer Edie Hart, while Herschel Bernardi as Lieutenant Jacoby keeps an eye on the private eye from afar (years before Bernardi takes the lead in the short-lived but extremely likable CBS series, *Arnie*, 1970–1972). *Peter Gunn* also teamed producer/director Blake Edwards with music maestro Henry Mancini, who would later partner on hit feature films like *The Pink Panther* franchise and many others. But for the moment, Edwards utilized his unique film noir style for the small screen images on *Gunn* coupled with Mancini's riveting theme music. It was this effective combination that captured the viewers' attention, including the ever-insightful Ed Spielman who, while growing up in Brooklyn, "wanted to *be* Peter Gunn."

"I thought he was the coolest guy," Spielman said. "I loved the jazz music, and I still love it. I wanted to be [like him] because he was cool. Peter Gunn lived the kind of romantic life I wanted for myself and frankly, that's actually the life that I got. I don't literally walk around with a gun and hang out at a jazz club, but the show really inspired me."

Peter Gunn also impressed Spielman on a professional level because the series accomplished so much visually, from its opening to closing credits, and in every creative way, with a relatively minimal production budget. "Blake Edwards was such a masterful producer," Spielman said. "He created a whole world with very little [money]. The show was quite artfully done and very revolutionary with the use of the Mancini jazz music. That whole 'cool' thing…took you away…to another place, and gave you a sense that not only did that [place] exist somewhere but that you could also aspire to go there. The idea that [any form of] media can take young minds and let them know that they can aspire to something…it's very, very powerful."

From *Gunn* to *Cannon* which, while nowhere near as stylish, was still astutely executed if with a completely different style and by a completely different producer and, as TV writer Larry Brody explained, a very dedicated lead actor in William Conrad:

"*Cannon* was another Quinn Martin production. We tried to make it more subtle than most detective shows of the era. Probably, we failed. Most interesting thing about it: The star, William Conrad, had left his wife and lived, full-time, in his trailer dressing room. Think about all the implications of that kind of lifestyle.

"*The Streets of San Francisco* taught me a great deal about writing for actors as opposed to just writing. And watching Karl Malden do his thing was the way I learned what the term "brilliant acting" really meant."

QM Productions, which produced the show was, according to those like actor Michael Douglas, who starred with Malden on San Francisco, "a wonderful place to work. Quinn cared not just about the shows and their ratings but about everyone who worked for him and went out of his way to show it."

Brody also wrote for the oddly-titled NBC crime-drama, *David Cassidy: Man Undercover* (1978–1979), which began as a special two-hour episode of the network's anthology series *Police Story* (1973–1977), which also gave birth to two other spin-offs: *Police Woman* (starring Angie Dickinson from 1974–1978) and *Joe Forester* (starring Lloyd Bridges from 1975–1976; the same seasons that CBS aired a similar show [about a senior policeman] called *The Blue Knight* [starring George Kennedy]). In essence, *David Cassidy: Man Undercover* was designed as a change of image platform for the former teenage idol. As Brody recalled:

"I was doing triple duty on the show at that time—producer, story editor, writer, so after I wrote the outline and got it approved, I hired another writer to do the teleplay. The first draft came in and was, as I'd say if I were working in the U.K., 'lovely.' I made the usual revisions and polishes, and then—only then—did we start thinking about who to cast.

"The head of the studio and executive producer of the series, David Gerber, came up with the idea to use David Cassidy. The episode was about a cop who goes undercover as a high school student, Cassidy looked young enough to carry it off, and Gerber was very much into 'popcorn casting,' which he defined as casting actors who'd been in previous huge hits, and we all know what a massive hit *The Partridge Family* had been for the same studio.

"Cassidy proved to be a much better actor than anyone, including David Gerber, had expected, and he did a terrific job as the undercover cop who feels so bad about lying to and betraying high school kids in order to shut down a drug ring that not only does he swear to never do it again, at the end of the episode he turns in his badge, resigning from the police force.

"There had never been any talk about designing the episode as a pilot. If there had been, we never would've had Cassidy's character resign. For that matter, we wouldn't have gone on record with the value judgment-theme that pretending to be a kid and ratting out other kids was a very bad thing, which, frankly, was for me the entire *raison d'etre* for the show.

"Everybody involved was very surprised when, about a week after the episode aired, NBC wanted to turn it into a series. Everyone assumed that I would run the series and our character would continue doing something that both he and I found ethically repugnant. I turned down the show. Didn't produce it. Didn't write an episode. *Nada*. NBC went ahead with it anyway, and the rest was history: 13 episodes and out.

"I can say, though, that not only I, but my whole family, thoroughly enjoyed *The Partridge Family*. My oldest daughter was a huge *Partridge* fan. Before working on *Police Story*, I'd done a series called *Gibbsville*, and when *Partridge* [actress] Susan Dey guest-starred and was on-set on my daughter's birthday I brought them together and had the chance to be the kind of hero every dad wants to be."

The importance of just how much one actor on any TV show, but specifically, a private detective show, has the power to connect with the audience was significantly addressed by entertainment journalist Ed Robertson in his *Television Chronicles Magazine* profile of *Harry O*, which starred David Janssen, former lead on *The Fugitive*. As Robertson said, "the failure of a pilot to sell usually spells the end of the project.

But there have been some exceptions to this basic rule of television. *Harry O* is one of them because while the Harry Orwell character may have come across as sullen, David Janssen himself tested well before an ASI audience that previewed the pilot. ASI is a Los Angeles-based research organization that arranges for members of the public to screen TV pilots prior to broadcast. The audience responds to the program by rotating a special dial located on the armrests of their chairs. The composite responses are recorded electronically and correlated second-by-second with the content of the show.

"The ASI audience really liked David," said Jerry Thorpe. "That was the impetus for why we made the second pilot." Indeed. *TV Guide* said the test audience wanted to see Janssen "firm and capable, with a good amount of toughness but, underneath, sensitive, understanding and a 'bleeder' for the problems of others—qualities that make him vulnerable on several levels."

"These, of course," Robertson said, "...were many of the same qualities that endeared Janssen to television viewers worldwide during his four seasons as *The Fugitive*." As Robertson went on to explain, convincing ABC to finance a second pilot for *Harry O*, after an initial first test episode failed to win any fans at the network, was another matter. Robertson said ABC asked *Harry O* producer Howard Rodman to provide the network with a memo outlining the merits of the project. Rodman responded with a 30-page document discussing the philosophy of *Harry O* (the series and the character) in detail.

The following quotes from Rodman's treatment appeared in *Murder on the Air*, which referenced excerpts of the otherwise unpublished document as part of its chapter on *Harry O*, saying the character of Harry Orwell "...had to be a guy who was totally honest, the sort of guy who would listen to you, and then say calmly, 'That's bullsh--"...I liked that. I liked it because it was reassuring. One of the qualities of the world I live in is that nothing is fixed and steadfast anymore. Everything changes so fast from day to day, that I have to learn new rules. Even 'changing against change' is change. What verities remain then? Well, certain ways we [the viewers] like people to behave—like a man who says, *Bullsh-- is bullsh--.*"

"In other words," Ed Robertson decided, "*Harry O* was a man of old-fashioned values."

For that same issue of *Television Chronicle*s, Robertson interviews actor Henry Darrow, who had a supporting role on *Harry O*. Robertson described the series as "a good detective show [and] also a show about a guy who happened to be a detective" (correlating somewhat with the previous assessment that *Life Goes On* was a show about a family who just happened to have a child with Down syndrome). Darrow agreed and went on to credit Rodman's contribution as key to the show's heart and success. "Howard gave [Harry, the character] a lot of little quirks, which David [Janssen] turned into wonderful moments of television. Like those shots of him sitting in his little car, waiting for it to start...and waiting...and waiting. And, of course, he always has his tie loose around his neck, with the blue shirt unbuttoned, and the gray jacket open. That was his thing."

This was a realistic trait that proved relatable to the audience. Most men most likely would prefer not wearing a tie today, nor during the '70s when *Harry O* aired. So, having Orwell do something as incidental as keeping the top button of his shirt open with a loose tie provided an identifiable connection with male viewers, if possibly, on a subconscious level.

Chapter 23

Stefanie Powers starred as *The Girl From U.N.C.L.E.* [Credit: Author's Collection]

A television crime show like *The Untouchables*, due to its government agents, such as Eliot Ness, as played by Robert Stack, could also be categorized as a secret agent series. In his article for *Who's Who in Television and Radio* in 1960, Stack discussed the success of his show, episodes of which were based on true crime stories of Chicago gangsters in the 1930s:

"Eliot Ness and the hoodlums he fought are not figments of a writer's imagination—they were real people. And although some license must be taken at times for better dramatic presentation to protect innocent survivors of the mobsters depicted, it's always the aim of the show to maintain that realism.

"That, I think, is the secret of the success of *The Untouchables*—or any good detective show. Crime in the past may have been more open, more colorful, but it is still with us, still powerful, still of great concern to everyone. The prime purpose of our show, of course, is to entertain. But I like to think that the example of Eliot Ness and his aides will arouse interest and inspire more strong blows against our common enemy—organized crime."

Decades later, in early 2014, journalist Colleen Curry, of *Yahoo News*, noted how some of our most popular cultural touchstones got their start during the Cold War; namely, James Bond, which Curry called "one of the greatest fictional spies in Western culture." As she explained, Bond is a British Secret Service agent who made his way into pop culture "under the shadow of the Cold War and the battle against communism" by way of Ian Fleming's first spy novel, *Casino Royale*.

In years to come, Hollywood would adapt Fleming's work into an extremely successful motion picture franchise that would cast several actors in the lead, including Sean Connery and two classic TV stars: Roger Moore, who appeared in shows like *Maverick* (ABC, in only the 1960–1961 season), *The Saint* (NBC, 1967–1969), and *The Persuaders* (ABC, 1971–1972); and Pierce Brosnan, who co-starred from 1983 to 1987 on NBC's *Remington Steele* with Stephanie Zimbalist.

Stephanie is the daughter of Efrem Zimbalist, Jr., star of ABC's *77 Sunset Strip* (1958–1964), as well as *The FBI*, a hit follow-up series that aired from 1965 to 1974—and which became one of the most popular government agent shows in history. As authors Tim Brooks and Earle Marsh explain in their TV reference book, *The Complete Directory to Prime Time Network and Cable Shows*, the Federal Bureau of Investigation has been the subject of several highly popular radio and TV programs, but none so imbued the "cool, professional operation of the agency so thoroughly" as *The F.B.I.* Zimbalist, they said, "personified the calm, business-suited government agent who always tracked the quarry down, scientifically and methodically, and with virtually no emotion whatsoever."

As Brooks/Marsh went on to reveal, and as with *The Untouchables*, episodes of *The F.B.I.* were allegedly based on legitimate government files, which ranged across America and involved counterfeiters, extortionists, organized crime, radical bombings (during the Vietnam War), and of course, Communist spies. The show earned the commendation of real-life F.B.I. director J. Edgar Hoover, who granted the series full government cooperation and even allowed filming of some background scenes at the official FBI headquarters in Washington.

In one of his last interviews, Zimbalist, who died at age 95 in May 2014, said fans of the show occasionally approached him to say they had joined the FBI or had become police officers because of his portrayal of the calm and authoritative government agent, Inspector Erskine on the series. "I get more joy from that than anything in my life," the actor said. "When you learn that you inspired someone, it's a huge honor." As the *Times* also conveyed, Zimbalist was named honorary special agent, the real FBI's highest civilian honor. The badge was presented by FBI Director Robert Mueller, who praised Zimbalist as an icon who inspired a generation of FBI agents.

Primetime television continued to mimic James Bond with other secret agent entries like ABC's *The Avengers* (1961–1969), which was imported from England (and is not to be confused with the Marvel comic book franchise of the same name; *I Spy* (NBC, 1965–1969) which (as noted elsewhere in this book), became the first show to feature an African-American male lead (in the guise of Bill Cosby); the ABC/Aaron Spelling 1963–1966 series *Burke's Law*, which in its third season became *Amos Burke, Secret Agent*, and from which a spin-off, *Honey West,* emerged (making a star of Anne Francis). *Burke,* starring Gene Barry, was regurgitated by Spelling with one more season from 1994–1995, this time for CBS (in the show's original detective form).

Also spied on TV was *Mission: Impossible*, which ran on CBS from 1967 to 1973, and which, as NBC did with Burke, was later remade by ABC (if for one brief season during a writer's strike, 1989–1990). From 1968 to 1970 on NBC, Robert Wagner portrayed Alexander Mundy on *It Takes a Thief* (around the same time that CBS featured Robert Conrad as James West on the secret agent Western *The Wild Wild West* (1965–1969). There was even a secret agent sitcom or two, namely the Mel Brooks/Buck Henry creation called *Get Smart* (NBC, 1965–1970 starring Don Adams, who later gave his voice to Inspector Gadget, and a secret animated series).

Though technically a superhero series, *The Six Million Dollar Man* began as a monthly secret agent series in the fall of 1973 on ABC's Saturday night *Suspense Movie*. Starring Lee Majors, formerly of the networks' 1960s Western hit *The Big Valley* and the 1970s legal series *Owen Marshall, Counselor at Law*, his half-man/half-machine super cyborg Col. Steve Austin was first portrayed as more of a James Bond type (who dressed in tuxedos, etc.). But that all changed once the show went weekly in January 1974. Steve was still a government agent, but less rigidly so (which better-matched Majors' casual charms). Two years later, Steve's cybernetic love, Jaime Sommers on *The Bionic Woman*, starring Lindsay Wagner, played out in a similar way in its first few episodes.

In the 1980s, *MacGyver* arrived on ABC, starring the network's former *General Hospital* soap stud Richard Dean Anderson, and produced by its former *Happy Days* star Henry Winkler. As Curry pointed out on Yahoo, *MacGyver* "became famous for being a scientist able to combat the KGB and the Cold War-era weapons by using his brains and a Swiss Army knife."

In the 1990s and 2000s, ABC, more than the other networks, kept the secret agent TV business thriving with many shows like the stylish, if very short-lived *Spy Game* (1997) and *Alias* (2001–2006) and, on ABC Family for 12 inventive episodes was a unique production titled *The Middleman*. Based on the graphic novels by Javier Grillo-Marxuach and Les McClaine, this show was about an aspiring artist who was recruited by a secret agency to battle evil. A highly visual series, somewhat along the lines of *Max Headroom* (ABC, 1987–1988), *The Middleman, unfortunately,* proved too high-wired for the mainstream.

Other more recent spies in the TV game include *La Femme Nikita* (USA, 1997–2001), *Nikita* (The CW, 2010–2013), *Homeland* (Showtime, 2011-Present), and *The Americans* (FX, 2013-Present), which *The Daily Beast* in 2014 called "the best spy show on TV."

Two of the most memorable classic TV spy shows are *Secret Agent* (CBS, 1965–1966), and *The Man From U.N.C.L.E.* (NBC, 1964–1968) which, like *The Six Million Dollar Man*, spawned a female sequel series, *The Girl From U.N.C.L.E.* (NBC, 1967–1968), starring Stefanie Powers (who later turned married-detective with former *It Takes a Thief* star Robert Wagner on ABC's *Hart to Hart*, 1979–1984).

To help keep the TV secret agent business in perspective is documentary filmmaker and classic TV fan John Scheinfeld, an Emmy, Grammy and Writers Guild Award nominee, and Telly Award-winner who is perhaps best-known for the theatrical documentaries *The U.S. vs. John Lennon* (2006) and *Who Is Harry Nilsson…?* (2010), Scheinfeld also produced, wrote, and directed the hit 2004 TV miniseries, *The 100 Greatest TV Characters* as well as numerous retrospectives about show business legends such as The Bee Gees, Nat 'King' Cole, Jimmy Durante, Bob Hope, Dean Martin, The Marx Brothers, Ricky Nelson, Jack Paar, Peter Sellers, Frank Sinatra, Andy Williams, and Jonathan Winters.

Guilty of watching "far-too much TV as a kid," Scheinfeld shares his insight as to why classic shows *The Man From U.N.C.L.E.* and *Secret Agent* in particular were and remain standouts of the genre:

"There is nothing secret about how famous Robert Vaughn and David McCallum became playing Napoleon Solo and Illya Kuryakin—an American and a Russian, working together as secret agents, proving that humanity could overcome politics. This working relationship really captures the hopeful, optimistic spirit of the 1960s and engages viewers in a unique way. While other series were played strictly for laughs (*Get Smart*) or drama (*Secret Agent*), or drama with jaunty good humor (*I Spy*), *The Man from U.N.C.L.E.* had tongue firmly planted in cheek. This made it not only fun but seriously cool. One cannot underestimate the cool factor—every week there were cool gadgets, cool villains, seriously cool and curvy femme fatales, not to mention Kuryakin's very cool black turtleneck. It was when tongue-in-check drifted into camp that the ratings started to go downhill. But what would-be-recruits for The United Command for Law and Enforcement will always remember is the extraordinary chemistry between Vaughn and McCallum. Even today, viewers still enjoy the fun they're having every week working with each other and battling nefarious scoundrels to save the world.

"What makes *Secret Agent* such a classic is its star, Patrick McGoohan. One of the most charismatic actors in the history of television, viewers absolutely cannot take their eyes off him. Every gesture, every turn of the head, a hint of a smile, his uncompromising nature, and silent sense of control carries such weight and intensity that the audience is left perpetually on the edge of their seats. That the scripts are smart and the plots and characters complex (not to mention the hero, John Drake, uncharacteristically does not carry a gun or kiss a girl), makes it that much more compelling."

Chapter 24

God has materialized one way or the other on TV over the years with shows like *Touched By An Angel*, and more recently, *God Friended Me*. Certainly, too, with annual airings of classic feature films like Cecil B. DeMille's 1956 epic *The Ten Commandments* (starring Charlton Heston as Moses) or 1965's *The Sound of Music* (starring Julie Andrews as a postulant). The Creator of the Universe has also been a pervading presence on episodic television (*Life Goes On*), and in TV-movies (*The Abduction of St. Anne*, ABC, 1975); in reality documentaries as one-shot specials (*The Real Face of Jesus*, The History Channel, 2014); as scripted mini-melodramas for Sunday morning shows (i.e. *Lamp Unto My Feet*, CBS/1948–1979, Father Ellwood "Bud" Kieser's *Insight*, Syndicated/1960–1984); with children shows like *Davey and Goliath* (Syndicated, 1960–1977); on Bishop Fulton Sheen's historic weekly hour *Life Is Worth Living* (DuMont/ABC, 1952–1957); by way of future TV evangelists like Billy Graham, Pat Robertson, and Joel Osteen; while various TV families through the years have frequently been seen "saying Grace" before meals or attending church (as on *The Donna Reed Show*, *Leave It to Beaver*, *Father Knows Best*, *The Andy Griffith Show*, and *The Waltons*).

[Credit: The Classic TV Preservation Society]

Of the all the inherently-religious or directly spiritually-driven shows, Insight is a stand-out. Originally airing in the 1960s, '70s and '80s, this remarkable series remains one of the most unique TV shows in history. The show may be likened to *The Twilight Zone* with a spiritual twist, divided into two main categories of story-telling: reality-based, and fantasy. The series features an A-list of talent, in front of and behind the camera, including actors Carol Burnett, Nichelle Nichols, Martin Sheen, Ed Asner, Beau Bridges, Jerry Houser, Tim Matheson; writers like John Furia, David E. Kelly, and Tom Fontana; directors such as Jay Sandwich.

At the heart of it all was a Father Kieser, the Emmy Award-winning Roman Catholic priest who blended religious commitment with a passion for making socially aware programming.

Father Kieser succumbed in 2001 to cancer at only 71-years-old, but author Father Mark A. Vilano has fully documented Kieser's show in the book, *Insight: The Series*. Vilano shared his thoughts on what he believes are *Insight's* optimum episodes:

"If I had to pick a few, I'd include Michael Crichton's 'The War of the Eggs,' starring Bill Bixby and Elizabeth Ashley, depicting an intense conversation between a husband and wife that unfolds in a hospital waiting room. It gives an example of the modest production values of the show while showcasing the emotional power of the writing, acting, and directing. I find some of the fantasy episodes fascinating, like Jack Hanrahan's 'Old King Cole' or John Zodrow's 'All Out.' They show how the series was always open to finding new ideas and genres to explore. Lan O'Kun wrote a number of episodes and one I like very much is 'And the Walls Came Tumbling Down' starring Martin Sheen and Jack Albertson. It's like a church homily in dramatic form. Fr. Kieser also wrote several episodes and the one that stands out to me is 'God in the Dock,' starring Della Reese and Richard Beymer."

Meanwhile, an almighty presence was showcased in one-hour dramatic episodes of shows like *Route 66*, including "Legacy for Lucia" (with Arlene Martel, 11/25/1960), and "Blue Murder" (Suzanne Pleshette, 9/29/1961). In both cases, guest characters sought religious or spiritual counsel or were seen praying for help through their various trials and tribulations. Such activity is rarely seen on contemporary TV shows, if at all. Writer Larry Brody explained why that is—and why such scenarios were so prevalent on a series like *Route 66*:

"Although I didn't watch much *Route 66* during its day, many years afterward I worked with Bert Leonard, who owned it, and Sam Manners, who was the *nuts-and-bolts* producer-production manager. They were proud of the fact that the show presented a more realistic view of human beings than most TV before, during, or since and were well aware that one of the ways it did that was by having characters who actually believed in something beyond the generic and material. Sam Manners, especially, made the point to me that back in the day religion and its place in society wasn't as controversial as it has since become. It provoked neither angry letters or kudos but just *was*. I think Sam mentioned that Leonard was always worried that they'd get network flak when he saw the church in a script but they never did. Maybe Leonard was prescient because even a whisper of any specific religion drives network executives into a frenzy of fear today."

The fear of God was present in the miniseries *Greatest Heroes of the Bible* (CBS, 1978–1979) in which this time a "Man Upstairs" was voiced by the distinguished veteran actor Peter Mark Richman, who some may remember as Reverend Snow, saintly father to Suzanne Somers' Chrissy on *Three's Company* (ABC, 1977–1984). As he recalled of playing God in *Heroes*, "When I was recording the show, the producer wanted me to be stronger in my declamations. In response, I said, 'God doesn't have to shout. He gently leans on your shoulder and whispers in your ear.' The producer agreed with Richman, who mused, "I won."

As fate would have it, the producers so enjoyed working with Richman they asked him to make a visual appearance in the series as a character he describes today as "the total opposite role" of God. "The King of Sodom and Gomorrah…the wicked king! It was so cold [in Utah] where we filmed, I could never warm up. And sloshing around in slimy, gray mud, wearing period costumes and foot coverings was not by any means a holiday."

Besides "the wicked king," Richman portrayed his share of villains over the years, on everything from detective shows like *Kojak* to mystery series like *Murder, She Wrote*. But he's done so without the need to utilize any extreme form of violent action or vulgar language, as is, unfortunately, the case with much of TV today. He talks about how overt verbiage and behavior is unnecessary when a villainess character is deftly written; how there's no requirement to utilize graphic images and profanity when portraying or displaying an "evil" character; how it's the job of the actor, the writer, and the director to impress upon the audience a villain's evil intent with talent rather than viciously severe imagery or verbiage: "I've made my living more times than I care to count playing very bad guys. Bad guys are human and they have to go to the bathroom, and so forth. I always remember that so that I don't get carried away or [go] over-the-top in [interpreting] an evil character. The eyes carry a lot of weight and the verbal intensity is explosive in a close-up. Of course, a good script helps to exemplify what the actor wants to express with simplicity. Years ago, there was no course language [in scripts], so I didn't have to say things I objected to."

When asked if he believes that television shows will ever be produced with the same quality as those from days gone by, Richman replied: "There are always good scripts, but unfortunately most readers [those hired by producers to peruse pre-sold material] are not perceptive enough to recognize them. In the old days of live TV, there were quality shows and there was something to be said about reading the script aloud and hearing how it sounded before going on the air [eight or nine days later]. And the authors and producers were willing to listen and improve the script. It was like going out of town for [a try-out]. And you were under the gun because air time loomed before you and you had to come through LIVE!…for millions of people watching. It was exciting and nerve-wracking, too! Good shows, bad shows…it's all cumulative. It all leads to experience. It's like life. The total experience is what adds quality to the actor's humanity."

One of Richman's earliest TV performances had a particularly positive impact on society. It was for a show called *Play of the Week*, an anthology series he filmed in New York. His episode was titled, "Emmanuel," originally airing December 19, 1960, and, as he explained, "I played Joseph to [famed classic TV actress] Lois Nettleton's Mary—and they were on their way to Bethlehem to have the Christ Child. [It was] a tender love story."

Such religious and specifically Christian images were also prevalent throughout television comedies in the '60s. In October of 1962, ABC premiered *Going My Way* which, in perspective, may most likely be defined today as a dramedy. Based on the 1944 Bing Crosby motion picture of the same name, the TV edition featured Gene Kelly as a carefree, young priest named Father Chuck O'Malley, stationed at an inner-city parish in New York City. Leo G. Carroll, later the secret agent superior on *The Man* (and *Girl*) *From U.N.C.L.E.*, portrayed Father Fitzgibbon, an older more conservative priest to Kelly. Dick York, one year before becoming the first Darrin on *Bewitched*, played Tom Colwell, a childhood friend of O'Malley; and Nydia Westman rounded out the cast as Mrs. Featherstone, the rectory's housekeeper. *Going My Way* was a sweet show with a gentle comedic manner, but it seemed dated, even for its time. The pace was slow, and everyone appeared a little too saintly. The series was a valiant attempt to bring God to the table in a more direct and weekly basis, but it had no staying power and left the air after only one season.

A few years later, and following the cancellation of *Gidget*, Sally Field reemerged from underneath her teensy surfboard and donned an older more reverend sister's floppy habit as *The Flying Nun*. Both *Gidget* and *Nun* aired on ABC, which also broadcast *Going My Way*. Whereas that series failed to make heavenly headway, *The Flying Nun* caught wind and soared in the ratings for three seasons. Based on the novel *The 15th Pelican* by Tere Rios, indirectly inspired by *The Sound of Music*—and unlike TV's slow-going *My Way*, *Nun's* pace was swift, mostly because the energetic Field transmitted her zesty voice and charisma from playing Frances "Francie" Lawrence on *Gidget* to the snappy (and sometimes singing) Sister Bertrille on *Nun*.

Peter Ackerman, son of *Father Knows Best* star Elinor Donahue and *Gidget/Nun* executive producer Harry Ackerman, is a former actor and production assistant. Today, he's formally known as The Reverend Father Peter Ackerman and more casually referred to as Father Peter, an Episcopal priest and rector for the parishioners at St. Christopher's Episcopal Church in Springfield, Virginia. As he viewed it, "There is a sense of vocational joy shared by Sally Field" in playing Sister Bertrille. "And that is probably why my dad knew that Sally was the ONE person who came to mind for the lead role in *The Flying Nun*. I cannot think of any other actress from that time period [who could have played that role, and that's] probably a huge reason why my dad could think of no other actress to play the part. She totally brings forth a sense of true ebullient joy that I find myself in ordained ministry…a joy that is probably present for anyone who finally doing what they love."

Like *Going My Way*, *The Flying Nun* was lighthearted fare, but the latter more productively hooked the viewers with a fanciful gimmick that allowed the show to spread its wings more easily and not take itself too seriously. *Going My Way* became the first weekly hit scripted television series to feature characters of a religious order, in the guise of clerical Roman Catholic characters. *The Flying Nun*, which credited members of the Church as advisors, did the same but attained higher ratings due to its fantasy premise—a format that became increasingly popular in the '60s; as was the case with *Bewitched*, another of Harry Ackerman's fancifully happy hits from the era. Here, Samantha and Darrin became the first married couple to sleep in one bed because she was not considered a regular (i.e. human) housewife, just like Sister Bertrille became the first nun allowed to have a spunky personality because she had the added fantasy element of flight. *Nun's* Bertrille was also similar to Julie Andrews' Maria in *The Sound of Music*, as Field's sister was a novice, and not fully vested in her order. So, Sister Bertrille was allowed even further leniencies.

Moreover, both *Going My Way* and *The Flying Nun* were two of TV's first weekly scripted shows that displayed statues of Jesus and Mary, the Blessed Mother. Such icons would not appear again until two other spiritually-set series hit the airwaves decades later: *The Father Dowling Mysteries* (NBC/ABC, 1987–1991), a traditional mystery series (in the vein of *Murder, She Wrote*, but not nearly as well-executed), and *Nothing Sacred* (ABC, 1997–1998), a much different drama series that caused an uproar in Catholic communities around the country.

Based on the novels by Ralph M. McInerny, *The Father Dowling Mysteries* starred Tom Bosley (upon his exit as Sheriff Amos Tucker on *Wrote*) in the lead, alongside Sister Stephanie ("Sister Steve"), played by Tracy Nelson, daughter of former TV rock idol Ricky Nelson (*The Adventures of Ozzie and Harriet*). Mary Wickes, who played her share of nuns on the big screen (in movies like 1966's *The Trouble with Angels* and 1992's *Sister Act*) was cast as a housekeeper at the rectory.

[Credit: *The Classic TV Preservation Society*]

Nothing Sacred was created by a Jesuit priest named Bill Cain and producer David Manson. Kevin Anderson portrayed Father Ray, an earnest and intense priest/teacher who questions his calling, existence, and faith as he confronts the challenges and issues of the less fortunate and very troubled. As documented in 1997 by *The New York Times*, The Catholic League and specifically Alan Keyes, on its board of advisors, declared *Sacred* a "sacrilege," and said it was "propaganda dressed up as entertainment [infused with] belief that there are no moral absolutes."

For one brief season in early 2005, a similar controversy arose from another such series, NBC's *The Book of Daniel*. This time, the unconventional main clerical character was Aidan Quinn's Reverend Daniel Webster, an Episcopal priest. "The fault of that show," said Minister Peter Ackerman, "…is that they tried to cram so much into one episode that it became comical."

"Having not seen *Nothing Sacred*," Peter said, "I can only assume that the Catholic Church missed an opportunity to show what the vocational role is like.

There are so many assumptions, many incorrect, about ordained people of faith. As an Episcopal priest, people are still surprised to hear that I have been married to a wife for 27 years and that we have two children. Clergy stance on social and political issues may vary vastly from those of more conservative nondenominational churches. I wonder if the Roman Catholic Church was invited to assist and guide in the development of *Nothing Sacred*, as my dad allowed in *The Flying Nun*."

"Ministry is fun," he added, "and full of adventures and people of all types and dispositions. It is truly a challenging vocation that is lived out daily and not just Sunday mornings. I do wish people could be exposed to some of the behind-the-scenes work we clergy professionals engage in…they might have a bit more appreciation for what we do, as opposed to what they think we do."

Even though David Carradine's Kwai Chang Caine was periodically referred to as a priest on ABC's Eastern-Western '70s hit, *Kung Fu*, the show's star defaulted that claim in 1992, saying, "Technically, that was not true. He was a monk." To further clarify, Caine was a half-American/half-Chinese Shaolin monk from the Far East who traveled the Old West bestowing spiritual knowledge and utilizing his martial arts expertise to protect the underdog. The show's 90-minute TV-film pilot (debuting February 22, 1972, as part of ABC's heralded *Movie of the Week*) was the first American-made martial arts film (for the big screen or small). In construction and content, *Kung Fu* was the inspiration for virtually all such TV shows and motion pictures that followed. It became one of television's most popular and unique Westerns, and one of the medium's most successful and endearing spiritually-based dramas ever to air. As previously noted, the series was also the first to introduce the elegance of Asian thought and culture to the mainstream American audience on a weekly basis—while President Nixon held historic talks with China's Chairman Mao.

Nearly twenty years after ABC canceled *Kung Fu*, CBS premiered *Touched by an Angel*, which enjoyed a lengthy run from 1994 to 2004. An upgraded edition of Michael Landon's hit, *Highway to Heaven* (NBC, 1984–1989), *Touched* touted stars Roma Downey, Della Reese, and John Dye, whose last name ironically denoted his character, Andrew, *The Angel of Death*. (Sidenote: Dye passed away in 2011 at the much-too-young age 47.)

In the pilot, elder angel Tess (Reese) informs novice angel Monica (Downey) of a promotion: She's now a caseworker, up a notch from search-and-rescue. The new position allows Monica to be seen by and interact with humans, who fascinate her, and for whom she has a grand affection (along with a new addiction to coffee). Her first assignment: stay close to David Morrow, a 10-year-old (played by T.J. Lowther), and his father Nick (Mark Metcalf), a run-down police detective. Both are trying to put their lives back together following the death of David's infant sister. Nick's wife and David's mother, Christine (Linda Hart) became distraught and fled the family. It becomes Monica's job to heal all hurts and reunite the Morrows.

Every episode of *Angel* is touched with hope, joy, and an uplifting spirit, signified by a white dove that flies away with each weekly closing credit. In the end, Monica, Tess, or Andrew, later, new angel Gloria (as played by Valerie Bertinelli who appears on the show from 2001 to 2003) make sure to relay to whoever needs it the most that "God loves you." Never had so directed a weekly religious message been relayed for such a lengthy period of time on a scripted series.

Today, Downey is married to producer and business partner Mark Burnett (*Survivor*), and together they have produced hit 2013 miniseries, *The Bible*, for The History Channel (and then NBC), and its subsequent re-working into the motion picture, *Son of God*. As *TV Guide* reported in April 2014, Burnett and Downey promoted *God* and *The Bible* on NBC's third-hour edition of *The Today Show*, hosted by Kathie Lee Gifford and Hoda Kotb. "We had huge hopes that America, one nation under God, would embrace the Bible series," Burnett said.

Downey then talked about how she and Burnett reached out to the Anti-Defamation League to make sure they presented the story in a way that was sensitive to the Jewish community. "We have worked across denominations and reached out to the Jewish community through Abe Foxman at the ADL to make sure that we told this movie sensitively, setting up political and historic context, presenting the story in a way that really just emphasized the love of Jesus and Mr. Foxman gave us a great endorsement from the ADL," she said.

As *TV Guide* went on to document, recent religious TV productions like *The Bible* are on the upswing and have "been a godsend." In 2013, the History Channel's miniseries averaged 11.4 million viewers, igniting an interest in religious-themed and faith-based programs. ABC's new drama, *Resurrection*, had averaged 10.2. million viewers in early 2014, and the popularity of big-screen movies like *Heaven is for Real, Noah, God's Not Dead*, and *Son of God* (a shortened-edition of *The Bible*) has inspired Hollywood power-players to start investing in similar-type programming over the next few years.

As *TV Guide* continued to report, Burnett and Downey were developing other spiritual properties: *The Dovekeepers*, for CBS, about the attack on Masada; and NBC's *A.D.: Beyond the Bible*, measuring Christianity's development. WGN America is developing a 10-part series of modern tales based on the Ten Commandments (the laws and not the 1956 motion picture); and Lifetime Television at one point was developing *The Red Tent*, a feminist interpretation of the life of Dinah, daughter to Jacob from Genesis in the Bible (the book and not the miniseries); and *The One*, which was to chronicle the lost early years of Jesus.

In 2015, OWN, Oprah Winfrey's network, will debut a seven-part documentary called *Belief*, which was to profile variant religious believers from around the globe. As Winfrey then relayed to *TV Guide*, "[This] is what I care about most on the planet Earth, "and the reason I put my name on a channel." Further still, CNN is developing a new show called *The Jesus Code* which, as also noted *TV Guide* revealed, will employ both archaeology and forensics as it explores the historical events laid out in the New Testament. Even reality programming, to a lesser extent, has gotten spiritual: *Preachers' Daughters* is a hit for Lifetime, while Oxygen is moving forward with a spin-off of *Preachers of L.A.*, which will profile religious leaders in other cities. Burnett and Downy are even rumored to be working on a reboot of *Touched by an Angel*, the long-running hit she starred in on CBS from 1994 to 2003.

The Reverend Peter Ackerman summed it up as such:

"I think spirituality in any and all forms on TV is a good thing. Whether 'God,' or 'Higher Power," it mirrors life…that there is a source that guides us, and is available to all. My biggest job as an Episcopal priest is getting people to see that God's love is available to them and for them to share with others. I have seen lives transformed through this. Thus, having shows, that even in a minor way, show a connection to something outside of ourselves is a good thing."

The TV families that pray together, stay together, as was showcased on *Father Knows Best* (left), *Hazel* (middle), and *The Beverly Hillbillies* (right) *[Credit: The Classic TV Preservation Society]*

Chapter 25

From holy water to the miracles of *Fantasy Island*, television has always been an oasis for inspiring programming, including sea-worthy adventures like *Sea Hunt*, and fellow sci-fi standouts such as *Voyage to the Bottom of the Sea* and *SeaQuest*. Other water-shedding moments were widespread on family shows like *Flipper* while ocean-geared police and detective shows have proved particularly popular over the years, namely, *Hawaiian Eye*, *Surfside Six*, and *Hawaii Five-0*, the original CBS version (1968–1980), and the same network's recent reboot (2010–Present).

Larry Brody penned two scripted episodes of the initial *Five-0* and wrote the story for a third. The original series featured the charismatic, if rather stone-faced, Jack Lord and ran consistently on Thursday nights for twelve years. For Brody, the experience was exhilarating:

"*Hawaii-Five-0* had the most dedicated bunch of writers I've ever seen. We were serious about everything and determined to have a unique style. Scripts were long—sometimes almost 70 pages—and everything was shot, after which the footage was

Dawn Wells played Mary Ann on *Gilligan's Island*
[Credit: Courtesy of Harlan Boll]

whittled down, down, down into the fastest-paced series of its time. And, of course, we had Jack Lord. To me, being in Jack's presence was like being in the presence of God. The man's mien absolutely demanded respect. And obedience. When I think of the show and him now, one word always pops into my mind: 'Yikes!'"

After the first *Five-0* ended in the spring of 1980, CBS replaced its Thursday-night slot the following fall with *Magnum, P.I.*, another Hawaiian-based series, this time making a star out of the mustached Tom Selleck, who got his start in commercials as the Marlboro Man and on game shows like *The Dating Game*. As *Magnum* scholar J.J. Walters explains on his website www.MagnumMania.com, the show remains an influential classic for several reasons:

"The show was a near-perfect blend of action, drama, comedy, and mystery. It is sometimes (somewhat incorrectly) referred to as a 'dramedy.' The action was usually very well done, often near movie caliber with some fantastic stunts. The drama ranged from the absurd to light fluff, to serious themes, to melodrama, to relatively unexplored themes and everything in between, including fantasy elements. The comedy, at first unexpected, was often subtle, farcical, and side-splittingly funny. And the mystery, while a relatively minor element of the show and would never be confused with *coup de theatre*, could often be quite good…Few shows have achieved a near-perfect cast. *Magnum, P.I.* did just that. Tom Selleck, John Hillerman, Larry Manetti, and Roger E. Mosley were the perfect choices for these roles. In the defining moments of their careers, Selleck and Hillerman in particular really shined in the show and they will forever be associated with the characters of Thomas Sullivan Magnum and Jonathan Quayle Higgins. Like few have done before, they truly *owned* these characters."

With regard to Selleck's interplay with Hillerman as Higgins, in particular, Walters said, "Simply put, these are two of the most interesting, fun to watch, characters ever seen on television! Both characters are richly complex with multiple layers of depth. Their dynamic, ever-evolving relationship forms the heart and soul of the show. What fun it is to watch these two men from opposite worlds, with vastly different personalities and interests, interact with each other. The playful fighting, the subtle humor, the witty dialog, it's all so much fun! An endless source of comedy, many of the most memorable scenes from the show involve these two together. It's interesting to see their relationship grow from cautious skepticism to respectful admiration to full-blown friends for life. Higgins is the father figure Magnum never really had and Magnum is the son Higgins never had."

Walters clarified how *Magnum, P.I.* presented a positive portrayal of Vietnam Vets. "Thomas Magnum and his close friends Rick and T.C. were the first Vietnam veterans to be featured in a primetime drama on American television. The characters went against the stereotype of Vietnam vets as psychologically devastated, bitter, homeless, drug-addicted people who had a hard time readjusting to society. Instead, they were refreshingly presented in a positive light as laudable role models. At the same time, the show also accurately dealt with the state-of-mind and psychological scars that Vietnam vets bear daily. The disillusionment. The indignation. Friends who never made it back. And yet, Magnum, T.C., and Rick all share the same key characteristic, one that would become a main theme of the show—An idealistic American spirit!"

Walters also noted how *Magnum, P.I.* signified the "value of friendship…unwavering, immutable, altruistic friendship and inspirational camaraderie is a theme sorely lacking in many TV shows, yet was a crucial element in *Magnum, P.I.* How many guys would kill to have friends like Magnum, Rick, T.C. or Higgins? They are fiercely loyal and always help when called upon. They have great personalities and are fun to be around. They possess laudable morals and values (yes, even Rick)."

Four years after *Magnum* debuted, NBC aired *Miami Vice*, a sea-based police action-adventure drama that made superstars of the dashing Don Johnson and Philip Michael Thomas, both of whom, among other things, inspired a popular line of clothing. Socks were optional, as Johnson not wearing them on the series became the male fashion statement of the era.

Vice resulted from a tall order placed in a short note from then-network president Brandon Tartikoff who told his staff to think "MTV cops." Tartikoff's instincts proved correct for its time as *Vice* went on to help catapult NBC to the top of the ratings in the '80s, along with other series like *The Cosby Show*. It went on to influence carbon copies, such as *Hawaiian Heat* and *The Insiders*, both of which had short runs on ABC. But *Miami Vice* itself was not an original, with regard to its core biracial casting of the Caucasian Johnson and an African-American Thomas.

In 1976, ABC had aired *Caribe*, starring Stacy Keach and Carl Franklin a racially-mixed police team stationed in Miami who probed the Caribbean. But whereas *Vice* soared in the ratings, *Caribe* sunk.

The 1960s shipwrecked hit *Gilligan's Island*, along with '70s staples like *Fantasy Island* and *The Love Boat* did pleased viewers seeking more lighthearted fare. The same could be said, too, for the '90s benchmark, *Baywatch*—but with more beneficial elements.

A ratings failure during its initial season on NBC, *Baywatch* flourished for eight more seasons in first-run syndication. The show became an international phenomenon, breaking ratings records and cultural barriers. In the fall of 2009, a report by National Public Radio placed *Baywatch* atop the list of most popular TV shows of all time, with some episodes viewed by more than 1 billion people of every heritage around the world.

With former *Knight Rider* star David Hasselhoff as its leading-life guard Mitch Buchannon, the show featured the various visual charms of an attractive cast that alternated over the years. For example, in 1991, Pamela Anderson left her role as Lisa, the tool girl on *Home Improvement*, to play C.J. Parker the lifeguard on *Baywatch*. While the original NBC edition of the show was more family-oriented, all of its adaptations provided a measure of socially-redeeming qualities. "Beyond its entertainment values," Hasselhoff said, "…*Baywatch* has enriched and, in many cases, helped save lives."

Former *Hardy Boys* star Parker Stevenson played lifeguard Craig Pomeroy in the first season NBC version of *Baywatch*. He said the show contributed to water safety measures not only in California, but across the country and the planet:

"*Baywatch* gave a worldwide television audience the chance to spend just a little bit of time on the sun-drenched beaches of Southern California and in the company of lots of friendly, fit, and attractive people dressed mostly in their bathing suits. What's not to like about that? The globally successful eleven-year run of the show attests to the universal appeal of an attractive cast in an appealing environment with suspenseful action sequences. While the audience may not have remembered the specifics of each episode's storyline, the dangers of rip currents, jellyfish stings, and shark attacks definitely were and David Hasselhoff's heroic portrayal of Mitch Buchannon significantly raised the public profile of lifeguards worldwide."

As to just how much power TV has in general, from both a positive and negative perspective, Stevenson said:

"My hope is that television at its least can be an escapist relief from the trials and challenges of life and at best an inspirational connection to ideas and dreams that might enhance our experiences of life. Intelligent storytelling can raise our awareness of the universality of our shared experiences and challenges.

"My own television viewing experiences have often not only been entertaining and relaxing but also enriching and intellectually stimulating experiences.

"My hope is that today's rapidly broadening entertainment outlets will provide new opportunities for the creative community and support and nurture their efforts to further raise the quality of future programming.

"The majority of thanks I have received over the years from viewers of shows I have been in, relate to moments when they were sorely tested by illness, personal hardship, or emotional challenges. These thanks consistently express gratitude for the comfort found watching shows during difficult times or for having been able to share a viewing experience with someone they loved and deeply cared about. The idea that in some way I have been of comfort to someone I don't even know amazes me and is probably the only true legacy of real value from my years acting and appearing on television."

The charismatic appeal of stars like Parker Stevenson plays an important role in the success of a television show, as well as helping to expand whatever positive message that television show may or may not have. The more popular an actor, the better chance that actor's show may share its positive message with a large measure of a mainstream audience.

Chapter 26

Lassie was top-dog on TV *[Credit: Courtesy of Jon Provost]*

While specific TV performers possess what might be termed animal magnetism, certain animal-oriented classic television shows with charismatic actors co-starring alongside non-human characters, as was the case with *Daktari* (CBS, 1968–1969), which featured a visually-impaired lion named Clarence; *Lassie* (CBS, 1954–1971; about a boy and his dog), *Mister Ed* (CBS, 1961–1965; about a man and his talking horse); *Gentle Ben* (NBC, 1967–1969; a boy and his bear) and, though technically a water-based show co-starring a mammal, there was *Flipper* (NBC, 1964–1968; a boy and his dolphin). In other cases, former superhero stars like Lindsay Wagner (of *The Bionic Woman*) were featured alongside animals in short-lived shows like *A Peaceable Kingdom*, a short-lived series from 1989, while shirtless superheroes were portrayed by actors like Ron Ely on *Tarzan* (NBC, 1966–1968).

Daktari, which is the Swahili word for "doctor," was a noble contender. This one-hour series starred Marshall Thompson as Dr. Marsh Tracy, a veterinarian who operated an animal study center in Africa, with the assistance of his daughter Paula (Cheryl Miller), Jack Dane (Yale Summers), and a native named Mike (Hari Rhodes). The series lasted four seasons and was filmed largely in "Africa, USA" near Los Angeles. Some scenes used actual locations in Africa, and still other segments were filmed in Florida., In either case, *Daktari* served a significant purpose. While early syndicated "reality" shows like *Wild Kingdom* showcased animals in their natural habitat, *Daktari* became the first weekly scripted series to present human actors performing beside animals (which also including a chimpanzee named Judy).

Tarzan, too, made its mark on TV, as it had for decades in other forms of media.

The Tarzan character was based on the novels of Edgar Rice Burroughs who told the story of a shipwrecked male infant on the shores of West Africa Tarzan is adopted by the Great Apes, a fictional species created by Burroughs who are different from gorillas. Tarzan goes to his Great Ape mother to find out why he is different.

Eventually, he encounters his first human—Jane Porter, a curious young explorer, and both of their worlds are never the same again. The first film to feature Tarzan was *Tarzan of the Apes* (1918) starring Elmo Lincoln. He played Tarzan again in two other films while four other actors (Gene Pollar, P. Dempsey Tabler, James Pierce, and Frank Merrill) portrayed the character in silent films before Johnny Weissmuller took on the role in *Tarzan the Ape Man* (1932). (Tarzan had many different big-screen adventures afterward, including an '80s excursion directed by John Derek, starring his then-wife Bo Derek, best known from the 1979 feature film, *10).*

When *Tarzan* came to television with Ron Ely, the character would reach more TV viewers in one evening, than any weekly shows of a feature film at the movie house.

Along with Patrick Duffy of *The Man from Atlantis*, and Clint Walker from *Cheyenne*, Ely, now in his mid-seventies, appeared at the *Paley Center's Retro Action-Adventure-Thon* in Beverly Hills. As opposed to utilizing what *Los Angeles Times* reporter Susan King called the "same monosyllabic tone" employed by Weissmuller, Ron Ely was more in tune with coloring or tone to Burroughs' original vision of the character…a cultured intellectual abiding in the jungle who, as King added, "preferred loincloths and whose best friend was a chimp named Cheetah."

In the fall of 2012, Warner Archive released *Tarzan* on DVD, along with *Cheyenne* and *The Man from Atlantis*. As Ely told King at the *Times*, "It's something of a mystery to me the way it sort of regenerated and picked back up. It's almost as if people were waiting for these [DVDs] to come out. The production quality of the show was not top-notch by virtue of the fact we were on location" [in Brazil and Mexico].

As the actor continued to explain, he performed all of his own stunts on the series. "I didn't insist on it, but it became a necessity," he said. "The important thing is you try to make something seamless. I didn't want publicity out on the fact I was doing the stunts, but then the injuries began to pile up."

As King revealed, journalists were on the set when Ely took an unfortunate tumble from atop a tree. "It was first reported as fact that I was dead," the actor recalled. "That is when it came out I was doing a little more than people expected."

Still, the king of all animal shows featured a queen, as in *Lassie*. While *Rin Tin Tin* (ABC, 1954–1959) attained a significant following in the TV dog series category, it's the *Lassie* TV show character that remains most beloved. Lassie, the character, like Tarzan, was introduced to the American psyche by way of other mediums (such as the 1943 feature film *Lassie Come Home*, starring Elizabeth Taylor; which was based on the 1940 novel by Eric Knight), but it was the original version of the TV series (starring Jon Provost and June Lockhart) that inspired many children across the country to beg their parents for a collie.

At the same time, too, the show became influential in more significant ways.

For a time in the mid-2000s, Dr. Jeff Werber, a real-life veteran of the ninth generation of Lassie animal-performers hosted *Lassie's Pet Vet* on PBS. Seen previously appeared in a varied capacity on CNN, Fox News, and CBS Sunday Morning, among other television spots, Werber was now featured alongside the famous canine on *Lassie's Pet Vet*, where he shared pet-care tips, pet-related trivia, and information on the intricate relationship between pets and their owners.

As *Scholastic News* reported in 2007, Lassie is not Werber's first well-known client. As a celebrity pet vet, the good animal doctor has cared for the pets of some of Hollywood's biggest stars, including Ben Affleck and Julia Roberts.

As a vet, of course, Dr. Werber worked with a number of different animals, but some of his favorites are cats and dogs…all of which led to his hosting *Lassie's Pet Vet*. The same year that show premiered on PBS, *Entertainment Weekly* voted Lassie one of "The 50 Greatest TV Icons," alongside Henry Winkler, Larry Hagman, and Johnny Carson.

Lassie's classic TV influence in American pop culture had been officially sealed…not with a weak whimper but a loud and firm bark.

PART 5
TRANSFORMERS

"I have found that having is not so pleasing a thing
as wanting. It is not logical but often true."
—Mr. Spock, *Star Trek*
(Episode: "Amok Time" – 9/15/1967)

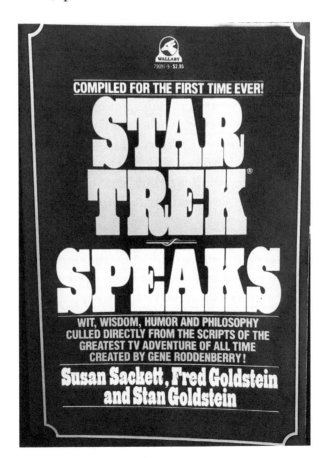

[Credit: Author's Collection]

Chapter 27

The half-hour sci-fi/fantasy sitcom is a peculiar animal.

It's not something that can be easily defined or effortlessly or swiftly produced. As with any creative property for TV, the big screen, or the stage, there are precepts for doing it right, specific laws by which to abide.

Bewitched, for one, did it right. Originally airing on ABC from 1964 to 1972, *Bewitched* made sense. Whatever transpired within its fantastical premise was explained with a specific "logic within the illogic." All the while, the series portended several social and family values. The show featured Elizabeth Montgomery as Samantha Stephens, a good witch who came to Earth seeking true love and found it with a mortal named Darrin (originally played by Dick York and later by Dick Sargent). She loved Darrin for who he was, and not for what he could do for her or buy her. She had no desire for material things. For whatever he could do for her, or buy her, she could "twitch" up something better with the wriggle of her nose.

While some viewers and critics of the series complained about Darrin's objection to Samantha's use of witchcraft, this demand not only set up the entire conflict for the series, butalso it represented his strong work ethic. Many episodes of the show addressed the hollowness of attaining material gifts without striving hard to achieve them. In short, *Bewitched* was a love story about two people of opposite heritage who cared deeply for one another in spite of their differences. Instead, they concentrated on what made them the same: their common humanity, even though Samantha was not human by design.

This concept of a "mixed marriage" was more realistically presented on *I Love Lucy* when Lucille Ball's Scottish-American Lucy McGillicuddy met and married Cuban bandleader Ricky Ricardo (played by real-life husband Desi Arnaz); and later, on CBS' one-season wonder, *Bridget Loves Bernie*, from 1972–1973, when Meredith Baxter's Irish-Catholic bride fell in love with David Birney's Jewish groom. The clash of cultures off-screen forced the show's cancellation.

Bewitched remained on ABC for eight hit seasons, leaving the air only because Montgomery sought to pursue other creative venues (such as her Emmy-nominated performance in groundbreaking TV-movies like *A Case of Rape*). The series was not, as has been erroneously reported over the years, canceled in its final season due to low ratings opposite *All in the Family* on CBS. ABC had renewed the series through 1974, but Montgomery opted out of her contract.

A few decades later, *ALF* also proved somewhat revolutionary, if not with the same lovingkindness displayed by Samantha and Darrin. It went against the grain of the usual fantasy sitcom template, and tossed TV tradition on its alien ear, with specific regard to one general but very important TV series rule: the lead character in a TV show, especially in a sitcom, must be likable.

Debuting on NBC in the fall of 1986 and airing until 1990, *ALF*, without a doubt, broke new ground for even sci-fi/fantasy sitcoms. The supporting cast, semi-regulars, and guest-actors of any series may deliver an unlikable character but not the show's lead character. In some cases, it is both the actor's performance and the character that is unlikable, as was the case with Dabney Coleman's featured role on *Buffalo Bill*, which resulted in the show's brief run and ultimate cancellation. And while Buffalo Bill, the character, was named after an animal, and really, the city in which he lived, he was still a human being (even if he didn't always act like one).

ALF, on the other hand (claw?) is an alien, from the planet Melmac. The rules for likability were relaxed, even if the character itself wasn't. ALF never allowed any of the show's other characters to relax, either, certainly not Mrs. Ochmonek, as played by Liz Sheridan. She was to ALF what Mrs. Kravitz (Alice Pearce/Sandra Gould) was to Samantha on *Bewitched*: a nosy neighbor who was frequently disturbed by the odd goings-on next door.

ALF's core association was between the lead alien, voiced by show creator Paul Fusco, a voice-over artist and character actor, and the conservative Willie Tanner, played by Max Wright, who headed the human family ALF came to live with on Earth, which also included his sweet and understanding wife Kate (Anne Schedeen), teen daughter Lynn (Andrea Elson), and her younger brother Brian (Benji Gregory)—all of whose lives were interrupted by ALF's fish-out-of-water (and many times crude) observations and interferences. As Fusco told *The Hollywood Reporter* in May 2012, "If you remember, toward the first season and second season, ALF used to drink, he was a party animal. He drank beer and everything, and once the kids and families started watching it, they said, 'ALF's not really a great role model if he's drinking beer; maybe you should pull that back a little bit.' And our response was 'He's 225 years old; he can drink beer…he can do whatever he wants to do.'"

Fortunately, the ALF character would soon sober up, and by the mid- to late-'80s, he was all over the place, guesting on other TV shows like *The Tonight Show starring Johnny Carson* or *Matlock*; he even had his own animated series, all of which further inspired lunch boxes, T-shirts, video games, plush dolls, even air fresheners. As *The Hollywood Reporter* observed, "Today, we make movies out of toys (see: *Transformers*, *G.I. Joe*, and *Battleship*), but back then, it was the ole 'ALFer's' character that sprung an empire…In an era of safe…television, he was proposing a twist on the standard nuclear family sitcom: a caustic, belching, destructive uncle from hell that came in the form of a wise-cracking alien who lived in the garage and tried to eat the family cat. With the pitch falling on deaf ears—it was a hard concept to sell, especially without imagery—out came ALF, from a plastic bag stashed beneath the table, ready to save the day.

"It looked like he was sitting at the table right next to Tartikoff, and it was just silence—they didn't expect that," Fusco told the *Reporter*. "And everyone was waiting for you to say something incredibly funny or something in the moment. And ALF didn't really say anything. ALF just kind of looked around the room and picked his nose and wiped it on Tartikoff."

Fusco's idea was bought, hook, line, and alien.

In the TV land of previous alien invasions, including *My Favorite Martian* (CBS, 1963–1966) or *Mork & Mindy* (ABC, 1978–1982), no such behavior would be acceptable. Fortunately, by the end of each episode, some measure of tenderness was displayed between its main *alien life form* ("ALF"), and any member of the Tanner family, mostly Max.

Such sentiment was pervasive on other classic sci-fi/fantasy sitcoms, such as *My Living Doll* (CBS, 1964–1965*), I Dream of Jeannie* (NBC, 1965–1970), *Nanny and the Professor* (ABC, 1971–1972), and even the relatively risqué ghost-comedy *Jennifer Slept Here* (NBC, 1984–1984), or with the twin horror-comedies *The Addams Family* (ABC, 1964–1966) and *The Munsters* (CBS, 1964–1966).

The Twilight Zone broke ground with Earth-shattering topics that otherwise might not have been granted airtime had it not been for the show's science fiction premise. For one, the pervasive TV topic of prejudice was presented in many of its fine scripts, some of which were written by its trailblazing host Rod Serling and other innovative minds such as Earl Hamner, Jr. (who would later create *The Waltons* for CBS).

One of Serling's most memorable *Zone* segments was "Eye of the Beholder," airing November 11, 1960, with Donna Douglas, before she played the whistle-calling, critter-loving country blond comic bombshell Elly May on *The Beverly Hillbillies*. In "Beholder," she was Janet Tyler, a desperate woman seeking plastic surgery to better fit her society's more "perfect" mold. It's unclear exactly which society that is or just how perfect that mold is supposed to be. When we first meet Janet, she's bandaged from the neck up (with a voice-over provided by actress by Maxine Stuart), awaiting the results of her procedure. Her "reveal" finally transpires with a story twist-ending that became a *Twilight* trademark: the bandages are removed, the surgery failed and, upon viewing Janet for the first time, her looks remain unchanged (attractive by our viewing standards, but repulsive to those in her world).

Serling's closing narrative was chilling:

"Where is this place, and when is it? What kind of world where ugliness is the norm and beauty the deviation from that norm? You want an answer? The answer is…it doesn't make any difference—because the old saying happens to be true. Beauty *is* in the eye of the beholder, in this year or a hundred years hence. On this planet or wherever there is human life, perhaps out amongst the stars…beauty is in the eye of the beholder. Lesson to be learned—in *The Twilight Zone*."

Douglas with her charming Elly May twang in check offered her personal take on the episode in the book, *Glamour, Gidgets and the Girl Next Door: Television's Iconic Women from the '50s, '60s, and '70s*: "People ask me about Janet all the time. Rod Sterling was a dear man. I enjoyed working on that show. It was really my first dramatic part, and it was rather easy. Janet…just wanted to be the same as everyone else. We all feel that from time to time, I reckon."

Serling penned several more noteworthy segments of the show, as did other writers of his ilk, each exploring variant social themes, plights, and causes that were woven into its framework as mortality plays. As explained in stellar books like *The Twilight Zone Company* by Marc Scott Zicree (Silman-James Press, Second Edition, 1992), *Dimensions Behind the Twilight Zone: A Backstage Tribute To Television's Groundbreaking Series* by Stewart T. Stanyard and Neil Gaiman (ECW Press, 2007), and *The Twilight Zone: Unlocking The Door To A Television Classic* by Martin Grams, Jr. (OTR Publishing, 2008), the show's development, presentation, and induction into the annals of TV history is a similarly worthy and riveting tale in and of itself.

Submitted for your approval: Exhibit A: Rod Serling. From the beginning, *The Twilight Zone's* popularity preyed upon his endless reservoir of ideas, originally inspired by his obsession with the past and his preoccupation with aging, mixed in with a measure of courage and faith and a few survival techniques he learned in the Army.

With monumental tenacity, Serling sought and gained rein over his creation on what became nearly a daily basis, all the while delivering top-notch scripts at a frenetic pace. With a strong desire to succeed, and an intense need for creative control, Serling, his genius, and his small-in-stature frame (he was only 5'5") proved to be a foreboding presence and talent. He took a no-holds-barred approach to get his product on the air—as he saw fit and so deemed, and settled for nothing less than optimum product along the way. He protected his turf, circumvented the typically charted waters of TV production, and opposed the demands placed forth by network executives, with a backdoor approach to realizing the fruition of his "other-worldly" dreams. Serling believed in his vision and rarely kowtowed to editorial invasion, fiercely guarding the end-results of his *Zone*.

Serling's *Twilight Zone* showcased weekly excursions into an unknown, yet familiar territory featuring characters with dimension that were introduced with arresting aplomb, many granted a second chance against the odds—much like Serling himself. Almost canceled twice before its original network demise, *The Twilight Zone* stayed afloat due to Serling's tactful maneuvers around Hollywood minds that were uncertain of anything—and everything—related to his *Zone*—except his undying passion for the series.

In the end, Serling proved to be a mere mortal like the rest of us, leaving this world too young, at only 50 years old, never reaching the twilight of *his* years, though not before he explored, unobtrusively, the senior mentality, and other untapped legitimate topics of conversation, with several, very-real trips into what seemingly became off-screen adventures into his own twilight zone of sorts; adventures that proved inspiring for the future journeys fictionalized on his most beloved TV series (among other creative properties).

From 1951 to 1955, he wrote more than 70 teleplays, including "Patterns," which aired January 12, 1955, on the *Kraft Television Theatre* anthology series. The story was about a power struggle between a ruthless president of a major organization, an aging vice-president who's pressured into resigning, and a new young executive brought in to replace him. As time would tell, this story may have eerily foreshadowed the frequent producer changes that took place behind the scenes on *The Twilight Zone*. But for the moment, Serling followed the success of "Patterns" with scripts for more of TV's most respected anthology series *Desilu Playhouse*, which produced his script for "The Time Element."

Serling had initially penned "Element" as a time-travel story for a show called *The Storm* back in 1951. But six years later, he expanded the story to sixty minutes and submitted it to CBS. The idea was then attained by Bert Granet, producer of the *Desilu Playhouse*, which Granet, in turn, begged the sponsor to fund filming for. "The Time Element" finally aired on November 24, 1958, and became a massive hit. Thanks to that and the positive reviews by the critics, CBS finally surmises Serling's genius. *The New York Times* review by Jack Gould (11/25/1958) was especially complimentary:

"Rod Serling is one of the pioneer television writers who still stays in the medium even though he is as articulate as video's expatriates about TV's limitations.

"Last night on *Desilu Playhouse*…he once again came up with an unusual and absorbing drama, 'The Time Element,' in which William Bendix showed anew that he is a fine serious actor as well as a clown.

"Mr. Serling's story was about a man visiting a psychiatrist. The patient complains of recurrent dreams in which he imagines he is living in Hawaii just before the attack on Pearl Harbor.

"In a series of flashbacks, the man is shown living with his knowledge of what has happened in the seventeen years since. He bets on sure winners in sports events, for example. But more particularly he seeks to warn a newly-married couple, newspaper editors, and anyone else who will listen that they will be attacked by the Japanese. But everyone is either too interested in a good time or too determinedly patriotic to give heed; the man only gets punched on the jaw.

"In a highly tricky ending, the psychiatrist is left looking at a blank couch and to steady his own nerves he goes to a bar to get a drink. There he learns his patient was killed at Pearl Harbor.

The humor and sincerity of Mr. Serling's dialogue made 'The Time Element' consistently entertaining.

"Mr. Bendix gave a finely drawn interpretation of the troubled man with the dreams; his warmth and insight gave the enigmatic script a living dimension. Martin Balsam was fine as the psychiatrist, as was Jesse White as the bartender."

"Where Is Everybody?" then aired on *Playhouse 90*, during the 1958–'59 season, showcasing a relatively unique, near cryptic story that brazenly concludes with a practical outcome. Along with "The Time Element," "Everybody" offered a fanciful, if credible, script that served as a backdoor pilot for *The Twilight Zone*, for which Serling soon exited *Playhouse 90* to establish.

Sterling created the core idea for what became the show when, one day, he took a walk through an empty studio lot at MGM. He felt the traces of a community but without any people. He sensed detachment and gloom; a foreboding feeling of what it would be like to wake up one day in a city with no residents. "Where Is Everybody?" appeared to be a story about the last man on Earth (played by Earl Holliman). Wherever he turned, there were traces of life, and yet no life. In the end, we learn it was all in his mind, party to an experiment for research into space travel. Scientists sought to uncover if man can withstand the isolation involved with an expedition to the moon. Holliman's character cannot. He loses his grip, and the scientists have their answer: Man must learn to conquer his own fears before he attempts to overcome the foreign elements connected with leaving home.

It was a pragmatic beginning to a television series that went on to explore more mystical possibilities in more imaginative ways. But the core essence of isolation was there, and all of it became familiar on future episodes of *The Twilight Zone* which by September 1959, CBS and General Foods, one of the network's major sponsors, ordered to become a weekly series.

Serling once described each episode as "complete in itself." The series was not, he clarified, "an assembly line operation. Each show is a carefully conceived and wrought piece of drama, cast with competent people, directed by creative, quality-conscious guys and shot with an eye toward mood and reality."

Zone ended production in January 1964 and was canceled. CBS president Jim Aubrey claimed he was tired of the show. He said he was tired of it after the end of the second season. By now, Serling knew that *The Twilight Zone* was not what it used to be—and he had been unhappy with it for quite some time. So he agreed to close up shop.

After *The Twilight Zone* folded, Serling continued writing with screenplays such as *Planet of the Apes*, released theatrically in 1968, and TV's *Night Gallery* (which tripped along for three seasons on NBC, from 1969 to 1971). He returned to Antioch College, as a professor, and rallied against the Vietnam War. (He was also a professor at Ithaca College.)

He died at only 50 years of age on June 28, 1975, from complications from bypass surgery. Many of the men in Serling's family died young. Serling's older brother Robert once said: "I didn't realize until *Walking Distance* [the *Twilight Zone* episode from the first season] that nostalgia for [Rod's] old hometown had played such a tremendous part in his life, how much he loved Binghamton, how much he wanted to go back to it, which in itself was kind of contradictory because he loved the glamour of Hollywood. He was almost like two people…He got his fill of the glamour every once in a while and had to go home to a simpler life."

Rod Serling himself once concluded: "Everybody has a hometown. Binghamton's mine. In the strangely brittle, terribly sensitive makeup of a human being, there is a need for a place to hang a hat or a kind of geographical womb to crawl back into, or maybe just a place that's familiar because that's where you grew up."

And that's where and when Serling subconsciously began to plant the homespun seeds for what became…*The Twilight Zone*. In a brief essay he wrote for *Who's Who In Television and Radio* in 1960, Serling concluded the following about his show's success:

"The case of *The Twilight Zone* seems to suggest…that there is ample room for variety in television programming. Matt Dillon can stand alongside Perry Mason; the panelists on *To Tell The Truth* alongside the strange and imaginative characters who people *The Twilight Zone* – without any overcrowding."

Chapter 28

Many popular daytime and evening soap operas have aired over the years. Afternoon serials have included *Search for Tomorrow* (CBS/NBC, 1951–1986), *Guiding Light* (CBS/NBC, 1952–2009), *As the World Turns* (CBS, 1956-2010), *The Edge of Night* (CBS, CBS/ABC), *Days of Our Lives* (NBC, 1965-Present), *One Life To Live* (ABC, 1968–2012), *All My Children* (ABC, 1970–2012), *Ryan's Hope* (ABC, 1975–1989), *The Young and the Restless* (CBS, 1973-Present), and *The Bold and the Beautiful* (CBS, 1987-Present). Primetime favorites have been *Peyton Place* (ABC, 1964–1969), *Dallas* (CBS,1978–1991/ TNT, 2012-Present), *Knots Landing* (CBS, 1979–1993), *Falcon Crest* (CBS, 1981–1990), and *Dynasty* (ABC, 1981–1989).

The expansive cast of *Dark Shadows [Credit: Courtesy of Dan Curtis Productions]*

But no series in the genre's history had more of a unique effect than *Dark Shadows*. Premiering on ABC in June 1966, *Shadows* first aired in black and white with just a basic mystery premise. The cinematography changed to color shortly after the addition of a devilish character named Barnabas Collins, a vampire played by the beloved Jonathan Frid. Such a persona injected new vitality into the series, which went on to tape 1,225 episodes until its cancellation in 1971.

Like *Star Trek*, *Shadows* took on a life of its own after its original run. The idea for the Gothic soap, with the slightly mysterious aura and a few minor ghost tales, had haunted series producer Dan Curtis in a dream. Although it was a concept that ABC bought into with eager immediacy, it just as soon became a nightmare. Upon its debut, the series got pelted in the ratings. Despite the presence of a famed former movie queen in the guise of Joan Bennett and the presence of stage-trained actors like Dennis Patrick, the *Shadows* began to fade.

In 1967, Curtis entertained a second vision. He decided to go all-out with the "spook stuff" and created Barnabas as a tortured bloodsucker. Curtis then continued to break all the soap rules by instructing his writers to inject something scary into every script, every day. If the vampire thing didn't work, he figured, "…we could always drive a stake into its heart."

But there was no need to take such drastic measures. The stakes, so to speak, were too high. Viewers came to love Barnabas, who was enamored by Collinwood governess Victoria Winters, as played by Alexandra Moltke, and then Kathryn Leigh Scott's Maggie Evans, who at first worked as a waitress at the

Collinwood Inn. Ratings would soon document 15 million viewers, 90% of whom were teens. Originally intended for a mere 2 or 3-week visit, Barnabas instantly becomes a permanent resident of Collinsport, or specifically—Collinwood—the centuries-old mansion with eerie ancestral family ties to the past, namely Barnabas himself. For indeed, he lived before—in the "old house" on the Collinwood grounds. The new house held the descendants of today's Collinwood family. But Barnabas is the one constant in all time periods…be it the 18th, the 19th or 20th Centuries, all of which are visited on the series (circa 1795, 1897, 1966, 1969–71).

Taped live, like a stage play, *Shadows* may have been considered camp by some, but that description did reflect the show's solid scripts, performances, and direction which, became some of the best daytime had to offer. There were a few missed or mispronounced lines, a randomly fallen set-piece, and other guffaws and gaffes. But even live stage productions and actors of the highest caliber face such challenges. There may have been a few rehashed ideas and retold stories, but each *Dark* script was an impressive adaptation of classic horror stories like *The Turn of the Screw, The Picture of Dorian Gray, Dr. Jekyll and Mr. Hyde, Dracula, Frankenstein*, and even H.P. Lovecraft's "The Call of Cthulhu."

Frid and his fellow DS repertoire of fine actors delivered solid interpretations of characters that were adored by millions of fans, most of whom were in their formative teenage years. Such legions did not fall in love with Barnabas because he was evil, but rather because he was an individual with a tortured soul. He was cursed with vampirism by the dejected romantic advances of the witch Angelique (played with cunning intensity by Lara Parker). With eyes only for Victoria and then Maggie, mostly the latter because she reminded him of his one true love from centuries before (Josette Collins, also played by Evans), Barnabas sought only peace for his discontent. He could not help be the night creature he became, despite the numerous trials made by Dr. Julia Hoffman (Grayson Hall) to cure him. Of course, the situation became even more complicated when Dr. Hoffman fell in love with Barnabas along the way.

The show's unique premise and presentation found a niche, as Frid's multi-layered performance as Barnabas displayed a conflicted soul who was simply cursed by a jealous love. Many viewers, young and old, connected with the very human traits and emotions of all the *Dark* characters who "just so happened" to be vampires, witches, and zombies (as with David Selby's Quentin Collins). The show utilized the horror-story mythology as a platform to address many merely human issues, gaining young developing minds as fans.

On primetime TV, there were witches, genies, and monster families. During the day—when the undead are supposed to be asleep—a vampire rose consistently at 3:30 (and later 4) in the afternoon. His name was biblical, but he was far from completely holy (at least in the conservative sense). The character was immortal, but the actor, Frid, was middle-aged, and, despite it all, the show became a pop phenomenon that only a few admitted watching but most adored.

Dark Shadows introduced scary new American sex symbols and canonized untraditional saints in the church of classic TV. It became the first *alternative* daytime serial, focusing on the lives of a bizarre troupe, instead of relatively *regular* ones (ages before NBC lets loose its supernatural daytime persuasion with *Passions* in 1999). Its audience was rare among soaps—legions of counterculture teens replaced their stereos with TVs. The show became the first non-primetime soap to be syndicated (eons before the onset of the all-soap channels). It premiered in a time littered with assassinations, illicit drug use, a sexual revolution, and a misbegotten war; many fans, with somewhat-lost souls of their own, pined to find themselves in another realm—a mystical realm.

Barnabas wound up on the cover of upscale magazines like *Time* and *Newsweek*. Before the term blockbuster became a part of the movie-going vernacular, *Shadows* spawned a feature film (1970's *House of Dark Shadows*) for which hordes lined up to see. A less-than-spectacular sequel was produced (1971's *Night of Dark Shadows*), while the TV series moved forward, then finally succumbed to a stake in the hard core of its appeal. Still, the show did not die. An updated primetime edition resurrected the franchise in the early '90s on NBC. Lunch boxes, books, memorabilia, and followers refused to gather cobwebs and instead gathered for bi-annual *Dark Shadows Festivals* (and not *conventions*).

As time went on, Frid tried to make sense of it all. "I suppose women see Barnabas as a romantic figure," he once said years after the show ended its ABC run. "Because I played him as a lonely, tormented man rather than a Bela Lugosi villain. I bit girls in the neck but only when my uncontrollable need for blood drove me to it. And I always felt remorseful later. As to his appeal with the younger crowd, he said, "Youngsters…are looking for a new morality. And he is Barnabas. He goes around telling people to be good, then suddenly sets out and bites somebody's neck. He hates what he is, and he's in terrible agony. Just like kids today, he's confused—lost and screwed up and searching for something. I'm a lovable and pitiable vampire. All the girls want to mother me."

Thus sums up the experience of *Dark Shadows*—not only one of daytime TV's most unique series but also one of the most unique shows of any genre to ever air, one that continues to enjoy a (good) "cult" following (despite a failed feature film remake from 2012 starring Johnny Depp as Barnabas and directed by Tim Burton).

The original series ended with this poignant farewell by Thayer David as the marble-mouthed Ben Stokes: "There was no vampire loose on the great estate. For the first time at Collinwood, the marks on the neck were indeed those of an animal…and for as long as they lived, the dark shadows of Collinwood were but a memory of the distant past."

Despite thousands of fan letters that formed a *Bring Back Dark Shadows* campaign, the lights went out, and *Dark Shadows* faded to black; at least, in its original form. Jeff Thompson, an English professor and the author of two books about the show's main creative force, producer-director Dan Curtis, said:

"*Dark Shadows* continues to gain and influence new fans every year, but I know that the 1966–1971 TV show had an enormous influence on us baby boomer fans who watched it when it aired on ABC. Many of us ran home from school to watch *Dark Shadows*, and all of us enthusiastically looked forward to every new episode. When we were not watching the TV show, we were experiencing *Dark Shadows* by reading the Gold Key comic books or Dan 'Marilyn' Ross's paperback novels, playing the *Dark Shadows* board game or working the jigsaw puzzles, looking at our *Dark Shadows* View-Master reels, and collecting the bubble-gum cards, Quentin postcards, 1897 pin-ups, model kits, masks, pillows, records, and other *Dark Shadows* merchandise.

"*Dark Shadows* attracted female and male fans of all ages and both genders, much more so than the dozen other soap operas on late-1960s daytime television. Fans felt an instant kinship with Laura, Barnabas, Angelique, and Quentin—the phoenix, the vampire, the witch, and the werewolf. The fans sympathized with, and often related to, the characters because they were "different." The sunburst of creativity that was *Dark Shadows* influenced many fans to pursue their own interests in writing, acting, singing, costuming, collecting, producing fanzines, researching history, exploring ruins, studying film music, discovering Gothic literature and film, and much more.

"The unique premise and presentation of *Dark Shadows*, as created by Dan Curtis and Art Wallace, allowed its fans to bond with the show in significantly productive ways. Jonathan Frid's multi-layered performance as Barnabas displayed a tortured, conflicted soul who found a kind of redemption through the TV storylines and the fans' adoration. Viewers, young and old, connected with the very human traits and emotions of the characters, who just so happened to be vampires, witches, werewolves, and phoenixes, yet they were much more than that. They were people who, according to *Dark Shadows* star Diana Millay, 'were looking for answers to their questions.'

"*Dark Shadows* utilized mystery, romance, and horror as a platform to address many basic human issues, and gained young developing minds as fans. Today, many of those fans are writers, doctors, professors, musicians, and artists just like their favorite TV characters. [More than 50 years later], its fandom is just as solid and devoted as those for *Star Trek* and *Doctor Who*."

Chapter 29

Hazel Court and Peter Mark Richman in "The Fear" episode of *The Twilight Zone [Author's Collection/Courtesy of Peter Mark Richman]*

Several one-hour science fiction/fantasy dramas in TV history have made a positive social impact, including *The Outer Limits* (ABC, 1963–1965) and *The Time Tunnel* (ABC, 1966–1967, which featured one history lesson after the next). But it's *Star Trek*, in any of its incarnations, that is by far the most influential of the genre.

William Shatner played Captain Kirk on the original series (NBC, 1966–1969) and in seven movies released between 1979 and 1991. As he explained in *Up Till Now* (St. Martin's Press, 2008), one of his many popular biographies, *Trek* made entertainment history, creating a multibillion-dollar franchise with beloved characters that have "been seen, and reseen and reseen, and in doing so we'd made an indelible impression on American culture and changed countless lives."

Even the Smithsonian Institution hosted a significant *Trek* exhibit, and the Las Vegas Hilton erected a special-theme attraction with amusement park rides and a live stage show titled *Star Trek: The Experience*. Shatner went on to express how his original *Trek* co-stars also experienced the *Trek* phenomena. Leonard Nimoy portrayed the Vulcan alien First Officer Mr. Spock, and DeForest Kelley played Spock's frequent sparring partner, medical officer Dr. Leonard "Bones" McCoy. Together, Kirk, Spock, and McCoy, known to *Star Trek* fans as "The Triad," represented, respectively, stability, logic, and emotion.

Shatner said Kelley's "greatest thrill was the number of people who told him that they had entered the medical profession because of him. Similarly, both Leonard [Nimoy] and I have often been told by people that they had become an engineer because of *Star Trek*, or a physicist, or an astronomer, or a pilot. Astronauts have told me they first started dreaming of going into space when they watched the show."

People like Steve Jobs, the genius behind the Apple Corporation was inspired by *Star Trek*, or at least its *Next Generation*, the first small-screen sequel that starred, among others, Patrick Stewart as Captain Jean-Luc Picard, LeVar Burton as Lt. Commander Geordi La Forge, and Brent Spiner, the android Data. In October 2012, the website *Tech-Ex* reported Spiner's belief that his *Trek's* generation not only influenced a connected society, but actually implied that the series was responsible for inspiring much of modern technology including the iPad, and stopped short of accusing Jobs of thievery.

Tech-Ex said Spiner was "confronted" outside of a grocery store and asked, "The iPad—was that really invented by you guys, 'cause you guys used a thing called the PADD." To which the actor replied with a wink, "Well, we invented everything."

It was then explained how *Trek's* PADD was an acronym for "Personal Access Display Device," which is reminiscent of today's iPad and other such electronic tablets. While Samsung didn't cite *Trek* in its patent against Apple, *Tech-Ex* mused, "…perhaps it should." [Samsung attempted to use director Stanley Kubrick's sci-fi feature film classic *2001: A Space Odyssey* as prior art in the case, but the technology giant was rebuked by the judge Lucy Koh].

Many future gadgets have been influenced by many of the *Trek* incarnations. The flip phone is quite similar to the communicator utilized on the original series, and Bluetooth headsets are reminiscent of the communications earpiece that was adorned by Nichelle Nichols as Lt. Uhura on the original show. As Spiner confirmed, "Of course, we did the Bluetooth; you remember Uhura with the Bluetooth; Captain Kirk had the flip phone, Captain Picard had a PADD in his office. We're soon going to be able to make ourselves transport from one place to another…matter of fact, I wish I could do that right now [to evade the paparazzi, it was assumed]."

As Geordi La Forge, LeVar Burton was Spiner's *Generation* co-star and Data's best friend. In September 2013, the actor (who first found fame as Kunta Kinte in the groundbreaking miniseries *Roots*, ABC, 1977) appeared at the third annual *100 Year Starship Symposium* conference which celebrates humanity's potential for space travel. In chatting with Miriam Kramer, staff writer for *Space.com*, Burton addressed the influential role the original *Trek* played in his life: "I was a young, black kid growing up in Sacramento, California, hooked on sci-fi. *Star Trek* was one of the few representations of the future that included me. I was really attached to Gene's vision…*Star Trek* always represented that hopeful aspect of this yearning we have. When I was a kid, that was the present I wanted to live in."

Burton expressed his dissatisfaction with contemporary sci-fi TV shows and noted how such productions could take a lesson from *Trek's* more uplifting vision of the future. "I wish there were more hope in the science fiction void," he said, referring to *Trek's* presentation of a common good, without allowing divisive issues of class, gender, or economics to invade or dismantle cooperation.

Burton wasn't the only *Trek* actor who began as a fan of the original series. Whoopi Goldberg, who played bartender Guinan on *The Next Generation*, remembers watching the show when she was growing up in the '60s. As she relayed on www.startrek.com, "When I was 9 years old, *Star Trek* came on. I looked at it, and I went screaming through the house, 'Come here, Mum, everybody, come quick, come quick, there's a black lady on television, and she ain't no maid!' I knew right then and there I could be anything I wanted to be."

In any of its forms, *Trek's* unique brand of sci-fi has without a doubt influenced the very real science of today. As Burton explained, "I was at a conference earlier this year in San Francisco. We are working on geosynchronous architecture in computers that will enable us to maximize the computing power and give us the opportunity to, in real-time, do more and complicated computations that would be required for something like a holodeck"—which was a reference to *The Next Generation's* holodeck—a reality simulator on the Enterprise starship that could replicate various environments.

NASA scientists are researching warp-drive technology, while medical devices similar to those of *Trek's* tricorders are fast becoming a mainstream possibility for the medical community. In September of 2014, NASA used a quote and theme music from *Star Trek* to add a little dramatic flair when officials from the agency announced that Voyager 1 became the first object built by humans to reach interstellar space.

In November 2012, *Reuters* and *Yahoo! News* reported how scientists in London are designing and testing what they hope might become the classroom of the future, inspired by the *Trek*-style multi-touch, multi-user desks that can boost math skills of children. A three-year project with 400 eight to

10-year-olds discovered that interactive "smart" desks can have benefits over doing math on paper and that students are able to improve their fluency and flexibility in math by working in unison. Liz Burd of Britain's Durham University led the study. "Our aim was to encourage far higher levels of active student engagement, where knowledge is obtained by sharing, problem-solving, and creating, rather than passive listening." Her research team, whose findings were published in the journal *Learning and Instruction*, designed software and desks that recognize multiple touches on a desktop that utilizes infrared light vision systems. The desks are built into the classroom furniture to help encourage more such collaborations and are networked and linked to a core smart-board. A live feed of the desks goes directly to the teacher who can intervene quickly to help a pupil while allowing group work to continue.

Burd's team uncovered that 45 percent of students who utilized a math program on the smart desk system increased the number of unique mathematical expressions they created, compared with 16 percent of those doing it on paper. The researchers said that using the desks helped children work together and solve problems employing inventive solutions. As Burd observed, "We found our tables encouraged students to collaborate more effectively. Such collaboration just did not happen when students used paper-based approaches."

Star Trek has also directly influenced the creative process throughout the entertainment industry itself. Before *Star Trek: The Next Generation* debuted in syndication in the fall of 1987, episodic TV shows had a beginning, middle, and end; story-arcs over several episodes didn't exist (beyond the daytime and primetime soaps), and "character development" was a periodic thing. For the most part, there were only episodic TV shows, and there really was no such thing as a "procedural." What happened in that one-hour dramatic (or half-hour episode comedic) episode stayed there and did not continue into any future segment or storyline. There may have been a periodic mention in some future episode that may have referenced a previous episode, but not on a regular basis.

This aesthetic change transpired gradually.

Millions of original *Trek* fans, code-named "Trekkies" or "Trekkers" (depending on the level of sophistication, dedication, or "geek-dom"), were anticipating Gene Roddenberry's *Next Generation*. For decades, they read books about the old show, whether in nonfiction or novel form, and attended conventions, which have become so all-pervasive today. When *NextGen* was announced, the fans, the artistic community, the sci-fi/fantasy community, and Hollywood (all of which intermingled at certain points) were in a tizzy.

Once the updated *Trek* debuted, some fans were startled by Stewart's Picard, a senior, hairless new captain of the Enterprise replacing the younger, more emotional persona of Shatner's Kirk. So, for many, something was not right. Also, too, *NextGen* seemed to be reworking *Original* episodes. Despite it all, the new show became a significant hit in first-run syndication as Roddenberry had grown weary of traditional network partnerships considering NBC canceled his original vision after only three years.

Because of *NextGen*, a new form of syndicated network was born, via Paramount and a host of syndicated network affiliates across the country. The show became a success, and a second season was ordered. But this is when things started to change. Gates McFadden, who played Dr. Beverly Crusher, left the series (if to return in the third year). For some Trekkers, *NextGen* became less campy, and more serious, specifically with the commencement of the story-arc. The one-hour self-contained episodes of the first season (and the *Original Series*) were no more. Episodes now ended, yet lingered. Many times, the viewer was left hanging or at least wondering as to what just happened. That happened on original *Trek*, but mostly to other characters beyond the actual Enterprise crew. On *NextGen*, the viewers did not have a clear take on what the regular crew members were feeling; emotions and motives became murky, and the stories were no longer concluded with a definitive ending.

Instead, the new *Trek* was like *L.A. Law—in Space*. The characters talked and talked, but no one went anywhere. Most of the episodes became "bottle shows," with all the action taking place on the Enterprise, and not out in space, on some new planet, exploring "strange new worlds." Whereas *The Original Series* lacked a regular dose of character development, *NextGen* had too much of it. The "A-Story" was the main story on *The Original Series,* while "The B Story" became the main story on *NextGen.* This mostly transpired due to producer Rick Berman. Roddenberry's health was failing, and Berman took the helm. But for many, this replacement was not as inventive as Roddenberry. Berman was inventive, but he wasn't Roddenberry. The sense of true fantasy and imagination that was a trademark of the original series was gone.

Beyond the world of *Star Trek,* Hollywood and the rest of the industry started producing television in the same way. Even a family show like *Life Goes On* started to change. For its first two seasons, this family series (which debuted on ABC in the fall of 1989) was an episodic hour; for its final two years, its episodes started to employ the "story-arc" technique, continuing the story from one week to the next with the same storyline. Other shows began to follow suit. The days of one-shot story episodes in dramatic television were quickly fading.

For some viewers, it was a positive thing; television programming, in their eyes, was maturing. For others, the days of classic storytelling on one-hour TV shows were over—no more happy endings were culminating at the 60th minute.

The heart and soul of *Star Trek* was somehow sustained in future syndicated sequels like *Star Trek: Deep Space Nine, Star Trek: Voyager,* and to a lesser extent, *Star Trek: Enterprise.* Each new syndicated series still presented the same vision of the original *Star Trek* series:

Hope for the future, set in a time when racism, world hunger, and other global horrors had been eradicated from Earth, where only peace and cooperation reigned between all peoples, cultures, creeds, countries, and nations. With our planet's priorities finally and securely in order, it was and will forever remain in reruns and on DVD and Blu-ray…time to explore strange new worlds aboard the Starship Enterprise, whose crew included a Russian navigator in the guise of Walter Koenig as Mr. Chekov (with a Beatles haircut), an African-American communications officer named Lt. Uhura played by Nichelle Nichols, and an Asian at the helm: Mr. Sulu, as portrayed by George Takei.

In one segment from the fourth season of the PBS series, *Pioneers of Television,* Takei explained just how important a prejudicial role *Trek* has played in the TV universe. "The inclusion of an Asian character was organic to Gene Roddenberry's vision for *Star Trek* and for our future. He told us that the Starship Enterprise was a metaphor for Starship Earth, and the strength of the starship lay in its diversity coming together and working in concert. So, you saw an African-American woman and an Asian man. Europe was represented by a Scotsman. And North America was represented by the Canadian Captain Kirk."

Classic TV fan Salvatore Amato, of Upstate, New York, weighs in on the *Trek* phenomena, completing his personal assessment of just how positive an impact certain programs can have on viewers: "If any TV show could give someone confidence to send their kids off into the world, it would be *Star Trek*. What could be better for my descendants than creator Gene Roddenberry's optimistic view of the future, with all races and both sexes contributing equally to a peaceful and prosperous galaxy? I now realize that while enjoying the adventures of the crew of the Enterprise most of my life, I unconsciously absorbed this optimism and passed it on to my children (and everyone else I know!) through everyday interaction. If we pass on the belief that this future is possible, maybe future generations will make it happen."

Amato concluded, "Escaping into the world of *Star Trek* instills in us the feeling of the way things *should* be, which should give us and our children something to work toward." In today's world, "we don't have heroes," Ed Spielman observed, as our contemporary universal mindset seems bent on suffering. "A generation can only rise to the height of its heroes, [but] we have a society that is actively deconstructing itself…whether it's the violence…the mass shootings…the indictment of a guy like Bernard Madoff or the crooks on Wall Street. All of these are instructive of a society that is in a moral decline."

Adam West was "The Bright Knight" version of *Batman* on screen, in the sci-fi/fantasy category of television *[Credit: Courtesy of Adam West/Author's Collection]*

Superhero feature films like *The Avengers, Captain America,* any one of the *X-Men* movies; *Man of Steel,* or the *Batman* trilogy have become hits at the box office. Yet, none may fully compare to the tried and true "happy" superheroes of classic television's past. While today's random Avenger seems so conflicted, moody, and sad, the super-charged do-gooders of the '50s, '60s, and '70s TV offered hope with an uplifting spirit.

Since the early days of the original *Superman* TV series starring George Reeves (ABC, 1952–1958), to the '60s premium cut cult classic *Batman,* to Lynda Carter's spine-twirling '70s "turn" as *Wonder Woman,* small-screen superhero shows have always held a strong presence in the lives of home viewers of every age group. While there was humor on the half-hour *Batman* series starring Adam West, it was sophisticated humor [as opposed to the trite musings of other 30-minute superhero shows (i.e. *Captain Nice* and *Mr. Terrific)*].

Other TV heroes were personified by Bill Bixby, post *The Courtship of Eddie's Father,* who took a double-take with Lou Ferrigno as *The Incredible Hulk.* Years after he was Friedrich in *The Sound of Music* (1965), Nicholas Hammond played Peter Parker and his web-slinging alter ego *Spider-Man* (CBS, 1977–1979). A few years following his co-star gig as Illya Kuryakin on *The Man From U.N.C.L.E.* (and decades before he became a regular on today's *NCIS*), David McCallum was *The Invisible Man* (NBC, 1975–1976), which later transmuted into a 1976 miniseries called *Gemini Man* (starring Ben Murphy after his exit from *Alias Smith and Jones*). Before playing Bobby Ewing on *Dallas,* Patrick Duffy starred as *The Man from Atlantis,* NBC's short-lived TV-take on DC Comic's *Aquaman* and Marvel's *Sub-Mariner.*

Atlantis began as four TV-movies that aired in 1976–1977, which led to a brief (13 episodes) but potent weekly series. In the fall of 2012, Duffy joined Clint Walker (from the *Cheyenne* Western) and others for the two-day *Retro Action-Adventure-Thon,* which took place in September 2012 at the Paley Center for Media in Beverly Hills, California.

In Susan King's coverage of the event for *The Los Angeles Times,* she talked about how Duffy was a young actor working as a carpenter between auditions when he got his first break as Mark Harris, an amnesiac with superhuman strength, webbed feet, and the ability to breathe underwater who was believed to be the only survivor of the lost city of Atlantis. As Duffy relayed to King, "The interesting thing about *The Man From Atlantis* is that I linger in people's memories. When I'm out in public people

Lynda Carter and Lyle Waggoner played Wonder Woman/Diana Prince and Steve Trevor in various editions of the *Wonder Woman* superhero-sci-fi TV series *[Credit: Courtesy of Lyle Waggoner/ Author's Collection]*

obviously say we are so glad *Dallas* is back [on the air on TNT with new episodes], but it's inevitable that one out of five say, 'You know, I remember *The Man from Atlantis.'"*

Duffy felt the show has a shelf life because of superhero adulation. "Look at what we are going through right now," he said. "It is the same syndrome with *Iron Man* and *Fantastic Four.* Superheroes offer some sense of hope. It seems to never fade."

Chapter 30

Two other more popular TV superheroes of the '70s remain *The Six Million Dollar Man* and *The Bionic Woman*, a dynamic duo of super shows that held a stronger-than-average influence on their viewers, the latter a spin-off series to the former. Debuting in the fall of 1973 as a monthly entry in the *ABC Suspense Movie* wheel, *The Six Million Dollar Man* starred Lee Majors as astronaut/test-pilot Col. Steve Austin. After a tragic plane accident, the government rebuilds Austin to be "stronger, faster, better" as a half-man/half-machine, a.k.a. *Cyborg*, which is the title of Martin Caidin's best-selling sci-fi novel on which the series is based (and also the name of a DC superhero). After the show was promoted to weekly status on ABC in January 1974, Steve Austin falls back in love with his high-school sweetheart named Jaime Sommers, played by Lindsay Wagner. She, too, is rebuilt after a tragic accident.

Lee Majors and Lindsay Wagner formed a Bionic bond on *The Six Million Dollar Man* and *The Bionic Woman* [Credit: *The Classic TV Preservation Society*]

Like Steve, she has one new bionic arm, and two bionic legs. But whereas Steve was granted a new super-powered right eye, Jaime has a new super-powered left ear. She was reborn as *The Bionic Woman*, died, and resurrected all in only four episodes. The ratings went through the roof and, after she was granted her own series, *The Bionic Woman* and *The Six Million Dollar Man* became unstoppable in the ratings.

In an interview with Allan Richter of *Energy Times Magazine* from March 2014, Wagner talked about just how important an influence TV and film actors and their characters can have on the audience. Richter referenced Wagner's 1988 TV-movie, *Evil in Clear River*, in which she played Kate McKinnon, a concerned mother who discovers that a respected high school teacher (played by Randy Quaid) is teaching Nazism and hatred of Jews to other students and seeks to have him removed from his position. As Richter went on to explain, Wagner has done a number of films that "have powerful messages and bring attention to issues that need attention: spousal abuse, domestic violence, racism."

When asked how she came to be involved with such projects, Wagner replied: "That's actually why I got into the business. I see this entertainment [industry] as a very powerful tool…I realized what a wonderful vehicle that could be for communicating…That was my passion about the business, much more so than the acting part of it. The acting was my vehicle, but my passion was in filmmaking and bringing my visibility to projects that could entertain and bring something to people. It was to help other people see themselves differently and see each other differently and hopefully accomplish something."

Both *The Bionic Woman* and *The Six Million Dollar Man* did just that. These shows introduced viewers to all the possibilities that rest with prosthetic limbs, not to mention one's true inner strength, the importance of self-esteem, and the potential of the mighty human spirit.

On one Facebook classic TV fan page, Martina Bonomo said, "You cannot imagine how much *The Bionic Woman* influenced my life. I didn't want to become a teacher or a tennis-pro or a government agent [like] Jaime. I wanted to grow up like her and develop into a woman with a heart like hers. *The Bionic Woman* was about values, about a vision of life. I'm still struggling on this path: forgiveness, loyalty, inner strength, freedom, and so much more. That's what a simple TV show taught me, and no other show, movie, or book managed to do anything similar."

A cybernetic connection was made amid a classic TV image and the real-life medical and psychological communities.

Steve Austin was the first post-Vietnam TV character to bring back the multi-dimensional, true-to-life hero in the white hat. By 1973, the American people were ready for some escape. The ideas introduced on both *Bionic* shows were lifted from actual scientific headlines. Both characters were fictional, but the futuristic possibilities of their super-powered prosthetics were quite real (much like the futuristic ideas employed on *Star Trek* that we use today).

Steve and Jaime were characters who believed it was more important to have inner strength than outer power; they were and remain popular because of their emotional and psychological mastery, to which their bionic abilities are merely an appendage. They are still socially and scientifically relevant:

intrinsic legitimate experiments have for years been conducted into the area of radar-like vision that was introduced by Steve Austin's right eye. The research was made possible because those in control of funding were fans of *The Six Million Dollar Man*. The scientific minds behind the real creations believed in what Steve and Jaime were presenting on screen, if alone, in terms of mere hope for the disabled.

Approximately five years after *The Six Million Dollar Man*'s debut, a man in Detroit lost the use of his right arm. After months of physical therapy and the delicately sophisticated technologies of prosthetic development (that were inspired by the Bionic shows), this man was able to lift more than 40 pounds with a newly-straightened and strengthened right arm.

ABC News Blogs writer Alyssa Newcomb said patients paralyzed by spinal cord injuries were taking their "precious first steps" at a Southern California hospital with the help of a battery-powered bionic suit that was first designated to help soldiers carry heavy loads. "Mentally, it's a wonderful feeling to be upright and moving," said Aaron Bloom, who was paralyzed in an accident in 2010. Then twenty-five years old, Bloom was told he would never walk again, but with each step in the Ekso Bionic Suit at Huntington Memorial Hospital, be began to defy the odds. "Right now," he said, "I don't really need anybody holding me. I can lift my hands up and put a little weight on these crutches and feel pretty comfortable."

Newcomb and Ekso Bionics, the company behind the groundbreaking technology, said the suit, priced at $150,000, was strapped on over an individual's clothing. Footplate sensors assist the center of gravity in order for the individual wearing the suit to maintain his balance with each step he takes. A computer is worn on the back to help drive the hip and knee motors. The entire super-garment weighs 45 pounds, but the load is transferred to the ground which takes the pressure off the patient not to bear the full brunt of the weight.

Newcomb said it required Bloom weeks of practice to feel comfortable using the suit, and he knew it wasn't an ideal solution, but, for the moment, it offered him a great deal of hope. "I have no doubt in my lifetime that there will be some sort of solution for spinal cord injuries," he said. "I firmly believe that I will be able to walk in the future. It's just a matter of time."

On October 20, 2013, 40 years to the day after the second *Six Million Dollar Man* TV-movie was broadcast, the Smithsonian Channel aired a documentary titled *The Incredible Bionic Man*. It was a TV special that chronicled engineers' attempts to assemble a functioning robotic body utilizing artificial parts that ranged from a working kidney and circulation system to cochlear and retina implants, and other body parts that came "tantalizingly close" to a real bionic man.

The parts arrived from 17 manufacturers around the world. Richard Walker was the lead roboticist on the project (and managing director of Shadow Robot, which designs and manufactures state-of-the-art anthropomorphic robotic hands and related systems). As he told *The Associated Press*, "[It's] an attempt to showcase just how far medical science has [come]." That week, the robot made its first appearance in the U.S., at the New York Comic-Con festival, having crossed the Atlantic enveloped inside two metal trunks—and following a brief delay in customs. Walker said the robot had a 60 to 70 percent functioning capacity in comparison to a real live human being. It stood six and a half feet tall, and it could step, sit and stand with the assistance of a Rex walking machine that's employed by those who've lost the ability to walk as a result of a spinal injury. It also had a functioning heart that uses an electronic pump to beat and circulate artificial blood, which carries oxygen just like human blood. An artificial, implantable kidney, replaces the function of a modern-day dialysis unit.

The parts used in the robot work, but components are a long way off from being utilized in humans. The kidney, for example, is only a prototype. And there are some key parts missing: there's no digestive system, liver, or skin; and…no brain. The bionic man was modeled after Bertolt Meyer, a 36-year-old social psychologist at the University of Zurich who was born without his lower left arm and wears a bionic prosthesis. The man's face was created based on a 3D scan of Meyer's face.

"We wanted to showcase that the technology can provide aesthetic prostheses for people who have lost parts of their faces, for example, their nose, due to an accident or due to, for example, cancer," said Meyer, who felt uneasy when he first took notice of the robot. "I thought it was rather revolting to be honest. It was quite a shock to see a face that closely resembles what I see in the mirror every morning on this kind of dystopian-looking machine."

Meyer has since warmed up to it, especially after the "man" was outfitted with some clothes from the U.K. department store Harrods. The cost? As it turns out, this bionic man comes cheaper than his six-million-dollar sci-fi cousin. While the parts used in the experiment were donated, their value is about $1 million.

In December 2013, Kathy Matheson of *The Associated Press* wrote about Titan Arm—a robotic device invented by University of Pennsylvania engineering students that can help its wearer carry an additional 40 pounds; it is ideally designed and suited for those who need either physical rehabilitation or a little extra strength for their job.

Titan Arm's design impressed Yong-Lae Park, an assistant professor of robotics at Carnegie Mellon University in Pittsburgh, who watched a video demonstration. Park's research is focused on making the "exoskeletons" less noticeable—"more like a *Spider-Man* suit than an *Iron Man* suit," he observed.

In more direct terms, an actual episode of *The Bionic Woman* played an integral role in saving a young woman's life. As was explained in *The Bionic Book* (BearManor Media, 2007), shortly after the series was canceled, a young girl, hitch-hiking in Modesto, California, was picked up by a deranged man, who then drove her to an isolated cabin, where he attacked and left her to die with her limbs completely severed from her body. The girl was a fan of *The Bionic Woman* and during the ordeal, she remembered certain techniques presented in the second season episode, "Biofeedback" (1/12/1977), which had to do with a high-profile scientist (played by Granville Van Dusen), who develops a body/mind/spirit control device. The techniques saved her life and helped her to rehabilitate her physical and emotional well-being.

Wonder Woman star Lynda Carter talked about one of her many heroic real-life plights in a recent interview with www.lifescript.com, which is dedicated to healthy living for women. The actress advocates for those afflicted with irritable bowel system (IBS), which she watched her mother suffer from for years. "She began having symptoms in her early 40s and wasn't diagnosed [with] IBS until she was 60," Carter said.

Now in her sixties herself, the actress is hoping to spread the word on digestive health for all and admits to eating healthier today than she did while filming *Wonder Woman*. Like Lindsay Wagner and *The Bionic Woman*, Carter and her *Wonder* TV persona did much for the Women's Liberation Movement in the '70s. But as she admitted to www.lifescript.com, "I didn't eat very much or well back then. I was under a lot of pressure to be a certain size, so I would forsake my health for crash and fad diets." She always struggled with her weight, she added and tried every diet imaginable. "I was on an all-grapefruit diet, one where you eat just one food all day, and those slashed whole food groups." All that did, she said, was make her hungry and upset her digestive system. "I didn't notice that these would lead to occasional bouts of symptoms similar to my mother's."

But she knows better now, as does her mother, who's doing well today. And *Wonder Woman* fans, and those who admire Carter in general, are following her heroic lead.

With such reel-to-real life transactions, and the motivations to develop medical research, and the display of true inner-heroics, *Wonder Woman*, *The Bionic Woman*, *The Six Million Dollar Man*, and other superhero TV shows from the past, as well as all classic TV shows in general, have time and again not only proved to be entertaining, but educational, psychologically nutritious, and lifesaving.

PART 6
EXTENSIONS

"I love Brian Piccolo. And I'd like all of you to love him too.
And so tonight, when you hit your knees, please ask God to love him."
—Gale Sayers, *Brian's Song*
(*Movie of the Week*: 11/30/1971)

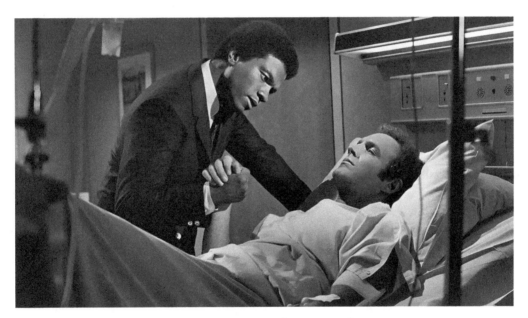

Billy Dee Williams and James Caan captivated the TV audience in *Brian's Song*
[Credit: The Classic TV Preservation Society]

Chapter 31

In a profile of classic TV performer Tina Cole, co-star of *My Three Sons* (ABC/CBS, 1960–1972) and *The King Family Children* (ABC, 1967), Editor-in-Chief David Laurell made the following observation in *Life After 50 Magazine*:

"As the first generation to grow up immersed in the programs, personalities, characters, and culture of television, baby boomers—unlike their parents or offspring—lived through that pre-cable extremely-limited-choice era when everyone, of every age, watched or was familiar with the same shows. Throughout the 1960s and '70s, variety shows and situation comedies attracted cross-generational viewing and, when it came to the holiday season, just about every family gathered around the tube for 'specials' hosted by a cavalcade of entertainers such as Perry Como, Bing Crosby, Bob Hope, and Andy Williams."

The Christmas specials hosted by Bob Hope, namely his overseas journeys during the Vietnam War to entertain the troops, were some of the most inspiring programs to ever air, holiday or otherwise. In these instances, television brought a measure of peace and joy to the war-torn grounds abroad, and to families in the States who ached from the absence of those sons and daughters, brothers and sisters, mothers and fathers, cousins and friends who so courageously served their country.

When the Vietnam conflict ended in 1972, Hope and others, like his good friend and former film co-star Crosby, continued to make holiday TV specials in our homeland. What would American television have been like in December without Hope's annual rendition of "Silver Bells" (variedly performed with Shirley Jones, Barbara Eden, and other well-known female TV stars)? Who can forget Crosby's "Little Drummer Boy" duet with David Bowie from his Christmas special in 1977? Or Perry Como and John Denver's periodic Christmas visits to the Colorado Rockies and other locations? Or when Andy Williams taped his holiday specials inside a studio, surrounded by his real-life family members who were incorporated into the show? Or how Lawrence Welk made sure to add annual Christmas segments with his musical family every December?

Every holiday was represented throughout the year with various broadcasts geared toward Easter, Valentine's Day, Easter, the Fourth of July, Halloween, Thanksgiving, and so forth, but it was (and remains!) the Christmas programs that most hold dear. Be they music-variety-oriented, animated programming (in traditional animation or claymation), or TV-movies, it is the Christmas programs that stand out. And while Christmas TV-movies, in particular, have aired through the decades (a tradition that networks like Lifetime and The Hallmark Channel have revived in recent years, airing more than 40 new Christmas TV-movies every season combined), for many viewers, the fondest of all Christmas airings is *Rudolph, the Red-Nosed Reindeer*, an animated one-hour story based on the classic holiday tune of the '40s. This one-hour special, more than any other children's' special, Christmas or otherwise, also happens to be filtered with the most insightful and caring life lessons.

Directed by Kizo Nagashima and Larry Roemer, and written by Robert May and Romeo Miller, *Rudolph* debuted on CBS in 1964. It's a "true love" story with pervading messages about maturity, responsibility, pride, prejudice, ambition, and acceptance that goes to great lengths to decipher things like "deer pressure" from "elf-improvement." Need to dispel the fear surrounding a visit to the dentist; to learn that no toy is happy unless it is truly loved by a child? It's all in there, as are some of the most tender and telling Christmas carols ever composed ("There's Always Tomorrow"; "Silver and Gold"), and one of the happiest ("Holly Jolly Christmas"). What else could anyone want in a Christmas TV special?

Broadcast every year in late November or early December, this perennial classic always signals the commencement of the holiday season like no other, reminding viewers to slow our pace and shine on until the morning—and beyond. Featuring the stellar vocal talents of Burl Ives as Sam the Snowman—who we first meet in the North Pole midst a field of Christmas trees ("Yep—this is where we grow 'em!"), and Billie Mae Richards as the leading reindeer, *Rudolph* shines from one moment to the next!

For example, shortly after Rudolph arrives on the Island of Misfit Toys with his friends, Yukon Cornelius (the Arctic prospector, voiced by Larry Mann) and Herbie/Hermie (the elf who wants to be a dentist, vocals by Paul Soles), he buckles up and ventures full-speed ahead to fulfill his destiny. He does so by breaking off a piece of land-ice and using it as a drift-device to carry him on his way through the Arctic sea. [Sidenote: The elf is referred to as "Herbie/Hermie" because his name actually changed from the first half of the show to the second due to a production mishap. But for the sake of clarity, from here on he will be referred to as "Hermie."]

As Rudolph drifts across the frigid waters, he wistfully bids farewell to his dear friends, saying, "Goodbye, Cornelius. I hope you find lots of tinsel. Goodbye, Hermie. Whatever a dentist is…I hope someday you will be…the greatest."

This scene is by far one of the most poignant moments in the entire special and speaks volumes about Rudolph's touching and massive heart, leaving the viewer with food for thought…especially what he says to Hermie:

Without understanding in the least anything about Hermie's intended profession, Rudolph wants only the best for his friend. Not only does Rudolph want Hermie to succeed, to find his joy, to find his bliss, he wants Hermie to be the best at what he aspires to be. It's an inspiring moment that offers the most charitable of the show's morals: to be happy for others, to wish only the best for friends and family members, to send only good thoughts for the increase and happiness of every kind.

Without a doubt, *Rudolph, the Red-Nosed Reindeer*, with all its insight and magic, year after year, remains the perfect representation of just how wonderful a program the medium of television has the power to produce and bring to millions.

Additional heartwarming Christmas animated specials have aired over the years.

- *A Charlie Brown Christmas* (CBS, 1965): Directed by Bill Melendez. Written by Charles Schulz. Young voice-over talent Peter Robbins made his indelible mark as Charlie Brown in this poignant holiday classic that spawned a series of similar specials for every holiday. Here, Charlie Brown searches for the true meaning of Christmas and the perfect tree. While directing a school play, he finds both, though not before our young low-achiever confronts a number of obstacles. Not the least of these conflicts is presented by his own dog Snoopy's obsession with winning first prize for a local decorations competition or by his mean-spirited peers who mock his choice of a tiny, sickly tree. Through it all, Charlie continues to struggle for peace of mind in his December time, when he is forced to visit with his pseudo-psychologist friend (and foe) Lucy, who offers him a 5-cent therapy session. Following a desperate plea (during which he screams, "Can't anyone tell me what Christmas is all about?!"), Charlie Brown finally hears the real deal—from Lucy's young brother Linus, of all people. "I can tell you," Linus reveals. And in one of the most uniquely animated moments in the history of the genre, Linus goes on to quote the Biblical story of the first Christmas. In a matter of moments, Charlie Brown's misguided pals realize their inconsideration and, with the help and reconfiguration of Snoopy's prize-winning decorations, breathe life into a once-listless tree—further uncovering and "illuminating" the true meaning of Christmas. "Hark the herald" these young animated angels then all sing.

- *How the Grinch Stole Christmas* (CBS, 1966): Directed by Chuck Jones and Ben Washam. Written by Bob Ogle and based on the book by Dr. Seuss. Director Ron Howard and actor Jim Carrey made a valiant attempt to bring Whoville to the live-action big screen a few years back, but that film does not compare to this original—especially due to the vocal brilliance of Boris Karloff.

- *The Little Drummer Boy* (NBC, 1968): Directed by Jules Bass, Arthur Rankin, Jr. and others. Written by Romeo Muller. Two years after CBS got heavy with *A Charlie Brown Christmas*, the Peacock network delivered this equally-deep and spiritual take on an animated Christmas TV special. Based on the classic song (that was later historically performed by Bing Crosby and David Bowie on one of Crosby's traditional NBC holiday specials), this poignant special featured the vocal character prowess of Jose Ferrer, Paul Frees, June Foray, and narration by Greer Garson.

- *Santa Claus Is Comin' To Town* (ABC, 1969): Directed by Jules Bass and Arthur Rankin, Jr. Written by Romeo Muller. Taking its cue from *Rudolph*, this smart Christmas tale expands on the popularity of a Christmas song and threads a charming tale about the origins of St. Nick—here voiced by Mickey Rooney. Also along for the ride: Fred Astaire (serving the narrator purpose, as did Burl Ives on *Rudolph*) as the Christmas Mailman. This also features the vocal gymnastics of Keenan Wynn, Paul Frees, Joan Gardner, and Robie Lester.

- *Frosty The Snowman* (CBS, 1969): Directed by Jules Bass and Arthur Rankin. Written by Romeo Muller. Here, Jimmy Durante (like his cartooned colleagues Burl Ives and Fred Astaire before him) serves as narrator to yet another Christmas carol come to life—along with Frosty. A sequel (*Frosty Returns*) later followed (with John Goodman, years before he donned the live-action edition of *The Year Without a Santa Claus* in the Frosty role originally voiced by Jackie Vernon). But it wasn't the same. This special also featured the voices of the great Billy De Wolfe (*The Doris Day Show*) and Bass/Rankin/Miller stalwarts Paul Frees and June Foray.

- *A Christmas Carol* (Syndicated, 1970): Directed by Zoran Janjic. Written by Michael Robinson and based on the classic novel by Charles Dickens. Who says television isn't educational—and this production introduced to the grand literary mind of Charles Dickens to American children in a visual and vocal way. Up until this point, "cartoons" meant only *Scooby-Doo, Where Are You!* This special featured the voice-over talents of Alistair Duncan, Ron Haddick (as Scrooge), John Llewellyn, Bruce Montague, Brenda Senders, and many others.

- *The Night the Animals Talked* (CBS, 1970): Directed by Shamus Culhane. Written by Peter Fernandez, Jan Hartman, and others. This unique special was just about as far away from Dr. Doolittle as you can get; we learn what the animals were thinking at the birth of Christ. They are granted the gift of gab—and we are granted the gift of insight. Mind-boggling and eons ahead of its time, this special featured the voices of Patricia Bright, Ruth Franklin, Bob Kaliban, Len Maxwell, Joe Silver, Frank Porretta, and others.

- *The Year Without A Santa Claus* (ABC, 1974): Directed by Jules Bass and Arthur Rankin, Jr. Written by William Keenan and based on the novel by Phyllis McGinley. Mickey Rooney returns as Santa, this time joined by Shirley Hazel Booth as Mrs. Claus in a witty take that may be sub-coded *Santa Takes A Holiday*—as the jolly one gets sick and decides to take a break from Christmas. A sophisticated animated tale is delivered, along with an astounding message and pristine dialogue. This cartoon proved so impressive, it spawned a live-action TV-movie (starring John Goodman) in 2006.

- *'Twas the Night Before Christmas* (CBS, 1974): Directed by Jules Bass and Arthur Rankin, Jr. Written by Jerome Coopersmith and based on the poem by Clement Moore. Producers/directors Bass and Rankin steered away from stop-action animation (*Rudolph, Santa Claus Is Comin' To Town*) and headed into the then-more traditional animatronics of the era. What's more, it's also told in a 30-minute format (as opposed to the aforementioned 60 minutes, though first completed a few years before with *Frosty the Snowman* in 1969). But their style is still evident especially drawn in the eyes and "heart" of each character. The result: a sweet narrative delivery of a perfect holiday rhyme. Featuring the voices of Patricia Bright, Scott Firestone, George Gobel (*Hollywood Squares*), Broadway giant and film legend Joel Grey, and Tammy Grimes (the original choice for Samantha on TV's *Bewitched*).

A few exceptional live-action Christmas TV specials and movies have also appeared through the decades.

- *The House Without a Christmas Tree* (CBS, 1972): Directed by Paul Bogart. Written by Eleanor Perry and Gail Rock. Based on the book by Rock. Jamie Mills (Jason Robards) has grown bitter over the years after losing his wife a decade before. He no longer celebrates Christmas and refused to put a tree. But this is no run-of-the-mill take on Scrooge—especially after watching Jaime's young daughter Addie (Lisa Lucas) drag a decorated tree through town and into the Mills' living room. If the TV viewer is looking for their heart, they'll find it in *The House Without A Christmas Tree*, in which too, veteran actress Mildred Natwick offered her usual stock performance, here—in a supporting role—as Robards' mother. With a sparse budget, *Tree* was produced on videotape, which, in the end, adds to the movie's poignant reality.

- *Miracle on 34th Street* (CBS, 1973): Directed by Fielder Cook. Written by Valentine Davies, Jeb Rosebrook (and others). It's not the original 1947 feature film classic, but it's more touching than the overblown remake from 1994. This version featured Sebastian Cabot (Mr. French from TV's *Family Affair*), David Hartman (soon to be an early-rising staple on ABC's *Good Morning, America*), and Jane Alexander (who's just about to find super fame playing Eleanor Roosevelt in a series of TV-movies for ABC). In solid supporting roles: Roddy McDowall, Jim Backus (*Gilligan's Island, Mr. Magoo*), James Gregory (*Barney Miller*), Conrad Janis (*Mork & Mindy*), Roland Winters, and David Doyle (*Charlie's Angels*) and Tom Bosley (*Happy Days*), who have been cross-identified by viewers for years, and who appeared on screen together for the first time. Add its slick production values (for its time), nostalgia (on so many fronts), and a straightforward "logic within the illogic" script, and this film becomes everything a Christmas TV-movie (or any TV-movie for that matter) should be.

- *Father Knows Best: Home for Christmas* (NBC, 1977): Directed by Norman Abbott and based on the original TV series created by Ed James. Like *The House Without a Christmas Tree*, this reunion TV flick was produced with a low budget and videotaped (whereas the original *Father* series was filmed). But little matter; the script is in place, the story is home-made-for-TV, and the cast is dynamite, including all members of the initial show: Robert Young (*Marcus Welby, MD*), Jane Wyatt (Spock's mom on *Star Trek*), Lauren Chapin, Elinor Donahue (who later married the much-older executive producer Harry *Bewitched* Ackerman; and who also guest-starred on the original *Trek*), and Billy Gray.

- *Saint Maybe* (1998, CBS): Directed by Michael Pressman. Written by Robert W. Lenski. Based on the book by Anne Tyler. Not technically a Christmas movie, this film is infested with the spirit of one. Thomas McCarthy plays a lonely teen who works past a tragic car accident that kills his sister and forces him to care for her three children. Moving, pristine, and downright awe-inspiring. Also starring Blythe Danner, Edward Herrmann (who co-starred with Jane Alexander in those *Roosevelt* TV-movies), the appealing Melina Kanakaredes, Mary-Louise Parker (*Weeds*), and former TV-movie queen Glynnis O'Connor.

- *Christmas on Division Street* (1991, ABC). Directed by George Kaczender. Written by Barry Morrow. On loan from *The Wonder Years*, Fred Savage delivers yet another fine performance, this time as the privileged offspring of wealthy parents who learn the true meaning of Christmas from their son (who learns it from a homeless man). Hint: It doesn't have anything to do with buying lots of expensive, materialistic gifts for people on Black Friday. Also starring Hume Cronyn, Badja Djola, Cloyce Morrow, Kenneth Welsh, and Kahla Lichti.

- *A Dad for Christmas* (a.k.a. *Me and Luke*, 2006, CBS). Directed by Eleanore Lindo. Written by Alan Hines. Based on the novel ("Me and Luke") by Audrey O'Hearn. Newcomer Kristopher Turner plays a compassionate teen-father who sets out to protect and claim his newborn son from the likes of the child's selfish mother. The Oscar-winning Louise Fletcher, as the Turner's grandmother, steps up to the plate as the first-time dad's main ally. Also starring Philip Akin, Lindsay Ames, among others.

- *Borrowed Hearts: A Holiday Romance* (1997, CBS): Directed by Ted Kotcheff. Written by Pamela Wallace and Earl W. Wallace. This time, Roma Downey is no angel. Hector Elizondo is also in this flick, which also stars Eric McCormack, pre-*Will & Grace*. Bottom line: She's poor. He's her rich, snobby corporate boss—and they're brought together by her daughter Carly (Janet Bailey)—with a little help from Elizondo.

- *It Happened One Christmas* (1977, ABC): Directed by Donald Wrye. Written by Lionel Chetwynd and Philip Van Doren Stern. Before the rest of the universe realized the wonder of Frank Capra's 1946 feature classic *It's A Wonderful Life, That Girl* star Marlo Thomas reworked it here with a female twist. And the results were impressive. It's probably because of this remake's success that people became enamored with the original. Also starring Orson Welles (as Mr. Potter), Wayne Rogers (*M*A*S*H*), Cloris Leachman (*The Mary Tyler Moore Show*), Dick O'Neill, Cliff Norton, Christopher Guest, C. Thomas Howell, and Doris Roberts (*Everybody Loves Raymond*) as Ma Bailey.

- *A Christmas Carol* (1984, CBS). Directed by Clive Donner. Written by Roger O. Hirsen and Charles Dickens, The Dickens classic had been remade several times before, but this version starring George C. Scott stands above the rest. It's an A-List production from every angle, also starring Frank Finlay, Angela Pleasence, Edward Woodward, David Warner, Susannah York, Roger Rees, and many other fine actors.

The Night They Saved Christmas (CBS, 1984): Directed by former child star Jackie Cooper, and written by Jim Moloney, this film is much grander than its simple title implies. Starring *Charlie's Angels* Jaclyn Smith, Art Carney (*The Honeymooners*), Paul Le Mat (who starred opposite *Angels* co-star Farrah Fawcett in 1985's groundbreaking TV-movie, *The Burning Bed*), June Lockhart (*Lost in Space*), songwriter Paul Williams, Scott Grimes, and others.

Chapter 32

General TV-movies and miniseries are benchmarked in the history of classic television with several notable entries.

A few standout small-screen films include *My Sweet Charlie* (starring Patty Duke and Al Freeman, Jr., CBS, 1970), *Duel* (starring Dennis Weaver and directed by Steven Spielberg, ABC, 1971), *Don't Be Afraid of the Dark* (starring Kim Darby, ABC, 1973), *Queen of the Stardust Ballroom* (Maureen Stapleton, CBS, 1975), *The Glass Menagerie* (Katharine Hepburn, ABC, 1973), *The Execution of Private Slovik* (Martin Sheen, NBC, 1974), *Trilogy of Terror* (Karen Black, ABC, 1975), *Suddenly Love* (Cindy Williams, NBC, 1978), *Friendly Fire* (Carol Burnett, ABC, 1979), *All Quiet on the Western Front* (Richard Thomas, CBS, 1979), and *The Day After* (Jason Robards, ABC, 1983).

Top miniseries include *Captains and the Kings* (Robert Conrad, NBC, 1976), *Sybil* (Sally Field, NBC, 1976), *Fresno* (Carol Burnett, CBS, 1986), *Shogun* (Richard Chamberlain, NBC, 1980), *Masada* (Peter Strauss, ABC, 1981), *The Thorn Birds* (Richard Chamberlain, ABC, 1983), *The Winds of War* (Robert Mitchum, ABC, 1983), *Heidi* (Jason Robards, The Disney Channel, 1993), and many more in either category.

Cicely Tyson in *The Autobiography of Miss Jane Pittman*, one of the most revered TV-movies of all time. *[Credit: The Classic TV Preservation Society]*

In his book, *The ABC Movie of the Week: Big Movies for the Small Screen*, Michael McKenna explains the influence and scope of the television film format in particular. "The genre was proliferating, a TV-movie might have been deemed a ratings disappointment if it had only drawn an audience of 12 to 13 million viewers. In the modern medium, with a larger, if fragmented audience, an equivalent viewership would almost surely land in the top ten rated programs for the week. It should also be noted the collective viewership of the movies in the 1970s far outpaced the number of people viewing feature films in a theatre setting."

As McKenna also observed, NBC was the first network to ignite the TV-movie format. In 1964, under the guidance of executive Robert Kintner, the Peacock network bartered a deal with MCA/Universal (with whom the network is more closely aligned than ever) to produce what is documented as the first film to be made specifically for the small screen: *See How They Run*, which premiered on October 17,

1964. Featuring popular TV actors like John Forsythe, Jane Wyatt, Leslie Nielsen, and George Kennedy, *Run* was about three children who were hunted down after they unknowingly gathered information that would indict a corrupt international cartel who had just killed their father. Approximately six weeks later, NBC broadcast *The Hanged Man*, a second TV-movie, this time starring Robert Culp and Vera Miles. Here, a gunman seeks vengeance on those he believes murdered his friend and becomes entangled with corrupt labor union politics. Both films scored solid ratings, but it would be two years before NBC would air a third movie.

ABC would screen its first homemade film, titled, *Scalplock*, on April 10, 1966. As McKenna points out, this movie, featuring Dale Robertson, was produced as a pilot for the weekly Western *Iron Horse* (which aired from 1966–1968). McKenna said this development was "illustrative of an emerging trend" in which TV-movies would be utilized as platforms for future regular weekly shows.

As time went on, TV-movies became more of a regular fixture on NBC, which in the 1966–1967 season, aired eight films under the umbrella title *World Premiere Movies*. Eventually joining in the game on a regular or weekly basis were CBS and ABC, the latter of which in 1969 premiered its very popular *Tuesday Movie of the Week* series, which it later paired with the *Wednesday Movie of the Week*. All the networks still aired first runs of feature films (under titles like *The ABC Sunday Night Movie* or *CBS Thursday Night at the Movies*), but it was ABC's 90-minute TV-film format that became the most popular (if by the mid-1970s later influencing each of the networks to utilize the term, *Movie of the Week*, or M.O.W. as a generic description of all films that were made specifically for the small screen). Many have credited then-leading ABC executives Leonard Goldberg, Martin Starger, and Michael Eisner for paving the way for the TV-movie explosion at the network, while others have crowned their colleague Barry Diller as the one who created MOW concept. But McKenna said "…the seminal concept for the MOW did not emanate from the ABC executive offices, but rather from veteran TV producer Roy Huggins. As the creator and producer of highly-successful shows, such as *Maverick*, *The Fugitive* (both for ABC), and *The Virginian* (on NBC), Huggins had built a strong reputation as a man who got a series on the air. Huggins formulated the basic concept of the MOW on New Year's Day 1968 while walking on a California beach."

As Huggins posed to author Leonard Goldenson in his book, *Beating the Odds: The Untold Story Behind the Rise of ABC: The Stars, Struggles, and Egos That Transformed Network Television by the Man Who Made It Happen,* "I asked myself, must we do two-hour movies on TV? I came up with the idea doing a show called *Movie of the Week* that would start at 8:30 and run ninety minutes."

Whoever was responsible for the development of the core 90-minute TV-movie format, the results were significantly productive, in view of heralded small-screen motion pictures like, for starters, *Brian's Song* (1971) and *That Certain Summer* (1972), both airing on ABC's *Movie of the Week*. *Song* was based on the true story of football players Brian Piccolo and Gale Sayers who struck up a friendship while playing for the Chicago Bears, only to learn that Piccolo would soon die of cancer. The film featured James Caan, soon to become a massive movie star by way of *The Godfather*, and Billy Dee Williams. The supporting cast featured Shelley Fabares, late of *The Donna Reed Show,* and several charismatic big-screen performances (alongside Elvis and Rock Hudson).

That Certain Summer dealt with the controversial topic of homosexuality which, while featured with a periodic reference on any one of Norman Lear's TV comedies, had never been so directly addressed in such a dramatic and poignant way on television. Starring Hal Holbrook and Martin Sheen as lovers, the thrust of the story was about Holbrook's older character and his relationship with his son, Scott Jacoby, who struggled with his father's lifestyle.

While *Brian's Song* told the tale of true platonic love between two men, *That Certain Summer* addressed the romantic and sexual nature of what could and did develop between two adult males in love and how it affected extended family members. Both films received awards and made significant headway with the home viewer on several levels. Junior high and high school teachers began assigning the novel adaptations of *Brian's Song* as required reading (which proved especially encouraging to high-school football players who increased their reading capacity), and *That Certain Summer* resulted in never-before-heard conversations between young and older family members in living rooms around the country. ("Mommy…What's a homosexual?" "It's when one man likes another man." "Oh.")

More innovative TV films were to follow. In 1974, *Bewitched* star Elizabeth Montgomery delivered an Emmy-nominated, career-changing performance in NBC's *A Case of Rape*. She played a woman who is raped not once but twice, only to find herself battling the stigma and bureaucratic issues associated with her horrific experience. Before this, the subject matter of rape was rarely presented on primetime or daytime television dramas (if only by this point, in a 1967 episode of ABC's *NYPD* which, that same year, in another episode, had also explored homosexuality). Critics praised the film. Gary Deeb of *The Chicago Tribune* called it "one of the most shocking, painful and socially provocative TV programs of the season." Said Larry Williams of *The Memphis Commercial Appeal*, "What could have been sensationalized was not, and here is where television triumphed, where perhaps a movie for theatrical release would not." Bob Williams of *The New York Post* said it was "probably the best made-for-TV-movie of the home-screen season." Cecil Smith of *The Los Angeles Times* named it "the best effort NBC has had all season in a form it used to call its own—the television movie." Jack Anderson of *The Miami Herald* called it "moving and thought-provoking…an eloquent argument for a review of existing statutes on sexual assault."

A Case of Rape not only became one of the Top Ten highest-rated TV-movies in history, but it also helped to change the congressional laws on rape to better and more substantially protect the rights of all rape victims.

Another TV-movie that changed the pace was CBS-TV's 1973 entry, *The Autobiography of Miss Jane Pittman*, which chronicled the life of a fictional former slave played by the Emmy-winning Cicely Tyson. A few years later, author Alex Haley's generational epic, *Roots* (ABC, 1977), based on his best-selling novel, dealt with the same topic and created an entirely new form of television movie: the miniseries. Both *Pittman* and *Roots*, notably, addressed on television the horrific developments in slavery decades before *12 Years a Slave* did so on the big screen in 2013. Not a miniseries, nor just a one-shot TV-movie, *Divorce His Divorce Hers*, pairing Elizabeth Taylor and Richard Burton in their first venture just for TV, and the syndicated miniseries, *QB VII* starring Ben Gazzara, were each innovative in its way. But it was *Roots* and other miniseries such as *Rich Man, Poor Man* (ABC, 1976) that brought the genre home to the viewer like no other.

Roots not only helped to increase awareness of human suffering and cruelty, but the miniseries encouraged viewer interest in family heritage. *Rich Man, Poor Man*, based on the novel by Irwin Shaw, not only ignited a sequel, *Rich Man, Poor Man, Book II* (ABC, 1978), but it allowed well-known TV actors like Ed Asner and Robert Reed (*The Brady Bunch*) a chance to spread their theatrical wings beyond the roles for which they were most known.

Asner appeared in *Roots* and *Rich Man, Poor Man*. In *Roots*, he played Captain Davies, the morally conflicted captain of the *Lord Ligonier*, the slave ship that brought Kunta Kinte (the film's main character, as played by Le Var Burton) to America. The role earned him an Emmy Award, as did the similarly demented part of Axel Jordache, the father to both the brothers, Tom and Rudy Jordache, as played by Nick Nolte and Peter Strauss in the *Rich Man, Poor Man*.

While playing Axel on *Man*, Asner had an epiphany: "I don't think I ever identified or sympathized with a role as much as I did that one. In the beginning, everyone was saying, 'Oh, what a rotten bastard!' I felt badly because I identified with the man. God knows how or why but I liked what I saw in him. I was delighted that as the filming progressed and people began to realize what there was to him! And the saving graces that occurred in the film, not in the book but in the film, I was very pleased with the reception he got and I got for doing it."

Indeed, there was so much heart in Asner's performance, particularly one scene in which Axel comes to retrieve Nolte's Tom from school after the boy made certain bodacious comments about a well-endowed female teacher. "He slapped his son around," Asner recalled of Axel, "but he'd still bail [Tom] out [of a jam] if he needed to."

In the original novel, it was Strauss' Rudy character that makes the remark and not Tom, prompting Axel to travel from upstate New York to Ohio to get his son, instead of the lengthier distance from New York to California as is explained in TV edition. Asner was impressed with the changes. "That extra mileage in the [miniseries] also made me realize what he was willing to put himself out for because he had no money to [travel that far]."

The actor's favorite scene in the television version of *Rich Man, Poor Man* occurs after Axel finishes beating Tom for fighting Rudy. At this point, Axel retreats to bed with his wife Mary, as played by Dorothy McGuire, who pulls the cover over her head and says, "Jesus, Mary, and Joseph!"

Axel then looks at his wife and responds, "Jesus, Mary and Joseph...and you! Four saints in one bed...[that's] one too many for me!"

For Asner, "little asides like that indicated" that the Axel character was complicated but not pure evil. But in reality, the actor Asner could not be any further from Axel. He remains one of the most beloved performers of his generation, beloved from the early days of anthology television (he played the same character in the original and subsequent remake of *Hawaii Five-0*). His versatile talent on-screen is equaled by his compassionate heart and generous spirit and manner off-screen.

Asner was born in Kansas City, Missouri, and raised in an Orthodox Jewish family. His Russian-born parents were Lizzie, a housewife, and David Morris Asner, who ran a secondhand shop. He attended Wyandotte High School in Kansas City, Kansas, and the University of Chicago in Chicago, Illinois. He later worked on the assembly line for General Motors, served with the U.S. Army Signal Corps, and appeared in plays that toured Army camps in Europe.

In short, Asner was raised with modest beginnings, which allowed him to retain a level perspective and priorities upon arriving in Hollywood. After hundreds of performances on TV, in film, and on the stage, he found fame playing Lou Grant on *The Mary Tyler Moore Show* (CBS, 1970–1977) and then in a spin-off series of his own (*Lou Grant*, CBS, 1977–1982). While other performers of his caliber, talent, and level of success were driving brand-new BMWs, he was still navigating Tinseltown in a 1977 Oldsmobile Cutlass Supreme. To this day, he is down-to-earth and approachable and donates his time, efforts, and money to various charitable causes, sometimes to his detriment. While filming *Lou Grant*, his liberal political leanings cost him his job, and the series was canceled before its time. A former president of the Screen Actors Guild, he continues to perform and remains a vital and outspoken advocate for human rights on the stage of real life.

"I came from middle-class," he said. "My father couldn't read or write English. He had morals and standards." As Tom and Rudy feared Axel on *Rich Man, Poor Man*, Asner feared his father because his four older siblings "made me afraid of him. And yet he never laid a glove on me. I was a mama's boy. Up until second grade we lived in railroad apartments that were above my father's junkyard. My classmates were Mexican. The junkyard was across from a farmer's packing house. So, I had humble beginnings in terms of ostentation. We moved to what I regarded as a white bread village. I made friends in the class."

Being the youngest in the family, Asner was more sheltered than the rest of his siblings who, before long, left home and, as he said, "I was on my own. I encountered whatever I encountered on my own." He became a success in high school but in his sophomore year in college, he dealt with a few challenging friendships, and he "anticipated the tragedy." Most of his friends were invited into fraternities, while he was not, and Asner "saw which way the wind blew. For me, I had been the class clown up to that point."

He said to himself, "Okay—I can't look to friendship to be surrounding me, so, I've got to excel."

So, he began excelling and achieving. But his "greatest regret was joining a college fraternity. In my senior year, it was totally unnecessary. But my buddies were in it, so I thought I'd join. And I betrayed my standards by doing so." After the first year and a half in college, he became involved in acting. He then took on a series of jobs, "all of them, blue-collar—and I suppose that…signifies two things: that I was *typed* and that I identified with, and I'd always would be identified as a common middle class working stiff."

An audience of his peers and fans identified with and responded to all of Asner's roles throughout the years, including and beyond his Lou Grant persona. His TV-movie/ miniseries performances on *Roots* and *Rich Man, Poor Man*, as well as the Christmas special *The Gathering* (ABC, 1977) each earned him one industry award after the other, accompanied by high ratings with the home viewers.

Certain other TV-movies and their actors did not fully register with the audience or specific members of the Hollywood community, such as the 1980 CBS TV-movie called *Playing for Time*. Written by Arthur Miller and musician Fania Fénelon and adapted from Fénelon's autobiography, *The Musicians of Auschwitz*, *Time* featured Vanessa Redgrave as Fénelon—when she was a prisoner in the Auschwitz concentration camp. She and a group of classical musicians were spared the atrocities of their time in return for performing music for their captors. The film, co-directed by Daniel Mann and Joseph Sargent, was also adapted as a play by Arthur Miller.

"You had people in TV who were executives who didn't even have the decency to choose an appropriate person to play a Holocaust survivor," Spielman said. "Instead, they [chose] someone, who was very literally anti-Israel, to create viewership."

And most of those standards were adhered to with the majority of classic TV-movies and miniseries.

Chapter 33

Alex Trebek was the optimum game-show host
[Credit: The Classic TV Preservation Society]

Comedy-variety hours of the 1950s at times morphed into sitcoms starring musical performers (i.e. *The Danny Thomas Show/Make Room for Daddy*), and game shows periodically transformed into talk and variety shows hosted by substantial name performers (like today's talk/variety programs combine elements of game shows: i.e. *The Ellen DeGeneres Show*, *The Tonight Show starring Jimmy Fallon*).

From 1950 to 1961, NBC aired *You Bet Your Life*, hosted by Groucho Marx. As was the case with many of TV's earliest series, *You Bet Your Life* began on radio, specifically in 1947 (with Groucho then serving as both announcer and host). *This Is Your Life*, created by host Ralph Edwards, began on the radio (first on NBC then CBS) in the late '40s. It then transferred to television (only on NBC) from 1952 to 1961. Ten years later, the series returned to television, this time with a syndicated version, and became one of the most popular off-network shows on the air. Before Bob Barker began his historic run as host of *The Price is Right* (CBS, 1972–2012), first hosted by Bill Cullen (from 1956–1965), he was the face of *Truth or Consequences* (CBS/NBC, 1951–1958; and later in a '70s syndicated edition).

Other popular game/variety shows from TV's early years include: *What's My Line?* (CBS, 1950–1957; Syndicated 1968–1975), its twin, *I've Got a Secret* (CBS, 1952–1967), and *The $64,000 Question* (CBS, 1955–1958). *Twenty-One* premiered on NBC in 1956, but it lasted only until 1958 due to and culminating with the infamous game show scandal of the era when a few unsavory producers were providing answers to contestants and rigging the results (all of which was later dramatized in the 1994 movie, *Quiz Show*, directed by Robert Redford).

With the onset of color television, and the '60s and '70s, arrived a new slate of uplifting game shows, less the trials and tribulations: *The Dating Game* (ABC, 1965–1973) and *The Newlywed Game* (ABC, 1966–1974) and popular updates of the celebrity-geared *Password* (CBS/ABC/NBC, 1961–1982), and *Match Game* (NBC/CBS/Syndicated, 1962–1981). *The Hollywood Squares* hosted by Peter Marshall took the shining star panel to new heights with a tri-level, tic-tac-dough-like set; while *American Bandstand* host-turned-media mogul Dick Clark kept upping the ante with his *$25,000* to *$100,000 Dollar Pyramid* game show format.

In the '80s, Merv Griffin hit the jackpot with his daily-double screenings of *Wheel of Fortune* (a circular-take on the famed "Hangman" word-guessing game) and *Jeopardy!*—both of which remain super hits long after his passing (in 2007).

Jeopardy!, hosted for decades by the revered Alex Trebek, in particular has consistently rated as one of the most popular shows in American TV syndication. Screened every weeknight on a network of local affiliates, the show has gained a cult-like following amongst trivia buffs and game show fans. The theme song has become immediately recognizable (as with *The Twilight Zone*) and has long been referenced in most every pop-culture platform since its original daytime run on NBC from March 30, 1964, to January 3, 1975.

In wake of the public's growing frustration of the game show scandals of the '50s, this early edition of *Jeopardy!*, hosted by Art Fleming, became a breath of fresh air and fair play. To further distinguish itself, the show turned the format on its head by having its contestants voice their answers in the form of a question. But it was canceled for the same reason all shows are eventually canceled: low ratings. The show was briefly revived in 1978, but that edition was also canceled due to a lack of audience interest. In 1984, CBS picked up the series, which also began in syndication, both new editions hosted by Alex Trebek. And the show has been on the air ever since, a powerhouse in the ratings, a pop-culture sensation.

The same could be said for *Wheel of Fortune*, the title of which was briefly utilized on a CBS game show from 1952–'53 that lasted only one season. The host was Todd Russell, and the contestants were billed as Good Samaritans. A wheel was turned to win prizes and, while it was a noble attempt at the genre, this *Wheel* wasn't fortunate enough to garner high ratings.

Approximately twenty years later, NBC hired Chuck Woolery and Susan Stafford to co-host a new *Wheel of Fortune*, which began as a one-hour edition of the half-hour format beloved by millions today. Game show historian B. F. Schumin, from www.Chris-Place.com, said Woolery left the 60-minute *Fortune* after a contract dispute and was replaced by Pat Sajak. In December 1982, Stafford also departed the series (on good terms), and Vanna White took her spot in turning letters on a board located next to the famous wheel. And Pat and Vanna have become the king and queen of game show television ever since.

Other game shows, combining charismatic hosts, celebrities and candid camera angles have entertained viewers for decades, while Alan Funt created a new kind of game show with a reality-series bent before the term was invented: *Candid Camera* (ABC, CBS, NBC/Syndicated, 1948–1978), which later inspired everything from ABC's long-running *America's Funniest Videos* (airing since its debut in 1993), and Ashton Kutcher's also-long-running-but-now-defunct *Punk'd* (MTV, 2003–2012).

For a brief time, celebrities left the panels of game shows including an entire list hosted by Bert Convy (*Tattletales*, CBS, 1974–1978; *Super Password* (NBC, 1984–1989), *Win, Lose or Draw* (CBS, 1987–1990, with Vicki Lawrence); they competed on primetime specials like ABC's celebrity-sports hybrid *The Battle of the Network Stars* (hosted by Howard Cosell in 1976) and CBS's *Circus of the Stars* (1977–1979)—all of which decades later transmuted in today's reality shows like the Donald Trump NBC shows, *The Apprentice* and *Celebrity Apprentice*; while celebrities have not (yet!) been castaway on CBS reality shows like *Survivor* (2000-Present) and *The Amazing Race* (2001-Present).

A quaint show called *Bowling for Dollars* was one particular TV sporting event that managed to turn everyday people into humble celebrities. In doing so, this unique game show format also captured the hearts and the high ratings of viewers. Like *Bozo the Clown*, *Bowling for Dollars* was a franchise property that was syndicated across the country with individual-geared editions that utilized local bowling enthusiasts. The former Claster TV Productions in Baltimore, Maryland syndicated the show in 25 markets including Buffalo, Syracuse, and Rochester, New York.

On March 14 of 2015, Alan Morrell, a reporter for *The Democrat and Chronicle* of Rochester chronicled the history of that city's edition of the series, which aired on Channel 13 (then WOKR-TV, now WHAM-TV) during two periods in the '70s and early '80s. The longtime host was Ron DeFrance, and segments were usually broadcast live (sometimes taped) from Channel 13's studio, where two special bowling lanes were constructed just for the show.

Local residents appeared on the show, and it was an immediate hit. The premise was simple: they bowled two consecutive strikes and won a jackpot shared with a "Pin Pal" drawn from a barrel of mailed-in cards from viewers. Fellow *Democrat Chronicle* journalist John Czarnecki recounted in 1974, "There are many who couldn't roll one strike and gutter balls are in evidence. There is the uneasiness of being on TV, which affects everyone."

As Czarnecki went on observe, the show's success fell into "a failsafe structure…Get as many people on the air, spout names continually, be personable … and give away money to thousands and don't stop until every possible viewer within range becomes a 'name' on the program. It is basic. Simple."

In other words, the local TV audience enjoyed tuning in to see people they knew and liked to hear their names mentioned on-air. DeFrance asked contestants, "Who'd you bring with you?" and in-studio supporters dutifully stood and waved to the camera when their names were called. When DeFrance asked whom they wanted to say hi to at home, "Some would pull out a shopping list of names and read the roll … some even said hello to their pets," Czarnecki wrote.

DeFrance's carefree style and amiable persona suited the show, while it also helped put shy contestants at ease. As he noted in 1974, "These people aren't used to being on television. That's why I try to make it enjoyable for them. No doubt, it's a very big thing in their life."

Craig Heslor was the production manager at WOKR, and the former director of *Bowling for Dollars*, which was canceled due not to low ratings, but high production costs. "It was a very expensive show," said Heslor, who has worked for Channel 13 for 50 years. "We were giving away cars and trips, neat stuff like that. They weren't Cadillacs, but they were brand-new cars. We were always number one in the ratings, but it had to be a 'strong' number one because of all that we were giving away."

Within its first year, the Rochester *Bowling for Dollars* had given away more than $100,000 in prizes to more than 2,300 contestants and received more than 825,000 "Pin Pal" cards. That type of payout caught up with the show, and the first version ended after about five years, said Heslor of the now-named WHAM-TV.

Channel 13 attempted to bring back *Bowling for Dollars* a few years later with the local celebrity host Joel Loy, but that incarnation did not last, while a Detroit-area TV station also tried to resurrect the show for its market briefly in 2013. But the magic was gone. The world became too complicated. The stakes became too high on other game shows and sporting events. The simple treasures once so significant on *Bowling for Dollars* of old became less worthy in today's news-oriented world.

But when a simplistic show like *Bowling for Dollars* worked, it triumphed and the winning prize was the joy viewers experienced in the simplicity of seeing their neighbors on TV, whether or not they won the competition.

With the article titled "The Spice is Right" published in the 1960-1961 edition of *Who's Who In Television and Radio*, original *Price is Right* game show host Bill Cullen shared his thoughts on the success of game shows as a particular brand of TV programming.

"*The Price is Right* is right as a TV show that gives the public all one could ask for when it comes to entertainment," he said. "It's lots of fun to do, and judging by the demeanor of the contestants, everybody's having one whale of a time."

"Women seem to have that extra sense of values and according to figures do lots better than men," Cullen continued. "The ladies must have an added bit of perception to walk away with the super-prizes offered on the show. And have you noticed the animation these women have when they come close enough to win? It's as if a Christmas tree were lighted up to surprise to someone who never expected such a thing to happen. And do you know, that exuberance, that extra spice, affects the show personnel, including myself to such an extent that we can't help but join the frolic."

"Drama here is created by the contestants in the studio and that suspense is [delivered] into millions of homes of viewers," he added. "You just can't stifle any of the excitement. I understand that the prizes cover the desires of every woman, man, or child, which is in itself an accomplishment. And of course those extras they just add to the general melee of 'what next?'"

"People are people," Cullen concluded. "But what takes place when people react like people and literally lose themselves in the goings-on is unbelievable. If you ask me, *Price* is an adult *Alice in Wonderland*. You never get enough of this show. And that goes for me, too. And the people you meet are enough to give you the greatest family in the TV world today."

In the same magazine that Cullen shared his thoughts on game shows, famed *What's My Line?* panelist Arlene Francis shared hers with an intricate lesson in American grammar and history:

"It is only in the latest dictionaries that one finds the word 'panel' relating to television or radio. The earliest definition of the word gave me rather a jolt, and I quote, 'panel – a wooden saddle for an ass.'

"I like to think we have gone a long way since then, but I am confident there are some detractors who feel we haven't advanced one iota and that the chairs behind the long tables are still serving the same old purpose! Let the Philistines think what they please. Happily, they are outnumbered."

Panel shows such as *What's My Line?* Francis said, "owe their success to the fact that audiences equate themselves with those of us whose business it is to unravel the riddle. If we miss [an answer], we're as dumb as the boy next door, and if we get it we're as bright as they are – or somebody gave us the answer."

"In that way," Francis continued, "I like to think we do a lot of good."

"Twenty-six million people," she approximated, "all are feeling superior to us. And since *What's My Line?* has survived for [then] eleven years, I feel we must have made at least 14,852,000,000 people happy just by missing once every Sunday night."

Francis said the panel quiz show uncovered a dangerous predilection on the part of celebrities. It permitted them to speak their own lines instead of the "pre-cooked sentences of playwrights and scenarists. With a little encouragement from the studio audience the actor became more emboldened to express himself until today he can carry on a conversation just like anybody else!"

"This remarkable discovery catapulted the art of talking into a succession of television programs devoted to [taking] the tongue out of the cheek and wagging it," Francis added. "People as well as performers are anxious to appear and exchange bon mots and life experiences. It is exhilarating to realize that perhaps in the not-too-distant future, audiences seeing the success of free-wheeling conversation on the screen may try turning to each other for a little philosophic comment and thereby become dazzled at the miracle of sustained thought put into words.

"This business of people conversing at home might eventually mean the end of television, which would, of course, include the demise of the panel show which started the whole thing off."

"That is why we feel for the research people of the future, the following data should be recorded," Francis mused.

Not only were episodes of *What's My Line?* recorded, but the show itself, along with many classic game shows, have been recently rebooted for the modern TV age.

PART 7
CURRENCIES

"I can't handle a love triangle. I'm not a Kardashian."
—Sue Heck, *The Middle*
(Episode: "The Diaper Incident" - 10/2/2010)

[Credit: The Classic TV Preservation Society]

Chapter 34

For many, *Frasier* is considered the last great traditional sitcom of the classic TV age, measured somewhere between 1946 and 2000, when stories were told with distinguishable characters that spoke unique lines of dialogue interpreted with likable performances from actors who played off each other and not to the camera. After *Seinfeld*, the sitcom was redesigned, reconceived, and redefined with shows like *Curb Your Enthusiasm* (HBO, 1999–2011) and NBC's hit trio from the past decade: *The Office* (2005–2013), *30 Rock* (2006–2013), and *Community* (2009–2014) each produced with a hip, edgy style all their own. Prior to these, *Everybody Loves Raymond* (CBS, 1996–2005) celebrated the blue-collar standard, while the Standards and Practices departments of yesteryear TV networks may not have granted a passing grade to 2000 CBS sitcoms like *Two and a Half Men* (2003–2015), *Mike & Molly*, *2 Broke Girls* (2011–2017), or even *The Big Bang Theory* (2007–2019), the latter two of which at least attempted to foster humanity and acceptance beyond one's physical appearance or level of intellect.

Some labeled *2 Broke Girls* vulgar, while others said the same of *Two and a Half Men*, namely one of its former stars: Angus T. Jones, who in *Men* played young Jack Harper, son of Jon Cryer's Alan Harper character, and nephew of Charlie Sheen's Charlie Harper (replaced in recent years with Ashton Kutcher's Walden Schmidt).

Jones exited his role as Jack in 2013 following controversial statements he made about working on the series, which he lambasted and beseeched viewers to tune out. "If you watch *Two and a Half Men*, please stop watching [it]," he said in a video streamed online. "'I'm on *Two and a Half Men*, and I don't want to be on it. Please stop watching it. Please stop filling your head with filth. Please." Jones later regretted his comments with a public statement. "I apologize if my remarks reflect me showing indifference to and disrespect of my colleagues and a lack of appreciation of the extraordinary opportunity of which I have been blessed…I never intended that."

In March 2014, the actor gave an interview to Houston television station KHOC, and once more professed his shame of *Men*, which he said opposed his core Christian beliefs. In a report by *The Wrap*, Jones said the series makes "light of topics in our world that are really problems for a lot of people" and that he was "a paid hypocrite" because even though he wasn't pleased with the show's creative direction, he still kept performing on it.

Jones was raking in approximately $250,000 per episode and now, unfortunately, has not worked steadily on any major television series since. His heart was in the right place, but he may have shot himself in the foot. He could have stuck to his beliefs—and the series—and merely tempered his thoughts more carefully. A young actor with good intentions and a solid set of priorities would have at least been able to communicate his personal views more productively. Instead, his strong opinions silenced any positive impact he may have had by continuing to play a character on a mainstream hit television show that was viewed and would have continued to be viewed by millions; all the while, he would have also continued to *make* millions. This potential alternative might have also allowed him to confer with *Men* producer Chuck Lorre about an episode that might have explored certain ethical questions (and answers!) about life, maybe the same questions that Angus was addressing in his reality. But that never transpired, and the opportunity for positive impact was lost—in a mainstream, large-scale way—on a relatively non-family show.

On the flip side, contemporary sitcoms like ABC's double play which began in 2009, *The Middle* and *Modern Family,* have raised the bar from the beginning, both receiving stellar reviews from day one. Verne Gay of *Newsday* said the show's "writers have great ears for 'real' dialogue and not a single line here feels like a dead ball. The characters, too, arrive fully formed and believable. First impressions are absolutely vital in TV, and *The Middle* makes an excellent one." Jonathan Storm of *The Philadelphia Inquirer* called it a "lively show with no canned laughter, where love has no chance to conquer all the family deficiencies but does make them not only bearable, but fun." David Zurawik, of *The Baltimore Sun* wasn't "yet ready to say *The Middle* is a great sitcom, but it sure seems in sync with the mood of Middle America today."

TV producer Heather Konkoli is known for specials like *The 100 Greatest Moments That Changed TV*, which aired in 2014. She said *Modern* "made it okay to laugh *at* someone and *with* them simultaneously because we can all see ourselves—for better or worse—in the flawed and funny characters. This sitcom broke barriers by making the inner lives of gay couples more accessible and acceptable to mainstream America without sugar-coating them. They were as flawed as every other couple featured. *Modern Family* also proved what at first appeared to be a superficial May-September/gold-digger type relationship was really based deeply in love and appreciation and provided the curmudgeonly patriarch a much-needed second chance at fatherhood. And it shined a light on the fact that the traditional nuclear family was the farthest of all from 'normal' with an overly neurotic mother, moonlighting magician father, and three scheming kids who were often wiser than their parents."

The show's inclusion of characters who are gay, namely, Mitchell Pritchett (Jesse Tyler Ferguson) and Cameron Tucker (Eric Stonestreet), has helped the mainstream acceptance of the Lesbian Gay Bisexual Transgender community (LGBT), just as *Will & Grace* did on NBC from 1998 to 2006, and like ABC's *Life Goes On* family drama accomplished from 1989 to 1993 with assisting the mainstream acceptance of members of the disabled community (as well as those afflicted with AIDS).

Actor Ty Burrell plays Phil Dunphy, *Modern's* brother-in-law to Mitchell and Cam. In September 2012, he talked about the show's impact with *The Hollywood Reporter*. "I have family members that I don't necessarily need to name, that felt one way [about gay rights] five years ago [when the show debuted] and feel a different way now. And I think that sort of …weirdly enough…banality…is revolutionary."

As *Hollywood* reported, "The series is a mix of incisive dialogue, sharp storytelling, and broad humor about universal conflicts, hardly the recipe for subversive programming." The trade magazine documented how polls in America reflect a shift toward the acceptance of same-sex marriage, while Burrell added:

"I know several conservative people that were saying one thing five years ago, and are now changing their tone," Burrell said. "Some super conservative people I know are not necessarily prepared to advocate for gay marriage, but I hear them defending gay people. I mean, literally, if something is said about gay people, I have heard those very same people who would have been on that other side of the argument, saying like, 'Well, you know, it's not easy for them. They're trying their best.' Even if it's still a little patronizing, it's changed its tone."

As TV writer Bill Persky explained it, for a sitcom to be funny, it has to be based on reality, which in turn may contribute to educating the audience in some manner. "That was the fun of *The Dick Van Dyke*

Show," he said, referring back to that classic CBS series of the 1960s. "It gave the audience something they identified with…the kind of a mild precursor to the type of humor that was later presented on *Seinfeld*… the little incidental stuff. And that's the thing that's been lost in today's shows. If they couldn't say 'vagina,' *2 Broke Girls* wouldn't be on the air. They just set up opportunities to have sex. And my biggest hatred is for [the show] *Girls* on Showtime. I think [that series creator and star] Lena Dunham is brilliant, but it bothers me that she doesn't use her talents to elevate people. Not that everything has to be elevating… but there was a common denominator of decency in the classic shows, even with the characters that were made fun of, we did so, lovingly."

When asked what he would do if he was in charge of *Girls*, he replied, "The laundry…because in two years there's never been a scene where they did the laundry. You've never seen anyone change those sheets that have been so violated and corrupted by every kind of perverse sex in the world. It's slovenly and it just bothers me a lot."

In reference to his famous *Dick Van Dyke Show* episode, "That's My Boy??" which dealt with race relations, a then-taboo subject of the '60s, Persky said, the topic "was handled in such a gentle and loving way that you weren't hit over the head with it. And it was just the beginning of a whole opening of dialogue. Whereas today—everything is thrust in your face and pounded into you. There's no grace in anything….no subtly. They only do shows to have the opportunity to be smutty."

A few recent contemporary sitcoms had appealed to Persky, such as *Modern Family*. "There's a dignity [in that show] in the way everyone is treated and it's funny. But all the other comedy shows…they look for ways to debase people and characters. They're almost like bullying. I don't watch *The Big Bang Theory*. I mean, it's funny and those characters are interesting, I guess. But I don't watch it. I *will* watch *Mike & Molly*…because I think [Melissa McCarthy, who plays Molly] is so funny. I'll watch to see somebody rather than the show…but they're all jokes. And I can honestly say that I have never written a joke. And by that, I mean, I never thought, 'Oh, it would be funny to say this'… 'Or how about we do that?' It was always, 'This is where the story is taking us.' And [from there, one of the writers] would do a twist [on the story] that made it funny. But it was not like we set out to work a joke in somewhere. It was taking what you were given and making it funny."

Be they past or present, first run, or rerun, syndicated or networked, via cable or broadcast TV, if a situation comedy is properly and professionally executed, the reward is a loyal following of fans and high ratings. But if a sitcom presents its laughter with class, distinction, and humanitarian content and effort that result in a sincere joy that's delivered to a multitude of watchers, the reward becomes something much more significant than attaining high ratings.

Chapter 35

It's a *Mad Men* world, and we're all just living in it.

So, it would seem with regard to the increasing popularity of the A&E period drama that has captured the hearts and minds of viewers since its debut in 2007.

Mad Men's success was measured not only by companies like Mindset Media but also by high-profile viewers like the Oscar-winning director Bernardo Bertolucci, one of the show's biggest fans. During a tribute in his honor by the American Academy a few years back, Bertolucci said he was disappointed with the Hollywood feature film world that once inspired him. Instead,

[Credit: The Classic TV Preservation Society]

he preferred to watch television shows like *Mad Men*. Bertolucci, who directed movies like *Last Tango in Paris* (1972), *Novecento* (1976), and *The Emperor* (1987), once told *The Hollywood Reporter* that TV programming such as *Mad Men* offers superior casting and direction above and beyond current movie-house productions. His generation, he added, had an "affair with American culture, there's no doubt about it. A street lamp and a fire hydrant made me sing in the rain...but the American films I like now do not come from Hollywood studios but from television series," such as *Mad Men*.

Producer Heather Konkoli has worked specials like the TV Guide Network's *Story Behind: Mad Men*. As she saw it, "You could say *Mad Men* has shown us how far we've come and how far we still have to go when it comes to sexism and discrimination in the workplace and in society in general. While alcohol-swilling, womanizing Don Draper [played by Jonathan Hamm] isn't exactly a role model, he is still a very inspirational character that completely reinvented himself from a 'poor nobody' to an 'Ad King of Madison Avenue' by swaying people with his confidence and raw talent. The same thing could be said for [characters like] Peggy Olsen [Elizabeth Moss] and Joan Harris [Christina Hendricks] who clawed their way to positions of power however painstaking it may have been. All these characters and their level of 'moxie' very much parallel show creator Matthew Weiner in his undying and uncompromising efforts to get the show made and to maintain its high level of quality and integrity throughout *Mad Men's* seven groundbreaking seasons."

Whether Weiner realized it or not, his '60s-based series presented itself like classic shows of days-gone-by—and not only with regard to premise, setting, and style. The series is a nostalgic period piece of a bygone era (the work-world of classic TV advertising man Darrin Stephens on *Bewitched* is pervasive throughout the show). Still, there is nothing organically revolutionary about its core content and general presentation.

Mad Men was an innovative series, but its production was innovative. Audiences had seen this style before, executed time and again by any number of classic television programs and feature films. With its lengthy, still-camera shots on its actors like Hamm and others, and minus the manic-pacing and swift dialogue exchanged between the characters (a style that was overtly-ignited by *Gilmore Girls* in the early 2000s), *Mad Men* displays a tranquil eloquence and sophistication that harkens back yes, to a more fashionable era, but it did not pave the way for genius on TV.

That path was already set in stone by *Perry Mason*, *Peter Gunn*, *Route 66*, and even *Father Knows Best*. Each of these properties, and hundreds more, were produced in the traditional manner of filming a television show (or feature film, for that matter): there were no spastic camera angles, no hand-held cameras, and no constant, chronic musical score that is sometimes employed to hide a less-than-worthy script. Music was utilized almost as a character and for certain emotional effects but not in every frame (as is the case today with many new TV-movies). Actual stories and characters were allowed to develop and evolve, as opposed to being thrown at the audience, begging for their attention. Unfortunately, such strategies are utilized on contemporary programs (and in big-screen movies) to prevent viewers from changing the channel (or exiting the theatre).

Conversely, in one of his many assessments of *Breaking Bad*, which aired on AMC from 2008 to 2013, Tim Goodman, the popular TV critic for *The Hollywood Reporter*, called this extremely successful show "one of the most acclaimed series of all time and one of my favorite series ever." A recent poll of anonymous *Breaking* fans, conducted by Larry Brody's TVWriter.com, provides a few answers as to why *Bad* is considered so good by so many:

- "As someone who watched and enjoyed every episode, I felt like it was one of the few shows that really kept me on the edge of my seat, made me relate to the characters even as they underwent big transformations, and always kept me longing for more at the end of each episode. Also, it's a smart show that really rewards its vigilant viewers when it comes to setting things up and paying them off. There was no spoon-feeding plot points. You had to pay attention and use your own intuition to follow along. Everything was there for a reason. No red herrings. But you had to sometimes be patient for things to come back around or to finally make sense."

- "It is intriguing because it chronicles the transition of an ordinary suburbanite chemistry teacher and others around him into an increasingly dark world as a result of ambiguous moral choices. Basic premise: He is dying of cancer and chooses to manufacture meth as a way to make money for his family when he is gone. But the choices start to snowball from there. Plus, it is hilarious as a dark comedy as well.

- "…his brother-in-law is a drug cop that takes him along one day to make a drug bust…being a chemist he then decides to go into making crystal meth and is very good at it. The next four years are filled with excitement and suspense. It is so popular because every man out there (can relate) to what this man will do for his family…but at the very last episode, we find a surprise about that."

- "I haven't watched it…but my oldest [son] was just tonight saying that he recently 'caught up' with all of the seasons using Netflix, is going to watch the series finale tonight, and says it's probably the best TV drama ever."

An anonymous reader offered this different view and covered the entire spectrum of scripted dramatic and comedic programming from the classic to contemporary eras:

"I've never seen *Breaking Bad*. But it's about a [chemistry] teacher who made and sold crystal meth. The series got darker and darker. The acclaim comes from (and my friend who loves the show swears by this) outstanding writing, direction, and performances. Hey, you can't argue with those three areas. The plot just doesn't appeal to me. I never watched it. I've never watched *The Sopranos*, either. I'm sure they are well-made TV series. They just don't appeal to me. The darkest series I ever watched was *The Shield* (FX), and I had to leave the series mid-way because it became too dark and disturbing for me. I do love series such as *Law & Order, Law & Order: SVU*, and *Law & Order: Criminal Intent*. Excellent shows that I also have to take frequent breaks from. I'm realistic towards life and TV. But my real life is stressful enough. I have to watch what I watch. I'm an intense person, so I'm careful what I expose my mind and heart to. I soak things up like a sponge. That includes TV and films. I most enjoy *The Big Bang Theory, Modern Family, The Middle, Once Upon A Time, The Golden Girls* [and] *The Munsters*."

Then, almost 30 years before *Euphoria* and *13 Reasons Why* were making headlines for their complex, mature portraits of teenage life, *Beverly Hills, 90210* was laying the foundation for the genre as we know it. It's then-revolutionary exploration of the social and sexual drama of high-school life became appointment viewing on a then-fledgling Fox network and turned its mostly little-known cast into celebrities who incited mall mobs. It aired for 10 seasons and spawned both a successful spin-off, *Melrose Place*, and a CW reboot, simply titled, *90210*.

In the late summer of 2019, the show's original cast reunited for a six-episode documentary-style series. Present were Jennie Garth, Tori Spelling, daughter of original *90210* producer Aaron Spelling, Jason Priestley, Ian Ziering, Gabrielle Carteris, Brian Austin Green, and Shannen Doherty. The only missing member was Luke Perry, who suffered a fatal stroke shortly before the project's announcement.

In essence, the new *90210* was a heightened reality show.

But for many, the stage of contemporary reality programming has been defined as mean-spirited, as evidenced with non-scripted shows like *Survivor, Jersey Shore* (MTV, 2009), *The Real Housewives of Beverly Hills* (Bravo, 2010-Present), and to some extent, even musical competition shows such as *American Idol* (Fox, 2002-Present), *Dancing with the Stars* (ABC, 2005-Present), and *The Voice* (NBC, 2010-Present).

Ed Spielman once more offered his straightforward insight, regarding one reality show in particular that has become one of the most popular of the genre in recent years: *Keeping Up with the Kardashians*, which debuted on E! in 2004, and which profiles the wealthy family headed by Kris Jenner, once married to former Olympic athlete Bruce Jenner (who has now transitioned into Caitlyn Jenner); their two children Kylie and Kendall, and three other daughters, Khloe, Kourtney, and Kim, from Kris's previous marriage to the late (and former attorney to O.J. Simpson) Robert Kardashian.

With regard to Kim, formerly married to musical artist Kanye West, Spielman said, "As far as I know, this young Kardashian woman is not trying to cure cancer. She cannot play the harmonica. She cannot tap dance; she's not gifted in any particular way. The only cultural contribution, if you want to call it that, is a sex tape that showed up on the internet. That same woman is now doing endorsements. Why... because there's no shame and because there's no public standard of morality. And nothing could be more instructive than that.

"Because there is no shame, there is no standard and the question is: Why would somebody like that be on the cover of every supermarket magazine. Now it's violence for its own sake without a moral point. It's not the good guys up against the bad guys and now you have fame for its own sake like the Roman Colosseum. The fame itself is the goal and not famous like Jonas Salk because [he] cured polio, not famous like Dwight Eisenhower because he was one of the great military leaders of any century so he got on *Time Magazine*. You have people *Keeping Up with the Kardashians*. Today, a sex tape on the internet is considered [a productive] marketing [technique], which is how Kim was introduced to the mainstream media, beyond being one of Paris Hilton's good friends.

"So, what's the answer? Unless you can—by whatever device—restore a public standard of morality, you're going to have a diminution of the quality of life in the populace," said Spielman. "The fact that America is printing money and is broke; the fact that a kid cannot go out in the street and play unless the parents want to be arrested for child endangerment. What we have is a society that has been deconstructed into people who are materialists. They simply are consumers and taxpayers. That's what the prevailing lack of values has accomplished," while at the same time, "TV always had the limits of what could and could not be shown. When you go to the movies, doesn't it seem like you're seeing commercials or trailers for the same movie? It's all the same."

In life, Spielman said, "Things are either evolving or devolving. Nothing ever stays the same." As he first conveyed, "[film and television productions have] removed the moral judgment as to what the conflict was about and the violence itself became the entertainment. Well, because people are in constant need of enhancement, they'll never digest the same thing again and again, so you have to raise the level of violence." With reference back to director Sam Peckinpah's feature film, Spielman said, "I'm not a big fan of The Wild Bunch, but that is a perfect example of where at the end, the bloodletting, the carnage, became the entertainment itself."

Fellow writer Bill Persky shared similar insight from a recent movie theatergoing experience. "There were six coming attractions, and not one of them was a human story," he recalled. "There wasn't one movie just about a regular person. [Apparently], without explosions [played out in the plot], there'd be no movies. And then once cable TV came along…I think [that] destroyed the country on many levels. For one, there is too much news. So much so, that everyone is running around interviewing people as their family members are dying…and they [news journalists] feel it's their right to be in people's faces at their moment of tragedy and people accept that, and feel that's what is expected of them to do [to share their most intimate feelings for all the world to see]."

Television scribe Arnie Kogen likened the association between "The Tube" and society to that of courtship between human beings. "TV has turned out to be a bad date. It started out as a beautiful, exciting, enchanting thing and then, over the years, slowly started to disintegrate." In the early days of television, specifically from the late 1940s to the early 1950s, "it was this wonderful thing," he said. As Kung Fu creator Ed Spielman pointed out, families would gather around their eleven-inch DuMont TV set and watch variety shows hosted by the likes of Milton Berle, Sid Caesar, or Ed Sullivan, or a Western such as Gunsmoke. "It was truly a family event," Kogen intoned. But six decades later, the family is isolated.

"When was the last time [that] Mom, Dad, the two kids, and Aunt Hilda all sat down together to watch a network show in prime time? I think it was in 1971. Today Dad is in his man cave watching a DVR of a football game, Mom is viewing a cat video on YouTube, the teen daughter is texting, the teen son is Skyping, and Aunt Hilda is on her iPad uploading a picture of herself to a strange guy on Craig's List. Family togetherness has gone the way of the manual typewriter."

Fortunately, many of the programs to which Kogen, Persky, Spielman, and so many other wonderful TV writers have contributed scripts are still accessible via networks like the beloved Hallmark Channel and TV Land (or for outright purchase on DVD). But there is little doubt about the increasingly violent and vulgar content of TV programming that was nowhere present in the "Golden Age" of the '50s, the "fantasy-fun" days of the '60s, or even the revolutionary content of the '70s.

In his article for Variety magazine titled "Brave New World: Cable TV Pushing Boundaries," columnist Brian Lowry once expressed thi:

"Networks are [now] pushing sexual boundaries on their shows to stand out from the crowd. But there's a fine line between provocative programming and prurience." And the audience is not only taking notice, but they're also putting the networks on notice.

In the Feedback portion of The Los Angeles Times "Calendar" section, L.A. resident Rena Moretti expanded the point with her response to an article written by Mary McNamara ("The Giant Leap To TV," 9/15/2015), about the recent film-to-TV migration of many classic shows. In addressing the small and big screen's ever-changing landscape, with particular regard to television's increasing descent into edgier programming, Moretti complained, "We are living in a dark age for movies and TV," then agreed with

McNamara's take on TV-movies from the 1970s: "They were of a higher level than anything Hollywood puts out now."

Around the same time, classic TV legend Dick Van Dyke offered his assessment of reality shows, specifically *Dancing with the Stars*, on which he has repeatedly refused to compete and appear. "I do hate it, I must say," he opined. "I know [they are] inexpensive to do, but I don't think it's entertainment. Those shows encourage bad behavior."

Epilogue

[Credit: The Classic TV Preservation Society]

On December 6, 1951, the National Association of Broadcasters (NAB) adopted a set of ethical standards called the Code of Practices for Television Broadcasters (PTB). Compliance with the code was represented by the "Seal of Good Practice," which was displayed during closing credits of most American TV shows from 1952 to the early '80s. In part, the code "prohibited the use of profanity, the negative portrayal of family life, irreverence for God and religion, illicit sex, drunkenness and addiction, presentation of cruelty, detailed techniques of crime, the use of horror for its own sake, and the negative portrayal of law enforcement officials."

The PTB also regulated how performers should dress and move to be within the "bounds of decency" and how news reporting was to be "factual, fair and without bias" (with commentary and analysis required to be "clearly defined as such"). The networks were to make time for spiritual broadcasting and were "discouraged from charging religious bodies for access," and the PTB rules limited the commercial minutes per hour.

In the wake of a settlement with the Justice Department, the Code was suspended in 1983. Seventeen years later, Angela J. Campbell authored the essay "Self-Regulation and the Media," which concluded that, applying the Code of Practices for Television Broadcasters to "digital television public interest responsibilities and privacy on the Internet" [as] "self-regulation is not likely to be successful in these contexts."

The "Seal of Good Practice" is relaxed with most new television programs. Today, a TV show does not require a moral or a message to succeed, nor should it. But when a new series does succeed, more times than not, it does so while the "Seal of Good Practice" is no longer required or enforced.

The lack of diversity in casting that disavows contemporary programming has distinguished classic TV shows. The cast on any new TV series more times than not looks the same. And if they don't look the same, they resemble or speak in the same way—with very few unique characteristics or qualities in sight or sound. Most of the lead male characters are young, good-looking, and white—with brown hair and brown eyes, or black hair with blue eyes, or somewhere not so far from in-between. Most of the leading female characters are young, good-looking, and white, with brunette hair and light eyes, while most, if not all male or female characters speak swiftly with acerbic tones.

Conversely, classic TV shows series from the '50s to the early '80s, received the "Seal of Good Practice," and were ahead of their time. *Marcus Welby, M.D.*, for one, starring Robert Young, showcased a senior male lead with gray hair and blue eyes, a young white associate with alabaster skin and brown eyes (James Brolin), and a fortysomething female office manager of Latin descent with light brown hair and eyes and olive skin (Elena Verdugo).

Tune into a retro '70s segment of *Bridget Loves Bernie* and view a male Jewish lead (David Birney) and a blond white female lead (Meredith Baxter-then-Birney), surrounded by a supporting cast of all ages with various degrees of brown, blond, black, and white coloring (David Doyle, Audrey Lindley, Harold J. Stone, William Elliott). Turning the world on with her smile during any episode of *The Mary Tyler Moore Show* is the white mid-western woman (Mary Richards, played by Moore) intermingling with a thirtysomething Jewish girl (Valerie Harper's Rhoda), a heavy-set, short and balding middle-aged white man (Ed Asner's Lou Grant), a silver-haired middle-aged male fox (Ted Knight's Ted Baxter), a middle-aged female blond with piercing blue eyes and a healthy sex drive (Betty White's Sue Ann Nivens), and a take-charge, middle-aged female blonde with a bouffant hairdo (Cloris Leachman's Phyllis Lindstrom).

Investigate *Mannix* and find an Armenian lead male detective (Mike Connors) with a female African-American secretary (Gail Fisher).

The Golden Girls showcased four female seniors, each unique in appearance: one, tall with a low voice (Bea Arthur as Dorothy); another, tiny with a big voice (Estelle Getty's Sophia); a Southern confident (Rue McClanahan's Blanche); and an innocent bystander with a heart of gold (Betty White as Rose).

Frasier presented two male sibling psychologists who act and sound alike but, in essence, are two very different people (Kelsey Grammer and David Hyde Pierce as the brothers Drs. Crane). Surrounding them are a tall, thin British woman with brown hair (Jane Leeves as Daphne Moon), a midwestern straightforward female with red hair (Peri Gilpin as Roz Doyle), and a gray-haired physically-challenged man with a cane (John Mahoney's Martin Crane).

Have breakfast or lunch with *Alice* and be served by a grumpy middle-aged man who operates Mel's Diner (Vic Tayback's Mel Sharples), a dark-haired girl from Jersey (Linda Lavin), a redheaded spitfire from Texas (Polly Holliday), and a pin-thin, Olive-Oyl-like (as in *Popeye*) high-school graduate (Beth Howland).

Swim on over to *Gilligan's Island* and discover a skinny little buddy with a white cap (Bob Denver in the lead), who pals around with a heavy-set, sandy-haired Skipper (Alan Hale, Jr.). Into that mix is a pre-*Big-Bang-Theory* Professor with his khaki-beige science duds (Russell Johnson), a stuffy millionaire and his wife (Jim Backus and Natalie Schafer), the demure and dark-haired down-to-earth country girl in ponytails and shorts (Dawn Wells as Mary Ann), and the tall, slinky, redhaired movie star with an attitude (Tina Louise as Ginger Grant).

Throughout the '50s, '60s, '70s, and to some extent, the '80s, TV casts were a diverse bunch. But where are the distinct personalities today? Where are the uncommon looks? Does *every* character have to be sarcastic, sardonic, quick-witted, and edgy? Does *every* actor cast have to be young and beautiful? Does *every* character/actor have to mumble and garble their words with abandon and without proper diction?

For some, it is this lack of authenticity, combined with the relaxation of the "Seal of Good Practice," that has contributed to a near-obscene miscalculation in contemporary television, a mismatch of monochromatic, mundane, and sometimes horrific and profane images and language that pervades today's all too "dark" and "edgy" approach to programming.

Michael Drew, a blogger for *The Huffington Post*, made a case in his article, "The Argument for Authenticity in Popular Culture." He wondered if authenticity is "a quest" or "a sign of our times… [Can] we recognize it when we…see, hear or read it?…We live in an age when people are moved less by spectacle and more by what they consider to be actuality—what feels real."

Drew added, "As anyone…who's watched even a portion of the many televised singing-competition shows on the air, contestants are singing their hearts out. But that doesn't mean they're singing well, or that their feelings, however earnest they seem, are genuine, or that they can convey genuine emotion. Loud and lamenting doesn't equal real and raw."

In the history of classic television, The Beatles' performance on *The Ed Sullivan Show* was assuredly authentic—for those who enjoyed it live in the theater and for the home audience. Ed Spielman's experience of watching TV as a child in Brooklyn was authentic. Noble sentiment remains at the core of his *Kung Fu* series, and many classic TV shows. From *Batman* to *The Waltons*, from Johnny Carson's respect for every guest he interviewed to each time Carol Burnett earnestly tugged her ear, the TV hits of the past and their stars remain heroic in their individuality.

The modern techniques of TV storytelling may be innovative but not altogether clarified. Just who exactly are all those characters talking to when they are seen on camera, being interviewed in all those modern show interstitials? For what documentary are they granting these interviews? How long is this documentary supposed to go on—and when will it be broadcast?

And what about that manic, portable-cam shaky effect that seems mandatory on all contemporary series? Does one wonder what any new half-hour comedy, one-hour drama, or other new presentation would do without it? If this technique were not utilized, the camera would actually have to stay on the contemporary TV actor for a lengthy amount of time instead of frequently jagging to the left and right or bobbing up and down.

What would they do then?

While there are several funny new characters on TV sitcoms today, they might better be defined as caricatures. In most cases, on most new programs, there is no true interaction between any characters. Instead, it seems as if each is performing some kind of stand-up material on the stage of their family living rooms or at their office desk, walking in and out of their scenes, cuing each other on who's to "go on" next.

To better integrate themselves into the homes of TV viewers, contemporary characters might stop behaving like caricatures and act more like people. They may have at one time evolved from them, but sitcoms are not variety show skits. As Buster Keaton once relayed to sitcom queen Lucille Ball, "You have to play comedy dead straight. You have to believe that your *nose is on fire*" (a reference to the classic *I Love Lucy* episode, "L.A. at Last," in which Ball's Lucy Ricardo accidentally sets her snout a flame). The innovations of the modern age undoubtedly contribute various new ways of storytelling on television (or the big screen). But while the shaky camera angle effect may have its place in today's fast pace—both a result and reflection of the world's present manic state—no jazzy, flickering screen image will ever take the place of a good story created with fine words that solidify a sound beginning, middle, and end. Movie theaters may be ignited with an assortment of *Avengers* and *X-Men*, displaying brains and brawn, cunning and cache, daring and diligence, all of which may be transferred to the small screen by way of DVD or Blu-ray.

But there is a measure of hope amidst some innovation in contemporary comedies, as television has at least tried to do itself some good in recent years.

In late June 2019, *Los Angeles Times* reporter Randee Dawn interviewed Simon Rich, creator of *Miracle Workers*, on how modern TV audiences have helped shift programming toward more ethical mores. "People are gravitating toward shows that try to post some kind of explanation for the deeply flawed world we find ourselves in," Rich said.

The following July, Netflix offered a couple of retro-styled, minority-geared sitcoms that were filmed in a traditional manner. Observed *Los Angeles Times* TV critic Robert Lloyd at the time:

"As Netflix prepares to take us back to 1985 with the third season of *Stranger Things*, it's also looking backward with two new sitcoms, the recently premiered *Mr. Iglesisas* and *Family Reunion*…Both series focus on people of color and are filmed, multi-camera style, before a live audience, as was the network's Latinx reboot of *One Day at a Time*" (then canceled and subsequently salvaged by Pop TV, owned by CBS).

In early November 2019, Lloyd pointed out how "For years, the go-to metaphor for TV was a 'vast wasteland,'" a term coined in 1961 by FCC Chairman Newton Minow. While one can't help but wonder if the S.S. Minnow from *Gilligan's Island* was named after Newton, Lloyd wrote, "But in the premium platinum post-*Sopranos* age, we reflexively proclaim that television is not just better than ever—Bryan Cranston said it in just those words at [2019's] Emmy Awards—but possibly the Best. Thing. Ever."

In January 2021, from the Marvel Cinematic Universe arrived *WandaVision*, a high-concept semi-situation comedy that premiered on Disney+. Inspired by a few sequences that ignited a romantic spark between Elizabeth Olsen's telekinetic Wanda Maximoff (otherwise known as the Scarlet Witch) and the robotic Vision, played by Paul Bettany, this show, created by Jac Schaeffer, finds the two living as a couple in a surreal world that reboots the history of TV comedy, where they are surrounded by "normal people," who cannot find out their true identity. As Lloyd observed once more, "With *WandaVision*, the sitcom gets a fresh makeover. It's the rare Marvel property where humor is more than just decoration."

However, nothing saves the day more than a sweet, charming visit with the real thing; the actual classic TV sitcoms or any kind of retro show with a few cordial family members, friends, and happy hours—in our living rooms after hours or work. Nothing soothes the classic TV soul like listening to the lilting musical theme of *The Donna Reed Show*, inviting us back to a simpler time in a way that not even a later-day movie like *Pleasantville* attempted to portray. The colorful opening credits of shows like *Love, American Style* and *Wonder Woman*, particularly the '40s-based first season, accompanied by their pulsating themes songs, have a measure of super power to entertain an increasingly-complicated world if even for just a few moments.

For many, TV's past and perfect mothers and fathers, sons and daughters, brothers and sisters, aunts and uncles, cousins, girlfriends and boyfriends, co-workers, A-types, B-types, cougars, lions, *Mister Ed* horses, *Gentle Ben* bears, and *Lassie* canines can all be found, each made in a simpler time. The harsh realities of the contemporary world continue to intensify amidst sophisticated technologies and a barrage of violent and vulgar images allegedly directed at "mature audiences only," as if maturity had anything to do with cursing or committing crimes.

In our educated world, common words and common acts of no valor are all too frequently spoken by uncommon people. The freedoms of speech and expression have been abused and have long outworn their welcome. Historians would argue that it was not the vision of our Founding Fathers to have freedoms that threaten decency and dignity. What purpose does any of that serve if the result is the ultimate fall of humane behavior (or even humanity)?

When the power of intimate media comes into play, as it does with actors, writers, producers, directors of television programming of any genre, should those same individuals make only dignified choices?

We may all curse when we stub our toes or grow impatient in unending traffic. But does that validate hearing a TV character curse every two seconds just because the relaxed rules of cable television have granted such flexibility? This is frequently the case without any legitimate creative cause to the character, and mostly, to the detriment and at the expense of the given character's true definition.

"With great power comes great responsibility."

So said Peter Parker's gentle and wise Uncle Ben (as played by Cliff Robertson) to the young web-slinger (Tobey Maguire) in the first major live-action *Spider-Man* feature film (of 2002).

The same could be said for the creative touch on television.

Arguably the most influential communication device created in the last century, or possibly ever, television has remained a fully-untapped resource for education—beyond the more direct approach of PBS. If in the creating and displaying of multi-layered stories with textured characters on shows, movies, specials, documentaries, is it such a bad thing for the TV audience not only to be entertained but to walk away all the wiser and kinder?

TV variety show pioneer Garry Moore may have had the answer long before the question was ever answered. Moore shared the following thoughts in an article he wrote in 1960 for *Who's Who in Television and Radio*:

"To me, the best thing about working in television is that the people who watch it, and they alone, are the ultimate and final judges of your efforts. In some quarters, I know, there is a tendency to speak of the 'mass audience' with some condescension, to peg public taste at a low level. The experience of television has proven that this is a fallacy. The trite, the unimaginative, the phony or dishonest elements that inevitably creep into such a vast enterprise as television occasionally are just as inevitably uncovered, to be quickly dismissed from the TV scene. A public that simply will not tolerate inferior entertainment can do just that by turning the dials on their TV sets."

To keep viewers tuning in and interested and entertained, "this is the greatest challenge to all of us in television," Moore decided. "Each season, we all try to meet it as best we can, to outdo our efforts of the previous season."

Fortunately, classic TV shows will live on in every season, via DVD and Blu-ray, or through syndication and/or streaming on retro networks like Get-TV. In October of 2015, Jeff Meier, then senior vice president of programming for Get-TV, shared his affection for classic TV *with the Los Angeles Times*; he delighted in the historic synergy of having, for one, reruns of *The Judy Garland Show* air on a network that is based on the Culver City, California, studio lot where Garland made several of her movies for MGM. "Goose bumps go through me when I think of that," Meier said.

In the process, the more family-oriented of the retro series will forever serve as a template for an ideal life.

Lucille Ball remains a staple of classic TV family programming. In *Here's Lucy*, she starred with her real-life children, Desi Arnaz, Jr. and Lucie Arnaz, and Gale Gordon, one of Ball's favorite actors. *[Credit: The Classic TV Preservation Society]*

For many, classic or any form of television has become a saving grace of escapism and academics and continues to inspire. Television has talked and walked us through the footsteps of Kwai Chang Caine on *Kung Fu*. At its highest, most productive level, TV has offered options on how to hold in reverence the creeds of all good religions and spiritual beliefs; to honor our parents as gracefully as Beaver and Wally Cleaver; to raise our children with the type of lovingkindness that Uncle Bill showered upon Buffy, Jody, and Cissy on *Family Affair*; to liken ourselves to Samantha and Darrin, and respect each other's differences by concentrating on what makes us the same; to be as likable and charming as Ann Marie and that boy Don Hollinger on *That Girl*; to influence our doctors to more readily resemble the caring *Marcus Welby, M.D.*; to protect the laws of humanity, as valiantly as *Perry Mason* and *Barnaby Jones*; to have as strong a work-ethic as Rob Petrie and Mary Richards; to comprehend how true power comes from inner strength, as so nobly displayed by *The Bionic Woman*; to be like *The Waltons*, and appreciate every morsel of food and every moment of family time. And mostly, if only, to make one another laugh as much as Lucy does for each of us.

Or as Professor James K. Howard, played by Jimmy Stewart on *The Jimmy Stewart Show*, once said, in turning to the camera, "My family and I wish you peace and love and laughter.""

Appendix:
Selective Classic TV Milestones

In the Beginning

From left: *The Beulah Show*, Nat King Cole, *The Nelsons* – Ozzie, Harriet, David and Ricky, Raymond Burr and Barbara Hale from *Perry Mason* [Credit: The Classic TV Preservation Society]

- The Dumont Network was the first major television broadcast network.
- The Seal of Good Practice appeared at the end of most television shows that aired from the 1950s through the early part of the 1980s.
- *Kukla, Fran and Ollie* (CBS, NBC, 1947-1957) was one of TV's first popular kiddie-shows along with *Bozo the Clown*.
- Though controversial for its stereotypical presentation of the American Indian, *The Lone Ranger* (Syndicated, 1949-1957) still was the first to showcase an interracial crime-fighting team.
- Before *Julia* and *I Spy*, *The Beulah Show* (ABC, 1950-1953) was the first TV series to feature African-American stars, but unfortunately, was condemned for stereotypical portrayals.

The 1950s

- Though canceled due to racist complaints, *Amos and Andy* (Syndicated, 1951-1953), which began with white actors playing Black roles, was the first TV show to feature African-Americans in leading and supporting characters. Like any other white sitcom of its day, the comedy was exaggerated. Unfortunately, the Black cast, which were reaping the rewards of success, was devastated, when the show ended, abruptly.
- *I Love Lucy* (CBS, 1951-1957): Lucille Ball and Desi Arnaz, married in real life, played TV's first interracial man and wife, while Ball would later become one of the first women to own and operate a television studio and production company.
- Anyone who ever really watches *The Adventures of Ozzie and Harriet* (ABC, 1952-1966) soon realizes that it so very far from homogenized programming. With a slice of "about-nothing" life that was later touted on *Seinfeld, Ozzie and Harriet* was funny, witty, and entertaining, the latter more so, when rock legend Rick Nelson would sing.

- As a drama with comedy, *Father Knows Best* (CBS, NBC, 1954-1960) is one of the best written half-hours in TV in history. Stereotypical only in the eyes of those who never watched it, this realistic series showcased a family of the late 1950s with imperfect characters; a mother, father, and three children who didn't always get along, but loved each other dearly.
- *Lassie* (NBC, ABC, Syndicated, 1954-1974) joins *Flipper* and *Gentle Ben* as one of the most popular pet-oriented TV series in history.
- As by far the best western of early television, as well as the longest-lasting (with twenty seasons), *Gunsmoke* (CBS, 1955-1975) which began on radio, went on to make stars of James Arness, Dennis Weaver, Amanda Blake, and Milburne Stone. It also presented some of the finest writing in television across the board, particularly in the initial half-hour episodes from the first six years.
- Before *Police Woman* and *Charlie's Angels*, there was *Decoy* (Syndicated, 1957-1958), a half-hour crime drama starring Beverly Garland as a female cop. Garland would later join the cast of *My Three Sons*, and then own and operate one of Hollywood's most popular hotels (The Beverly Garland).
- Along with *Gunsmoke*, and later replicated with a female lead on *The Big Valley*, *Bonanza* (1959-1973, NBC) as a weekly staple in American living rooms for years. It was also the first TV show to be screened in color.
- Submitted for the audience's approval, again and again: The genius of Rod Serling kept ground the morality plays presented in the science fiction/fantasy realm of *The Twilight Zone* (CBS, 1959-1964).
- The Beatles premiered on *The Ed Sullivan Show* (CBS, 1948-1971) and popular music and the world, was never the same again.
- The super talented and charismatic Nat King Cole was the first African-American to host a musical variety show (NBC, 1953-1959).
- The ever-mellow Bob Keeshan, in the form of *Captain Kangaroo* (CBS, 1955-1984), guided pre-school young mind for decades with his weekday morning series.
- *Leave It To Beaver* (CBS/ABC, 1957-1963) stood out from the crowd of family sitcoms because it presented family life from the children's point of view.
- *The Donna Reed Show* (ABC, 1958-1966) featured a strong-minded housewife played by its star who also broke ground by serving as the sitcom's co-executive producer with her husband Tony Owen.
- Countless attorneys and other legal professionals pursued their careers because of *Perry Mason* (CBS, 1957-1966) starring Raymond Burr and Barbara Hale as his loyal secretary Della Street.

The 1960s

Rose Marie enjoys TV, and an *I Dream of Jeannie* bottle design by Mario Della Casa *[Credit: The Classic TV Preservation Society]*

- Most episodes of *Route 66* (CBS, 1960-1964) were written by the show's creator Sterling Silliphant. In many segments, the extended dialogue sometimes did not match the characters, but the sentiment and "TV noir" style of the series is unmatchable.

- Was there ever a more bucolic place to live then Mayberry on *The Andy Griffith Show* (CBS, 1960-1968)? Not likely. When Griffith left the series, Ken Berry took the lead in the equally-charming sequel, *Mayberry RFD* (CBS, 1968-1971).

- *The Flintstones* (ABC, 1960-1966) may have been inspired by *The Honeymooners*, but it was much more sophisticated. As a prime-time animated series for adults, it addressed the husband-wife dynamic, while also tackling topics like adoption.

- It was called *My Three Sons*, (ABC/CBS, 1960-1972) but really, there were four. After Tim Considine left, Don Grady became the oldest brother to Stanley Livingston, and real-life sibling Barry Livingston, who later joined the cast as the adopted son in Fred MacMurray's male-dominated world. That is, until Beverly Garland and were added to the cast in this charming show's final years.

- *The Dick Van Dyke Show* (CBS, 1961-1966) delivered laughs with a whole lot of talent. While Van Dyke's Rob Petrie and co-star Mary Tyler Moore's wife Laura sang, danced, worked and took care of their little son Richie (Larry Mathews), they also had multi-talented friends and co-workers like Sally Rogers (one of TV's first career women) and Buddy Sorrell (who became the first Jewish character to be have a bar mitzvah on television).

  It was on the *Van Dyke Show* that Moore met then-advertising executive Grant Tinker who was working behind the scenes. Her spirited Laura Petrie had no issue wearing the pants in the family, while Moore and Tinker would later marry and forge MTM Enterprises, which would produce *The Mary Tyler Moore Show* (CBS, 1970-1977) the first of many hit quality comedies and dramas in their company's wheelhouse.

- *Hazel* (NBC, CBS, 1961-1966) as played by the Oscar-winning Shirley Boothe (*Come Back, Little Sheba*, 1952), may have lacked a formal education, but her winning "everywoman" logic and what would later be defined as "emotional intelligence, always prevailed.

- Along with *Ben Casey*, *Dr. Kildare* (NBC, 1961-1966) starring Richard Chamberlain and Raymond Massey, was one of television first compelling medical dramas.

- Lucille Ball continued to break ground with *The Lucy Show* (CBS, 1962-1968), which was the first to feature not only a widow with children (Ball as Lucy Carmichael), but a female divorcee with children (Vivian Vance as Vivian Bagley).
- *The Beverly Hillbillies* (CBS, 1962-1971) were rich country fish out of water with a whole lot of money and heart, if not too much brains.
- *The Fugitive* (ABC, 1963-1967) starring David Jansen, is considered one of the best written, acted, directed and produced dramas in the history of entertainment. A 1993 feature film version starring Harrison Ford marked one of the better small-to-big-screen adaptations.
- Television viewers were hard-put to find a cozier series than *Petticoat Junction* (CBS, 1963-1970), which featured Bea Benaderet as a widowed mother with three daughters and a feisty, lazy Uncle Joe. Together they ran the Shady Rest Hotel in the fictional country town of Hooterville, through which ran the charming Cannonball train.
- Although populated with stereotypes, *Gilligan's Island* (CBS, 1964-1967) proved that people from all walks of life could get along and "survive" as family.
- With her intelligence, wit and beauty Elizabeth Montgomery's Samantha Stephens – the witch with a twitch – charmed not one but two TV husbands on *Bewitched* (ABC, 1964-1972). In the process, the show represented a strong work ethic, true love, and advocated against prejudice.
- *The Munsters* (CBS, 1964-1966) may have seemed like a silly supernatural sitcom, but many of its episodes stressed the importance of family and "inner beauty," and advocated, directly or indirectly, against prejudice and fears of those who are different.
- *Flipper* (NBC, 1964-1967): The melodic theme music sang it all.
- Before she was an Oscar and Emmy winning actress, Sally Field made her television debut on *Gidget* (ABC, 1965-1966) in which she delivered an energetic, heartfelt and sincere performance as an American teenager.
- Before *The Girl From U.N.C.L.E.*, *Honey West* (ABC, 1965-1966), starring Anne Francis and John Ericson, was TV's first female James Bond-like spy-series.
- With its solid scripts, fine acting, and morality tales, *The Big Valley* (ABC, 1965-1969) starring big screen legend Barbara Stanwick, is one of the most underrated television westerns of any era.
- The first season of *Lost in Space* (CBS, 1965-1968) took itself more seriously than in later years, but each episode showcased the importance of family, even in outer-space.
- The positive social influence of *Star Trek* (NBC, 1966-1969) is immeasurable. Cell phones, desktop computers, and laptops. All of that and more were inspired by the show, which presented diversified, unified representatives of Earth on a starship that soars through the galaxy abiding by one major "Prime-Directive" universal law: Don't disrupt the development of other cultures.

  William Shatner's Captain Kirk represented stability. Leonard Nimoy's Mr. Spock was all logic. DeForest Kelley's Dr. McCoy was emotion. Together, they were the Triad of *Star Trek*, which along with *The Twilight Zone*, turned science fiction on its ear with originality, morality plays, and style.
- Was there ever a more fun show than *Batman*? (ABC, 1966-1968). But really. Who needs *The Dark Knight* when there is *The Bright Night*?
- *Dark Shadows* (ABC, 1966-1971) was filled with vampires, witches, werewolves, ghosts, zombies, and other supernature creatures of the night. But airing during the day, this gothic soap showed that even otherworldly beings have feelings.
- In the history of television, there is not a more likable romantic on-screen young couple than Marlo Thomas and Ted Bessell who on *That Girl* in the 1960s played to the innocence of a troublesome decade.
- Mike Connors starred in *Mannix* (CBS, 1967-1975) a detective series with complex plots that somehow all came together at the end. Co-starring the Emmy-winning Gail Fisher as secretary

Peggy, who along with *Star Trek's* Nichelle Nichols, and Diahann Carroll on *Julia*, was one of the first African-American females to be featured on a weekly series.

- Despite some complaints that the show did not present a legitimate perspective of African-American life, *Julia* (NBC, 1968-1971) starring Diahann Carroll as a nurse, was a groundbreaking platform for minorities.

- Charm, charm, and more charm. That describes *The Ghost and Mrs. Muir*, (NBC/ABC, 1968-1970) starring Hope Lange and Richard Mulhare who shared a chemistry that fed the romance of the series, more so in the first season (and similarly in the beloved 1947 feature film of the same name starring Rex Harrison and Gene Tierney).

- A mixture of romance, Western pioneers, drama, and comedy, all in one family show. That's the best way to describe *Here Come the Brides* (ABC, 1968-1970) a sort of TV version of the big screen's *Seven Brides for Seven Brothers*.

- *Adam-12* (NBC, 1968-1975) is party is one of the several Jack Webb crime-dramas that present a realistic view of police work.

- Arguably the most popular Saturday morning cartoon of the 1970s, and possibly of all time, *Scooby-Doo, Where Are You?* (CBS, 1969-1970) ignited a franchise that bled into live-action feature films. Warm and cuddly, funny and scary, and delightfully inspiring kids to think, *Scooby-Doo* hit all the right chords, especially with its rousing theme song.

- Norman Lear and *All in the Family* (CBA, 1971-1979) changed television forever.

- The Children's Television Workshop changed educational television forever with programming like *Sesame Street* (PBS, HBO Max 1969-Present)

- Based on the 1963 feature film of the same name, *The Courtship of Eddie's Father* (ABC, 1969-1973) was one of TV's initial dramadies. Filmed like a movie, within a half-hour format, the show also was one of the first to include a respectful presentation of an Asian character (played by Oscar-winning actress Myoshi Umeki, *Flower Drum Song*, 1961)

- Inspired by the 1968 feature film, *His, Hers, and Ours*, *The Brady Bunch* (ABC, 1969-1974) was one of the first TV sitcoms to showcase the blended family, while also igniting a franchise that would cover every format with sequels and spin-offs and reboots (including animated series, variety show, feature films, and stage plays).

- Premiering the same year as *The Courtship of Eddie's Father*, *Room 222* (ABC, 1969-1974), like that series, became one of TV's first half-hour dramedies. Following in the foot-steps of *Mr. Novak*, and paving the way for *Welcome Back, Kotter*, it was also one of the first shows to deal realistically with life for kids in school. Who says TV isn't educational?

The 1970s

ABC's Wednesday hit *Charlie's Angels*, the first season of which starred Jaclyn Smith, Farrah Fawcett, and Kate Jackson. Friday night staples featured Freddie Prinze, Sr. with Jack Albertson on NBC's *Chico and the Man*, and ABC's *The Partridge Family* starring Shirley Jones, David Cassidy, Susan Dey, Danny Bonaduce, Susan Crough, and Jeremy Gelbwaks and Brian Forster (sharing the role of Chris Partridge). CBS rules the 1970s on Saturday night with *All in the Family*, *M*A*S*H*, *The Mary Tyler Moore Show*, *The Bob Newhart Show*, and *The Carol Burnett Show* [Credit: The Classic TV Preservation Society]

- *The Mary Tyler Moore Show* (CBS, 1970-1977) turned the entire world on with its countless smiles, and inspired more career women into independence including Oprah Winfrey.
- Rock Hudson made a massive comeback with *McMillan & Wife* (NBC, 1971-1977) which made a star out of Susan Saint James, while introducing the world to Nancy Walker and John Schuck. As a most likable cog in the mystery wheel series, *The NBC Mystery Movie*, *McMillan & Wife* would most likely not be made today due to the age disparity of its leading married couple. But it sure made a lot of viewers happy in the early 1970s. The show featured four very likable characters portrayed by four very likable characters who became family to each other and the audience at home: Rock Hudson, Susant Saint James, Nancy Walker, and John Schuck.
- From 1972 to 1978 on CBS there was "That uncompromisin', enterprisin', anything but tranquilizin', Right on *Maude*!"
- Though set in the 1930s, and originally airing in the 1970s, *The Waltons* (CBS, 1972-1981) represents a realistic family of any era with characters who laugh, cry, get angry, and love and forgive each other.

- *Brians Song* was one of several "issue-oriented" 90-minute ground-breaking TV-movies that aired on ABC's popular Tuesday and Wednesday *Movie of the Week* series (1969-1975), which were later replicated to some extent by NBC and CBS. The film, based on the true story of cancer-stricken football player Brian Piccolo made stars of James Caan and Billy Dee Williams, and addressed true friendship beyond racial disparities.
- *The Partridge Family* (ABC, 1970-1974) made a pop superstar out of David Cassidy, who co-starred with his stepmother Shirley Jones as one of TV's first widowed, self-sufficient working mothers.
- Produced by David Victor (*Dr. Kildare*), and nicknamed *Doctor Knows Best*, *Marcus Welby, M.D.* (ABC, 1969-1976) was the ideal follow-up starring vehicle for Robert Young (*Father Knows Best*). His warm and kind-physician was one of the last to make house-calls, while the show itself (along with *Medical Center*, starring Chad Everett), made sure to have medical professionals on board behind-the-scenes as consultants.
- *Alias Smith and Jones* (ABC, 1971-1973) ultimately inspired by the big-screen's *Butch Cassidy and the Sundance Kid*, changed the way TV westerns were produced and filmed shortly before *Kung Fu* did the same with its non-technicolor manner, and decades before Clint Eastwood's *Unforgiven* feature film.
- *The Brady Bunch* bled into Saturday morning with *The Brady Kids* (ABC, 1972-1973) the first in a long line of sequels to the original live-action family-oriented series.
- The writing, the acting, the directing, and the producing makes *The Street of San Francisco* (ABC, 1972-1977) one of the most realistic, gritty crime-dramas in the history of TV, premiering ten years before *Hill Street Blues*.
- Before he blazed the cinematic trail with the trailblazing *Blazing Saddles*, Cleavon Little starred first with James Whitmore in *Temperatures Rising* (ABC, 1972-1974) which was later revamped as *The New Temperature's Rising Show* with Paul Lynde (seen here).
- She was Catholic and he was Jewish, but no matter because *Bridget Loves Bernie* (CBS, 1972-1973), a landmark series starring a pre-*Family Ties* Meredith Baxter (daughter of *Hazel* star Whitney Blake), and David Birney – who later married each other in real life.
- For some, the first two seasons of *M*A*S*H* (CBS, 1972-1981) are considered the best. For others, it's the remaining, more "serious" nine years. But either way, the show remains one of the most beloved, best produced, directed, written and performed programs in TV history.
- In another reverse of the male white bigotry presented on *All in the Family*, *Sanford and Son* (NBC, 1972-1977) starred Redd Foxx as a male Black bigot who frustrated his infinitely more understanding and compassionate son (played by Demond Wilson).
- Though there were complaints because David Carradine was not an Asian actor in the lead, *Kung Fu* (ABC 1972-1975) introduced the Asian culture to the mainstream American viewer, just as China's Chairman Mao was holding historic talks with President Nixon. In the process, the show was the first to present non-stereotypical Asian characters, while keeping hundreds of Asian-American actors (including Keye Luke, seen here) employed for years.
- Not only has *Emergency* (NBC, 1972-1979) inspired many to get into the medical field, but the show itself, with its on-screen instructional procedures, have saved lives off-screen.
- Buddy Ebsen proved that he "still had it," when he followed his lengthy stint as down-home millionaire Jed Clampett on *The Beverly Hillbillies* to play a senior crime-fighter *Barnaby Jones* (CBS, 1972-1981). Would such an older-generation-led series be popular today in a youth-oriented culture?
- We loved him for years on *Bonanza* and *Highway to Heaven*, but it was *Little House on the Prairie* (NBC,1974-1983) for which Michael Landon will forever be best remembered. Based on the

novel by Laurel Ingels, *Little House* along with *The Waltons*, represented rural/period family programming at its best.

- *The Six Million Dollar Man* (ABC, 1973-78) and *The Bionic Woman* (ABC/NBC, 1976-1978) gave birth off-screen to many scientists, medical professionals, and government agents, all the while helping to advance technology in cybernetic limbs.
- Circa 1974-1977, CBS most likely showcased the most historic Saturday night line-up in television: *All in the Family*, *M*A*S*H*, *The Mary Tyler Moore Show*, *The Bob Newhart Show*, and *The Carol Burnett Show*.
- Cicely Tyson united all cultures in compassion with her Emmy-winning performance in the 1974 TV-movie, *The Autobiography of Miss Jane Pittman* (based on the novel by Ernest J. Gaines).
- *Chico and the Man* (NBC, 1974-1978) made a household name out of Freddie Prinze, who starred with veteran Jack Albertson in this ground-breaking Caucasian-Latino mix of a sitcom.
- "Temporary lay-offs"? Not a problem for the family of *Good Times* (CBS, 1974-1979) because the harder the times, the more love they shared. Another benchmark series from the Normal Lear stable, which also includes *Maude*, from which *Good Times* initially sprang.
- The first season and a half of *Happy Days* (ABC, 1974-1984) plays more like a sweet version of the big-screen 1974 classic flick *American Grafitti*, both of which star Ron Howard. After graduating from *The Andy Griffith Show*, Howard went on to play boy-next-door Richie Cunningham in *Happy Days*, alongside Henry Winkler as The Fonz, the hood with a heart. *Happy's* popularity soared after it switched to filming before a live audience, and increased Winkler's airtime. The sitcom's positive impact was verified after countless viewers went on to get library cards following Fonzie's lead.
- Produced by Saturday morning genius siblings Sid and Marty Krofft (*H.R. Pufnstuff*), *The Donny and Marie Show* (ABC, 1975-1979) brought variety back to prime-time in a big and bright way.
- Like *Mr. Novak* and *Room 222* before it, *Welcome Back, Kotter* (ABC, 1975-1979) presented a relatively realistic view of life in the classroom. It also introduced the world a future superstar in John Travolta.
- On *One Day at a Time* (CBS, 1975-1984), Bonnie Franklin was TV's first liberal-minded female divorcee with children (played by Mackenzie Phillips and Valerie Bertinelli). From the wheelhouse of Norman Lear's machinated mind, the show also starred Pat Harrington and Richard Masseur.
- *The Jeffersons* (CBS, 1975-1985) was a spin-off from *All in the Family* in more ways than one. The show featured a lower-middle-class-turned-high-class African-American bigot (played by Sherman Hemsly) married to an African-American wife with a huge heart (Isabel Sanford), as opposed to *Family's* no-class Caucasian bigot Archie Bunker (Carrol O'Connor) married to a Caucasian woman with a huge, if a little ditsy, heart (Jean Stapleton). But more than anything else, *The Jefferson's* historic hinge-pin remains its proud showcase of a minority family who "finally got a piece of the pie."
- With its Latino and Caucasian leads, *CHiPs* (NBC, 1975-983) carried the torch of diversity in partnership, which was ignited by *I Spy* ten years before.
- As a kind of Lucy-and-Ethel physical comedy for the 1970s (yet based in the late 1950s and early 1960s), *Laverne & Shirley* (ABC, 1976-1983) offered blue-collar workers across America a voice (of nostalgia) to identify with.
- *Rich Man, Poor Man* (ABC, 1976) made stars out of Peter Strauss and Nick Nolte, making history as TV's first mini-series.
- The scripts were sometimes silly, the acting wasn't always top-level, but there's no denying that *Charlie's Angels* (ABC, 1976-1981) inspired female independence in immeasurable ways in the 1970s and beyond.

- *Roots* debuted in 1977 and television was never the same again.
- As the first hour-long drama to be spun-off from a half-hour sitcom, *Lou Grant* (CBS, 1977-1982) soared in the ratings until it was shot-down in its prime by the controversial politics of star Ed Asner.
- *Three's Company* (ABC, 1977-1984) was frilly and silly but groundbreaking, as it became the first TV series to feature a character who at least pretended to be gay.
- *The White Shadow* (CBS, 1978-1981) became another groundbreaking TV platform uniting culture and advocating for racial diversity
- On *The Facts of Life* (NBC, 1979-1988) Geri Jewell, born with cerebral palsy, became the first actor to portray TV's first character with a disability.
- *Schoolhouse Rock* interstitials combined education and entertainment for Saturday morning television on ABC in the 1970s and early 1980s.

All generations were covered in the "Big '80s," including Beatrice Arthur, Rue McClanahan, Betty White and Estelle Getty from *The Golden Girls*, to Caryn Richman, star of *The New Gidget*. [Credit: *The Classic TV Preservation Society (left) & Courtesy of Caryn Richman (right)]*

The 1980s

- *Hill Street Blues* (NBC, 1981-1987) forever changed the way TV crimes shows were produced, filmed, acted, written and directed.
- *Murder, She Wrote* (CBS, 1984-1996) was part of the senior-TV-resurgence in the mid-1980s that included *The Golden Girls*. Hollywood legend Angela Lansbury played an Agatha Christie-type writer/amateur detective (a role that was originally intended for Jean Stapleton, who turned it down).
- Alex Trebek was the star of *Jeopardy!* (Syndicated, 1984-Present) which, along with *Wheel of Fortune*, was created by talk show host Merv Griffin. Two game shows that entertained and educated millions of viewers for decades.

- *The Golden Girls* (NBC, 1985-1992) proved that life begins at 55.
- *The Wonder Years* (1988-1993) about family life in the 1960s, premiered in the 1980s, and was rebooted in 2022 with an all-black cast. Both editions dealt forthrightly with the tumultuous Age of Aquarius.
- The first few seasons of *Seinfeld* (NBC, 1989-1998) are nothing short of brilliant. Though the characters are unlikable, the performances are likable. As the seasons continued, not so much. But the show addressed topical issues with diversified characters (including the hearing-impaired and "little people"). As far as how it directly affected society in a positive way, one young boy awakened from his coma in his hospital room when he heard the show's theme music on his television.
- Nick at Nite in the late '80s and early '90s helped with the resurgence of appreciation of classic television.

The 1990s

- *Baywatch* (NBC, Syndicated, 1989-2001) once documented as the most popular TV show on the planet, went on to save lives on screen and off, inspiring many to become lifeguards and medical professionals in real life.
- Playing characters with AIDS, and Down syndrome, Chad Lowe (who did not have AIDS in real life) and Chris Burke (who does have Down's) proved that indeed...*Life Goes On* (ABC, 1989-1993) no matter the circumstances or challenges on the ground-breaking series from the early 1990s. As the first weekly series to feature a regular character with a disability, this show broke the mold of family entertainment, long before *This Is Us* (NBC, 2016-2022).

Chris Burke (left) and Chad Lowe (right) from *Life Goes On [Credit: The Classic TV Preservation Society]*

- *Frasier* (NBC, 1993-2004) is arguably the last, best and most sophisticated comedy in the history of television. Unlike many sitcoms that would follow it, *Frasier* played it for real, with credible characters, who sometimes went over the top, but didn't live there.
- *Touched By An Angel* (CBS, 1994-2003) reworked *Highway to Heaven* and soared in the ratings as one of the most non-violent mainstream series on the air from 1995 to 2005.
- As a kind of *Honeymooners* for the late 1990s and early 2000s, *King of Queens* (CBS, 1998-2007), proved that true love in marriage doesn't always run smooth, but can always be funny. Kevin James and Leigh Remini starred with a late-blooming Jerry Stiller (fresh off his stint from *Seinfeld*) as her father who shares their residence.

The 2000s

- The Hallmark Channel, more than any other contemporary television network, has not only utilized a return to family programming, but featured classic television stars in new productions.

- As one of the last great "old-fashioned" (yet not) sitcoms, *Reba* (The WB, The CW, 2001-2007) proved that dysfunctional families can still make it all work with a smile, amid divorce, teenage pregnancy and a host of other issues.

- Upon it's debuted, *Mad Men* (A&E, 2007-2015) was considered ground-breaking in the way it told its stories, narratively and visually. But the truth is, its stories were just simply told like they used to be on TV. Though because the techniques had become so high-tech by the time the series aired, it was considered unique.

- *The Big Bang Theory* (CBS, 2007-2017) proved that not all nerds can fall in love, too, and beauty is in the eye of the beholder.

- Like many recent sitcoms, *The Middle* (ABC, 2009-2018) was a little over-the-top, with larger-than-life characters. The simplicity and reality of traditional comedies was replaced by swift camera cuts and stand-up-like performances. But the show was not without its charms.

The Hallmark Channel harkens back to the past with a modern mix of traditional and progressive programming, featuring veteran television stars and contemporary actors *[Credit: The Classic TV Preservation Society]*

The cast of *Reba* (from left): Melissa Peterman, Christopher Rich, Reba McEntire, Joanna Garcia, Steve Howey, Scarlett Pomers, Mitch Holleman *[Credit: The Classic TV Preservation Society]*

Bibliography/Sources

Books

Andrews, Bart (with Blythe, Cheryl), *The Official Cheers Scrapbook*, New York: New American Library, 1987.

Arden, Eve, *Three Phases of Eve: An Autobiography*, New York: St. Martin's Press, 1985.

Bloom, Ken, and Vlastnik, Frank, *Sitcoms: The Greatest TV Comedies of All Time*, New York: Black Dog and Levanthal Publishers, 2007.

Burns, George, *Gracie: A Love Story*, New York: G.P. Putnam's, 1988.

Burnett, Carol, *One More Time: A Memoir by Carol Burnett*, New York: Random House, 1986.

Cali, Dennis D. (edited by), *Faith and the Media: Reflections by Christian Communicators*, Mahwah, New Jersey: Paulist Press, 2010.

Duke, Patty, and Turan, Kenneth, *Call Me Anna*, New York: Bantam Books, 1987.

Durkee, Cutler (Editor), *Television Shows That Changed Our Lives: Great Moments and Guilty Pleasures*, New York: People Books/Time Home Entertainment, 2010.

Ebsen, Buddy, *The Other Side of Oz*, Newport Beach, CA: Donovan Publishing, 1993.

Edelman, Rob, and Kupferberg, Audrey E., *Angela Lansbury: A Life on Stage and Screen (Revised and Updated)*, Secaucus, New Jersey: Citadel Press, 1999.

Eden, Barbara (with Leigh, Wendy), *Jeannie Out of the Bottle*, New York: Crown Archetype, 2011.

Frost, Tony (Editor), *FAREWELL: Stars We Loved and Lost in 2009*, Periodic and Book Association of America/Distribution Services, Inc., 2009.

Garner, James (and Winokur, Jon), *The Garner Files: A Memoir*, New York: Simon and Schuster, 2011.

Garver, Kathy (with Mark, Geoffrey), *The Family Affair Cookbook*, Albany, Georgia: BearManor Media, 2009.

Green, Joey, *Hi Bob: A Self-Help Guide to The Bob Newhart Show*, New York: St. Martin's Press, 1996.

Hamner, Earl, and Giffen, Ralph, *Goodnight John-Boy: A Celebration of An American Family and the Values That Have Sustained Us Through Good Times and Bad*, Naperville, Illinois: Cumberland House, 2002.

Herz, Peggy, *The Mork & Mindy Story*, New York: Scholastic Book Services, 1979.

Herz, Peggy, *TV 74*, New York: Scholastic Book Services, 1973.

Herz, Peggy, *TV Talk: Your Handy Guide to Faces and Places in TV-Land*, New York: Scholastic Book Services, 1975.

Herz, Peggy, *TV Talk 2: Exploring TV Territory*, New York: Scholastic Book Services, 1976.

Herz, Peggy, *TV Time 78*, New York: Scholastic Book Services, 1978.

Herz, Peggy, *TV's Fabulous Faces*, Gabe Kotter and His Sweathogs: *Welcome Back, Kotter*, New York: Scholastic Book Services, 1977.

Hez, Peggy, *TV's Top Ten*, New York: Scholastic Book Services, 1976.

Hotchner, A.E., *Doris Day: Her Own Story*, New York: William Morrow and Company, 1976.

Javna, John, *Cult TV: A Viewer's Guide to the Shows America Can't Live Without*, New York: St. Martin's Press, 1985.

Jewell, Geri, with Nichelson, Ted, *I'm Walking as Straight as I Can: Transcending Diability in Hollywood and Beyond*, Toronto, Ontario, Canada: ECW Press, 2011.

Jones, Gerard, *Honey, I'm Home*, New York: St. Martin's Press, 1992.

Jones, Shirley, and Leigh, Wendy, *Shirley Jones: A Memoir*, New York: Gallery Books, 2013.

Kaufman, David, *Doris Day: The Untold Story of the Girl Next Door*, New York: Virgin Books, 2008.

Manago, Jim, with Manago, Donna, *Love is the Reason for it All*, Albany, Georgia: BearManor Media, 2008.

McDonough, Mary, *Lessons from the Mountain: What I Learned from Erin Walton*, New York: Kensington Publishing, 2011.

McClay, Michael, *I Love Lucy: The Complete Picture History of the Most Popular TV Show Ever*, New York: Warner Books, 1995.

McNeil, Alex, *Total Television: A Comprehensive Guide to Programming From 1948 to the Present* (Second Edition), New York: Penguin Books, 1984.

Meehan, Diana M, *Ladies of the Evening: Women Characters of Prime-Time Television*, New Jersey: Metuchen, 1983.

Mitz, Rick, *The Great TV Sitcom Book*, New York: Richard Marek Publishers, 1980.

Reuter, Donald F., and Turtu, Anthony, *Gaborabilia: An Illustrated Celebration of the Fabulous, Legendary Gabor Sisters*, New York: Three Rivers Press, 2001.

Rios, Tere, *The Fifteenth Pelican: The Incredible Adventures of a Nun Who Discovers She Can Fly*, Garden City, New York: Doubleday and Company, 1965.

Santopietro, Tom, *Considering Doris Day*, New York: Thomas Dunne Books, 2007.

Scott, Kathryn Leigh, and Pierson, Jim, *Dark Shadows Almanac*, Beverly Hills, CA: Pomegranate Press, 2000.

Shulman, Arthur; Youman, Roger, *The Television Years*, New York: Popular Library Publishers, 1973.

Smith, Ronald L., *Sweethearts of '60s TV: Interviews and Photos of the Real Women Behind TV's Most Memorable Female Characters*, New York: S.P.I. Books/Shapolsky Publishers, Inc., 1993.

Story, David, *America on the Rerun: TV Shows That Never Die*, New York: Citadel Press/Carol ublishing Group, 1993.

Tucker, David C., *Shirley Booth: A Biography and Career Record*, Jefferson, North Carolina and London, McFarlund, 1962.

Waldron, Vince, *Classic Sitcoms: A Celebration of the Best in Prime-Time Comedy*, New York: MacMillan Publishing Company, 1987.

Periodicals

Abramovitch, Seth, "Todd Bridges on TV Dad Conrad Bain: 'He Treated Me Better Than My Own Father,'" *The Hollywood Reporter*, January 16, 2013.

Ames, Denise, "One-on-One with Susan Olsen," *Tolucan Times/Canyon Crier*, August 14, 2013.

Archerd, Army, "Army Archerd Calling...," *Movie Life Magazine*, January 1969.

Barnes, Mike, "*Dallas* Actor Larry Hagman Dies at 81," www.hollywoodreporter.com, November 23, 2012.

Barnes, Mike, "Actress Bonnie Franklin Dies at 69," www.Hollywoodreporter.com, March 1, 2013.

Barnes, Mike, "Dale Robertson, Star of TV Westerns, Dies at 89," www.Hollywoodreporter.com, February 28, 2013.

Barnes, Mike, "*Happy Days* Writer-Producer Bob Brunner Dies at 78," *Hollywood Reporter*, November 8, 2012.

Barnes, Mike, "Norman Felton, Co-Creator of *The Man from U.N.C.L.E.*, Dies at 99," *The Hollywood Reporter*, July 5, 2012.

Barton, Chris, "Cos' Effect," *Los Angeles Times*, June 18, 2012.

Bauder, David, "Report Shows Persistence of TV Violence," *Associated Press/Yahoo News*, May 2, 2013.

Bawden, James, "Eve Arden: 'Better to Remain Just Me,'" *Classic Images Magazine*, December 2013.

Berg, Sandi, "Barbara Eden Shares Insights on Her Career, Keeping Fit and Aging," *Life After 50 Magazine*, March 26, 2012.

Berg, Sandi, "Diahann Carroll – The Barrier – Breaking Beauty on Acting Activism and Aging," *Life After 50 Magazine*, August 3, 2011.

Blake, Meredith, "For Gays, Reality TV Can Be A Path To Acceptance," *Los Angeles Times*, October 3, 2012.

Bomboy, Scott, "What If JFK Had Survived His Assisination?", *National Constitution Center* via www.news.yahoo.com, November 23, 2012.

Bulik, Beth Snyder, "You Are What You Watch," *Advertising Age*, November 1, 2010.

Bunting, Sarah. D., "Erik Estrada on 'Chupacabra vs. The Alamo': I'm A Cop Who Acts Once in A While," *Yahoo TV News*, March 23, 2013.

Carter, Bill, "Why Studios Keep Cranking Out TV Remakes, Despite the Flops," *New York Times*, December 28, 2009.

Carter, Jack, "The Stars of *Father Knows Best*: Where Are They Now?", *Globe*, February 18, 2013.

Cooper, Gael Fashingbauer, "Michael J. Fox on Return To TV: "I Never Really Went Anywhere," www.Today.com, September 25, 2013.

Curra, Jennifer, "Diahann Carroll Says, "We're All Very Grateful," September 23, 2013.

Day, Patrick Kevin, "Valerie Harper Has Brain Cancer," Los Angeles Times, March 7, 2013.

Dawg, Big, "How to Write a Reality Show," *eHow.com*, September 28, 2013.

Doyle, Paul, "Jack Shea, Acclaimed Director and CIMA Founder, Dies," *Tidings*, May 3, 2013.

Drew, Michael, "The Argument for Authenticity in Popular Culture," www.huffingtonpost.com, March 4, 2013.

Erskine, Chris, "Lunching with One Legend at Another," *Los Angeles Times*, September 7, 2013.

Franklin, Garth, "Gidget Gets Film & TV Reboots," *Dark Horizons*, May, 2010.

Gelineau, Kristin, "James Earl Jones to Star in *Driving Miss Daisy*," *Yahoo News!*, January 7, 2013.

Gelt, Jessica, "Carol Burnett awarded Mark Twain Prize for American Humor," *Los Angeles Times*, October 21, 2013.

Gillman, Greg, "Hollywood's Disabled Actors Protest NBC's 'Ironside' Casting – When Is it Their Turn?", *The Wrap*, May 21, 2013.

Goldberg, Leslie, "*Two and a Half Men*: Carl Reiner Navigates Holland Taylor, Amber Tamblyn, *Hollywood Reporter*, September 18, 2013.

Gil, Virginia, "Mary Tyler Moore Meets "Sex" Meets "Girls," *DoYouRemember.com*, September 26, 2013.

Goodman, Tim, "*Breaking Bad*: Looking Back at a Revealing Interview with Creator Vince Gilligan." *Hollywood Reporter*, September 29, 2013.

Guider, Elizabeth, "Humanitas Prods. Hires Mandalay TV Exec," *Hollywood Reporter*, March 13, 2010.

Johnson, Ted, "Media Congloms Fear Proposed FCC Rule Change Will Hinder Station Sales," *Variety.com*, September 25, 2013.

Joseph, Jackie, "What A Difference A Day Makes: One-on-One with Doris, Parts 1 and 2," *Tolucan Times*, April 10 and 17, 2013.

Kahn, Jennifer, "The Country Doctor Is In," *Parade Magazine*, March 3, 2013.

Keck, William, "Keck's Exclusives: Sally Struthers Remembers All in the Family Mom Jean Stapleton," *TV Guide Online*, June 6, 2013.

Kelland, Kate (edited by Paul Casiato), "*Star Trek* Desks: Classrooms for the Next Generation?" Thompson Reuters via www.news.yahoo.com, November 23, 2012.

Keveney, Bill, "Burnett Recalls How Variety Spiced Up TV Life," *USA Today*, September 11, 2015.

King, Susan, "Lightning Strikes for a Latino Pioneer," *Los Angeles Times*, September 15, 2012.

King, Susan, "A New Heyday," *Los Angeles Times*, January 6, 2012.

King, Susan, "Bill Persky, That Guy from *That Girl*," *Los Angeles Times*, January 2, 2013.

King, Susan, "Like Old Pals," *Los Angeles Times*, September 22, 2011.

Kirby, David, "Need A New Show, Just Dip into Television's Past," *America Online News*, August 19, 2002.

Kissell, Rick, "Rudolph, Victoria Lift CBS on Tuesday," *Variety.com*, December 5, 2012.

Kolker, Robert, "The O In Network," *New York Magazine*, March 29, 2010.

Korn, Steven, "Beatrice Arthur, *Golden Girls* star, dies at 86," *Entertainment Weekly*, April 25th, 2009.

Klofer, Dan and Poppy, Nick, "Bill Cosby: 'I Wanted to Take the House Back' from Kids," *Yahoo News*, June 6, 2013.

Kramer, Miriam, "How *Star Trek* Vision of Future Inspired Next Generation Actor LeVar Burton," *Yahoo! News*, September 29, 2013.

Laurell, David, "The Perceptive Woman," *Life After 50 Magazine*, September 2013.

Laurell, David, "Julie Newmar Explains Life on Earth," *Life After 50 Magazine*, March 2012.

Lewis, Andy, "*The Jetsons* Turn Fifty Today," *Hollywood Reporter*, September 23, 2012.

Lewis, Hilary, "M.I.A. on NFL Legal Battle: What About Madonna's 'Sexually Provocative' Underage Dancers?" *Hollywood Reporter*, September 24, 2013.

Malcom, Andrew, "Sotomayer: Inspired by *Perry Mason*," *Los Angeles Times*, January 15, 2013.

Lieberman, Matthew, "Hollywood Take Note: Here's What TV Viewers Really Want," *Hollywood Reporter*, September 25, 2013.

Lowry, Brian, "Brave Nude World: Cable TV Pushing Boundaries," www.Variety.com, October 8, 2013.

Manikar, Sheila, "Asner on *Mary Tyler Moore*, Broadway, Yahoo!, December 12, 2012.

Mann, Chris, "Re-imagined TV," *Los Angeles Times*, September 27, 2011.

McCaine, Florine, "Marlo Thomas: What She Had to Do to Become A Star," *TV Radio Show Magazine*, October 1967.

McNamara, Mary, "The Giant Leap to TV," *Los Angeles Times*, September 15, 2013.

McNamara, Mary, "Modern Issues," *Los Angeles Times*, September 24, 2012.

Moore, John, "Michael Jackson's 'Thriller' Resonates at 30," *Denver Post*, November 29, 2012.

Morretti, Rena, "A Dark Age for Movies and TV," *Los Angeles Times* (Feedback), September 22, 2013.

Morrison, Patt, "Another Day," *Los Angeles Times*, January 7, 2012.

Morrison, Patt, "Seriously Funny," *Los Angeles Times*, June 20, 2012.

Myers, Jack, "How Spongebob and Rugrats Influenced This Election!" *Mediabizbloggers.com*, November 6, 2012.

Nelson, Valerie, "Dann Cahn Dies at 89; Editor on *I Love Lucy*," www.latimes.com, November 26, 2012.

Newcomb, Alyssa, "Bionic Suit Helps Paralyzed Patients Walk Again," Yahoo! News, December 22, 2012.

Noland, Claire, "Gary Collins, Actor and TV Host, Dies at 74," *Los Angeles Times*, October 13, 2012.

Oliver, Myrna, "Frances Bay, 1919-2011: Late Start Led To Success For Busy Character Actress," *Los Angeles Times*, September 17, 2011.

Poniewozik, James, "Serial Killing: How TV Dramas, Good and Bad, Have Become Addicted to Blood," *Time*, March 11, 2013.

Portantiere, Michael, "Florence Henderson – From Broadway to Brady and Beyond," *Life After 50 Magazine*, August 22, 2011.

Pullella, Philip, "Bernardo Bertolucci Says TV Shows Better Than Hollywood Now, *Reuters*, May 28, 2013.

Radar, Dotson, "Ready to Roll," *Parade*, September 9, 2012.

Rogers, John, "Beav's brother Tony Dow Now An Abstract Artist," *Associated Press*, September 22, 2012.

Rooney, David, "The 65th Primetime Emmy Awards: TV Review," *Hollywood Reporter*, September 23, 2013.

Rose, Lacey, "*Modern Family* Writer Reveals Emotional Backstory of 'Historic' Gay Marriage Proposal," *Hollywood Reporter*, September 26, 2013.

Rothaus, Steve, "Former Child Star Brandon Cruz Keeps Alive Memory of *Eddie's Father* TV Dad Bill Bixby," *Gay South Florida*, November 7, 2012.

Schiffman, Steven Mitchell, "Shari Lewis: The Lady Who Talks to Puppets," *TV Gold Magazine*, #7, December 1986.

Seaman, Don, "TV Not History," www.MediaBizBloggers.com, October 9, 2013.

Slezak, Michael, "Rue McClanahan Remembers Bea Arthur," *Entertainment Weekly Online*, April 26, 2009.

McLellan, Dennis, "Producer-Director Boosted the Career of Carol Burnett," *Los Angeles Times*, June 16, 2001.

Stanton, Kate, "Trailblazer Diahann Carroll presents with Kerry Washington at the Emmys, Compliments TV's Attractive Men," September 23, 2013.

Thomas, Marlo, "From *Peanuts* to *Grinches* to Elves – Time for Those Christmas Classics," www.huffingtonpost.com/marlo-thomas, December 7, 2012.

Thomas, Marlo, "Marlo and Sofia's Special Family Affair," www.HuffingtonPost.com/marlo-thomas.com, November 19, 2012.

Trachtenberg, Robert (Photographer), "Reunions: *The Carol Burnett Show*," *Entertainment Weekly*, October 14/21, 2011.

Trounson, Rebecca, "Mom on TV's *One Day at a Time*," *Los Angeles Times*, March 2, 2013.

Tucker, Ken, "Bea Arthur: A Magnificent *Maude*, a *Golden Girl*, a Mighty Woman," *Entertainment Weekly Online*, April 25, 2009.

Valby, Karen, "Why Funny Gals Rule the World," *Entertainment Weekly*, October 14/21, 2011.

Weber, Bruce, "Bea Arthur, Star of Two TV Comedies, Dies at 86," *New York Times*, Sunday, April 26, 2009.

Wilson, Craig, "Carol Burnett Chats About Mother-Daughter Love Story," *USA Today*, April 8, 2013.

Woo, Elaine, "Former Mouseketeer Excelled at Dancing," *Los Angeles Times*, November 20, 2012.

Zacharin, Jordan, "Greetings from Melmac: *ALF* Creator Paul Fusco on His Star Alien and Potential Comeback," Hollywood Reporter, May 22, 2012.

Zacharin, Jordan, "Ty Burell: *Modern Family* Helps Move Gay Rights Forward," *Hollywood Reporter*, October 3, 2012.

TV Guide

Amory, Cleveland, "Review of Sesame Street," *TV Guide*, February 14-20, 1970.

Amory, Cleveland, "*Review of The Andy Griffith Show*," *TV Guide*, July 31-August 6, 1965.

Amory, Cleveland, "Review of *The Andy Williams Show*," *TV Guide*, January 24-30, 1970.

Amory, Cleveland, "Review of *The Advocates*," *TV Guide*, April 11-17, 1970.

Amory, Cleveland, "Review of The French Chef," *TV Guide*, March 30-April 5, 1968.

Arras, Jean, "The Long and Short of It," *TV Guide*, December 30-January 5, 1973.

Asimov, Issac, "William: An Introduction to William Shakespeare for Younger Viewers," *TV Guide*, December 30-January 5, 1970.

Barnard, Charles N., "Some Questions for Miss Walters," *TV Guide*, December 30, 1972-January 5, 1973.

Bedell, Sally, "Too Hot to Handle," *TV Guide*, October 8-14, 1977.

Becker, Angela, "Flower Power from Boston," *TV Guide*, August 17-23, 1970.

Buckley, William F., "Midwiving an Insight and Confuting the Devil," *TV Guide*, January 24-30, 1970.

Chagall, David, "The Child Probers," *TV Guide*, October 8-14, 1977.

Davis Jr., David E., "Watching the Cars Go By – Fast!" *TV Guide*, July 31-August 6, 1965.

Diehl, Digby, "He's Finally Combing Those Feathers Out of His Hair," *TV Guide*, March 30-April 5, 1968.

Diehl, Digby, "He's the Apostle of Life After 30," *TV Guide*, January 24-30, 1970.

Diehl, Digby, "The Oldest Living Teenager," *TV Guide*, February 14-20, 1970.

Doan, Richard K., "Every Night Is Election Night," *TV Guide*, March 30-April 5, 1968.

Doan, Richard K., "How Television is Waging a Summer Campaign for Racial Understanding," *TV Guide*, August 17-23, 1968.

Doan, Richard K., "They Make Good Television in Hershey, Too," *TV Guide*, February 14-20, 1970.

Durslag, Melvin, "From Back Alleys to Ballrooms," *TV Guide*, January 24-30, 1970.

Efron, Edith, "Can TV Drama Survive?" *TV Guide*, September 25-October 1, 1965.

Efron, Edith, "The Magnificently Opinionated Victorian Institution," *TV Guide*, December 6-12, 1969.

Gehman, Richard, "Women's Home Companion," *TV Guide*, July 31-August 6, 1965.

Graff, Richard, "Dear Sir: You Cur..." *TV Guide*, April 11-17, 1970.

Hickey, Neil, "*Hee Haw*-ing All the Wat to the Bank," *TV Guide*, October 8-14, 1977.

Hobson, Dick, "Four Days with the Remarkable Mrs. Morton," *TV Guide*, March 30-April 5, 1968.

Keck, William, "Sally Struthers Remembers *All in the Family* Mom Jean Stapelton," *TV Guide*, June 6, 2013.

LeBlanc, Jerry, "Making Peace in the Army...with Television," *TV Guide*, December 30, 1972-January 5, 1973.

Lipton, James, "Soap Operas Are for Real," *TV Guide*, February 14-20, 1970.

MacKenzie, Robert, Review of *Soap*," *TV Guide*, October 8-14, 1977.

Mead, Dr. Margaret, "Our Leaders Do Not Understand Television," *TV Guide*, December 6-12, 1969.

McGinniss, Joe, "A Talk-Show Host Talks Off Camera," *TV Guide*, August 17-23, 1968.

Morgan, Thomas B., "How Sweet It Is – Or Is It?," *TV Guide*, September 25-October 1, 1965.

Musel, Robert, "Englebert Humperdink by Any Other Name," *TV Guide*, December 6-12, 1969.

Musel, Robert, "Wlodzimierz Has His Problems," *TV Guide*, March 30-April 5, 1968.

Nadel, Gerry, "Just About All Talk and No Action," *TV Guide*, October 8-14, 1977.

O'Hallaren, Bill, "No More Balloons," *TV Guide*, October 8-14, 1977.

Raddatz, Leslie, "Look What's Happened to These Dodge City Citizens," *TV Guide*, August 17-23, 1968.

See, Carolyn, "An Old Actor Stands Fast in a Changing World," *TV Guide*, March 30-April 5, 1968.

See, Carolyn, "Speaking of Life Styles..." *TV Guide*, April 11-17, 1970.

Shayon, Robert Lewis, "When Anybody Can Speak Out on Television...Anything Can Happen," *TV Guide*, December 30-January 5, 1970.

Wasserman, John L., "I Don't Even Like Apple Pie," *TV Guide*, December 6-12, 1969.

Whitney, Dwight, "The Anatomy of Success – In the Case of *My Three Sons*,' It Bears a Striking Resemblance to That Old Saxophone Player, Fred MacMurray," *TV Guide*, July 31-August 6, 1965.

Whitney, Dwight, "The Return of Oliver J. Dragon III," *TV Guide*, February 14-20, 1970.

Additional TV Guide References

"Courtship," *TV Guide*, March 30-April 5, 1968.

"It Was Typecasting," *TV Guide*, September 25-October 1, 1965.

"*Jeffersons* Star Sherman Hemsley Remembered by Friends at Funeral," www.Hollywoodreporter.com, November 23, 2012.

"Go Boutique," *TV Guide*, April 11-17, 1970.

"Good Morning, Ladies," *TV Guide*, July 31-August 5, 1965.

"Julie Newmar in Bed in the Middle of Times Square," *TV Guide*, February 14-20, 1970.

"Out of Sight, Out of Luck," *TV Guide*, October 8-14, 1977.

"Start With the Word Mexican," *TV Guide*, January 24-30, 1970.

Additional Sources

"Five Great TV Shows That Changed the World," *Reader's Digest Online* (www.rd.com), March 3, 2013.

"*Dancing with the Stars*: Celebs Who've Turned Down the Show," www.PopEater.com, February 26, 2013.

"*Dallas* Return with J.R. Ewing's Final Schemes, Murder and Mystery," *Associated Press*, January 23, 2013.

"Gracie Allen," http://www.biography.com/people/gracie-allen-9542415.com (accessed Aug 31, 2013).

"Lynda Carter," *The Biography Channel website* (http://www.biography.com/people/lynda-carter-10073461 (accessed Aug 31, 2013).

"Patty Duke," *The Biography Channel website*, http://www.biography.com/people/patty-duke-9542536.com (accessed Aug 31, 2013).

"Lindsay Wagner," *The Biography Channel website*, http://www.biography.com/people/lindsay-wagner-585880.com (accessed Aug 31, 2013).

"Barbara Walters," *The Biography Channel website*, http://www.biography.com/people/barbara-walters-9523127.com (accessed Aug 31, 2013).

"Jane Wyatt," *The Biography Channel website*, http://www.biography.com/people/jane-wyatt-218221.com (accessed Aug 31, 2013).

"Loretta Young," *The Biography Channel website*, http://www.biography.com/people/loretta-young-9542113.com (accessed Aug 31, 2013).

"Marlo Thomas: Sometimes You Have To Make Your Parents Cry," *TV Radio Show Magazine*, December 1966.

The Martin Milner Archives Online (accessed March 7, 2013).

"Spending Time with Sally Field," *TV Radio Show Magazine*, October 1967.

The Unofficial Isis Appreciation Page (accessed November 2, 2011).

http://www.bbc.co.uk/radio4/womanshour/2003_31_fri_03.shtml

"Doris Day: Exclusive Interview with Her Longtime Confidant," *Globe Magazine Special*, American Media, 2013.